MY CRAZY
CENTURY

MY CRAZY CENTURY

Ivan Klíma

Translated from the Czech
by Craig Cravens

Grove Press UK

First published in the United States of America in 2013 by Grove/Atlantic Inc.

First published in Great Britain in 2014 by Grove Press UK, an imprint of Grove/Atlantic Inc.

First published in Czech as two volumes: *Moje šílené století* by Nakladatelství Academia, Prague, and *Moje šílené století II* by Nakladatelství Academia, Prague.

Printed in Great Britian

ISBN: 9781611855708
eBook ISBN: 9781611859751

Grove Press, UK
Ormond House
26-27 Boswell Street
London
WC1N 3JZ

www.groveatlantic.com

NOTE FROM THE PUBLISHER

With the help of the author and translator, this edition has been abridged from the original Czech edition, which was published in two volumes. It is our hope that the full unabridged translation will be published in the future.

CONTENTS

PROLOGUE   1

PART I   3

PART II   219

EPILOGUE   415

ESSAYS   417

    Ideological Murderers   419

    Utopias   426

    The Victors and the Defeated   433

    The Party   438

    Revolution—Terror and Fear   445

    Abused Youth   452

    The Necessity of Faith   458

    Dictators and Dictatorship   467

    The Betrayal of the Intellectuals   475

    On Propaganda   481

    Dogmatists and Fanatics   491

    Weary Dictators and Rebels   496

    Dreams and Reality   503

    Life in Subjugation   507

    Occupation, Collaboration, and Intellectual Riffraff   511

    Self-Criticism   517

    (Secret Police)   522

    The Elite   530

MY CRAZY
CENTURY

PROLOGUE

A young Czech editor from BBC Radio, for whom I sometimes wrote commentary, once asked me, "Why don't you write about why you were a Communist in your youth? I think listeners would be very interested."

I realized that although I had used many of my experiences as material for my prose, I had avoided my several-year membership in the Communist Party, perhaps with the exception of a few mildly autobiographical passages in my novel *Judge on Trial*.

For quite a long time now I have considered the Communist Party or, more precisely, the Communist movement, a criminal conspiracy against democracy. And it is not pleasant to remember that, even though it was for only a short period, I had been a member of this party.

But was my young colleague from the BBC correct? Who today could be interested in the reasons why so many people from my generation succumbed to an ideology that had its roots deep in the thinking, in the social situation and societal atmosphere, of the turn of the nineteenth and twentieth centuries?

Marxism, which invoked a Communist ideology, is today somewhat forgotten. Its revolutionary theories have been refuted by practice. These days people are threatened much more by international terrorism; instead of battling Marxism, democracy is battling radical branches of Islam.

But it is less ideology than the need of people, especially the young, to rebel against a societal order that they did not create themselves and do not consider their own. Besides, people need to have some kind of faith or goal they consider higher than themselves, and they are inclined to see the world and its contradictions in unexpected, apparently simple relationships, which appear to explain everything that is important, everything they are going through, or everything with which they do not agree. And for these often deceptive goals they are willing to sacrifice even their lives.

All ideologies of the past that led to murder could evolve only when they had purged from the minds of the people everything they considered inappropriate and compelled the people to fanatical loyalty to their ideas, which they proclaimed appropriate. In this they did not differ from contemporary ideologies that lead to terrorist murder.

Perhaps this attempt of mine to recount and analyze what took place in my life might have meaning even for those who consider communism a long-dead idea. In my account, I mainly concentrate on the circumstances that, in this crazy century, often led mankind astray, sometimes with fatal consequences.

PART I

1

My first memory is of something insignificant: One day Mother took me shopping in an area of Prague called Vysočany and asked me to remind her to buy a newspaper for Father. For me, it was such an important responsibility that I still remember it. The name of the newspaper, however, I no longer recall.

My parents rented two rooms and a kitchen in a house that was occupied by, in addition to the owner, a hunting dog with the elegant name of Lord. Birds, mainly blackbirds and thrushes, nested in the garden. When you are four or five, time seems endless, and I spent hours watching a blackbird hopping about the grass until he victoriously pulled a dew worm out of the earth and flew back with it to his nest in the juniper thicket, or observing how snowflakes fell on our neighbor's woodshed roof, which to me was like a hungry black-headed monster, gobbling up the snowflakes until it was sated and only then allowing the snow to gradually accumulate on the dark surface.

From the window of the room where I slept there was a view into the valley. From time to time, a train would pass, and at the bottom of the vale and on the opposite slopes huge chimneys towered into the sky. They were almost alive and, like the locomotives, they belched forth plumes of dark smoke. All around there were meadows, small woodlots, and thick clumps of shrubbery, and when the trees and bushes were in bloom in the springtime I began to sneeze, my eyes turned red, and I had trouble breathing at night. Mother was alarmed and took my temperature and forced me to swallow pills that were meant to make me perspire. Then she took me to the doctor, who said it was nothing serious, just hay fever, and that it would probably afflict me every spring. In this he was certainly not wrong.

It was in one of those chimneyed factories, called Kolbenka, that my father worked. He was an engineer and a doctor, but not the kind of doctor who cures people, Mother explained: He cured motors and machines and even invented some of them. My father seemed larger than life to me. He was strong, with a magnificent thatch of black hair. Each morning he shaved with a straight razor, which I was not allowed to touch. Before he began lathering his face, he sharpened the razor on a leather belt. Once, to impress upon me how terribly sharp it was, he took a breakfast roll from the table and very gently flicked it with the blade. The top half of the roll toppled onto the floor.

Father had a bad habit that really annoyed Mother: When he walked along the street, he was always spitting into the gutter. Once when he took me for a walk to Vysočany, we crossed the railway tracks on a wooden bridge. A train was approaching, and to amuse me Father attempted to demonstrate that he could spit directly into the locomotive's smokestack. But a sudden breeze, or perhaps it was a blast of smoke, blew my father's new hat off and it floated down and landed on an open freight car heaped with coal. It was then I first realized that my father was a man of action: Instead of continuing on our walk, we ran to the station, where Father persuaded the stationmaster to telephone ahead to the next station and ask the staff to watch the coal wagons and, if they found a hat on one of them, to send it back. Several days later Father proudly brought the hat home, but Mother wouldn't let him wear it because it was covered in coal dust and looked like a filthy old tomcat.

Mother stayed at home with me and managed the household: She cooked, did the shopping, took me on long walks, and read to me at night until I fell asleep. I always put off going to sleep for as long as I could. I was afraid of the state of unconsciousness that came with sleep, afraid above all that I would never wake up. I also worried that the moment I fell asleep my parents would leave and perhaps never come back. Sometimes they would try to slip out before I fell asleep and I would raise a terrible fuss, crying and screaming and clutching Mother's skirt. I was afraid to hold on to Father; he could yell far more powerfully than I could.

It is not easy to see into the problems, the attitudes, or the feelings of one's parents; a young person is fully absorbed in himself and in the relationship of his parents to himself, and the fact that there also exists another world of complex relationships that his parents are somehow involved in eludes him until much later.

Both my parents came from poor backgrounds, which certainly influenced their way of thinking. My mother was the second youngest of six children. Grandfather worked as a minor court official (he finished only secondary school); Grandmother owned a small shop that sold women's accessories. Her business eventually failed—the era of large department stores was just beginning and small shops couldn't compete.

Grandpa and Grandma were truly poor. The eight-member family lived in a two-room flat on Petrské Square, and one of those rooms was kept free for two subtenants, whose contribution ensured that my grandparents were able to pay the rent. Nevertheless, they made certain their children got an education: One of my aunts became the first Czech woman to get a degree in chemical engineering, and my mother graduated from a business academy.

Two of Mother's brothers were meant to study law, but they went into politics instead. I hardly knew them and can't judge whether they joined the Communist Party out of misguided idealism or genuine solidarity with the poor, who at that time still made up a sizable portion of the population. After having immigrated to the Soviet Union, both of them returned to the German-occupied Protectorate of Bohemia and Moravia on orders from the party. Given their Jewish background, this was a suicidal move and certainly not opportunistic.

My mother was fond of her brothers and respected them, but she did not share their convictions. It bothered her that the Soviet Union meant more to them than our own country and that they held Lenin in higher esteem than they did Tomáš Garrigue Masaryk.

On the day I turned six, Masaryk died. For my birthday, my mother promised me egg puffs, which were an exceptional treat. To this day I can see her entering the room with a plateful of the pastries and sobbing loudly, the tears running down her beautiful cheeks. I had no idea why; it was my birthday, after all.

Father seldom spoke about his childhood. He seldom spoke to us about much of anything; he would come home from work, eat dinner, sit down at his worktable, and design his motors. I know that he lost his father when he was thirteen. Grandmother was able to get by on her husband's tiny pension only because her brother-in-law (our only wealthy relative) let them live rent-free in a little house he bought for them just outside Prague. When he was studying at the university, my father supported himself by giving private lessons (as did my mother), but then he got a decent job in Kolbenka and managed to hang on to it even during the Depression. Still, I think the mass unemployment that affected so many workers influenced his thinking for a long time afterward.

I hadn't yet turned seven when the country mobilized for war. I didn't understand the circumstances, but I stood with our neighbors at the garden gate and watched as columns of armored cars and tanks rolled by. We waved to them while airplanes from the nearby Kbely airport roared overhead. Mother burst out crying and Father railed against the French and the English. I had no idea what he was talking about.

Soon after, we moved across town to Hanspaulka. Our new apartment seemed enormous; it had three rooms and a balcony and a large stove in the kitchen. When the stove was fired up, hot water flowed into strange-looking metal tubes that Father called radiators, although they bore no resemblance to the radio from which human voices or music could be heard. It was in this new apartment that my brother, Jan, was born. The name Jan is a Czech version of the Russian Ivan, so if we had lived in Russia our names would have been the same.

When Father brought Mother and the newborn home from the maternity hospital, there was a gathering of both our grandmothers, our grandfather, and our aunts, and they showered praises on the infant, who, in my opinion, was exceptionally ugly. I recall one sentence uttered by Grandfather when they gave him the baby to hold: "Well, little Jan," he said, "you haven't exactly chosen a very happy time to be born."

※

Until then I had never heard the word "Jew," and I had no idea what it meant. It was explained to me as a religion, but I knew nothing about religion: My school report card stated "no religious affiliation." We had the traditional visitation from Baby Jesus at Christmas, but I had never heard anything about the Jesus of the Gospels. Because I had been given a beautiful retelling of the *Iliad* and the *Odyssey*, I knew far more about Greek deities than I did about the God of my ancestors. My family, under the foolish illusion that they would be protecting my brother and me from a lot of harassment, had us christened. Family tradition had it that some of my mother's distant forebears had been Protestants, and so my brother and I were christened by a Moravian church pastor from Žižkov. I was given a baptismal certificate, which I have to this day, but I still knew nothing of God or Jesus, whom I was meant to believe was God's son and who, through his death on the cross, had liberated everyone—even me—from sin and death.

Father may have been upset with the English, but one day my parents informed me that we were going to move to England. I was given a very charming illustrated textbook of English called *Laugh and Learn*, and Mother started learning English with me.

I asked my parents why we had to move out of our new apartment that all of us were fond of. Father said I was too young to understand, but he'd been offered a good job in England, and if we stayed here, everything would be uncertain, particularly if we were occupied by the Germans, who were ruled by, he said, an upholsterer, a good-for-nothing rascal by the name of Hitler.

One snowy day the Germans really did invade the country.

The very next morning complete strangers showed up at our apartment speaking German—or, more precisely, shouting in German.

They walked through our beautiful home, searched the cupboards, looked under the beds and out on the balcony, and peered into the cot where my little brother began crying. Then they shouted something else and left. I wanted to know who these people were and how they could get away with storming through our apartment as though they owned it. Mother, her face pale, uttered another word I was hearing for the first time: *gestapo*. She explained that the men were looking for Uncle Ota and Uncle Viktor. She lifted my brother from his cot and tried to console him, but as she was so upset, her efforts only made Jan cry harder.

At dinner, Father told Mother it was time to get out. But in the end, we didn't move to England because, although we already had visas, Grandmother's had yet to arrive. To make matters worse, our landlord, Mr. Kovář, served us with an eviction notice. He didn't want Jews in his building anymore. Naturally no one told me anything, and I still had no idea that I was so different from other people it might give them a pretext to kill me.

We moved into a newly completed building in Vršovice, where again we had only two rooms. Immediately after that, the war began.

I can no longer recall exactly how that apartment was furnished. I vaguely recollect a green ottoman, a bookcase on which an azure blue bowl stood, and, hanging on the living room wall, a large map of Europe and northern Africa where Father followed the progress of the war. Apparently it was not going well. The German army swiftly occupied all those colored patches on the map representing the countries I had learned unerringly to recognize: the Netherlands, Belgium, France, Denmark, Norway, Yugoslavia. To top it all off, the good-for-nothing rascal Hitler had made an agreement with someone called Stalin, who ruled over the Soviet Union, decreeing that their respective empires would now be friends. This news took Father by surprise. I also understood that it was a bad sign, since the area on the map marked Soviet Union was so enormous that if the map was folded over, the Soviet Union could completely cover the rest of Europe.

When we first moved into our new home, there were lots of boys and girls to play with. Our favorite game was soccer, which I played relatively well, followed by hide-and-seek because there were many good hiding places in the neighborhood.

Then the protectorate issued decrees that banned me from going to school, or to the movies, or into the park, and shortly thereafter I was ordered to wear a star that made me feel ashamed because I knew that it set me apart from the others. By this time, however, Germany had attacked the Soviet Union. At first Father was delighted. He said that it would be the end of Hitler because everyone who had ever invaded Russia, even the great Napoleon himself, had failed, and that had been long before the Russians had created a highly progressive system of government.

Of course it all went quite differently, and on the large map, the vast Soviet Union got smaller each day as the Germans advanced. Father said it couldn't possibly be true. The Germans must be lying; they lied about almost everything. But it turned out that the news from Hitler's main headquarters was mostly true. Whenever they advanced, they posted large V's everywhere, which stood for "victory," while at the same time they issued more and more bans that eventually made our lives unbearable. I was no longer allowed out on the street at night; I couldn't travel anywhere by train; Mother could shop only at designated hours. We were living in complete isolation.

Father's beautiful sister, Ilonka, managed to immigrate to Canada at the last minute. We were not permitted to visit Mother's eldest sister, Eliška, or even mention her name, since she had decided to conceal her origins and try to survive the war as an Aryan. Father thought she would have a hard time succeeding, but in this, once again, he was wrong. Mother's youngest sister fled to the Soviet Union, and her Communist brothers went into hiding for a while before they too fled. When the party recalled them to work in the underground here, the Germans quickly tracked them down, arrested them, and shortly thereafter put them to death. Mother's other sister, Irena, moved in with us. She was divorced, but it was only for show, since her husband, who was not Jewish, owned a shop and a small cosmetics factory that, had they not divorced, the Germans would have confiscated. The family had no idea, since very few people had any such ideas then, that they had offered my aunt's life for a cosmetics business.

In our apartment building there were two other families wearing the stars—one on the ground floor and the second on the top floor. In September 1941, the family living on the ground floor, the Hermanns, were ordered to leave for Poland, apparently for Łódź, in what was called a transport.

I remember their departure. They had two daughters slightly older than I was, and both girls were dragging enormous suitcases on which they had to write their names and the number of their transport. As the Hermanns left, people in our building peered out from behind their doors, and the more courageous of them said goodbye and reassured them that the war would soon be over and they'd be able to return. But in this, everyone was wrong.

My parents rushed about trying to find suitcases and mess tins, and they bought medicines and fructose in a recently opened pharmacy. They couldn't lay in any other supplies because everything had to be purchased with ration coupons, and we had been allotted scarcely half of what those not wearing stars were given. Less than two months after the Hermanns were taken away, Father received a summons to a transport. He didn't go to Poland, though, but rather went to Terezín, a town not far from Prague built long ago as a fortress to protect our country from the Germans, which, Father said, had never been used for that purpose. His was the first transport to Terezín. Father also had to write his name and number on his suitcase. Mother was distraught. What would become of us now? she sobbed. How were we going make ends meet and would we ever be together again? Father tried to console her and said that although the Soviets might be retreating, they were doing it only to lure the Germans into the depths of their enormous land, as they had lured Napoleon. The terrible Russian winter was about to begin, and that would destroy the Germans. In this he was not wrong; it just took longer than he'd imagined.

Several days later, we too were assigned to a transport. The very same day, America entered the war against Japan, and the insane Hitler immediately declared war against the United States. Our neighbors, who helped us hastily pack, assured us that Hitler had now signed his own death warrant, and in this they were not wrong.

In the Terezín ghetto, they put us in a building called the Dresden Barracks. In a small room they referred to as our "quarters," they crammed thirty-five people, all of them women except for my brother and me.

The fact that so many of us had to live in a single room and that we all had to sleep on the floor depressed most of the women. We had been allowed to bring our mattresses from home, but there was so little space here that they could be laid down only end to end. The first evening I remember hearing a woman sobbing, and someone was walking through the room and few of them could sleep. But even though I didn't like going to sleep, I managed to sleep pretty well that first night on the floor. The next morning they announced breakfast, and so I went with my mess kit, wondering what I would get. It wasn't good: bitter black ersatz coffee and bread. I don't remember our first midday meal, but lunch was almost always the same: soup with a little caraway seed and a piece of turnip or a couple of strands of sauerkraut and, for the main course, several unpeeled potatoes in a sauce. The sauce was made from paprika, mustard, caraway seeds, and sometimes also powdered soup, and once in a while there was even a mouthful of meat floating in it.

Perhaps my memory is deceiving me by driving out unpleasant recollections, but today it seems to me that I was not aware of any particularly cruel suffering. I accepted whatever happened as an interesting change. I had lived apart from other people for a long time; now this isolation was broken. Several children my age also stayed in the barracks, and I was able to get together with them. Foremost in my memory is a moment of one of my greatest achievements in life until that point. In the courtyard, the only place where we were allowed out during the day, several boys were playing soccer. I didn't know them and it never occurred to them to invite me to play. I stood some distance away and waited. Finally the ball came in my direction and I stopped it and dribbled it into the game. I kept possession of the ball for almost a minute before they were able to take it away from me. They stopped the game, divided the players again, and let me play.

After a week, Father showed up in our room, but he said he'd dropped in only to repair the electricity. The lights were always going off and it was around Christmastime and the days were very short, so we either groped about in the dark or burned the last of our candles that we'd brought from home. He embraced Mother and us and then quickly shared news that the Germans were fleeing Moscow and that the entire German army had frozen to death. The war would soon end and we could return home. He was talking to Mother, but the other women in the room were listening, and I felt a sense of relief and hope fill the air. The mood in our living quarters improved, and sometimes in the evenings— when the windows were shut and blacked out—the women would sing. I didn't know most of their songs and I didn't know how to sing, but I liked listening to them. But right after the New Year they started handing out orders to join transports that were going somewhere in Poland.

Some of the women cried, and those who were stronger—or perhaps it was just that they had less imagination—reassured them that nothing could be worse than this place. Those whose names were on the list packed their few belongings and got ready for a new journey, which for most of them would be their last, though of course they could not have known that. Over the course of a few days our room was all but emptied, but it wasn't long before fresh transports arrived in Terezín, and the living quarters began to fill up again. I understood that from now on, the people around me would come and then leave again and that it made no sense to try to remember their names.

For the time being we didn't go on a transport because Father had been among the first to be sent to Terezín in a group that was assigned to build the camp, and the Germans had promised that these men and their families would remain in Terezín. I accepted this promise as ironclad, not yet comprehending how foolish it was to believe promises made by your jailers.

Each day was like the next: The biggest events were lineups for food and water and for the bathroom and for outings in the courtyard. Mother said she would tutor me, but we had neither paper nor books, so she told me stories of long-ago times about the Emperor Charles, who founded Charles University in Prague (though I had no idea what a university was and I didn't want to ask), and about Jan Hus, the priest they burned at the stake in Constance. My mother stressed that justice never flourished in the world, and those in possession of power would never hesitate to kill anyone who stood up to them.

My brother Jan also listened to her stories, even though he didn't understand anything she was saying because he was barely four years old. From several toy blocks that he had brought from home, and from the sticks that we were given in winter so that we could have a fire in the stove, he would build fortresses on the floor between the mattresses.

Then Mother's parents were also forced to come to Terezín, along with my other grandmother and Aunt Irena. They were assigned to our barracks. They told us what was going on in Prague and how the Germans were winning on every front: In Russia they were nearing the Volga River. But Grandfather claimed no one would ever defeat the Russians because Russia was huge, and no one had ever occupied it.

I was fond of Grandfather because he talked to me as though I were already grown up. He told me how our allies had betrayed us and about collaborators and Fascists who informed on anyone the Germans didn't like.

Suddenly, in the summer of 1942, the ghetto police disappeared from the gates of our barracks and we could go into the streets of the town, which was surrounded by ramparts and deep moats. I ran outside, happy as a young goat let out of the barn, knowing nothing about his fate.

Then we were moved again, this time to the Magdeburg Barracks, where a lot of prominent people lived. They put us in a tiny room above the rear gates, where we could live with Father and the grandmothers and Grandfather and our aunt, and where there was a single piece of furniture: a battered old kitchen cabinet. Father was in charge of everything in the ghetto that had to do with the electrical power supply, and as a perk, we were allowed to live together. Next door to us were three painters with their wives and children.

One of the painters, Leo Haas, asked me if I would sit for him as a model, even in my ragged clothes with the yellow star on my jacket. I gladly obliged, not because I longed to have my portrait done, but because it allowed me to escape the dispiriting grind of life in the barracks. When Mr. Haas was finished, I plucked up my courage and asked him if he could let me have several pieces of paper. He replied that paper was a rarity even for him because he had to steal it. But he gave me a sheet and I tried to sketch a lineup for food in the forecourt.

When our Nazi jailers learned that the artists, instead of working at the tasks they were assigned, were drawing and painting scenes from the ghetto, they immediately arrested them, even though we were all de facto prisoners already. The painters ended in Auschwitz, and their wives and children were sent to the Small Fortress in Terezín. The only one to survive was Mr. Haas and, miraculously, his little son, Tomáš, who was scarcely five years old. What also survived, however, was a cache of the pictures and drawings all the painters had hidden beneath the floorboards.

⸺◦⸺

I was too young to work and so had lots of free time. We hung out in the courtyard or behind the barracks. There was a blacksmith's shop there where Mr. Taussig shod the horses that pulled the wagons, sometimes laden with food and sometimes with garbage or suitcases left behind by the dead. Anything that had belonged to the dead now belonged to the Germans. Mr. Taussig had a daughter, Olga, who was about my age and had long chestnut hair and seemed very pretty to me. Two large trees grew in front of the blacksmith's shop—I think they were linden trees—and we strung a rope between the trunks and outlined a playing area with stones and then we played volleyball. I was usually one of the two captains and could choose my team. I always chose Olga first so the other captain wouldn't take her and I then tried to play the best game I could, full of spikes so that if we won, she would know it was my doing.

We also played dodgeball and windows and doors, and we stole things. Sometimes it was coal and, very occasionally (it was too dangerous to do it often), potatoes from the cellar. Once we broke into a warehouse, where I stole a suitcase full of the sad personal effects of someone who had died, including a pair of climbing boots. Through the glassless bay windows we also tried to throw stones at the fleeing rats. I never managed to hit one, but since the barracks were infested with fleas and bedbugs, I became a champion flea catcher. When it was raining, we would simply wander up and down the corridors while I amused the others with stories. Sometimes they were stories I remembered from my Trojan War books about the wanderings of Odysseus, and sometimes I made up stories, about Indians, for instance (about whom I really knew nothing at all), or about a famous inventor who built an airplane that could fly to the moon (I knew even less about astronomy and rocketry). Then, for a short time, the Germans allowed us to put on theater performances in our barracks and even, to the accompaniment of a harmonium, operas. For the first time in my life I saw and heard *The Bartered Bride*.

I also started attending school in the barracks. My classmates and I had not been able to go to school for several years, so teaching us must have been hard work. The teacher was already a gray-haired lady and she spoke beautifully about literature and recited from memory poetry that had been written by people I had never heard of. At other times we would sing Moravian and Jewish songs, or she would teach us spelling. She urged us to remember everything well because the war

would one day be over and we'd have to make up for the lost years of
our education.

Once we were assigned a composition to describe the places we
enjoyed thinking about. Most of my classmates wrote about the homes
they had left behind, but I wrote about the woods in Krč and the park
on Petřín Hill in Prague, even though I had probably been in either
of these places only once. But in Terezín, where there was nothing but
buildings, barracks, wooden houses, and crowds of people everywhere,
I longed for woods and a park. Such places were as unattainable as
home, but they were open and full of smells and silence.

The teacher liked my composition so much that during the next
lesson she asked me to read it aloud to the others. Though they were
bored, I still felt honored. Perhaps it was at this moment that the determination was born to start writing when I got home—I imagined
writing whole books—but our lessons lasted no more than a few weeks,
since the transports began leaving again, and one of them swallowed
up our teacher. That was the last I ever heard of her.

Soon Grandma Karla fell ill; they said she had a tumor. She was
bleeding and the room was full of a strange and repugnant smell. Mother
wept, saying that Grandma would certainly die in such conditions, but
there was no alternative. Grandma rapidly went downhill. She stopped
eating and drank only water, which I brought in a bucket or in my mess
tin after I stood in line for it.

Whenever she could, my mother sat by Grandma and held her
hand and told her over and over again that everything would be all
right, that the war would soon end, that Grandma would return home
to Prague, and we would go for a walk around Petrské Square. As she
spoke, her tears flowed, but Grandma didn't see them because her eyes
were shut; she didn't respond, just breathed in and out, terribly slowly.
Then Mother sent me and my brother outside and asked us to stay
there for as long as possible.

Behind the barracks was a fresh pile of beams from the old wooden
houses. Jan and I climbed about on it and then we went to see what

Mr. Taussig was up to. Olga came outside and wondered what we were doing out in the evening, since it would soon be eight o'clock and if we weren't back by then, we could be in serious trouble. I explained that our grandmother was dying. And indeed, when we returned, the room was dark and the window was half open. Grandma's narrow wooden bunk was empty and a candle burned beside it.

—⁂—

We heard that some people had gone missing from Terezín, but the population could be counted only with great difficulty because so many were dying every day. The Germans were uncertain how many people actually lived in our closely guarded town, so they decided to count us. Early one rainy morning on a gloomy autumn day—probably in 1943 because Father was still with us—they herded everyone out of the town and onto a huge meadow. We were each given a piece of bread, margarine, and liver paste, and they kept arranging and rearranging us in lines while the ghetto police trained their guns on us. People were constantly running up and down the lines, and then some SS officers appeared. I had never seen them before. Perhaps they'd come to reinforce the ghetto police—people were saying things were not looking good.

We stood for the whole day while the rain kept getting heavier; the light started to fade, and we had to remain there all that time without moving. The women were wailing that this was the last day of our lives, that they would shoot us or toss a bomb into our midst. And as if to confirm their fears, a plane with a black cross on its wings passed overhead. Some could no longer stand by themselves, so others held them up, and some, mostly the very old, simply toppled into the mud and stayed, though others warned them that the SS officers would shoot anyone who collapsed.

I promised myself that even if everyone else collapsed, I would remain standing because they couldn't possibly kill me just like that. But my little brother, who was cold and afraid, cried and kept asking to go home.

The SS men ran about, shouting at those who had fallen, kicking them till they stood up again. They kept on counting but they seemed incapable of arriving at a final tally because, as Father said, they were trained to kill, not count. Late in the evening one of the SS officers in command gave the order to return. We all crowded in through the gates, eager to be back in our smelly flea-bitten holes. As bad as they were, they were our homes.

Then something strange happened. Shops began to open in Terezín. The SS moved people out of select places and brought in goods to sell, mostly things taken from the suitcases of the deceased. In the town square they built a bandstand for a real orchestra to play, and in a little park below the ramparts they began to build a nursery school. We were also given paper money—not the real thing, merely bills printed for our ghetto. On the face of the bill was an engraving of a bearded man holding a stone tablet in his arms. Mother explained that this was Moses and that carved on the tablet were ten laws according to which people were meant to conduct their lives. They also moved everyone out of several dormitories and crammed these people into the attics of other barracks. Then they brought normal furniture into the emptied dwellings and moved in specially chosen tenants—not thirty to a room, as was common, but only two or three.

By this time everyone was talking about how a delegation from the Red Cross was on its way to Terezín and that it was possible the Red Cross would take over the camp from the Germans and we would all be saved.

A delegation did in fact visit, and to this day I remember that for lunch there was beef soup, veal with potatoes, cucumber salad, and finally a chocolate dessert, none of which we had ever seen or tasted before or since in Terezín. The delegation was shown around by several SS officers bearing the death's-head insignia on their caps. We recognized some of them and knew they beat anyone who didn't salute them or who didn't have the yellow star fastened properly or whom they simply didn't like. We stood up when they entered, but they smiled affably and gestured for us to sit down again.

The Red Cross did not take over the ghetto. Quite the contrary: Shortly after their visit, the transports started leaving for Poland again, one every two or three days, usually with about a thousand people in each. When the thirteenth transport had left, everything suddenly became quiet, literally so because by now the barracks were half empty, and the entire ghetto seemed hollowed out. The lineups diminished, and there was almost no one on the streets, which had previously been full of people in the evenings.

Around then Grandfather began to cough. He always had a cough because he'd smoked a lot before the war, but this cough sounded different. He began to perspire persistently and he had a fever. He was diagnosed with consumption and had to go to the infirmary, where the SS stockpiled those who were bedridden in an enormous room until they were dead. We couldn't visit, lest we be infected ourselves, but Grandpa survived there until the beginning of 1945, the last year of the war, and he occasionally sent us encouraging little notes via some of the attendants. He predicted that we would live to see liberation. He believed we would all meet again and that life would treat us better than it had treated him.

When he died, my mother couldn't even light a candle because we no longer had any. Aunt Irena was still with us and, in addition to noodles, she occasionally brought us news about how the Russians and their Western allies had entered German territory, and now the war really was nearing the end. From time to time squadrons of heavy American bombers would pass overhead. The skies belonged entirely to them; not a single German aircraft put in an appearance. Whenever the air raid sirens wailed, my brother and I always ran into the courtyard, and as we looked up at the sky I tried to explain to him that those aircraft meant the war would soon be over and we would be able to go home. My brother began to cheer and wave at the planes with both hands, or using his shirt with the star sewn on it. We never left the courtyard, not even when, shortly after the aircraft had flown over our heads, we could hear bombs exploding in the distance.

We survived, but the Germans took away all of my friends. I remember their names but I've forgotten their faces, and in any case they'd look different today.

―❦―

Many years later an American reporter asked me a question that most people were reluctant to ask: How is it that we remained in Terezín and survived when practically all of our contemporaries did not?

It's a strange world when you are called upon to explain why you weren't murdered as a child. But a similar question arises in relation to an utterly modern event: Why do the terrorists in Iraq release one prisoner and mercilessly behead another? Did someone pay ransom for the one they released? Was there a secret exchange of prisoners? Or was it merely the whim of those who claim the right to decide whether someone who falls into their hands should live or die?

To the question of how I survived, I can reply with certainty that I cannot take the least credit for it. When the last transports left for Auschwitz, I had just turned thirteen. The only ones in Auschwitz who could survive at that age would have been the twins on whom Dr. Mengele performed his experiments. He—or someone else in his position—sent all the other children to the gas chambers. I owe my survival above all to my father. As I've said, he went to Terezín on the first transport, which consisted entirely of young men whose task it was to prepare the town for the subsequent internees. Until 1944, these men and their families were not included in any of the transports headed eastward.

Why had they chosen him, of all people, to go on that first transport?

His own explanation was that some decent comrades had arranged for all of us to be quickly whisked away to Terezín because

Mother's brothers were members of the illegal Central Committee of the Communist Party and had been exposed and arrested. It was to be expected that the gestapo would come after their relatives as well. I found this explanation unlikely because those in the Jewish community who, on orders from the occupiers, drew up the lists of people to go on those transports to Terezín wouldn't have taken any interest in Mother's relatives, and it's unlikely they knew of either their arrest or their execution. It seems far more probable that Father's name had simply come up by chance or because those in charge of the future operation of the ghetto understood that a specialist such as my father would be needed in Terezín from the beginning.

In addition to looking after the electrical lighting, the motors, and various machines in Terezín, Father joined an underground cell of the Communist Party. As far as I know, the comrades were not preparing an armed uprising, but they certainly made an effort to maintain contact with the outside world, and they smuggled correspondence in and out, along with food, medicine, cigarettes, newspapers, and books.

At the time, of course, Father told me nothing about his secret activities, but he did talk to me about politics. What else could he have talked to me about? Practically speaking, I was not going to school. I read no books because none were available, and my friends didn't interest him. So he talked to me about the situation at the battlefronts and about the importance of the allied invasion, which to his great disappointment seemed never to come. He also tried to explain the difference between life in the Soviet Union and the countries called capitalist. In the Soviet Union, in his telling, mankind's ancient dream of a society governed by simple people, in which no one exploited anyone else and no one persecuted anyone on the grounds of his racial or ethnic origins, had come true. The Soviets persecuted only capitalists—the owners of factories or landowners—but that was a just thing to do because the capitalists had become wealthy from the labor of their serfs and led a profligate life, while those who worked for them went hungry. "Do you understand?" he would ask.

I did not understand why it was just to persecute anyone, but Father explained to me that although no one can help being born black or yellow or a Jew, a capitalist came by his property because either he or his forebears had exploited countless numbers of poor, enslaved workers and peasants. It was German capitalists, he added, clinching the argument, who had supported Hitler, and capitalists all around the world looked on passively because they believed that Hitler would destroy the Soviet Union, the very country where the people ruled.

That was how my father had worked it out in his mind, even though, as I came to understand years later, none of this was a product of his own thinking. But his thoughts on these matters interested me very little; if anything excited me it was news from the front. Once Father took a piece of paper and drew Moscow, Kiev, Kharkov, and Stalingrad; then he sketched in a line to indicate the farthest extent the German army had penetrated and another to show where it was now. Then he added the city of Prague and, a short distance away, the fortress of Terezín. So you see, he said, how Hitler's warriors have taken to their heels!

But I could tell from his sketch that the front was still a long way from Terezín, and I understood that freedom was therefore still far off and that a lot of terrible things could still happen before it came.

And sure enough, one summer day, they ordered Father to pack his things and appear the next morning in front of the Command Center.

We were all very upset. It never augured well when they unexpectedly summoned someone. Father was probably more terrified than the rest of us because he must have thought they'd found out about his underground activity and were going to take him to some torture chamber and try to extract from him the names of those he'd worked with to undermine the Reich. Even so, he reassured us that his good friends would remain behind and look out for us, and if we found ourselves in any kind of trouble we were to seek them out. He reminded my mother of the names of these friends, and she nodded, but I think she was unable to take in anything of what he was telling her.

We went along with Father and saw that he wasn't the only one summoned; two other men also showed up at the Command Center. Father recognized them from a distance and remarked that they were engineers and acquaintances of his. Then an SS officer appeared, checked their identity papers, and, to our astonishment, ripped off their yellow stars and threw them onto the cobblestones. Might this be a good omen? Might it be that for some scarcely comprehensible reason these three men had ceased to be Jews? Or was this just another one of those sadistic jokes that those who ruled our lives sometimes liked to play on us?

Several weeks later, Mother was summoned to the Command Center. An SS officer showed her a postcard and asked how someone from the Gross-Rosen camp might have gotten our address. The postcard was from Father. He wrote that he was well and hoped that we were too and said that we should be happy where we were and that under no circumstances should we leave. The SS must have thought this message was pure insolence, since it was hardly up to us to decide where we stayed or where we ended up. Mother explained how Father knew our address, and to our surprise the SS officer handed her the postcard and nothing further happened to us.

In Gross-Rosen they placed Father in a special unit whose task was to develop some improved technology—perhaps a miracle weapon —to help the Germans win a war they had already lost. But why would they have used prisoners—difficult to properly monitor—to give the prisoners' archenemies an advantage? Moreover, the Russians were not far off, and after several weeks the Germans abandoned the camp, and Father began a journey from concentration camp to concentration camp, and at the end of the war he was moved on foot in a mass exodus that came to be called the Death March.

It was only years later that Father discovered the reason for this strange journey. Sometime at the beginning of the war, when the Germans had begun their mass expulsion of the Jews from the Reich, one of Father's German colleagues, who was not a Nazi, wrote a letter to the Reich Main Security Office saying that he knew of three exceptionally good non-Aryan specialists whose knowledge the Reich might profitably put to use, and that these men should be allowed to continue working in their fields.

At that early stage of the war, when the Germans seemed close to victory and thus had no need for specialists who, in any case, were earmarked for elimination, no one paid attention to the letter. But when the Germans began to see defeat looming in the distance, someone dug out the letter and issued an order to locate these specialists. Coincidentally all three of them were in Terezín. Naturally the Germans couldn't reinstate them in their original positions, so they came up with the idea of creating a special unit in the concentration camps.

Shortly after Father's mysterious departure from Terezín, the largest series of transports to Poland began. We understood that we were no longer protected and that our turn—which was highly probable —could come at any time. For several weeks we lived in expectation of the moment that had so far passed us by and would mean a journey into the unknown. All we knew was that those who set out on it seemed to vanish from this world forever—as indeed most of them did. All my playmates had departed, and certainly Father's good friends and comrades had also gone, but we were still there. And we remained. We were still alive. Why?

When Father returned after the war, he was convinced that his comrades had saved us, as they had promised when he went away, and for the longest time, when I gave any thought to it all, I believed he was right. But now I'm not so sure. In a well-informed book about the Terezín ghetto, H. G. Adler claims that any person younger than sixty-five who remained in Terezín must have either been a member of a special group or had some personal relationship with the SS.

The special groups included the Danes, the Dutch, women who were working in the mica factory, and VIPs—members of the existing Council of Elders (earlier council members had all been murdered). None of those categories applied to us. The transport lists were drawn up by a group of people called the Jewish self-administration. The Germans in charge of the camp, however, provided them with lists of those to be included in a given transport as punishment (the final transports were assembled by the SS itself) and a list of those who, because they were useful to the Germans in some way, were not to be included. It's possible that when the German camp leaders received notice that Father was a highly qualified specialist whose skills were obviously recognized by their superiors (and the opinion of superior officers had the authority of law for every member of the SS), they put us on the list of those who were not yet to be sent to the gas chamber.

This is merely speculation, but whatever the reason for my survival, I can take neither credit nor blame for it. In this abominable lottery, I had drawn one of the few lucky numbers, and perhaps it had been slipped to me by Father or one of his comrades, or, paradoxically, by the very people whose primary aim was to eliminate me. And thus I survived the war.

Essay: *Ideological Murders,* p. 419

2

Finally it was peacetime.

We ripped off our yellow stars and threw them into the oven. Jan and I received a box full of goodies from the International Red Cross.

I assumed that we were free, another train would come, and we'd hop aboard and leave for Prague. But an epidemic of typhoid and spotted fever broke out in Terezín, and the town was placed under quarantine. Mother was desperate. Now that the long-awaited moment had arrived and we'd made it to freedom, they wanted to let us die?

But a few days later a light-haired, freckle-faced young fellow entered our quarters from another world. He embraced Mother and shook my hand. It was my cousin Jirka Hruška, who, thanks to his mother's decision not to declare herself a Jew, survived the war without a scratch. He had traveled to Terezín in a truck that was waiting a little outside of town to take us to Prague. Mother protested that this was against the rules, but my cousin said we'd go ahead and try anyway. Who was going to try to stop us? It was true: The SS men had disappeared; the policemen who had been guarding the fortress gates were nowhere to be seen; the higher-ups had most likely cleared out and found someplace to hide or fled altogether. And the rest probably thought it awkward to continue guarding innocent prisoners.

Mother wanted to start packing our things, but my cousin talked her out of it. We wouldn't be needing them just now, and we would have an opportunity to come back for them. It would be best to pretend we were simply going on a stroll.

From the window of our quarters you could see clearly the gate that I'd known for years was impossible to pass through and beyond which lay another world, a world where you could walk freely, where rivers flowed and forests grew, where cities spread in all directions, circumscribed by neither ramparts nor moats.

My cousin Jirka led us toward that gate. A Soviet soldier carrying a submachine gun was at that very moment walking through the gate, but when we passed him he didn't even glance up. And that's how we went through—we strolled through the "gate to freedom," as my cousin put it. He led us to the truck, which had a Czechoslovak flag flying from its bed, and on the side was written CONCENTRATION CAMP REPATRI-ATES! Several other escapees joined us.

Then we took off. The truck was an old clunker—the Germans had commandeered most of the decent vehicles for military purposes. Instead of gasoline it ran on wood fuel, which made the journey extremely slow, and at every little incline we had to stop and wait for the wood to produce a little more fuel. On the side of the road lay old, broken-down hulks of cars, yet every house and cottage was decorated with flags, and strangers would run out and wave to us.

And all of a sudden Prague emerged on the horizon. The truck had to negotiate the narrow gaps in the barricades, the houses were pock-marked with bullet holes, and I saw in the street a group of men and women wearing white armbands toiling away with paving stones, piling them in a heap. According to Jirka, these were Germans who only yester-day ruled over our land and decided who would live and who would die.

—❈—

Once again I was sleeping in a real bed. In the evening, for the first time in years, I could crawl into a bathtub full of warm water. I could go outside and take off wherever I wanted down the street. I could select whatever book I wanted to read from Aunt Eliška's library. That's how I spent an entire blissful week. Then we received permission to move back into our old apartment.

A locksmith came with us to open the door, along with our uncle, Pops, to see what we would need. The place on Ruská Avenue was the only home I'd ever known because I never considered the barracks a home. This is where I would return in my thoughts. This is where my Jules Verne novels were, my electric train, the metal bed that I slept on and that wasn't teeming with bedbugs. And the bathroom, the toilet, running water. Soap. Plates instead of metal bowls. A radio!

While the locksmith was opening the door, the apartment manager told us that our belongings had been removed, but we were not to worry because the SS man who had lived in our flat while we were away had left behind all of his own furniture, which, as we would soon see, was brand-new. The bastard had lived there barely six months.

The furniture was indeed new. In the living room stood an enormous writing desk, a large four-section wardrobe, and a couch. But there wasn't a trace of my Jules Verne, electric train set, or bed. The bed in the master bedroom was even bigger than the writing desk, but the feather duvet was missing. Uncle told us not to worry; he'd find us a duvet. Then he looked at my brother and me and said to Mother that the revolution was over, and schools were operating again. Jan was still too little—he'd just turned six last November—but I had missed so many years that Uncle said I shouldn't waste a single day.

Mother agreed and sent me to ask the apartment manager, who had a son my age, if he knew which school I was supposed to attend.

The next day I set out for the secondary school in Heroldovy Gardens. The principal was somewhat at a loss for what to do with me. "Have a seat, young man. Did you attend school in Terezín?"

I explained to him that schools had been prohibited.

The principal asked me how old I was, and when he found out that I'd be fourteen in a few months, he told me that I belonged in the ninth grade. "If we place you in a lower grade," he mused, "it would look like you'd failed, and that wouldn't be fair."

So he beckoned me to follow him down long, chilly corridors to a door marked 4a. He knocked and walked right in.

The classroom was full of unfamiliar boys and girls, and the teacher was writing something on the chalkboard. The students stood up, and the teacher hurried over to greet us.

"Boys and girls," said the principal, "please welcome your new classmate. Please be," he hesitated for a moment as if searching for the right word, "kind to him. He was locked up in what was called a concentration camp for four years. Completely innocent people were interned there, and he didn't have a chance to attend school." He considered that to be the worst thing that had befallen me. He turned to the teacher, who was peering at me inquisitively, and asked that he and his colleagues take this into consideration.

The principal left and the teacher showed me where to sit. Then he continued his explanation about something, which I almost immediately stopped listening to because it didn't make any sense. During recess, one of my classmates told me we had just sat through physics.

The worst thing for me was that this wasn't the end. We still had three more classes to go, and tomorrow six more, and in most of them I had no idea what they were talking and writing about.

It was clear that it would be pointless to test me on anything, except perhaps history and geography, and then only on the material that had been covered in the previous lesson. The teachers agreed that at the end of the year I would be given a certificate so I could apply to a high school. Fortunately, there were only a few days until vacation.

———

We waited to see if Father and our relatives, who had disappeared one by one, would return. I was also waiting to see if any of my friends would come back. I refused to accept that they were dead. They couldn't have killed everyone, all those they had carted off by the thousands to the East, could they?

Every day the radio broadcast lists of freed prisoners who had reported they were still alive. We sat waiting and listening to the invisible convoy of the rescued and anticipated hearing a name we knew.

Father's sister Ilonka reported in. Just before the war she had managed to escape to Canada, and Mother's sister Hedvika had fled to the Soviet Union, where she had lived a few years earlier. Two of Father's cousins returned, one of whom had survived Auschwitz; and Aunt Eliška's husband, Leopold, who had escaped via Egypt to England, where he joined our army abroad. Leopold, a former postman, had never, he assured us, even fired an air rifle, but he had achieved the rank of staff sergeant. He was shot in the leg at the Battle of Aachen and had a limp, though the way he described it, the war seemed to be nothing more than one thrilling adventure after another.

Finally we found Father's name on a list of rescued prisoners. He arrived on a flatbed truck with several other prisoners and was so emaciated we barely recognized him.

Once again we were sitting down together to a celebratory dinner, everyone in the family who had survived. Father, surprisingly full of energy, told us about his travels through the concentration camps and how they had marched from the camp in Sachsenhausen nearly all the way to the sea, thirty kilometers a day without food and almost without rest. When they had stopped for a minute by a farmhouse, a Pole who was being forced to work there gave him a piece of bread with lard, which had most likely saved his life.

Why did he give it to you, of all people?

"Because I was the closest," explained Father. "Life hung precisely on such threads. And on willpower. Your feet were chafed bloody and you didn't think you could raise your foot, but you went on nevertheless, and every step you thought would be your last. It would rain at night, and there was nowhere to take cover, so I took the single blanket I had and made a tent so I wouldn't get completely soaked. And the next day I just went on," he told us, and none of us uttered a word. "If I didn't get up or if I'd merely stopped, they would have shot me, and right now I'd be rotting God knows where in the ground."

Then Father began talking about the future. After everything he'd gone through, he realized our society was corrupt, that it bred inequality, injustice, poverty, millions of unemployed, who then put their faith in a madman. But the future belonged to socialism and finally communism, which would put an end to poverty and exploitation.

"You make it sound like a fairy tale," protested Uncle Pops, and he wondered if we too were going to found collective farms and nationalize factories, shops, trades, and finally even wives.

This question provoked Father, and he warned Uncle not to believe the Nazi propaganda. The only things that would be nationalized were large factories, mines, and banks. Uncle wouldn't have to worry about his measly cosmetics shop.

A few days later, Aunt Hedvika and her husband came to visit. She told us she had worked for a radio station in Moscow, but when the German army was getting close, everyone volunteered with picks and shovels to dig trenches on the outskirts of the city. Then she was evacuated to a town called Kamensk-Uralsky. Meters of snow would fall there, so they had to dig passages in the drifts, but there were some days when the temperature sank to forty degrees below zero, and no one went outside if he could help it. During the last year of the war, when she was back in Moscow, she saw Stalin up close. Stalin in the flesh.

I kept waiting to see if any of my friends would return, my cousins, my aunts, if the Hermanns and their daughters who lived below us would come back.

But no one at all returned.

———

From the beginning of the postwar days, Mother was doing poorly. She was always weak, and now she complained of fatigue and chest pains. Father took her to see a renowned Prague cardiologist, who pronounced a devastating diagnosis. Mother's heart was so bad that it wouldn't bear any strain, not even walking uphill or climbing steps. No excitement, not even a fever. (At the time we didn't know that this was a false diagnosis, and she lived another fifty years.)

Since we had miraculously survived everything, I was looking forward to setting off on vacation as we did before the war, but because of Mother's weak heart, this was off the table. Father decided, however, that at least my brother and I needed to get outside the city, and right away he took us to a camp on the outskirts of Prague, which was operated by a new organization that bore an unpoetic name, the Czechoslovak Union of Youth.

The fact that we had all just been reunited and now we had to part again depressed me so much that to this day I remember that vacation as a sort of exile. Jan took it even harder, and he asked Father to take him back home. He didn't want to stay in the camp. Father promised he would return to check on us soon, and it was my task to take care of my brother.

The camp comprised several wooden cabins and a sheltered communal kitchen. I didn't know any of the leaders or even any of my squad members. I also didn't know any of the things that all the other kids knew about: war games, rituals such as raising the flag or singing the national anthem. I never sat around the campfire, I didn't play any instrument, and my singing was awful. Nevertheless, I tried to somehow get acquainted with the others. I attempted to curry favor with three of my roommates by telling them about some of my wartime experiences, but they weren't the least bit interested. They were interested only in girls and wanted to know how it was with the girls in Terezín. This seemed indecent, even crude, because the girls I had gotten to know there were now dead. So in the evenings I visited my brother, who slept with kids his own age at the other end of the camp. I would go to their cabin, sit on a bunk, and think up a continuation to my fairy tale about a wacky poodle. During this time, Jan was kind of sad or maybe just a little frightened, but the word "poodle" for some reason always made him laugh.

Since we were in the early postwar period, there was a shortage of food. The supervisors obviously had not managed to obtain any extra allotments or any of the food brought by the UN, so we were always hungry. I was accustomed to going without food, but the other members of my squad were constantly grumbling. One evening when I was already in my bunk, they pulled me out of the cabin and asked me to help them procure some food.

We went to see the director. He let us in, heard us out, and then told us that he was hungry too, perhaps even hungrier than we were because he was bigger and received the same amount of food as we did. We had just gone through a war, and there were people starving more than we were, and we'd had supper today. Then he instructed us to follow him to one of the cabins that served as a warehouse. He told us that whatever he gave us would be at the expense of the others, and we certainly didn't want that. Then he took a handful of sugar cubes from a cardboard box and gave each of us two.

I ate one of the sugar cubes and saved the other for my little brother.

Life soared upon wings of rapturous celebration of victory and freedom, but in no time it collapsed into hatred and a longing for revenge.

During the first few postwar weeks, the Germans had to help dismantle the barricades. Sometimes, so I was told, one of them would be killed or even hanged from a lamppost or tree branch. I never actually saw anything like this, but had I come across such an event, I certainly would have stopped and looked on. I never suspected that often those who hanged another without trial were merely concealing their own misdeeds, and they did not care if the hanged were in fact guilty of anything at all.

At the beginning of the war, several German families lived on our street. In addition to German, they spoke Czech, and we children played together. Later, however, their parents forbade them to even speak with me.

From the moment I arrived in Terezín, the only Germans I met wore uniforms, and instead of the state symbol on their hats they had a skull and crossbones. Those skulls also adorned traffic signs that warned of particularly dangerous curves, which we called curves of death. The skulls on their hats proclaimed that the wearers were standing in a curve and beyond lay death.

Their deeds seemed to me so evil that I was convinced it was my duty to remind people never to forget the horrors the Germans had perpetrated. Over the school break I composed an article in which, with maudlin and artless pathos, I recalled my four Christmases in Terezín and concluded with a note about the end of the war.

> The spring brought us peace, the end of the war, which we had so much looked forward to, which we had awaited for six years. The end, however, brought such horrifying news. Of the hundreds of thousands of children and the elderly who were taken off to the East, not a single one returned. I think about my friends and cannot believe they're no longer on this earth, that the Germans managed to murder hundreds and hundreds of helpless children. I shudder with horror every time I realize that it was only due to a miracle that I survived. But since I have had the good fortune to remain alive, I pledge my word that I will do everything to ensure that what we were witness to during those final years of the war will never happen again. . . . My only wish is that you never feel pity for the Germans, even if they never did you any harm. Do not forget the horrors of the concentration camps and judge fairly and without mercy so that your children will not be forced into German prisons as we were, so that during Christmas, sitting over their bread and water, they will not have to despair over the fact that you were lenient on the German butchers.

I sent the article to a children's magazine called *Onward*, which printed it complete with several mistakes I had made.

My only experience had been the war, but it was a devastating one. My world was now divided into good and evil, with the Red Army and their allies embodying the good. The Germans embodied the evil. That was it. I knew nothing of other evils, other slaughters. I knew life from only one side, and I mistakenly assumed that I was entitled to sweeping judgments.

I wasn't alone in considering the Germans the embodiment of evil. Everyone nurtured in his memory how the Germans had dealt out blows. It was the Germans, after all, who had chosen Hitler as their leader. They had accepted his doctrine that they were the master race even though they had nothing in common with genuine masters. They made their way through Europe and believed they would rule forever. They pounced upon their neighbors and undertook to exterminate every single Jew and execute at least a hundred innocent Poles, Russians, or Serbs for every one German who had fallen outside of battle. And they did not alter their behavior even when they knew all was lost. Even during the last days of the war, they drove prisoners from the concentration camps, executing those who fell behind.

What had happened was an abrupt departure from the order of things whether human or divine. They went beyond all measure of arrogance, and the people clamored for some kind of justice.

Six weeks after the end of the war, the president established by special decree extraordinary People's Courts and a Federal Court to try former German leaders along with Czech collaborationists. The brief news reports of the trials usually ended with, *Condemned to death.*

The sentences were carried out immediately.

Obergruppenführer K. H. Frank, a man with thousands of human lives on his conscience, was even executed in public. I very much wanted to witness such a spectacle, but I was forbidden.

In a newspaper report from May 23, 1946, I at least found a photo of Frank hanging on the gallows.

Third Courtyard of Pankrác Prison, 12:58

5,000 people—the muffled drone of the courtyard as the sun beats down. The gallows are situated in a corner between two buildings, before which stand the executioner and his two assistants. At 13:02 the tribunal arrives, followed by Frank surrounded by four members of the prison guard. Through a translator, Dr. Kozák once again reads the sentence to Frank. Frank, however, at first simply stares into space, then he looks around. . . . The last question Dr. Kozák puts to him is: "Have you understood the verdict, K. H. Frank?" And a final "*Jawohl.*" "Do you have any last wishes?" "No."

13:31—the just punishment of K. H. Frank is carried out.

I read the brief article with a thrilling satisfaction: Justice does exist after all.

⚬⚬⚬

When a catastrophe blows over and mortal danger is past, euphoria prevails for a brief time. Not even the sorrow of those deprived of their loved ones, the anger of those who longed for retaliation, the final murders committed by the fleeing SS, or the powerful explosions of the Soviet liberators could wipe out the thrill of newly won freedom.

From the very first days, flags billowed from windows: Czechoslovak flags, red Soviet flags with some yellow symbols (which my cousin explained were supposed to be a hammer and sickle), American flags with sloppily stitched-on stars, and even British flags. Lord knows where people came by them so quickly.

Units of our armies abroad were returning, welcomed with ecstatic ovations. Flowers fluttered through the air, and after such long-lasting silence, shouts of rapture erupted everywhere. The mood of exaltation encouraged our dreams of a society in which we would live freely, effortlessly, and more safely than at any time before.

At the same time, reminders of war lay everywhere. The remnants of the barricades were disappearing only slowly from the streets; automobiles appeared only occasionally; people stood in lines in front of shops. Old Town Square was defaced by debris from the town hall, and bombs had demolished the Emmaus Monastery. This, however, did not last long. Signs soon appeared calling for the fulfillment of a two-year plan to restore everything the war had destroyed. Father added that we would soon have five-year plans just like those in the Soviet Union, and only then would genuine prosperity reign. I was too young, too affected by what I had gone through, to understand that nothing could be as simple, as effortless as it appeared to Father or to the enthusiastic orators on the radio.

Real school started after the holidays. I passed a test to get into the high school in Vršovice. A few days after the beginning of the school year I celebrated my fourteenth birthday. For breakfast I got cocoa (my aunt in Canada had sent it) and then gifts of a box of oil paints, a palette, and nonporous paper, so I could develop my fondness for painting. At the same time my father reminded me that the Germans had deprived me of five years of school. I should be two grades higher, so I'd better do everything I could to catch up, especially in mathematics, physics, and chemistry. I could paint only when I'd finished all my other obligations.

It was difficult getting used to school. I bought notebooks and managed to borrow some textbooks from a couple of upperclassmen. Some of the books had been printed before the war, and when I paged through them I found entire paragraphs blacked out, which had obviously contained unpleasant facts or ideas during the period of the protectorate. There were, however, no other textbooks to be had.

Our homeroom teacher liked to talk to us about life and the value and meaning of our future endeavors. The old man was supposed to instruct us in mathematics, but when he turned his attention to his subject he would start mumbling. We couldn't understand him, so we stopped paying attention. Since we had no idea that mathematics was a precise logical structure in which every breach threatened the entire construction, we neglected mathematics and clamored all the more insistently for him to talk about politics. Certain students would prepare questions that were meant to provoke him: Why didn't the Americans come to help during the Prague Uprising? What did he think about the nationalization of the film studios? What did he think about the National Front—wasn't that actually an undemocratic organization? Why did we have the National Police Force instead of police? Perhaps it was due to the feeling of sudden liberation after years of occupation, when he had to watch every word; perhaps it was an attempt to elevate us above our coarse natures, which had been intensified by our wartime experiences of violence; perhaps it was a belief that speaking about essential life questions and providing some life lessons was more important than mathematical equations—our teacher always let himself be provoked into speaking about things that had nothing to do with mathematics.

Fortunately, my father explained mathematics to me. And even though I excelled in it, I forgot everything later, whereas some of the teacher's life lessons remain with me today. One of them concerned gambling. Whoever spends money on lotteries or gambling pays only the tax imposed by his own stupidity. Whoever has money to spare should be generous and help the poor, the sick, and those in need.

—•—

Sometime before Christmas we were paid a visit by Vlasta Kratochvílová. This woman, my father told me beforehand, was the bravest person he knew. She had risked her life many times over—to deliver mail to Terezín, to acquire needed medicines, and even to procure weapons.

I was expecting a heroic-looking woman, but when she arrived I beheld a quite ordinary woman, dressed somewhat provincially and about as old as my mother. She had brought with her some cakes she had baked and a Marbulínek picture book for my brother. To my surprise, she and my father kissed at the door, and then we sat at the table drinking real coffee (sent by my aunt in Canada) and munched on the homemade cakes. Mrs. Kratochvílová reminisced about the various people she had met and sometimes asked what had happened to them, but she always received the same reply: They were no longer alive; they didn't come back.

Then she began to confide to Father her concern about what was happening. They were needlessly socializing everything, as if we hadn't seen the chaos that ensued in Russia. She also didn't understand why the Communists were behaving as if they alone had won the war. They were butting into everything and distributing false information about the resistance.

I could see Father didn't like such talk, and if not for Mrs. Kratochvílová's past he probably would have begun shouting at her, but instead he tried to explain that communism represented the future of humanity. The war had proved this. It was, after all, the Red Army that finally defeated Germany and chased the Germans out of our country. Only the larger factories, banks, and mines were supposed to be nationalized, and that was proper and just. Why should people be left to the mercies of some coal barons and the like who cared only about increasing their own profits? For them, the worker was merely a means. We needed a society that would ensure that nobody suffered, that people were able to live their lives with dignity. "I know what unemployment is. I worked at the Kolbenka factory and knew a lot of the workers. Most of them were masters of their craft, but they were let go anyway. What happened to them then? They went begging? Vlastička," he addressed her almost tenderly, "I do not hide the fact that I am a Communist, and I'm proud of it."

"But, Doctor," she said in disbelief, "you can't be serious. Do you think people are prospering under communism? I talked to their soldiers, and you wouldn't believe the horrors they spoke of. They've got concentration camps there, for heaven's sake. Nothing good will come from this quarter."

Her words astounded me. Was it possible that someone would dare speak like this about our liberating ally? Tension suddenly filled the air, and Father said in a raised voice, "Mrs. Kratochvílová, I would never have expected you to spread Goebbels's propaganda." Then he launched into a long lecture about English and French colonialists, who lived off the exploitation of millions of slaves in India, Africa, and China. There they didn't need to build any camps because the people were so poor they were living in a concentration camp already. The imperialists were not above even extracting work from children, whose wages amounted to a handful of rice.

Mrs. Kratochvílová said that she had never been in those countries, and even if what Father said were true, it did not excuse the atrocities taking place here or in Russia. After a moment she stood up. This time she didn't kiss Father but merely shook his hand.

After she left, Father paced about the room repeating almost brokenheartedly: "She used to be such a courageous woman, and now look what's become of her: a reactionary!"

───

At this time, entire gigantic tracts of land in the border regions were suddenly depopulated. I'd heard that interim governors had taken over some of the factories and enterprises, and entire divisions of the Revolutionary Guard carrying rifles and machine guns had set out for the border. In exasperation, Father said that instead of bringing life, these people had taken away everything that wasn't nailed down. They weren't called the Ransacking Guard for nothing. Of course, he quickly added that it wasn't only the guards who showed up there but also those without land so they could finally acquire some property.

None of the new arrivals, however, could replace the millions who had been forced to leave. Crops, usually poor ones, stood abandoned in the fields with no one to harvest them. Soon an old military word found a new meaning: *brigade*.

Although I was born in the city and had never lived in the countryside, thanks to the brigades I enjoyed a significant amount of farmwork: I thinned out beets; harvested potatoes, cabbage, and onions; tied sheaves of wheat; worked with the threshing machine; labored on hay mounds; picked hops; and loaded trucks with hay. (They didn't know about my hay fever and once sent me up to the hayloft. After a couple of seconds I was gasping for air—much longer, and I would have died.)

We did all of this work at the expense of our studies, but I thought harvesting, or rather saving crops from ruin, was much more important than agonizing over *consecutio temporum* in Latin sentences. The others did not share my opinion. I also welcomed every opportunity to escape the city and go somewhere near the forest.

Once our entire class arrived in a border village to help with the harvest. The trucks were arriving at the thresher, loaded with sheaves of grain. Our homeroom teacher selected four of us to pass the sheaves to a man who would toss them into the thresher. The man was a re-emigrant, a muscular farmer whose features were hidden behind a wet sponge he had attached to his face; clouds of dust poured from the thresher.

At first we took turns, but after about an hour I was the only one left with the man. I would hand him sheaves as fast as I could, but the dust bothered me so much that I started to suffocate. I was ashamed to quit, however, and leave him by himself.

My classmates considered me either a blockhead or a strike-breaker. But I was usually able to reestablish my reputation in the evening, when I would compose love letters for their absent loves, even verses.

On one brigade when we were pulling onions, I composed "Onion Blues" for our improvised jazz orchestra:

> *Evening falls*
> *My hands they reek of onion.*
> *Unspeakably tormented,*
> *I go on day after day,*
> *Till I myself become an onion.*

Before I give up my soul on these broad fields,
I want to sing my onion blues
Into your ear, my love.
My sad, my final
My onion blues.

—∞—

At the end of spring 1946, I came down with measles. Because of my age, it laid me out. For several days, my fever was so high I was delirious. When the illness finally passed, the doctor gave me a thorough examination and saw from the electrocardiogram that I'd had, or still had, myocarditis, an inflammation of the heart muscle. The doctor prescribed six weeks of complete rest: lying, lying, and more lying. At most I could get up to eat at the table.

My prostration was oppressive primarily because it plunged me into solitude. I had lost all my friends during the war and so far hadn't been able to make any new ones. It was as if I was afraid that every new attachment would end in tragedy.

I read a lot. This was actually the first time in my life that I had both the time and the opportunity. No books were to be had in Terezín. We didn't have a lot of books at home. Those that my parents had accumulated before the war were lost during the occupation. But at an old bookbinder's shop a few buildings down from ours, Mother purchased a buckram-bound copy of *War and Peace*. Finally I had something to read, something that promised to absorb me for several weeks. I read avidly, drawn into the flow of events. The translation was somewhat archaic, full of participles. But I soon stopped noticing the style. It belonged to a far-off time, full of noblemen—the somewhat awkward Pierre Bezukhov, the Rostov family, and Prince Andrei. Then there was the great conqueror Napoleon, who slogged through broad Rus, where he succumbed to defeat just like his miserable successor.

From this epic novel I came away with the conviction that greatness that cannot be measured in terms of good and evil is worthless.

It's possible to be happy in life, but whether anyone manages to or not depends primarily on his ability to detach himself from his own suffering and from his concern for things and property, because all happiness comes not from insufficiency but rather from superfluity.

During my illness I also listened to the radio a lot. Two big trials had just concluded: one in Nuremburg and the other in Czechoslovakia, which dealt with the government during the protectorate. Sometimes the second one was broadcast live. I followed it fascinated. Shortly before the beginning of the new school year, my desk mate Jirka came by to visit and promised he'd save my place next to him. Everyone in the class, he said, was looking forward to my return. I knew he was exaggerating. Then he presented me with a gift, which I opened right there in front of him. It was a wartime paperback edition of Plato's "Phelibus." My classmate's visit unexpectedly brought me back to life. I started looking forward to new encounters and thinking less about my dead friends.

That very evening I read Plato's dialogue about the truly happy life. Being used to fiction, I devoured the strange and abstruse morsels of Socrates's arguments. To this very day, I remember that there are clean pleasures and unclean ones, higher and lower, and that the intellect is much more beneficial than pleasure for human life and happiness.

In school I quickly caught up with the little material I'd missed; I had the advantage that Father, during his brief visits to Prague, was able to explain the parts of mathematics that the teacher couldn't, and Mother patiently helped me translate elemental Latin texts: *Qui dedit beneficium, taceat, narret, qui accepit. Accipere quam facere praestat irjuriam.*

My mother was a frail, silently suffering romantic and at the same time an ascetic. I never once saw her drink even a glass of beer. She never smoked, and you could not express in her presence a single word that was even a little vulgar. When she spoke about her childhood and youth, it was always memories of various miseries and injustices: hunger during the First World War, when she would stand in line for bread in the early morning darkness. The bread never arrived or only a couple of loaves were available, and she wouldn't get one. At barely eleven years of age, she was sent by a charity organization, the Czech Heart, to some rich farmer who considered her a useless little girl, a good-for-nothing, because she couldn't lift a full bucket of water.

She was well-read and loved Russian and French literature: *Anna Karenina* and Romain Rolland's *The Soul Enchanted* and *Jean-Christophe*. The first books that came into my possession I received from her: Anatole France and Stendhal. I was later guided by her taste and purchased short stories by Turgenev and Gogol.

In Terezín I once managed to filch from the storeroom a suitcase that had been left by a dead inmate, and I found some French novel, or maybe it was a book of poetry. I don't remember the title or the author, but it was one of the few things Mother brought home with her to Prague.

The main thing she brought back from Terezín was fear. Even after the war had ended and no one was after us, she never ceased to be afraid. She didn't want us to attend large gatherings of people and asked us not to speak about our time in the concentration camp, especially that we had been imprisoned on the basis of race. The word "Jew" never crossed her lips.

My mother created in me the image that women were frail and vulnerable. They were sufferers who needed protection. They were a combination of beauty and inaccessible corporeality, which they would prefer to be rid of.

⚬⚬⚬

Scarcely had I returned to school after my illness when I fell in love with one of my classmates. I could admire the object of my affection only from afar. To me she seemed beautiful, smart, and virtuous, and she was afflicted with a debilitated hip joint. I didn't dare reveal even a little of my feelings to her. I could only dream and, at least for myself, put my feelings into words. So I started writing my first novel.

It was a love story beyond compare—at first unhappy but later blessed with a happy ending—between a girl crippled in an auto accident and a poor medical student. I managed to cobble together the beginning and outline the initial complications caused by the uncomprehending parents and treacherous and scheming friends, along with the oppressive social situation of both protagonists. Then, as I couldn't wait for the denouement, I wrote the ending in advance. I used up several school notebooks, and in the story I made it all the way to kisses and embraces. In reality I didn't even come close to touching the object of my adoration.

Certainly, even something like this can be an impetus for a writer: timidity in love, the need to replace reality with fantasy and to project this fantasy into reality by endowing it with form. Literature, or any kind of art, can emerge from the life experience of the writer or from his fantasy, which elevates to reality.

I still remember the excitement I felt when on the first blank page in the black, narrow-lined notebook I signed my name and beneath that the title, *Great Hearts*. Beneath the title I wrote *A Novel*, which corresponded to my resolve to cover every single white page. The emptiness of the paper was thereby annulled. Then when I read over the sentences I had just composed, I trembled with joy when I saw that they formed a whole, a story that unfolded just like those in printed books. I couldn't believe I was capable of something like this.

Every boy experiences something similar the first time he succeeds in constructing a kite from sticks, paper, and string, which then literally soars into the air.

Imparting form to something formless provides a certain satisfaction. You are intoxicated with the work, even if the form is imperfect or derivative, as long as, of course, what you have just created is recognizable.

Art obviously does not begin when you succeed in generating form out of formlessness; it begins when you are able to judge the caliber of your creation and not fall into raptures over the sole fact that you have created one of countless paper kites. At the time, however, I had no clue, and never again did I feel anything like the excitement I had when I filled the notebook with my artless and untutored sentences. The enthusiasm over the creation does not correspond directly to the quality of the thing created. Just the opposite: The creator never rids himself of doubts as to whether his construction will hold up even during his lifetime. The writer of mass-produced, popular works, on the other hand, is a stranger to these doubts and is convinced of the quality of his creation.

When I solemnly penned the words "The End," I was ecstatic. I wasn't even bothered by the fact that I'd left out the whole middle of the story.

Later, when I was moving out of the house, I placed all my manuscripts in a cardboard box that I stored in a closet next to the gas meter. As soon as I had my own apartment, I planned to return and retrieve it. After many years (I'd had my own family and apartment for a while), Mother asked me to finally come and fetch the box. I opened the closet and took out the box filled with faded manuscripts. They reeked of coal gas. I opened one of the notebooks at random and then one of the folders containing my unfinished epic. The quality of what I read was appalling.

I asked Mother to give the entire box to the schoolchildren when they came to collect paper. Thus like a coward I shrank back from carrying out this expurgatory act myself.

❦

At the beginning of the war I had been baptized, but I didn't realize this would entail any obligations at school. The vicar who taught religion in elementary school found out that although I was a member of the Evangelical Church of Czech Brethren, I simply went home during religion class. He called me in and criticized me as an immoral blaspheming hoodlum and hooky player.

In the next class, unlike several of my evangelical classmates who considered religion class somewhere between school and the playground,

I sat quietly like a model student and listened to the vicar's enjoyable tale about how the Jews escaped from Israel. I couldn't raise my hand because I knew absolutely nothing about this story, which, according to the vicar, was incontrovertibly true. The next time he was going over the material I raised my hand, and I soon became the teacher's favorite pupil. Unfortunately, my education in God's commandments and the tales of the ancient Israelites came to a premature end upon the decree that as a descendant of the aforementioned Israelites, I was banned from school.

Mindful that it was a matter of duty and my own salvation, I never missed an hour of religion class after the war. Father, however, raised me in his rational world, where you were not allowed to believe in anything that could not be proved by experiment or at least rationally explained. Religion, though, was expounded through inexplicable natural phenomena; it offered a primitive cosmology at a time when the earth was still the center of the universe. What I heard in religion class I therefore saw as the entrance to a fairy-tale world where miracles took place: Whales swallowed and spat out prophets with whom God himself would then converse; one could walk on water, and the sea would part before a raised staff; water could be turned into wine; the dead were brought back to life (even though they died later anyway); the blind could see; and angels visited people as God's messengers, while evil spirits entered unclean swine. Now I was suddenly supposed to believe all of this: Jesus was the true Son of God, the God who in six days created the heavens, stars, earth, water, and every living creature. At the same time, however, Jesus was the father as well, since he was both Father and Son in one person, even though he was conceived by the Holy Ghost, and that was why he along with the Father and Son formed a Trinitarian being, which could not be understood by reason but only believed in.

Since childhood, I have been interested in the mystery of life, the inconceivability of eternity and infinitude, the inexplicability of the origin and eventual demise of the universe, the strange and abrupt divide between life and death. I had the firmest intention of penetrating the mysteries of being and without prejudice listening to all the conclusions people had hitherto arrived at. On Sundays I dutifully attended the church in Vinohrady and listened to the sermon. Even though it seemed removed from what I had experienced, I was all the more interested.

I was included among the confirmands, went through all the exercises, and memorized the necessary responses. After my confirmation I began to attend the youth meetings of our church. At these gatherings, which were attended by around fifteen boys my age, we prayed together, learned songs, and listened to a brief lecture or sermon. Sometimes we would go on an excursion or to the cinema, and, as was common at that time, we went on brigade trips, where all the participants, unlike my nonevangelical classmates, worked hard because pretending to work was dishonest.

Because I participated in these meetings and activities, and because I would pose interesting questions, the pastor suggested I become chair of our youth group.

It was my first serious appointment, and I resolved to take it responsibly.

Most of those who had been confirmed and came to the evangelical youth meetings had been raised in the faith. Since childhood they had attended Sunday school and church services, and they were used to praying. God, who sacrificed his Son to redeem humanity, was for them a given, and there was no need for speculation.

I, however, was raised in neither the Christian nor the Jewish tradition, and so everything I was now learning, everything I repeated and proclaimed, awoke within me questions and doubts.

I was fond of Greek mythology and had memorized entire passages retold in the *Iliad*, which would certainly have been blasphemous in the eyes of our vicar. There actually wasn't any fundamental difference between the Greek image of the gods in human form and the image of a single God in human form, even though in the end, unlike the Greek gods, Jesus takes upon himself all of mankind's powerlessness, and when he dies in torment calls out in the darkness that had gathered in the afternoon above the land of Israel: *My God, my God, why have you forsaken me?*

Homer, however, had written of his own will; he had merely captured the tales or songs of his ancestors, whereas the writers of the biblical texts wrote not of their own will, but by God's, and this guaranteed the veracity of their texts. This dogma did not convince me. Who was it who had claimed that the texts of the Bible arose from God's will? Only their adherents.

Essay: *Utopias*, p. 426

3

Even though after the war I assumed that the finest people were always doing their utmost to create an ideal society—one that would not wage war, would eradicate poverty, and would care for the ailing and the elderly—I never took the slightest interest in politics. In the tenth grade, a student who had been held back and was a member of the Communist Party joined our class. He had a steady girlfriend and the inauspicious fate of a student forbidden to advance to the next grade. He explained to us the meaning of political persecution. With an air of aloof independence, he pretended he'd been wronged and implied that he was the only adult among us. As a member of the party of the proletariat, he had found himself among the immature and unwitting dregs of the petite bourgeoisie and the offspring of the politically unreliable intelligentsia. Despite the fact that he obviously shared my conviction concerning mankind's Communist future, I did not like him.

At the beginning of 1948, the year of the putsch, my classmate Polívka came up with the idea of organizing an election. He brought to class an old margarine box, cut an opening in it, and gave everyone who wanted to vote four pieces of paper, each of which bore a stamp of one of the authorized political parties.

I participated not only in the voting but also in the tallying of the votes. Unlike the actual parliament, the Communists in our class suffered a defeat that would have been described as "crushing" by the press. Apparently, our class was full of opponents of socialism.

The election took place sometime around the middle of February. During recess we were expending our pent-up energy by playing soccer in the classroom, even though it was a breach of school rules. Instead of a ball, we kicked around chunks of coal. It was neither hygienic nor pragmatic because after every kick our ball would break into pieces, so after a while the front of the classroom was strewn with coal rubble. At the peak of our competitive frenzy and as fragments of heating fuel, which was then still in short supply, were whizzing through the air, the principal walked into the classroom and, as fate would have it, received a blow right in the face.

The mere look from our walloped ruler, a man of venerable appearance and with a name worthy of a principal—Fořt—froze us on the spot. He undertook to write down the names of the culprits in the class register. When he finished he said he would consider our punishment. At best we would get the principal's paddle and a C in behavior, at worst conditional expulsion.

The prospect of such serious punishment devastated me. Even though the others claimed that such a triviality would result in a B in behavior at the worst, I couldn't sleep for several days and lived in perpetual fear of retribution. I was completely unaware that elsewhere a fateful event was beginning to unfold, one that would utterly overshadow my petty deed.

Like most of my wiser and more hard-bitten fellow citizens, I had no idea of the impending changes. Whenever Father came home, he didn't have much time to talk to me. But I knew that he disapproved of the national managers who thought of nothing but getting rich. Here he differed from those in charge of the recently nationalized businesses. He believed that the economy would begin to function only when all businesses were in the hands of the people.

In the middle of the week, Father unexpectedly arrived to inform us that the day of reckoning with the reactionary forces was close at hand. The workers had had enough of the theft of property that belonged to everyone. He turned on the radio to listen to a broadcast from the trade union congress. Passionate and bombastic words blared from the radio along with even more enthusiastic applause and sloganeering.

"Sons of the working class, sons of poverty and struggle, sons of unbearable suffering and heroic endeavors, at last you are declaring: No more!" bellowed the speaker.

Excitement coursed through my body.

Then another speaker declaimed: "The reactionaries would gladly drown your movement in blood. They have forgotten, however, that we are in Prague, not Athens or Madrid. We will not learn democracy from those who form public opinion with the assistance of the atom bomb." To the ecstatic assent of the crowd, he went on to declare that when the workers in Paris demand bread, they are fired upon, but that this kind of democracy has come to an end here in Czechoslovakia. Our democracy was now under the protection of our big brother, faithful to the workers, our magnificent Slavic brother, our deliverer from the Fascist pestilence, the almighty Soviet Union, which was the guarantor that nobody would again ever fire upon the workers.

"With the Soviet Union forever!"

Father exulted, but Mother was frightened and asked if we could finally have peace and quiet and a normal life.

"Only now," explained Father, "will everything begin to move forward, when we have gotten rid of all those parasites who have bled us dry. And you shouldn't forget," he reminded her, "what your brothers gave their lives for!"

Then everything came to pass that would ensure a Communist future for our country forever. Everything happened so quickly and without bloodshed that in my naïveté I succumbed to the illusion that this was merely the will of the majority being fulfilled. I even asked Father if I could borrow his Communist badge.

He was surprised and wondered what I needed it for, but he finally lent me this metal talisman. The next morning, to show on whose side I stood at this historic moment, I pinned it to the lapel of my jacket, in fact just a little higher than where I'd previously been forced to wear the Star of David. For several days I proudly wore this metal badge bearing the letters *KSČ* until Mother rebuked me and told me not to pretend to be something I wasn't.

If someone had told me at the time that wearing the Communist Party badge was just as deplorable as wearing a swastika when the Reichstag was burning and Hitler was installing his dictatorship, I would have been astounded and offended by this base comparison.

It didn't seem to me that any big changes were on the horizon during the first spring of Communist rule. Father looked satisfied; Mother cried because the foreign minister, Jan Masaryk, so the papers told us, had committed suicide by jumping from the window of his apartment in the Czernín Palace. "Why did he do it?" she asked.

"I'm sure he accepted the new government," declared Father. "He was a decent man of the people." And he repeated what he'd most likely heard at a meeting or on the radio: that the sensitive minister was shattered by the reactionary forces and had taken the side of the workers.

The principal who had threatened us with the dreadful punishment was removed, and a severe-looking woman took his place. She announced over the public-address system that a new era was at hand. As in the magnificent Soviet Union, we were creating a more just society. This required a new and progressive intelligentsia. She demanded that we devote even more diligence to our studies. It was no longer merely in our own interest, she pointed out, but in the interest of all working people who, through their Socialist endeavors, were making this possible for us.

To me the speech seemed appropriate during this epochal moment, but most of my classmates did not share this opinion, as they demonstrated by coughing and snorting. Toušek even whinnied (he could imitate a horse perfectly), and the end of the principal's speech was drowned out by raucous laughter.

Soon after that, our homeroom teacher informed me that I was to go immediately to the principal's office.

In light of my recent offense, this unexpected order frightened me.

The principal, however, welcomed me and asked me to have a seat. For a moment she browsed through some papers and then she said, "I've heard you're a good comrade."

I didn't know what to say. No one had ever called me comrade before.

"I heard," she continued, "that you're related to the Synek brothers." I said they were my uncles.

"They were genuine heroes. You must be proud of them." I agreed.

"And are your parents in the party?" I said that only my father was.

"And you," she said reproachfully, "aren't even in the Union of Youth."

Then to my amazement she suggested I call her comrade. A new era had begun, after all, and everyone struggling to build socialism was equal. Teachers and students had to trust and help one another. She rose and offered me her hand. "I wanted to tell you, Comrade Ivan, that we're counting on you. Apply for membership in the union."

Her trust and encouragement flattered me, but the prospect of joining any sort of organization was alarming. I made bold to object that it didn't really make sense now at the end of the school year, but I would talk it over with my parents.

Essay: *The Victors and the Defeated*, p. 433

4

The following school year did not start out well for me. When I entered
the classroom and headed for my desk, I saw that the seat in front of
mine, where Rost'a usually sat, was occupied by Richter. He didn't
dare take my seat but correctly assumed that Rost'a would offer no
objection. Richter was truly the worst student in the class and also the
biggest bully. It was only by a miracle that he hadn't flunked (perhaps
the February coup had a hand in it, since as the son of a house porter
and a cleaning woman he had the best class origin of any of us). His
seat used to be always assigned, usually in the first row where he didn't
dare demonstrate his boredom. Sometimes, however, he was placed in
the back row so that his apathy would not depress the teachers. Rost'a's
seat in the very center of the third row was decidedly the most advantageous. He could copy from his classmates and at the same time hide
behind those in front of him.

   I shouted at Richter to clear out of Rost'a's seat. He replied that the
seat belonged to him because it was the beginning of the year and he'd
gotten there first. I told him he was behaving like an extortionist and
furthermore a Nazi, which was the worst name I could think of. Then
I tried to shove him out of the seat. We immediately started fighting.
Because there wasn't enough room in the aisles, we tussled our way
up to the front of the classroom, and a crowd of onlookers gathered
around us. One of the girls urged someone to tear us apart or we'd kill
each other. No one did, and why would anyone? So we traded punches
and Greco-Roman wrestling moves in which my opponent was more
competent. A moment later I was on the ground with the victorious

Richter kneeling on my chest and enthusiastically banging my head against the floor. But before he managed to batter the consciousness from my skull, his frenzy suddenly abated. He released me and calmly rose to his feet.

I sensed a curious silence in the room.

I stood up, wiped my bloody face, and only then looked around. Next to me stood an unfamiliar teacher, whose short plait of hair at the back of his head, like something worn by the Chinese in pictures I'd seen, held my attention. He spoke fluent Czech, however, and asked us our names, and then noted in the class register: "Richter and Klíma were brawling like two mongrels and would not stop even in my presence." In the meantime, Rost'a assumed his original seat, and before yet another fight broke out, a second unfamiliar man stepped into the classroom. (Our teachers were always changing now.) His appearance suggested one of those lightly graying gentlemen from British films that had until recently been playing in the theaters. He even addressed us in faultless English. When he concluded from our expressions that we understood not a word, he informed us in Czech that his name was Marek and, as we could see, not only would he be teaching us English but at the same time he would serve as our homeroom teacher, which, his colleagues had informed him, was the worst thing that could happen to him at this school. Then he opened the class register, examined it for a moment, and said, "Well, well. It seems my colleagues were not exaggerating. Considering the fact that school started five minutes ago, you really seem to be in a hurry. Klíma and Richter, stand up." He looked us over. "I am obliged to punish you severely. But first, what have you to say in your defense?"

Richter, as usual whenever he was asked anything, clammed up.

"I wasn't fighting," I objected.

"How am I to understand that?"

"He started it," I said.

The teacher grimaced and told us both to sit down. Then he spoke at length in English, which seemed to us flawless even though we didn't understand a word.

Moments after taking his seat behind the desk during the following period, he confided to us, "You'll never guess what I've been entrusted with. Mrs., that is, Comrade Principal has charged me with the collection of old paper, which most likely includes rags and bones. This was to be expected since I'm new here, and, through this politically beneficial activity I will have the opportunity to correct my contemptible efforts to propagate the language of imperialists, warmongers, and Shakespeare. I have no choice but to offer you the same opportunity to atone for the sin that you continuously commit by deciding to study."

He glanced around the room in which he knew only the two rogues who had started fighting before the new school year had begun.

He pointed at me. "Klíma, I daresay that not only are you capable of committing frightful offenses against school rules, but you're also able to cope with difficult situations. I see you as the most appropriate adept for this praiseworthy activity. I hereby appoint you collections officer of the entire school. You have a sense for the passive voice, I assume, so pay attention: From this moment you are put in charge." He grinned and added serenely, "I believe that in this function you will perform much better than in a fight."

I soon joined the Czechoslovak Union of Youth. Several students from our class did too. We were accepted at a meeting that took place in the art room. A smiling twelfth-grade girl in a white blouse with a badge of the union was acting as chair. She introduced herself as Milena. She welcomed us briefly and noted how wonderful it was that the organization was growing. Then she invited us on a cleanup brigade in the school neighborhood.

When the meeting was over, she approached me and said she'd spoken to the principal about me. She thought I should be the chair in our class.

Until then I'd been the chair of our church choir youth group. It seemed to me that these two functions didn't quite jibe. I asked her what she thought.

"It would be fine." She beamed. She went on to say that it wouldn't really be any work at all. I'd just call a meeting every now and then and if necessary get people to go on brigade work. She would always tell me about an event well ahead of time.

I liked her smile. If I'd been a little bolder, I would have perhaps invited her for a walk in the park, but I merely said I would think it over.

I had my hands full, as I had started publishing the school magazine with the consent of the principal. I cannot recall a single contribution, but I do remember that we had to return all the used duplicating paper to the office. I didn't suspect that having access to copy paper and a mimeograph was a great advantage in a land where not a single line could appear without being approved by the appropriate comrades.

The weekly newsreels showed clips demonstrating the constructive enthusiasm of the workers. Weavers were using an ever greater number of looms; miners were accepting obligations to extract more and more coal; smelters poured out white-hot gleaming steel by the ton. Also, with the help of youth brigades, new smelting houses and dams were being constructed along the Vltava River. At numerous and apparently unrelated meetings, participants would applaud enthusiastically and proclaim glory to the Communist party along with Comrades Stalin, Gottwald, Slánský, or Zápotocký. The comrades would smile amiably and sometimes during a demonstration bow down to accept a bouquet proffered by a young girl, whereupon the crowd would applaud all the more ecstatically. The newsreels also showed black marketeers covering up hundreds of bolts of cloth, pairs of shoes, or sacks of flour whereby they sought to destroy our market. It was only because of these vampires, we were told, that our goods were rationed.

The hours devoted to Latin in school were cut in half, and our new Latin teacher was an amicable woman who understood that Latin belonged to an entirely different era.

In civics class, instead of Plato's *Laws* or even our own, we studied the *Communist Manifesto*. "The history of all hitherto existing society is the history of class struggles. . . . The Communists disdain to conceal their views and aims. They openly declare that their ends can be attained only by the forcible overthrow of all existing social conditions." The gray-haired teacher, whom we had nicknamed the Snake Charmer, always lectured as if in melancholic contemplation, which contributed to the dullness of her lecture, as if she were saying, "I'm sorry to bother you with all this." "Let the ruling classes tremble at a Communistic revolution. The proletarians have nothing to lose but their chains. They have a world to win."

—∞∞—

They locked up our landlord, Mother told Father when he came home one Sunday. He was apparently in some sort of work camp; at least that's what his wife had said.

"He was a bougie," explained Father.

"I didn't know there were any camps in Czechoslovakia," my brother joined in.

"Obviously only for people like him." Father brushed him off. "It won't hurt him to do a little real work."

"She started crying when she told me," continued Mother. "She asked me if I knew what she should do. They hauled him away and didn't even say where they were taking him."

"Why wouldn't they have told her? Why do you insist on believing everything those people tell you?" Father pronounced the words "those people" with a grimace and went over to his desk, which was always heaped with stacks of papers covered with numbers and indecipherable sentences. He made it apparent that Mother's news didn't interest him.

Nothing had happened that should have upset her. After all, bougies were used to living off the work of others. It was only fair that now they'd be forced to work.

Of course our landlord was an ordinary building contractor, and I saw him almost every day as he left for work.

Every day during first period at school we announced who was absent. Usually somebody was sick and could be gone for several weeks. All the teachers would conscientiously write down the absences, and at the end of the year they would be added up and listed on your report card. Two of my classmates were absent for several days. One of them, Polívka, was the administrator of something like parliamentary elections in our class. We dutifully announced that they were absent, but one day our homeroom teacher informed us that we no longer had to report their absence because they would certainly not be coming back this year. We stared at him in surprise, but he remained silent. Instead, he went to the board and wrote: "It is better that ten guilty persons escape than one innocent suffer" (Sir William Gladstone). "Write this down if you're interested: 'good, better, best.' Which comparative is this?"

As we stared at him in dumb silence, he explained, "As the brightest would understand, if they were not absent right now: the irregular!"

Several days later, one of our classmates who lived on the same street as Polívka shared the news that both our classmates had been locked up and accused of some horrible antistate crimes.

I would have liked to hear more, but it seemed everyone was afraid to talk about it.

Not long after, our drawing teacher also disappeared. He was of Serbian heritage and had abstained from voting upon a resolution condemning Josip Broz (Tito), who had been until recently the magnificent son of the working people of Yugoslavia (now a traitorous agent of imperialism and a rabid dog). Our teacher had obviously been one of Tito's many spies. At least that was how our classmate, who, unlike myself, was actually a member of the Communist Party, had explained it.

Our teachers never mentioned their colleagues, just as they never gave us their opinion about what was going on.

—∞—

Graduation was approaching. It was a different kind of graduation from the one our parents had told us about. The teachers were no longer our fearsome overlords but comrades on our shared path to socialism. We wore Union of Youth shirts (everyone was now a member); some of the teachers had stopped wearing ties, while others dressed as inconspicuously as possible; and everyone pretended to be a mere worker in the field of education.

Now education was viewed as a reevaluation of what had previously been presented as the truth. This concerned primarily history. The Americans and English were no longer allies. Masaryk and Beneš were no longer our beloved President Liberators or Architects—they were now representatives of the bourgeoisie. History had become the story of class struggles.

The revolutionary spirit had affected even the evaluation of literature. Great poets were now shriveled-up apples or they completely disappeared. Above all of them loomed the *marvelous standard-bearer,* the author of *Red Songs,* Stanislav Kostka Neumann, along with Jiří Wolker.

Between the final written and oral exams, our history teacher called me into the staff room and informed me that the party caucus of the school had decided to offer me membership in the Communist Party. We all believe, she said with amicable sternness, that the party will assist you in your aspirations to achieve greater consciousness, and your work will be an asset to the party.

I said thank you.

At home I conscientiously filled out the application. My class origin was not exactly the best. I knew of not a single worker among my ancestors, but on the other hand two of my uncles had been executed and were prewar Communist functionaries and national heroes.

A few days after graduation, I was invited to a meeting of the party caucus, whose members, much to my surprise, were mostly teachers.

I sat through a boring lecture and a similarly unenjoyable discussion of it, but finally my turn came. The history teacher, who was apparently chairperson of the local organization, announced that the district council had approved my membership application. "So, Comrade, we welcome you among our ranks. Never forget that being a member of the party is an obligation for the rest of your life. You must always act faithfully, honorably, and unselfishly to defend the interests of the party, which stands at the head of our entire society on its path to socialism." She failed to add, "So help you God."

I received a party ID card and mumbled something; I don't remember a word of it. Most likely I promised not to disappoint them.

At home, I was surprised that my party card was not met with approval. Father merely said, "It was your decision!" Mother looked doubtful. "Couldn't you have waited just a little while?"

And thirteen-year-old Jan said that people like me in his class were called freshly hatched reds.

"They're in your school already too?" cried Mother in astonishment.

No, my brother explained, but all around us.

Essay: *The Party*, p. 438

5

I was nearly twenty years old when I graduated from high school. Despite the number of unlucky circumstances, I had acquired some knowledge of chemistry, physics, and geography along with ancient and medieval history and Czech literature. I excelled in mathematics and was able to translate some less complicated Latin texts. I also read Lev Tolstoy's "The Kreutzer Sonata" in the original Russian. Thanks to my aunt Eliška, who owned the collected works of Karel Čapek, I devoured almost all of his works. I knew a little German and even less English, even though our English teacher was a notable translator of Thackeray and studied at Oxford. I had read (not studied) several works by Plato and Aristotle. I had also read some of the books of the Bible, mostly *Ecclesiastes*, several times.

I still hadn't kissed a girl; I'd never been interrogated; I wasn't interested in the fates of those who had been unexpectedly arrested and condemned; and it didn't even occur to me to compare the activity of the current government to that of the Nazis. It was as if the walls of the fortress where I had been forced to spend part of my childhood had hindered me from seeing the world in its true colors.

Despite the prevailing conditions, most of my classmates were accepted into the university. What was I supposed to study when I figured out that the only work I might be any good at was some sort of writing?

How did a writer actually make a living? And who could tell me if anybody would be interested in my writing? The most appropriate thing seemed to be to become a journalist. Karel Čapek had been one, after all, and his was the only work I knew fairly extensively. At the same time, however, I wasn't aware that journalism had changed since Čapek's time. It had become one of the least free occupations and was in such ethical decline that any decent person would have avoided it.

I learned that journalism was taught at the University of Political and Economic Sciences. I knew nothing about this school, so I went to the dean's office to get some information. I was told I could apply in theory, but the school was unique in that it trained primarily political officers and therefore accepted only graduates of workers' training schools, not high school graduates. He didn't tell me—perhaps he himself wasn't aware—that journalism was no longer going to be taught. I applied even though I definitely did not want to become a political officer.

In the cadre questionnaire, I mentioned my two uncles who had been executed; it was definitely owing to them that I was accepted.

The very first day we were divided into groups. We were to help each other in our studies, *culturally nourish* one another, go on brigade work, and learn about the new relationships among comrades in general. My classmates were indeed originally blue-collar workers or Youth Union members or party functionaries. Most of them had attended a one-year—in some cases, a several-month—course that was supposed to replace four years of high school study. But even the school administration was aware that such hastily acquired knowledge was insufficient. And so half of the lectures covered high school material. Since time immemorial, the life of a student has always been arduous, but it offered many joys.

When I entered the university, student life was not inordinately merry. Any unauthorized gathering, unorganized debate, unregistered and uncensored written expression was considered antisocial or even antistate.

By some miracle, a small private shop selling stationery and books had survived on Albertov Street, where our lectures took place. Once I went in, and there was not a single customer to be seen, so I started talking with the owner about books. I complained that there were so many authors I'd heard or read about, but it seemed they had ceased to exist. You couldn't find their books anywhere.

He asked whom I had in mind, and I recalled Čapek and Dos Passos, whose *42nd Parallel* sounded like an ingeniously conceived novel.

The bookseller agreed and went on to explain the present state of book publishing. All private publishing houses had disappeared, and only a few were permitted to operate. These had to belong to certain organizations and they were told what they could publish and primarily —here he grimaced—what they could not publish. Then he asked what I was studying. Journalism, I told him, even though I had no desire to be a journalist. I wanted to write books. But at the same time I wasn't studying journalism, because the subject had been abolished.

"So, you're a budding writer." Most likely he'd intended it ironically, but then he said, "Wait here a moment." He disappeared into the back of his shop and brought out two leather-bound books. "These are two of the greatest American authors, but you won't find their books anywhere." They were Steinbeck's *In Dubious Battle* and Hemingway's *To Have and Have Not.*

To my shame I had not heard of either author.

—————

My mother noticed an article in the journal *Tvorba* mentioning the field of literary studies, which had just opened at Charles University's School of Humanities.

I went to the dean's office to inquire about the requirements for acceptance. Once again I learned that literary studies (considered an ideological field) did not accept high school graduates. He added, however, that I could of course submit an application.

So I did. I explained in the application that I wanted to change universities because the department of my studies had been abolished.

During this short period of my life, everything was panning out. It was certainly due to my membership in the party. I was accepted and could leave the school that was so senseless that it was closed two years later.

I knew that Charles University was an old and venerable institution. Three years earlier it had celebrated six hundred years since its founding. But I was unaware that the faculty had been purged that very year, and all of its traditions as a free university had been debased. The new students no longer had a chance to take part in those traditions, and the professors who were now here (most had entered the Communist Party) didn't even mention them. (Many of the professors had probably participated in the purge.) I had only a smattering of education and was blind. I paid no attention to the purges that had occurred not only at this university but at the others as well, along with all the newspapers, journals, and radio stations. I didn't even notice the news about sentenced, banned, or imprisoned writers. I didn't follow the discussions concerning socialist realism, the new type of hero, or ideology in literature.

Of course I understood well enough that subjects such as the History of the Communist Party of the Soviet Union, Introduction to Marxist Philology, or A Marxist View of Literature certainly could not until recently have been compulsory.

The university (like every school) thrusts a lot of knowledge upon the student, most of which he will never need and will sooner or later forget. The university should teach students a systematic and responsible approach to research. It should teach them how to seek out sources and work with facts. And the most important thing it can offer is contact with figures who can serve as mentors—an example for both the student's work and his civic conduct.

Besides a lot of useless knowledge, my university provided above all knowledge that I had to reject later on in my life because it was fundamentally untrue.

While most of the linguistic subjects were taught by professors and genuine philologists, most of the literature lectures and seminars were led by young assistants who had written nothing more than perhaps a brochure or newspaper article. All that was left of modern Czech literature for our lecturer was the realistic social branch and of course Communist authors. Interpretations concentrated on the content and their political assessments. Nobody really attempted literary analysis, and as a result second- and third-rate authors became prominent, whereas many of those whose works were superior were not even mentioned—they were considered Catholics, ruralists, legionnaires, decadents, or formalists.

In the class that treated progressive traditions in world literature, which was the only class on world literature, a young party journalist read to us the text of his own pamphlet, *Troubadours of Hatred*. It was the only lecture concerning contemporary literature that had come into being to the west of our borders.

> During the rise of Fascism and World War II, the intellectual had two choices, two sides between which to decide—the nation or betrayal, his own people or Fascism. The decision taken by Gide was tantamount to relegating himself to the trash heap. . . .
>
> Where are today's descendants of *Buddenbrooks*, Forsyth, Thibault? Today they are no longer creating a "world in and of itself." Today they stand as pawns in the game of the only predatory power: American imperialism. . . . American imperialism seeks to conquer the world. Their plans contain military, diplomatic, financial, cultural, and political elements. What will their cultural equivalent be? What elements of culture, and especially literature, correspond to their appetite for world domination?

In his lectures he belittled Camus, Sartre, Wilde, and Steinbeck. *The name of Sartre has become a symbol of decay and moral degeneration, a synonym for decadence, a prototype of the morass into which bourgeois pseudoculture has sunk.* There were no limits to the abuse he heaped on the aforementioned books and the simplifying interpretations meant to prove the decadence of the greatest contemporary non-Communist authors. *Sartre's* Troubled Sleep *is poison, death, which agitates, which stretches out its claws for living people. . . . Yes, let us ask what sort of people does a literature of degeneracy envisage? Take for instance Steinbeck's final series of California novels. What kind of human being is he reckoning upon when in* Wayward Bus *he introduces a repulsive series of human creatures. . . . Faulkner's* Light in August *is organized training for murder, hatred, and a willingness to hire anyone for a criminal cause. . . . The unprincipled adventurer, sentenced in 1924 to three years of hard labor for a burglary in Cambodia, André Malraux, wants to be both a Goebbels and Rosenberg to today's de Gaulle, his idol and leader. . . . The novel* For Whom the Bell Tolls *is the ideal work to further the foreign political goals of the United States. . . . Another mockery of the war in Spain was,* according to our lecturer, *Adventures of a Young Man* by Dos Passos (whose works I admired); also, *Eugene O'Neill revealed his degeneracy in his play* The Iceman Cometh. Albert Camus was *one of the apostles of decadence and morass;* Simone de Beauvoir advocated *the idea of cannibalism,* as did Robert Merle. And literary critics and historians? *The bourgeoisie sham-scholars, publicist nabobs, theorizing buzzards howl in unison like a pack of hyenas wrapped up in professorial garb.*

His way of thinking, and primarily speaking, appalled me, and even though I was still willing to consider the claim that art in non-Socialist countries was undergoing a decline, the abuses he showered on these authors was repulsive; I knew some of them, and what I had read seemed marvelous. From our assistant Parolek, who lectured on Russian literature, I learned how good literature comes into existence: *The politics of the party is critical both for culture and for literature. They actively participate in resolving questions concerning the battle for peace and the construction of the material and technical basis of communism. The politics of the party emerges from*

the scientific analysis of the international situation as well. It **directs***
*the development of Soviet society as well as Soviet culture on the ba-
sis of a scientific understanding of the sole proper direction.* Writers
should follow instructions that lead them in the proper direction.
The author himself need not search. Other, more competent people
searched for him. Soviet authors (and ours, as well) were supposed
to write about four points:

    *1. Depict the epoch-making victory of the USSR and demonstrate
its profound significance in all its aspects.*

    *2. Show the heroism of the Soviet people in their Socialist, constructive
activity in factories and in the fields of their collective farms.*

    *3. Battle for peace against reactionaries abroad. Go on the offensive
against bourgeois culture. Support the fight for peace by democratic forces
abroad.*

    *4. Uncover palpable attributes of future Soviet communism directly
in Soviet reality, primarily in the Soviet man.*

Fortunately there was at least one person among my colleagues
who knew something about world literature. Josef Vohryzek, like
me, should have died in a concentration camp, but his parents had
managed to send him to Sweden at the last minute. There he survived
the war living with some kind people. In a factory he learned to work
with metal and after the war he returned to Czechoslovakia, where he
searched in vain for his parents and relatives. He remained a blue-collar
worker, but in the factory where he worked he was chosen for workers' training. When he finished, he ended up in our department. He
knew Scandinavian literature. He'd also read many translated works in
Swedish, which had never been published in Czechoslovakia. After one
of Comrade Bouček's lectures, he heatedly announced that everything
that fellow had claimed was nonsense. You can't judge a literary work
according to a political yardstick. The extensive list of condemnable
authors, whom the assistant had tried to discredit, we should take

---

* Bold lettering indicates Klíma's emphasis.

rather as a recommendation. It was precisely their works that should
be read because they belonged to the best of world literature.

I managed to get hold of a translation of Camus's *The Stranger*
as well as Hemingway's *For Whom the Bell Tolls*. Both novels mesmer-
ized me.

One day in a tram I ran into my former English teacher, Marek.
He asked me what I was studying and how I was doing. When I mentioned the content of the lectures on foreign literature, he said it didn't
surprise him. Then he added, "You know, Klíma, whoever wants to
break a free spirit always attacks education. That's why the Germans
closed the universities, and that's why today they are reviling great souls
and confusing concepts and values. The goal is to undermine education
in its very foundation. He who truly wants to know must return *ad
fontem*.* I don't have to translate this for you. You did well in Latin."

⸎

I had been in the department barely two months when, after a lecture
on the history of the Communist Party in the Soviet Union, a girl
whom I'd never noticed before approached me. She began by apolo-
gizing for taking up my time, but she knew that I'd been accepted to
study literature even though I had a high school diploma (I had no idea
how she had found this out). She had tried to enter the department,
as well, but without success. They allowed her to study Czech only in
connection with Russian.

I didn't know what to tell her. She kept walking with me as if
expecting me to say something significant. We were no longer on the
topic of changing majors. We talked about literature. She also liked
Karel Čapek and Vladislav Vančura and had read a lot of poetry. She
loved Pushkin and even recited something about Tatyana from *Eugene
Onegin*. In class she was called Tatyana.

---

* To the spring, the source.

She confided to me that she had composed a few poems. Then we discovered that neither of us smoked or went to pubs, and then she told me that she sometimes felt very lonely. She used to go out with Tomáš, but they didn't understand each other and broke up. When you're with someone you don't understand, it's worse than being alone. We walked all the way to Letenský Park, where dogs and children dashed about. In the distance we could hear the jackhammers of the construction workers who were building the largest monument in the country, in Europe, and perhaps in the world (I had no idea of Jesus in Rio de Janeiro)—to Stalin. The acacias were already in bloom as well as the early roses. The air was filled with sweet aromas, and I tried desperately not to sneeze.

She said she loved flowers, roses most of all. A short distance from her house was a big park where she often studied.

I asked her where she lived, and she said all the way out in Líbeň. I didn't have to walk her the whole way home, but of course that was precisely what she was suggesting. But I was afraid my allergies would start up and I would begin sneezing, so I accompanied her only to the tram. The little marketplace near the tram stop sold flowers, and I bought her a delicate little pink rose which, in view of my financial situation, seemed to me a magnanimous gift.

I could see gratitude in her eyes, which were similar in color to mine, and suddenly tears appeared. Her tram was approaching, and she quickly wiped away the tears and thanked me again for the rose. She wanted to talk with me again sometime.

So we started seeing each other. I learned that she almost didn't remember her father, who had died when she was three, but she could still recall how she would wait for him in the evenings when he came home from work. He would pick her up and throw her into the air and catch her. Tears started flowing down her cheeks again as she told me about it. She told me how she fell in love with Tomáš in high school, and everyone in the class knew they belonged together, but they were actually very different. She was fond of poetry, whereas he preferred sports and engines. He was marvelous at basketball because he was almost two meters tall, and she could never even get the ball into the basket. Besides, such an activity seemed pointless. Why would you like running around a gym or basketball court?

Some days we just sat side by side in silence. At such moments she would peer, unblinking, into my eyes. She would stare at me so lovingly that it excited me more than words (we hadn't even embraced yet, just held hands a couple of times). She wanted to know if I'd ever been in love, and she asked about my childhood. When I told her about Terezín, tears once again streamed down her cheeks even though I didn't describe anything particularly brutal. The next day she told me she'd had a dream in which we were wandering down a long, dark tunnel with only a few intermittent flickering lanterns. We kept looking ahead waiting for light, but it never appeared. Then corpses were scattered over the tracks, and we had to step over them, but there wasn't enough room, and they kept reaching out their chilly hands for us. It was terrifying.

She struck me as delicate, gentle, and poignantly diffident.

Of course, now we sat together in class. When it came time for exams, we studied together, usually in an empty lecture hall and sometimes outside in a park. Once we took a tram all the way to the edge of the city and lay in a meadow somewhere above Spořilov. We were studying for a while, and then she suddenly leaned over and began kissing me. She didn't say so, but I'm sure she was thinking: since he's never going to get around to it himself.

Then came summer vacation. She left on a brigade to Ostrava, while I stayed in Prague. We promised we would think about each other every evening at nine o'clock, and she believed our thoughts would meet halfway. We would write as well.

It was out of love for her that I started filling the gaps in my knowledge of poetry. I brought home from the library a bundle of poetry collections, as well as Vítěslav Nezval's *Manon Lescaut*. The story of a great romantic love had me enthralled. I immediately identified with the couple from the narrative. Moreover, the rhythm of the verses penetrated into my mind, even my blood, like some rapidly proliferating microbe. For a while I lost my own voice. I wrote my sweetheart a romantic poem two pages long (I wrote it during class). A few of the verses still stick in my mind:

> *To die, I want to die for your love,*
> *I long to go for a walk with you tomorrow*
> *how distant is black Ostrava,*
> *living without you is like an execution.*
>
> *My love, my love till death,*
> *now alone somewhere in the shadow of a smelter,*
> *in my soul I stare into your soft eyes,*
> *do something so my heart does not burst apart.*

I rambled on about our love, which I compared to a mountain we were climbing together. There above, my dear, stands a castle with 365 rooms,

> *each created for a night and a day,*
> *may our love be glorified*

I was thrilled with my creation, and I was certain it would make an impression on my sweetheart as well. I waited impatiently for an answer.

It didn't come for a long time. Then I received an unusually cold and curt letter. She assured me that she wasn't at all lonely. She was experiencing marvelous and utterly new human relationships and didn't understand how, during this time of labor and constructive activity, I could scribble poetry about some sort of castles in the air so distant from real people and real life. She hadn't even wanted to mention my poetry, but she thought it only proper to say what she was thinking and feeling. Finally, she had lost the desire to continue corresponding with me.

The first time we were in the same class after vacation, she found a seat as far away from me as she could. She came over during the break to inform me that Tomáš too had been on the brigade, and she had realized she was still in love with him. I shouldn't be angry. During the trip, she had grown up and come to understand that life is not just poetry but also labor and the happiness that comes from work fulfilled.

———◦◦◦———

The accounting with members of the occupying offices, traitors, and collaborationists began immediately after the end of the war. Some of the trials were broadcast on the radio, and the larger ones were written about extensively. Most, however, were summarized in only a few lines that reported that a certain informer was sentenced to death, and the sentence was carried out immediately.

At first I followed the trials with unhealthy interest, but as traitors continued to be uncovered and incriminated in almost exhausting succession, I had stopped paying attention.

But suddenly an extensive and bewildering accusation appeared against a ring of conspirators whose members were leading Communist functionaries. At their head was the general secretary of the party, Rudolf Slánský. Almost all of the fourteen accused were Jews who were indicted of course not for their Jewish origins *but for supporting and protecting the activities of Zionists, this reliable agency of American imperialism, for . . . allowing the capitalist elements of Jewish origin to rob the Czechoslovak state on a large scale.* They were also in league with traitorous elements abroad, which were sheltering Trotskyites. The charges alleged they were attempting to bring back capitalism, committing sabotage, and working with imperialist and Titoist agents. They were also accused of attempting to assassinate President Gottwald. The prosecutor's speech took up several pages of the newspaper *Rudé právo*, which demonstrated the tremendous significance we were supposed to attribute to the trial.

Immediately after the accusation appeared in the paper, a weaver from Jaroměř shared her feelings with a reporter.

As I read the accusation against Slánský's band of traitors, I fully realized the danger threatening us, the working people. Slánský and his coconspirators were attempting to bring back the times of capitalism and do away with the democratic system of the people. Following the shameful example of their teacher Tito, they sought to bring back those times, which we working people, and especially the workers in the textile industry, remember very well.

The same day the builders of the Slapská Dam had their say:

We the workers constructing the Slapská Dam demand the severest punishment for the traitors. In reply to all our enemies, we pledge to work with even greater diligence to honorably fulfill our task before the birthday of J. V. Stalin.

The court had not yet even pronounced judgment, but writers began to join in with their condemnation. One of their articles, "No, They Are Not People," recalled court reporting before the war.

During trials of the most serious and hardened scoundrels, I have never encountered such figures as I saw in the courtroom during the antistate conspiracy ring led by Rudolf Slánský. . . . I remember the faces of robbers, safecrackers, and murderers that I saw in the courtroom, and I must say . . . yes: these fourteen accused monsters are not people!

A class-conscious poet who was present in the courtroom added his characterization of the accused: *Here before us sits abomination embodied in living creatures who were at one time human beings.*

There was something hideous about this language, as if they were writing about a group of SS murderers from the gas chambers.

The confessions of the accused and their witnesses filled a special edition of *Rudé právo.* Surprisingly, all of them repeated, with slight variation, the words of the prosecutor's speech. One of them, André Simon, until recently a distinguished journalist, when asked how he judged his actions, replied in the words of the prosecutor:

> I condemn myself as a criminal deserving the severest punishment. As a conspirator I am responsible for every deed and crime of each member of our conspiracy ring. I am of Jewish heritage. In which country does anti-Semitism grow freely? The United States and Great Britain. I was in contact with the intelligence services of these two countries. Which countries are reviving Nazism? The United States and Great Britain. I was in contact with the intelligence services of these two countries. In which country is there a law against racism and anti-Semitism? The Soviet Union. . . .
>
> I was a writer. It has been said that a writer is an engineer of human souls. What kind of engineer was I when I poisoned souls? Such an engineer of souls belongs on the gallows.

In his concluding speech, the former secretary general of the Communist Party, designated as the leader of this antistate conspiratorial ring, stated:

> I know that the sentence suggested by the state prosecutor will be fair to the utmost in light of all of the terrible crimes I have committed. I bear the main and most burdensome guilt of all the accused because I stood at the head of this antistate conspiratorial and espionage ring. It was I who created this ring, led its activities, and provided the instructions for all of my accomplices, which were not only my instructions, but primarily those of the American imperialists I served. They were instructions of betrayal and conspiracy, sabotage, subversion, and espionage. . . . The enemy within the ramparts is the most dangerous enemy of all because he can open the gates. I was an enemy within the Communist Party, within the Czechoslovak state, within the entire camp of

peace. The state prosecutor is correct when he says I disguised myself. I had to disguise myself to remain as an enemy within the ramparts. . . . I said I was against imperialist war, but I was preparing this war, I was carrying out sabotage, planting and protecting spies who would have formed a fifth column in case of war. . . . I committed the most perfidious crimes possible. I know that for me there are no extenuating circumstances, no excuses, no clemency. . . . I deserve no other end to my felonious life than the end suggested by the state prosecutor.

This trial was much discussed in our department. How was it possible that they could write about the accused as criminals deserving the death penalty when the verdict had not even yet been announced? Didn't that reflect a tampering with the law? Wasn't it bewildering that the same thing had happened before in the Soviet Union? Almost everyone there who had fought for the revolution and then led the country was in turn revealed to be a traitor. It seemed ridiculous that traitors, spies, and saboteurs were at the head of government. It was also odd that right after someone was arrested, he confessed. Even the war criminals at Nuremberg tried to defend themselves; they had denied their guilt or at least tried to minimize it.

I was surprised by the strange phraseology of the accused. Would evil-intentioned enemies and spies use the term "camp of peace" for the Soviet Union and its allies and condemn American imperialism? Would they employ the language of speeches that had been only recently delivered? Even now that they were confessing, why didn't they alter their choice of words? Was it possible they were speaking this way because they thought such an admission would be considered extenuating circumstances?

No extenuating circumstances were conceded. All but three were hanged.

At home Mother started to worry that they were going after Jews again. I waited for Father to object, to explain that communism was, after all, an international movement, and it condemned any kind of racism. But he remained silent.

When Mother was asleep he called me into the kitchen, where he worked and slept. He seemed to be considering whether or not to tell me why he'd called me in there. Then he said, "They're after me too."

I didn't understand.

He explained that several weeks earlier, four engineers under his supervision were arrested. They were constructing new high-tension motors for a Polish power station.

I didn't know what a high-tension motor was, but this clearly wasn't the issue.

Sixty motors had been ordered, continued Father, but no one at the factory had had any experience. It was a new factory where untrained women made so many mistakes in production that most of the machines barely functioned at all. He tried pointing this out, but no one would listen. Everyone was in a hurry to fulfill the quota. Now the bosses obviously wanted to hold them, the designers, responsible. "I wanted to tell you," he said, coming to the most important point, "if something happens to me, it's up to you to take care of Mother and little Jan. You're an adult and know very well that Mother cannot work."

I protested, saying that nothing could possibly happen to him, since he hadn't done anything wrong. Even if he'd miscalculated something, it wouldn't be considered a crime.

Father nodded and then simply smiled sadly.

Essay: *Revolution—Terror and Fear*, p. 445

6

Attendance at specialized lectures was still voluntary. Participation in military preparation, however, was mandatory and strictly monitored; the only absences tolerated were those due to an illness officially confirmed by a doctor. The first military seminar dealt primarily with regulations and basic information about the composition and organization of the army. The smallest unit is the squad; three squads form a platoon; three platoons, and in some cases one motorized unit, make up a company. There were differences between infantry units and motorized or tank units. We were taught how ordinary soldiers were armed. Everything we were told was secret, and we were warned that any mention of this information outside class would bring us before a military court—because the enemy never slept. Even an apparently minor detail could be of crucial significance. An unbelievably half-witted lieutenant colonel explained that the moment we disclosed some seemingly unimportant detail, we became open to blackmail, and the enemy would demand more and more serious information (as if we had any). All the instructors were officers and emphasized vigilance and readiness to confront imperialist aggression, and a hatred of German revanchists and their American employers.

Our notebooks for this class were likewise stamped SECRET, and at the end of class they were collected and locked up in a vault in the military department.

I'm not sure how it happened, but once at the end of winter when I had just come back from class, I discovered that I'd forgotten to turn in my notebook and accidentally stuck it in my briefcase. Now this notebook, chock-full of strictly classified notes on military duties, the firing power of howitzers, and the effective range of antiquated antitank weapons, was at home, where I'd been instructed it had no business being. I was quite rattled and wondered whether I should run back to school and turn in the notebook. But they would probably start asking questions: Why had I taken it? What had I been doing with it all day? On the other hand, I could take it to the next class and turn it in as usual, and no one would be the wiser. So I shoved it in among my other notebooks in my dresser and paid it no further mind.

The next morning the doorbell buzzed. When Father opened it, five men burst into the apartment. They reminded me of something that had happened a long time ago during the first day of the occupation, when gestapo agents burst into the apartment looking for my uncles. But the gestapo had merely walked through the apartment looking into various possible hiding places, and then they disappeared. These men pulled out some papers, shoved them at Father, and continued to conduct a thorough search of the apartment.

While my panic-stricken mother tried to elicit from them what they were doing, what right they had to dig through our things, my brother was still sleeping, and Father mutely looked on. At that moment, I was thinking about my notebook. If they found it, I would never be able to convince anybody that I'd placed it in my briefcase by mistake and not with the subversive intention of photographing its contents and handing them over to an agent of the CIA.

Occupied with my own paltry problem, I barely noticed the growing pile of documents with Father's calculations, and specialized books in German, English, French, Russian, and Hungarian. These strange investigators could not make sense of any of it (they knew no foreign languages and had no idea what the documents and books dealt with). Therefore, they found them suspicious. To the pile of books and calculations they added a camera, a projector, and binoculars. We didn't own anything else of value.

Then one of them walked over to my dresser, opened a drawer, and took out a notebook, which had notes in Russian. This fellow, who belonged to the ancient past as well as the present, asked: Is this yours?

I nodded

Are you a student?

I said I studied Czech.

He took another notebook, opened it, and gave it a good shake. A piece of blotting paper fell to the floor. He let it lie there for a moment but then it occurred to him that it might contain a message. He picked it up and held it against the light.

I didn't remember how far down the SECRET notebook was, just as he didn't know what he was supposed to be looking for in my dresser. I said, "That one's for Russian literature."

He put the notebook back and closed the drawer. I knew I was saved.

Father, however, was not. They led him away without even letting him say goodbye.

It looked as if a tornado had ripped through our apartment. Books, piles of paper, everything lay all over the chairs, floor, and dining room table. Some things they'd taken away, and the rest they'd just left lying wherever they'd thrown it.

Funeral music was playing on the radio at the time when Socialist songs should have been broadcast. Then a voice, tremulous with emotion or pain, announced: *The Central Committee of the Communist Party of the Soviet Union, the USSR Council of Ministers, and the Presidium of the USSR Supreme Soviet announce with profound sorrow . . .*

Yesterday we'd already heard the doctor's report about J. V. Stalin's serious illness, so I didn't have to wait for the end of the announcement. It was clear: Stalin was dead.

The next day, the newspapers' front pages were bordered in black and bore a youthful picture of the recently deceased. The Communist Party newspaper *Rudé právo*, on the very day of his death (I remember thinking it strange the paper did it so quickly), printed a text, which I cut out because of its remarkable combination of folk song and political phrasing (at the time I didn't fully understand the duplicity of the content):

> When our workers were given to understand this woeful news, they were stricken with boundless grief and wept bitter tears. They wept for the most painful loss that could afflict the Soviet land, the international working class, the working people of all countries, and the entirety of progressive and peace-loving humanity. *Farther on it continued in a decidedly nonlyric tone:* In vain did the imperialist hyenas base their hopes upon the death of the great Stalin. His work is unchallengeable and incontrovertible.

A period of national mourning was proclaimed; flags were lowered to half-mast or exchanged for black funeral banners.

My former love, Tatyana, who had taken a dislike to me, came to see me one day and asked if I had a moment.

We sat on a bench on the top floor of the building where students were waiting to take an exam in the dead languages of the Near East, and, as was her habit, she peered unblinkingly into my eyes. She said she knew how horribly she'd offended me and could imagine how alone I must feel after such a calamity.

I wasn't sure what calamity she was talking about. At first I thought she'd found out that my father had been arrested, but then she explained: How horrible it is that even the greatest of people must die. She said she also felt alone, completely alone. She placed her head on my shoulder and started crying.

In *Literární noviny* respected poets were expressing their grief. Milan Jariš lamented:

Each felt the cold in his heart
and the responsibility—we must continue apart
No, there is no one I loved more
than my father who is no more.

Stalin—The strength of the Soviet Union
Stalin—The author of future instruction
Stalin—The life of every future human
Stalin—The one that will destroy destruction.

The weekly newsreel showed the crowds at the funeral. You could hear the oaths of loyalty to his eternal memory, and black crepe seemed to blanket the entire world, which was apparently drowning in tears.

Tatyana confided to me that she'd made a tragic mistake with Tomáš. She had succumbed to the atmosphere there on the Ostrava Brigade. Life, however, is built not from bricks and mortar but from feelings and understanding. And now during these difficult and dismal days, she had realized it.

On the bench, looking out over the embankment and castle arrayed in black, we embraced each other and kissed.

On top of all this, President Gottwald died a few days later.

Once again crowds swarmed the funeral; oaths of loyalty were sworn to the sacred memory of the first workers' president; there were more black banners and tears. Cinemas and theaters were closed, and the only thing on the radio was funeral music.

We had no news of Father—where he was, what had happened to him, why they had taken him away. We didn't even know what we were going to live on.

Aunt Hedvika, who always talked about the great Stalin with such enthusiasm, stopped by. She said Father had certainly done nothing wrong, and she offered to contribute at least a little money until he returned. Then my aunt, the one who had lived so many years in the

Soviet Union and revered Stalin as a giant among men, said something that astounded me. Vilík is lucky the Leader has died. Maybe everything will change now, and these disgraceful trials will cease.

———⁂———

Mother had become desperate. She kept looking out the window as if thinking she would catch sight of Father, who couldn't be kept in prison, since he hadn't done anything wrong.

Because she was the sister of national heroes after whom a Prague square had been named, she steeled her resolution and wrote a letter to the new president of the republic. She said she'd known Father from their early student days and was quite certain he'd never done a single dishonest thing in his life. She knew that work meant everything to him, and every day he worked well into the night. She also knew that when he was working in Brno, he was attacked, and only because he'd urged people to do honest work. Such aspersions, however, have no place in our republic.

She racked her brain over every word, even over the closing. She knew she should end with the comradely *Honor to Work*, but that greeting never passed her lips, so she wrote just *With Deep Regards*.

Mother never received an answer to her letter, but about five weeks later we found a letter from Father in the mailbox with the stamp *Uherské Hradiště*. Father wrote that he was thinking about all of us and we shouldn't worry about him. He was lacking for nothing and hoped we too were healthy and were somehow getting by.

The letter was written on gray paper, which immediately brought to mind the notes we were allowed to write from Terezín now and then.

Paradoxically, it was during this time that my probationary period expired, and I was to be either accepted or rejected as a member of the Communist Party.

At the meeting, my admission to the party was the last item on the agenda. In the lecture hall, shrouded in tobacco smoke, the chairman acquainted the party members present with my case. I was an excellent student. For reasons of health, I hadn't gone on the summer work brigade. I had a good relationship to the collective. As far as my class origin was concerned, I had a white-collar background, but my uncles were national heroes and loyal members of the party who had fallen in battle against the Nazis. Now, of course, my father had been arrested, apparently for political reasons, so it would be necessary to consider carefully my possible membership.

I was given the floor in order to discuss my father's situation.

I said my father was the victim of some sort of mistake or a false accusation. He would definitely be proved innocent.

A comrade addressed me from the floor and asked about my relationship to socialism.

I replied that I believed in its future.

The comrade was not satisfied with my answer. My father had obviously not believed in socialism and hated it. Was I prepared to disown him if it turned out he had committed a crime against the state? I was not prepared for anything like this. It was unthinkable that my father would get mixed up in any criminal conspiracy, and I answered heatedly that my father would never perpetrate anything like that.

The comrade from the floor held his ground and demanded a straightforward and unambiguous answer: yes or no. To my great surprise, the chair intervened. He said I had indeed provided an answer, and there was no need to anticipate the judgment of the court. Since no one had any further questions, they took a vote on whether or not to admit me. I was certain there was no way I would be accepted, and it was with amazement that I observed my classmates, the young assistants from various departments, staff members of the dean's office, even the cleaning women raising their hands.

So I was accepted, and the chair invited me up to the table and congratulated me. My mood, however, was not at all celebratory. Instead I was oppressed by anxiety. It was as if I had been accepted into some kind of merciless holy order that could demand of you anything, even the renunciation of your own father.

—◆◆◆—

Father hoped that we would somehow manage to scrape out our livelihood without him, which of course meant that I was supposed to manage it somehow. We had no savings (even if we had any, they would have been worthless after the currency reform at the beginning of the summer). Mother continued to believe the diagnosis according to which she wasn't even supposed to be alive. Just as the mistaken doctor had advised, she tried to avoid any effort. She suggested that she could at least do some knitting at home, but there was no yarn to be had. She could also translate from French, but no one showed any interest.

On the bulletin board at the department I noticed an opening for a student assistant. Obviously no one had thought it worthwhile to apply. They paid only two hundred crowns a month for attending to library loans and cataloging book acquisitions.

I got the position and was at least able to pay for lunchtime meal tickets at the cafeteria, and for supper I always waited until the last minute before the kitchen closed, since the kindhearted cooks would give away part of the leftovers. So almost every evening I would bring home at least ten slices of lightly salted bread and a usually large military mess tin full of dumplings and some kind of sauce or at least thick soup from the very bottom of the pot.

My brother, who with surprising obstinacy had wiped from his memory everything related to our stay in Terezín, sometimes complained that the food from the mess tin reminded him of something unpleasant. Mother usually just nibbled on a piece of bread and said she had eaten some potatoes earlier. I had no idea what Father was eating. In my foolishness, I told myself that today's prisons could in no way resemble wartime concentration camps.

But we couldn't live like that for long. I knew I would either have to give up my studies or find some other, more lucrative source of income. But what did I know how to do? I had excelled in mathematics in high school, but I was already starting to forget it; and German, which I had picked up during the war, was also fading from my mind. I could paint a little, but I'd abandoned this hobby as well. All that was left was my writing.

Without a letter of recommendation, I set out after the holidays on a pilgrimage to the ever smaller number of newspapers and magazines and asked if they wanted me to do any reviewing. To my surprise, they offered me several books as a test. (Only later did I learn that lying around editorial offices are a great number of books, which almost every reviewer with any sense avoids.)

The selection of titles allowed for publication was meager. So I wrote about the stories of Karel Václav Rais, Mark Twain, and Maxim Gorky. Most of the books I was given to review were by officially approved Soviet authors. All of these authors wrote about the recently concluded war, a period that still fascinated me, and I was prepared to believe that the stories in these works would provide evidence of the new man, his bravery, and his Soviet patriotism. The texts had obviously been translated and brought out quickly. They were full of Russianisms and long-extinct participles. I certainly took in this cramped style, but at the same time there was the danger that it was affecting and perverting my own language.

I had no idea what was happening in the Soviet Union, the land that these authors so blatantly acclaimed and whose books I was recommending. But someone who has no idea should make an effort to acquire knowledge. If he does not succeed, he should at least keep quiet.

At the office of the Union of Youth daily newspaper, for which I sometimes wrote reviews, I was offered the chance to attend a conference on Alois Jirásek's novel *Psohlavci*. The conference was being held, appropriately enough, in Domažlice, where the novel takes place. Because the conference started in the morning, I was supposed to be there a day earlier, but I wasn't to worry because the newspaper would reimburse the cost of my lodging.

During a university lecture on Marxism, I was sitting (once again) next to Tatyana, and I told her that I would be gone for two days next week. I was going to a conference in Domažlice, and I wondered if she'd like to come with me.

She was surprised and nodded.

In case she hadn't considered it, I pointed out that we would have to stay overnight.

Yes, that's what she had assumed, since we would be there for two days.

The night before my first trip in the company of a girl, I slept poorly.

Did the fact that she had agreed to go with me mean that she had also agreed to spend the night with me in a single room or even amorously in a single bed? And what would I do if they didn't put us in a single room? Knock on the door of her room and try to spend the night with her? Wouldn't she see that as pure insolence? And what would I do if she let me in? I wasn't sure that I was really in love with her. And if I wasn't sure, then it wasn't proper to act as if I wanted to spend my whole life with her.

The next morning I took my entire month's pay from an envelope and in a state of extreme nervousness set off for the train station, where I arrived a half hour early. The train was just pulling in, and I managed to be the first one on and got two seats by a window in the last car. Then time dragged along unbearably as I waited for Tatyana. Three minutes before departure, I saw her running toward the train smiling, well rested, and toting a small overnight bag.

The train wheezed along in a cloud of its own smoke, and we sat across from each other with our knees touching. I realized we had two whole days ahead of us, which might decide our future. But it didn't seem appropriate to talk about it. We chatted about other, more abstract topics. What was beauty? To what degree did it depend on the time period, on social conditions? Did art have a duty to educate?

When we finally disembarked at the Domažlice railway station, she asked me where we were going, where I had reserved a room.

I hadn't reserved anything. It hadn't even occurred to me. I reassured her, however, that the organizers of the conference had surely taken care of our accommodations.

She was doubtful, especially concerning her own accommodations.

In the end, we discovered that they hadn't even taken care of mine. The hotel on the square was full. The receptionist explained to me that some sort of literary conference was supposed to be going on and advised me to inquire elsewhere. We wandered for at least two hours through town. On top of everything, it started to rain.

The idea of spending our first night together on a bench somewhere in the train station waiting room was certainly not encouraging. I realized with relief, however, that it would postpone the fateful moment of decision. Tatyana obviously did not share my feelings of relief. Her good mood had passed, and she remained stubbornly silent. As we blundered through the streets and alleys, soaked to the skin, a small sign attracted my attention: The building we had just passed housed the chapel of the Czech Brethren Church. The first-floor light was on, so I rang.

The pastor was young and looked the way people do when a complete stranger knocks at their door. I told him I was a member of the Vinohrady congregation and that I was very sorry to bother him, but my colleague and I (I wasn't lying; she was after all my colleague) had arrived for a literary conference, and we couldn't find lodging. He was our last hope.

He nodded that he understood. We were welcome. They had a room for guests, and of course we could spend the night. I gazed proudly at my bewildered companion. I hoped she appreciated my ability to find a solution to a difficult situation.

The pastor let us in and asked about my congregation. He'd gone to college with our pastor but hadn't seen him for a long time. Then his wife entered and offered us bread, butter, and tea.

She also told us that the room was ready for the young lady and asked if I would mind sleeping on the sofa in the office. The church rectory was not going to be an appropriate sanctuary for an amorous rendezvous. So I wished my sweetheart a good night without even kissing her and went off to a room full of religious tracts. Above my head was a portrait of Jan Amos Komenský, and on the opposite wall a reproduction of Jan Hus at the Council of Constance.

On a chair beside the sofa lay a Bible.

In the end, the conference was boring, and I noticed with a feeling of desperation the disapproval of the one person who mattered to me.

On the trip back in the train I nearly tied myself into knots trying to be amusing or at least create interesting conversation. My beloved Tatyana smiled at me now and then—with sadness, sorrow, and perhaps even understanding.

I realized that Tomáš would have reserved a room and certainly would not have dragged her to a rectory where even a good night kiss was improper.

Essay: *Abused Youth*, p. 452

7

A letter arrived from the legal advisory office in Uherské Hradiště. A certain Attorney S. informed us that he had been assigned the case of the engineer V. Klíma, which would be taken up on June 24. He had good news: Paragraph 135 (endangerment of the economic plan), according to which the accused was to be mandated, allowed for a punishment of only three months to three years. But he thought that in view of the current situation the maximum penalty would not be applied. Furthermore, the case would probably not be made public. The reading of the verdict, however, would be public and visitors would be allowed.

Mother burst out crying because she still believed that Father, who could not have done anything wrong, would one day be deemed innocent and released, whereas now he would be placed before the court like a common criminal.

My brother was intrigued by the word "situation." The verdict couldn't depend on some sort of situation, could it?

There were only three days until the hearing. Mother asked us if she should go to the court and immediately added that the trip there along with the trial would probably kill her. My brother offered to go, but Mother objected that he had to go to school, and if he did in fact attend the trial, he would most likely say something inappropriate because when he was angry he couldn't control himself. It would be best if I went because I was levelheaded and didn't start jabbering the first thing that came into my mind. So I left for Uherské Hradiště, a place where I'd never been and where I knew no one.

Father's attorney was so unprepossessing that nothing about him stuck in my memory except his small, gold-rimmed glasses. But these belonged merely to his external appearance, just like his gray jacket. He suggested we go to a café, where he said he had a table. He then offered me a cigarette (which I refused), addressed me as "my dear boy," and informed me that the prosecution, as he'd learned from the documents, was apparently trying to prove that my father had committed sabotage. As I was surely aware, certain changes of a general nature had occurred, and now, although he didn't want to promise anything, it looked as if he might be able to ask for an acquittal. He assured me he would do everything in his power, even though as I was certainly aware . . .

I said I had no idea what he was talking about.

These days, he explained, a lawyer could do less than— He looked around to see if anyone was sitting at the neighboring tables and said in almost a whisper, "A lawyer can accomplish less than a cleaning lady from the district committee."

When I entered the dreary courtroom, where the only décor was the state symbol and a picture of President Zápotocký, I felt a weight descend upon me.

The court entered, then five uniformed hulks brought in Father and four other accused. Father seemed the smallest. He was extremely pale but not unrecognizably emaciated the way he was when we first saw him after being liberated from the concentration camps.

He saw me sitting there, forced a weak smile, and acknowledged me with just a nod because he was handcuffed.

I was so flustered when I saw Father sitting on the bench of the accused that I nearly couldn't follow the prosecutor's speech. He spoke without any zeal, as if he were trying to put the court to sleep as quickly as possible. Then we were ordered from the room.

The next day toward evening I was let into the courtroom to hear the verdict.

"The defendant Klíma," announced the judge, who didn't bother with Father's academic title, "in his capacity as the director of the national enterprise MEZ Development, which he held from August 1, 1947, to June 30, 1951, did not see to proper labor organization. Furthermore," he continued, "he did not devote the proper care to the training of personnel, tolerated criticism of his work with difficulty, and systematically did not cooperate with the manufacturing plant even though he knew the machines he had designed could be built only by personnel who were both professionally and politically adept."

At the same time, the judge allowed that the machines Father had designed were so demanding that the personnel at the manufacturing plant could not even assemble such complicated apparatus.

The court also established that the accused attempted to refute most of the accusations by claiming he had tried to point out and warn against these shortcomings during the manufacturing process.

"The national economy, however, has suffered considerable damage, the extent of which it is impossible to determine without a thorough investigation," he continued in the voice of a weary shopkeeper who toward evening was already suspecting that no one would buy his limp produce. "Nevertheless, the court believes it cannot conclude that the accused is guilty of sabotage, for he attempted to rectify the situation."

Father and the other accused engineers were sentenced to thirty months in prison; father was also fined two thousand crowns.

Immediately after the trial, the agitated attorney ran up to me and led me aside where no one could hear us and said the court was supposed to sentence them only to the time they had served during the investigation, and because all of the accused had been given a year's pardon owing to the recent amnesty, they could go home immediately, but the blockhead of a judge did not take into consideration that Father had been arrested three months later than the others, so he'd actually given him three extra months.

I confessed that I had no idea what Father had been found guilty of, since he clearly had not done anything unlawful.

"But my dear boy," said the attorney, amazed, "it's a matter of how things are interpreted, not how they are in reality. That would smack of bourgeois rule, wouldn't it? Just a year ago, your father would have received at least twenty years for the same thing. And a year before that . . . It's best not to think about it."

⤨

When I next brought one of my reviews to the editorial office of *Mladá fronta*, I was asked if I'd like to take a trip to one of the border regions and write a news story about it. At that time, the Union of Youth had announced a big campaign of long-term agricultural brigades to the border regions, which had still not managed to recover from the mass deportation of their German inhabitants.

I said I'd be glad to try.

They also wanted to know if I had a special relationship with any particular part of the border regions, and, fearing they might change their mind, I said I liked Šumava.

Šumava appealed to them as well. A certain group of brigade workers in Kašperské Hory were promising to harvest the hay on fifty acres of mountain fields even though they had only two scythes. This time I had no one to invite to accompany me, so the next day I got on my bicycle and took off in the direction of Plžeň. Along with my ordinary things, I took with me a folding map from 1935, which displayed features that were missing from contemporary maps for reasons of secrecy. It also listed the population from 1930. I read that in the district of Sušice, where Kašperské Hory was located, there had been twenty thousand Germans. Now they were undoubtedly no more.

After nine hours, I rode into town, where it looked as if the war had ended only a few weeks ago. I climbed off my bicycle, went into a restaurant, and sank down on the nearest chair. At a long table sat two scruffy, ragged, and obviously somewhat drunken men who looked at me with apparent suspicion or perhaps even malice. In the tavern, which reeked of cheap cigarette smoke, beer, goulash, and mildew, sat several other half-drunken, scruffy fellows wearing overalls. In the corner of the room sat a group of young people bawling out a drunken song, or at least trying to.

After a while a similarly drunk waiter shambled over and wordlessly placed before me a glass of beer. Sometime later he appeared with a bowl of soup, and I asked where I could register for a room.

He was surprised it had occurred to me I could get a room here; maybe in Sušice at Fialka, he suggested. It was a big hotel. I said I couldn't make it to Sušice; there had to be someplace in town I could spend the night.

Maybe at the farmhouse where they took all the military bunks. There would certainly be a free spot there since half the brigade workers had already run off. He pointed at the group of young drunks sitting in the corner, and I realized that these were the brigade workers I'd pedaled nine hours to see.

There were ten of them, six boys and four girls. None of them was wearing the blue Union of Youth shirt. The girls seemed drunker than the boys. A quite pretty brunette was wearing a khaki military shirt almost completely unbuttoned with nothing covering her breasts. She was sitting on the lap of a boy dressed like a cowboy and giggling. When I walked over to the table, the boy pushed her off, lifted his cowboy hat, and waved to me. He was obviously the leader.

I asked him for a place to spend the night but I did not betray my journalistic profession. I said I was a student on vacation; this cheered up the brigade workers, and they wanted to know if I perhaps intended to leave the country. I denied any such intention, and this cracked them up again. They assured me I had nothing to be afraid of. Some of them had come to Šumava for precisely that reason, but then they discovered they couldn't leave through here because those green swine would start shooting right away. It's better to go through Berlin.

I tried to ask them what it was like living here. My inquiry struck them as amusing. Couldn't I see? There was nothing to do except get drunk. Sometimes there was some shooting going on. And the pigs squeal a lot because there's nothing to feed them.

Then they ceased paying attention to me, and I didn't dare disturb them.

The waiter chased us out sometime after midnight, and I skulked behind the singing brigade workers to the farm. In a large barn by the light of an oil lamp, I counted twelve military bunks with bare straw mattresses—two were empty. One of the girls reeled over to me carrying three blankets and suggested I put one under my head. There was a pump in the yard if I wanted to wash up.

When I awoke in the morning, the bedroom was already half empty. Two brigade workers were getting ready to go to the dentist in Sušice, and if I wanted a ride, the bus was leaving in a moment. The girl who had been sitting on the lap of the comrade wearing the cowboy hat was still asleep, with her head wrapped in a wet towel. Another was just walking into the room with a bucketful of water and a rag tied around a broom.

I said I would like to pay for my bed.

Payment was not necessary; the beds were free. She laid aside her broom and complained for a bit. If they didn't get a little milk from the cows and hadn't found some year-old potatoes in the basement, they would have died like the pigs here who are dying of hunger. Then she led me to the sty to see several gaunt and squealing swine. Behind them stood two filthy goats.

I went back to the pub for breakfast. The now sober waiter asked me how I'd slept. He then wanted to know which one I'd chosen. They're all sluts, he explained. Why did I think they had come here? They wanted to get rid of them at the factories, so they booted them to this place. Here they had plenty of customers, and he pointed to the tavern where several border guards were standing.

Afterward, I climbed a steep hill above the town. I saw several cows being watched by a boy around my age. He was sitting, leaning against a tree and smoking a small pipe. I recognized him as one of my bedfellows.

He was surprised I was still around. Did I perhaps relish the beauty of the wilderness? It was the asshole of the world is how he explained his relationship to the local splendor. I tend cattle, he added as if in apology. They couldn't find anything else for him to do.

He took from his wrist a copper bracelet embossed with grape clusters and rose blossoms and handed it to me to show what he used to do. He added that they'd sent him here as punishment for attending Mass on Sundays.

Here Mass is celebrated only once a month, but on the other hand you're closer to God. Or at least the sky.

I went back to the farm. Only the brunette with the wet towel on her head was there. She gave a sigh of apology, since she obviously looked so awful. She knew she shouldn't drink that much, but just let him try to tell her what to do. She opened one of the wardrobes and pulled out a bottle of rum and two mustard glasses. I said I didn't drink, and she poured one for herself. "I can't work anyway." She pulled up her military shirt, which was buttoned this time, and I saw on her belly a bloody, inflamed gash. She explained that they'd been fighting a bit. She'd probably gotten this from a pitchfork. She didn't remember much of what had happened. I asked if she'd seen a doctor. She waved her hand. She wouldn't get any sick leave, so what was the point? Again she offered me a glass of rum, and when I refused, she drank it. Then she stretched out on the bed, stared at the ceiling covered with cobwebs and damp plaster, and after a moment said, "I'll kill myself someday anyway. But before that I'm going to break somebody's jaw. I can't stand guys. Especially those clever swine who sent us to this shit hole."

Right away the next day I wrote a somewhat moralistic article in which I claimed that the brigade workers here, who had been dispatched into unexpectedly arduous circumstances, felt like outcasts. They had no idea how to live or work in these new surroundings, so they drank or they tried to save themselves by running away. At the editorial office, they were appalled. I was told that if I was going to mention the negative aspects, I had to balance them out with something positive. Then they asked if I'd stopped by the district secretariat of the Union of Youth. I admitted that I hadn't. After that they talked on the phone for a long time and then advised me to go to Dolní Krušec, where brigade workers were fulfilling the plan by 212 percent.

Thus I received my first lesson concerning what you were allowed or, rather, what you were forbidden to write about if you wanted to get your reportage published.

So what could I write about? Where was the border of what was allowed? Was it the duty of every journalist or writer to offer up only praise, only confirm the image of a society where, except for a few enemies and conspirators, everyone was enthusiastically building socialism?

It occurred to me that instead of an article, I could write a short story about the brigade I saw in Kašperské Hory. I composed it in one rather protracted evening. I invented a teacher and had her tell the story of her experiences on the brigade. In a remote spot where the workers were toiling away, morale was gradually disintegrating. Then a young boy got blood poisoning and had to be taken immediately to the doctor in town. The telephones were not working, and the only means of transportation was a tractor that the brigade workers had received for their labor. Unfortunately, at this critical moment the driver was so drunk that he couldn't get up from his chair in the pub. The teacher finally got behind the wheel of the tractor and drove the boy to the doctor. Everything ended happily and moreover brought the brigade workers around to see the error of their ways. Even though I had invented the entire story, including the happy ending, I thought I had actually said something about reality. In a paroxysm of pride, I took the story to *Literární noviny*, which I considered the most dignified literary platform.

To my surprise, the editors asked to publish my story under the title "Far from the People." Neither they nor I suspected that, despite the double happy ending, it could provoke the party overseers. But nonetheless I allowed myself to describe how the brigade workers were starting to get drunk and lose the sense of purpose of their activity.

> Perhaps you cannot imagine those long evenings in April and May. Not a soul outside, just rain and wind—and inside? Some go to the pub, others stay inside and remain silent. . . . I wanted to read, and then I was struck by the thought: Why should I read? Perhaps there are others who think everything here is pointless and without purpose—even work, because for us it has ceased to be something valuable. . . . None of us, after all, lives only to work off his hours in the field. . . . Everything is done for the people . . . and at the same time you see how people are going to seed before your very eyes. What are we doing here? If I had to live like this for a year or two, I would probably say: Why live at all?

I was called to a meeting of the editorial board where the chair of the Writers' Union himself, Jan Drda, would be speaking. The famous Jan Drda tried to analyze the subject of my prose. He said that I was obviously a talented and, in view of my youth, a promising author. He also praised my attempt to compose a story about the present day. But was reality actually so dreary? Can we really say that our young workers are losing their sense of the meaning of life, that the result of their collective effort is the question: Why live at all?

⁂

Father finally returned. This time there was no big family celebration. Aunt Hedvika stopped by with some real Russian pierogi filled with ground meat and cabbage.

Father ate them with relish and recounted his experiences to us as if he had just returned from foreign parts. He had spent the last three months with some convicted monks, a scout leader, and real-live thugs. The monks were truly saintly people who hadn't done anything wrong. Everyone in prison says he's innocent, though; even the safecracker or the accountant who had embezzled nearly a hundred thousand crowns had said he was innocent. But those monks were guilty of nothing except having at one time entered a monastery and then refused to renounce their beliefs.

Only now did we learn that they had held Father for nine months in solitary confinement and the whole time kept trying to convince him that if he wanted to get out of there he would have to confess to sabotage. They managed to turn everything he had accomplished into proof of his intention to undermine the building of socialism. They wanted to know why he wanted flee to England to escape Hitler and not go to the Soviet Union. According to them he had joined the Communist Party in order to undermine it sometime in the future. He had been severe on his subordinates because he wanted to discourage them and thereby ruin their work. He had given them such demanding tasks so they wouldn't be able to fulfill them and thereby would disrupt the five-year plan. And he'd convinced his cronies (that's how they referred to the other members of my father's team) to help him create erroneous calculations so that his motors wouldn't function properly. The other four saboteurs in his group had already confessed and were sorry that they'd allowed themselves to be led astray by him.

When he insisted he'd never purposely calculated anything incorrectly, they had him taken away. Then for perhaps a week nothing would happen, but then they would come for him in the middle of the night and repeat the same thing until morning. And then the entire next day. They took turns assuring him that they would hold out, not him. And from the very beginning they had kept telling him that he was lucky—prisoners were no longer beaten.

In the beginning, when he wasn't being interrogated, he kept trying to come up with a way to convince the inquisitors of his innocence. Finally he understood that they weren't interested in the truth. Their job was to get a confession out of him, and they had plenty of time. He also started to understand that the same thing was taking place in all cases like this. They forced people to admit to crimes they hadn't committed.

It didn't make sense to befoul his mind and waste time trying in vain to convince them. He couldn't write because they wouldn't give him pencil or paper. Fortunately he'd always had an excellent memory, so he started recalculating his design, trying to figure out if there had been any errors. It was taxing, but it also relaxed his mind, and he was proud he could manage even complicated calculations without a slide rule.

Finally he gave up and signed mountains of reports. Then for several weeks they prepared material for the prosecution. He'd already come to terms with the fact that he wouldn't get out of there for more than ten years. But they took him to the prosecutor, who surprisingly addressed him not as the "accused" but rather as "Mr. Klíma" and advised him to forget about everything he'd confessed to and/or signed. Originally it had been decided that he would get twenty years for sabotage, but now there was no need. Yes, he'd used the word "need."

"Now I was supposed to confess that I'd devoted too little time to the training of young people; I'd neglected the rules of job management and thereby disrupted the fulfillment of the five-year plan. Then I could go home. I didn't understand what was happening," explained Father.

Yes, you were actually lucky, agreed Aunt Hedvika, and she explained that when the Leader had died, everything started to change. New instructions had arrived from Moscow, and prosecuting attorneys were ordered to make sure that they didn't break any laws, that they didn't force confessions and convict the innocent.

The ordinary criminals he had been placed with, continued Father, taught him never to admit anything. Not even what you'd actually committed. Keep this in mind, he said, turning to us; you never know what you might run into.

Essay: *The Necessity of Faith*, p. 458

8

On one of my journalist excursions, this time to eastern Bohemia, I arrived at a village where placards announced that actors from the East Bohemian Theater would be performing that day. The performance took place on a small stage in the local pub. I bought a ticket and took a seat in the overcrowded room.

In this pretelevision era, the audience was quite grateful and applauded after each scene whether it was a song or speech. But sometimes I didn't really understand what was going on. The audience members would become extremely boisterous and burst out laughing. They would interrupt the actors with applause or shout out something that was apparently supposed to add to the dialogue of the theater troupe.

When it was over I went backstage, introduced myself to the actors as a correspondent from *Mladá fronta*, and said I would love to write about their performance.

They weren't much older than myself, and like most actors they wanted as much attention as they could get even after they had stepped down from the stage. It was with great pleasure that they described how they traveled during their free time around the provinces and sang folk songs along with the new revolutionary ones, recited classics, and added some progressive poets who composed verses about contemporary times. The greatest success was reserved for those sketches taken directly from daily life. They explained that a few days before they were supposed to perform, they would send their writer into the town to listen as the locals described the difficulties they were having, and whether something special or unusual had happened. Then he would put together a brief sketch in which the people would recognize themselves or their neighbors. Thereby the theater was returning to its ancient roots when people sat around the fire and talked or sang about their immediate concerns.

I was captivated by the image of an author seeking out stories among the lives of villagers and then concocting miniature dramas from them. I knew I could do it too, but I lacked actors along with everything else necessary for such an undertaking.

When I returned to Prague, however, ideas began flitting through my mind. We had foreign students in our department studying the basics of the Czech language, and I thought viewers would find them fascinating during this time when the entire country was locked behind impermeable borders. A few days later I learned that a Chinese woman, whose name in translation meant Doe Grazing in a Spring Meadow, had decided to study opera in Prague. An Italian by the name of Fabri played the accordion and knew loads of folk and revolutionary songs, and an officer in the Korean People's Army, Nam Ki Duk, was willing to talk in tolerable Czech about the horrors of the recent war. A pair of young Czech teaching assistants knew some satirical sketches they had already performed. Further inquiry led me to a group of girls who had formed a Moravian folk song trio, and one of my classmates, who had already published a collection of poems, was willing to go with me around the villages and compose satirical verses for other sketches. These would then be set to music and sung. There were plenty of students in the department who could recite poetry or read a text. I was convinced that the idea of forming a traveling troupe with such an appealing repertoire seemed realistic. Now all I needed was an audience.

Feigning apology, a secretary at the dean's office informed me there were no funds available for our enterprise, and she advised me to go to the Ministry of Culture.

I had to consult the telephone directory to locate the ministry and had no idea whom to see there.

An older female comrade in charge of folk art led me to an office that contained a cheap desk, a baroque bureau, and several marvelous Chinese vases, all apparently from the erstwhile palace the ministry had taken over. The comrade took a seat behind her desk, lit a cigarette, and gazed at me silently for a moment. Then she tapped her cigarette ash into a Chinese vase and bade me speak.

She listened to my story and had only one question: Had we prepared something from Soviet literature?

We were just working on that part, I managed to reply. But our singing trio had two Russian folk songs: "Volga, Volga" and "Stenka Razin."

The comrade gazed at me again for a moment, tossed her butt into the Chinese vase, and said that our project sounded interesting, but she had her doubts about the original sketches. She'd never heard of anything like it before, but we could at least venture an attempt. She leafed through her bulky diary and suggested she come next Wednesday at two o'clock to see our program. Unfortunately, she couldn't come sooner.

Her willingness to see our program in a week took me by surprise, but it was only Thursday, so we had six days. I said I'd be waiting for her at the porter's lodge.

The following Tuesday evening I was certain that all was lost. Both of our teaching assistants who had prepared a satire had left to attend a seminar; the soprano of the women's trio was down with a fever; the emcee who could recite verses of contemporary poets had a seminar he couldn't get out of; and our Italian accordion player had a funeral in Italy. The satirical sketches that were supposed to address local problems couldn't be written, and even if they could, we had nobody to perform them.

My comrade from the ministry arrived a half hour late looking contrite. She was accompanied by a colleague who looked rather skeptical.

I led both women to one of the lecture rooms on the third floor and acquainted them with the bad luck that had befallen us.

An unenthusiastic group composed of the remaining members of our nonexistent troupe was waiting for us in a spacious lecture hall with a view of Prague Castle. To my horror I noticed that the highlight of the show, my Doe Grazing in a Spring Meadow, was missing.

Both comrades seated themselves in the second row and fired up their cigarettes as a sign they were ready. I asked for a brief moment of their patience.

The comrade I was acquainted with fixed her eyes for a moment on Prague Castle and recalled how she had been sitting in this room in 1939. It was the last lecture on art history she had attended. Then the Germans closed the university. Suddenly the doors opened, and Doe entered dressed in a marvelous silk robe. I noticed that both comrades were staring at her delightedly.

I stood in for the emcee and announced that the opening number —an Italian revolutionary song, "Bandiera Rossa"—would not be performed because Fabri's father had unfortunately died. Also, the next satirical piece, which was supposed to take us directly to the floor of the UN, would not be performed because both of its protagonists had left for a conference in Ostrava. Then I invited the women's trio to perform folk songs from the Chodsko region, and when my two classmates took the stage I glanced apologetically at my comrades from the ministry to remind them that the third singer lay in a fever somewhere in the dormitory.

The satirical number, which was supposed to come next, hadn't yet been composed, but it would definitely not be absent during the actual performance.

The skeptical-looking comrade wondered why we hadn't written a sketch about the life of our department. Certainly there were plenty of themes we could use.

But Doe Grazing in a Spring Meadow had already mounted the stage. She sang a Chinese song and then an aria from Dvořák's *Rusalka*, "Song to the Moon," in her soft and supple Czech. Her singing was so spectacular that both comrades burst into applause.

Our program comprising only a handful of routines and a good number of apologies was already stumbling its way to the conclusion. The Korean officer Nam recounted how wonderful life was during peacetime and then came the horrible attack on his beautiful country by imperialist troops. Only one passage, which I heard many times, sticks in my mind: "After one battle I was walking through a village and came upon a corpse. It was a woman who had been carrying a baby who couldn't yet speak. He just cried and cried, and I took him to another village and gave him to a good woman, who fed him."

When it was over, the comrades stood up and said they would still have to review and discuss everything. I was to call the following week to learn their decision. The other performers and I remained in the lecture hall and agreed that what we had just performed, perhaps with the exception of our Chinese singer, couldn't hope for success even in an elementary school.

A week later I arrived the Ministry of Culture with a feeling of futility.

To my amazement, the board of the humanities department found our project interesting and was prepared to provide us with a bus and chauffeur. On top of that, we would be allocated money for meals. To the question of where we were planning to go first, I answered, still in a state of shock, to Šumava, as if I'd already made arrangements with all the local amateur theaters.

They asked if we had arranged accommodations yet, and when they heard we hadn't, offered us free housing at Castle Velhartice.

Only years later, when I started to see the connections, did I manage to explain to myself the unbelievable motivation and assistance we received. The same ministry employees (or their party superiors) had several years earlier silenced (often by imprisonment) hundreds of artists, but they did not trust even those whom they had "screened." Everyone still remembered democracy and its freedoms all too well, and could feign accommodation to the new regime. We of the young generation didn't remember anything, or remembered so little that we could still find credible the ideological fabrications about the past, present, and future. For them we were the ones, the appropriate generation, that would, according to the prediction of the ingenious Lenin, complete the building of communism. It was, therefore, politically correct to support us.

———&oo———

Immediately after our Šumava expedition, I left on a construction brigade to Most with my classmates. We took a bus, and there was no celebratory welcoming to greet us. The period of great construction brigades enthusiastically celebrated by newspapers and weekly newsreels was over. They also didn't charge us with building anything so magnificent and important as smelting plants or railway tracks in mountain terrain. Our task was to lay the foundations for a housing development.

The leaders of the brigade took us straight from the bus to a wooden barracks that reminded me of Terezín.

They gathered us together in the dining room, and to my surprise I was named the leader of an eight-member group that would work on block fifty-something. I didn't understand why I'd been chosen; I'd never worked on any construction project before and had no idea what was expected of me. None of the members of my group, however (most of them were in the same class as I was), protested my appointment. They all correctly assumed that when their work ended and they were free, the group leader would then have to review the completed assignments, fulfill various orders, consult with the foreman, and attend to other superfluous activities.

We were informed that work started at six in the morning, and fifteen minutes before that a truck would arrive to take us to the site. They also advised us to wear boots or at least galoshes. Because lunch would be served only after the shift had ended, we were to bring a snack. The foremen would explain the rest. The others were free to leave, but as the group leader, along with the others afflicted with this task, I had to wait and listen to a homily on workplace safety. The spokesman explained the Decalogue of Greatest Dangers, most of which I forgot immediately, but I do remember that suffocating in a crush of clay, loam, and rock was a horrible way to die. Anyone who stuck his head into the mixer risked losing it, and riding on the Japanese could have similarly tragic consequences not covered by insurance. (I had no idea what or who this Japanese was.)

In the morning I looked out the window at the yellowish dawn; the air reeked of sulfur and God only knew what other chemicals. There was a line to the toilet in the hallway, and the bathroom was crammed as well, but I was used to all this from Terezín.

As soon as the truck had dropped us off on a plain suffused with stinking haze, we set off uphill to the work site. The individual blocks were marked with numbers. In some places we saw construction ditches, and in others the ground was as yet untouched. Every now and then we'd pass grubby caravans and wooden shanties that stored work tools and bags of cement. When we finally found the block assigned to us, we saw that although the ditches had indeed been prepared for laying cement, they were flooded with water. Now I understood why we'd been told to wear rubber boots. When my coworkers looked over the terrain, they asked me, as the group leader, to protest immediately, for this was obviously the worst block of all. But our foreman had already arrived, a gaunt middle-aged beanpole of a man with a face Jack London would have described as weather-beaten and features usually referred to as craggy. He welcomed us with overt animosity and ordered us to get a pump from the storeroom and pointed to one of the wooden shanties. So instead of lodging a protest, I set off with two of my coworkers. Of course it was a manual pump and, as we soon ascertained, partially broken. No matter how hard we tried, it would spit out only a tiny stream of water. The entire time we spent in this inhospitable place, we referred to the area around the excavation pits as the shore.

The foreman skeptically observed our vain efforts as if asking himself what could be expected from a group of inexperienced students.

When he learned I was the group leader, he read to me the list of equipment issued to us from the storeroom; took me around the excavation pits, which were only slowly emptying of water; and showed me the staked-off area we were supposed to dig. He even specified the depth we were to reach, which I was to strictly monitor because he would check it himself. Then he addressed us all and pointed out that we had to work hard, damn it, otherwise we wouldn't earn enough for the mountain air we were breathing. He addressed us as little idiots and used this epithet every time even though he should have called us comrades.

The next day we were issued a mixer and a vehicle covered with encrusted cement. This was the Japanese that we'd been warned not to ride on. The warning was superfluous because no one would have voluntarily climbed onto it. We also received instructions on the ratio of water, cement, and sand, and the foreman reminded me that I was responsible for everything. If the foundation was not solid, he threatened, the house built atop it would collapse, and its inhabitants, including women and children, could die in the wreckage.

We took turns at the mixer, dragging half-ton bags of cement and pouring their contents into its maw, while the dust lodged itself in our lungs.

At first we tried to convince ourselves this was only temporary, and despite the toil and heat we carried on quite learned conversations. We finally realized, however, that such colloquy was inappropriate given our surroundings, and we began to argue about things like why there was water still flowing into our excavation pit, what grade of soil we were digging, or whose turn it was at the mixer tomorrow. The mixer sometimes stopped working, and none of us knew how to get it going again, so we were losing both time and money, and it was up to me to locate the repairmen. If they did not happen to be in one of the neighboring blocks, they were sitting in the tavern, drinking beer and sometimes playing cards.

The foreman gradually started to see that we were working more and better than he'd expected. But the norms had not been set for college students and probably not even for experienced construction workers. Instead, they were established so that no one could earn more than was necessary for daily subsistence. The employees made up for this by either purloining building material or sneaking off during work hours to make money on the side. We, on the other hand, as the foreman told me, wouldn't make a thing at this rate. We'd had the misfortune of being assigned to this block.

And there was more misfortune yet to come. During our third week, it rained continuously, and when we finally made it to the work site—it was a Saturday, and the shift ended at noon—we saw that part of our freshly dug pit had collapsed along one side and filled our hole with a considerable amount of new earth. Water spurted from the side, which was probably the source that filled our pit every night.

The foreman arrived, surveyed the destruction, and, as if we were the builders instead of him, concluded that we should have timbered the pit. So we'd have to dig out the earth once again, and of course no one would pay us for this extra work. Then he added that now it would be best to embed the whole thing in concrete, otherwise we'd have a lake on Monday, but we probably would anyway because we wouldn't be able to get it cemented by lunchtime. He sent me for the pump and said he was leaving to go see his family. Then he took off just like the others who weren't here working like idiots.

When we came back on Monday morning, the trenches were dry. The foreman stood over them almost in surprise and asked how we'd managed to do it. Then he invited me into his trailer, took a seat behind his unbelievably dingy desk, and asked me if I'd calculated how much we had earned for the previous week.

We'd always made very little, but this week as a result of the repeated breakdown of the mixer, the flooded excavation pits, two days of no work because of rain, and finally the collapsed wall that we had to dig out again, we didn't even make a hundred crowns apiece.

Then he asked how many times we'd had to use the pump. I said every day we were working last week. He pulled out a worksheet and wrote: manual transfer of pump, sixteen hours. Then he added carpentry work and manual transfer of wood, eight cubic meters.

I objected that we had timbered only on Saturday, and then only a few boards.

"Don't bother me when I'm working, you little idiot!" he replied.

He thought up several more operations I'd had no idea existed and calculated each of our wages to be three hundred crowns and some change.

At a loss, I started to thank him. "Don't thank me," he admonished me, and he added that he wasn't paying me out of his own pocket. They were swindling us as much as they were him.

This had been my first encounter with those we had been taught were the working, and thus ruling, class—if I don't take into account those who two years earlier had searched our house.

———— ❧ ————

It wasn't easy to select a topic for my seminar paper, let alone a senior thesis in the field I was studying. I could choose either some sort of historicizing topic of Czech literature: Czech national revival authors (most of them were revivalists rather than writers) or the rural realists, or perhaps I could heap praise upon one of the few prewar leftist authors or one of the many contemporary authors.

At this time appeared a slim pamphlet by a Soviet Slavist named Nikolsky praising the antifascist work of Karel Čapek, an author who until then had been blacklisted because he had been among the major personalities of the democratic republic. A friend of President Masaryk, Čapek had written an angry essay called "Why I Am Not a Communist" (one of my classmates had lent me a nearly illegible typewritten copy), and had attacked the Communist movement, especially in its early stages.

The fact that Čapek was published and praised in the Soviet Union somewhat befuddled those who were determining what was admissible in literature and what was harmful. Finally, his book *The War with the Newts* was allowed to be published with only minor censorship, and I decided to write my seminar paper on it. Čapek's political utopia entranced me so much that I decided to study his work further, and I began regularly visiting the university library reading room. Surprisingly, during a time when all "ideologically harmful works" in the area of politics, history, economics, philosophy, and social science, that is, all non-Marxist works, had disappeared from the libraries and bookstores (it was as if authors such as Camus, Hemingway, Sartre, Faulkner, and Kafka had never existed), in the reading room I could request any journal from the polemical anticommunist *Nebojsa* to anti-Semitic and Fascist tabloids such as *Arijský boj* or *Vlajka*.

I spent hours and hours poring over volumes of prewar *Lidové noviny*, *Přítomnost*, and dozens of other journals to which Karel Čapek had contributed.

Eventually I was given permission to write my thesis on Čapek, which was supposed to address the antifascist elements in his work. But the works that were imprecisely designated antifascist, as far as I understood them, simply consummated Čapek's lifelong efforts to warn against any form of totalitarianism, whether it was a technological civilization or the Nazi regime. In the end, my thesis treated Čapek's entire oeuvre.

<hr />

The Twentieth Congress of the Communist Party took place at the end of February 1956. The press wrote about the congress in the usual spirit. The Communist Party members proudly reviewed the successes achieved as they were rebuilding their war-ravaged land and offered dizzying glimpses into the future. The people were following closely behind the country and a Leninist government of the party and the country. But there was nevertheless something astounding: a criticism of Stalin's economic mistakes! The Soviet Communists also admitted that capitalism might temporarily achieve better economic results than Socialist economics. The congress concluded with elections in which the recommended candidates were unanimously approved.

A short time after, late in the evening Father called us together to the radio, which he'd acquired when he was released from prison. It was usually tuned to the news from Vienna rather than Prague. Although I was slowly forgetting my German, and although the radio was sometimes mostly static, I understood that at some sort of secret and closed meeting of the Central Committee in Moscow, Stalin's successor, Nikita Khrushchev, had delivered a heretical speech in which he spoke of his predecessor as a criminal who had on his conscience the illegal persecution of innocent people, the torture of prisoners. According to Khrushchev, this all led to mass murder based on lists drawn up by Stalin himself or at least approved by him. Stalin had also apparently underestimated the danger of a German attack, and owing to his military ignorance he was responsible for a nearly hopeless situation on the fronts during the first months of the war. It wasn't the content of the speech alone that struck me as unbelievable; it was that something like this could be said at the Congress of Soviet Communists, moreover by its highest member.

Shortly thereafter, Aunt Hedvika, who had spent so many years in the Soviet Union and was well-informed, came to visit. She seemed extremely agitated. Not only was everything we heard true, she assured us, but this was only a small part of it. And she, who had never said a single bad or even critical word about her time in Russia, began to talk. When she was working in Czech broadcasting at the Moscow radio station, people she was working with would be there one day and then gone the next, and no one dared ask where they were or what had happened to them. No one even dared pronounce their names. And if one of the disappeared had happened to write a book or an article, not a word of it could be cited, and the book was immediately removed from the library and destroyed. Merely cracking a stupid joke or just laughing at it was enough for the security forces to come for the unfortunate person. Sometimes the police would come that very night and sentence him to ten years in a camp in Siberia. Or he would disappear completely, and at most his family would receive a package containing his clothing.

I asked why she'd never told us about this, why she hadn't warned us after she'd lived through it.

She explained that she couldn't precisely because she had lived through it. No one was watched more than those who had lived in the Soviet Union and could testify to these horrors. No one would have believed her anyway

A few weeks later at a party meeting of the department, excerpts of Khrushchev's heretical speech were read.

I was surprised that a lot of people had not heard about the speech, or, if they had, thought the whole thing was an invention of the enemy. Now they were stunned. Some of the women started sobbing, and I remember hearing the hysterical cry: "You deceived us."

It appeared that things were actually starting to change. At meetings and previously boring seminars on Marxism-Leninism, people started speaking more freely. If innocent people had been condemned in the Soviet Union, what had happened here? Wasn't it necessary to reconsider all the political trials? Shouldn't the Communist Party, which had apparently deceived its members, step down?

At a party meeting we resolved that an extraordinary congress would convene to undertake rectifications.

Like so many other people, I still believed in the possibility of rectification, or, deceived by the sudden feeling of freedom, I unreasonably and senselessly placed my hopes in it.

It was in this atmosphere of intoxication that we began to prepare for the student Majáles—the traditional May celebration (whose origin is centuries older than the garish May Day festivities). We constructed masks and trudged singing from our department along the bridge in the direction of the exhibition ground where we planned to choose the king of Majáles. I don't remember who came up with the idea that I don a crumpled broad-brimmed hat and tattered coat to represent an unfortunate and persecuted kulak. Along with the others I sang "Gaude-amus Igitur" and was proud to be a student of one of the world's oldest universities and that I was helping to renew the venerable tradition of so-called academic freedom.

When I got back to the department, two men stopped me at the entrance, showed me some sort of document, and demanded my iden-tity card. They led me behind the porter's lodge into the Youth Union committee room and began their interrogation.

Where was I coming from?

A procession.

What did I mean by procession?

At that moment I recalled Father's recent advice not to say any-thing about what you were doing. Even if you were doing nothing at all.

It was a procession of students.

Who had organized it?

I answered that I didn't know, but they could certainly find out. (Everything was always organized by either the party or a Youth Union committee.)

They yelled at me not to tell them what to do. They wanted me to tell them who had invited me to the procession.

I really didn't remember.

What had I been disguised as?

I hadn't been disguised. I'd never possessed a disguise in my whole life.

One of the men started shouting at me not to start pontificating. Who was I pretending to be?

A man in a hat.

They started to shriek that if I was trying to make fools of them, this would all end unpleasantly.

I probably wanted to look like a farmer, I explained.

Why? Did I have a farmer's background?

I said nothing.

Why had I shouted antistate slogans?

I said that I didn't shout anything because I don't shout slogans on principle.

Then who was shouting antistate slogans if not you?

I said I hadn't heard anyone shouting any slogans.

Two more detained students were brought in, two of my classmates dressed in Moravian folk costumes.

My two men were obviously in a hurry to move on. The one who had been asking the questions now emphatically warned me not to think that the time had come for any sort of counterrevolutionary activity. The working class had made it possible for us to study so that we might become useful members of a Socialist society, not so that we could walk around the streets shouting antistate slogans.

The other one pointed out that they had my name, and if they ever caught me again at similar provocations, I wouldn't get out of it so easily.

It occurred to me in the tram that nothing essential had changed so far. Academic freedom had certainly not begun to apply.

Essay: *Dictators and Dictatorship*, p. 467

editor in chief called me in for a discussion. He had nothing against me personally, but I had to realize that everywhere I went I was representing the magazine, that is, the publisher as well. It was not appropriate for thousands of people to see me hurtling along the streets of Prague every day carrying a briefcase. What if somebody recognized me? Then he would go around saying we employed a nutcase who didn't even earn enough for a tram ticket. If I traveled like a normal person, that is, not running, it didn't matter if I came by foot or by tram.

This was my first act of wrongdoing during the few months I was employed at *Květy*.

The editor in chief at the time, at least in name, was a bad writer whose only merit, besides membership in the party, was that he'd composed a novel in which he assiduously and mercilessly denigrated exploitation in Tomáš Bat'a's factories. However, he never strayed into the offices; even his paycheck had to be sent to him by mail. In reality his deputy headed the magazine. He was a diminutive man of indeterminate age but somewhere under fifty, and was perpetually afraid an article that could be considered inaccurate or even provocative would leak into the magazine. Another class-conscious bigwig worked here, the venerable widow of the Communist writer Egon Ervín Kisch. This comrade likewise did little actual work; instead she watched over everything that went on in the editorial offices and apparently did not take kindly to the fact that youngish and insufficiently class-conscious people were employed there who, in her opinion, threatened the quality, but most of all the party mission, of the magazine. By her side stood the chairwoman of the party organization (she sometimes wrote as well on women's issues, that is, mostly fashion), who was always prepared to call a party meeting and raise the issue of how something unseemly could happen. Among other worthy comrades was the foreign desk editor, who limited his reporting to articles on other friendly Socialist countries and telephone calls with opponents of Western imperialists and devotees of revolution throughout the rest of the world. I found myself for the first, and actually last, time in an environment ruled by

prominent Communists, who were always resolved to advocate whatever the party leadership required. I was stunned by how the environment bubbled over with rancor, continual suspicion, malicious gossip,
and personnel screening.

Once my colleague Kabíček and I set off on an assignment to
southern Bohemia and instead of a photographer we took along a
graphic artist, a woman who was approximately our age. We thought
it would be interesting to have her drawings instead of photographs
enliven our text.

This deed scandalized the reputable widow. At a meeting, she
accused us of using editorial funds to organize a sex excursion, which
had tarnished the magazine's reputation. The artist burst into tears, and
we tried in vain to convince everyone that we hadn't touched her. We
got off with a warning and instructions that similar excursions would
not be approved in the future. From now on, only our photographers
could accompany us on assignments.

All these petty affairs, however, faded in significance before the
momentous events taking place on the international stage. The first
thing we heard was the distant thunder of a workers' strike in Poland,
and then the Hungarians began to defy the Communist regime. At the
same time the so-called Suez crisis broke out. Not a word was to be
found about these events in our journal; in our editorial offices, however, the only thing people talked about was the situation in Hungary.
The chairwoman of the party organization would call a meeting once a
week to discuss the political situation. Worthy Communists cautiously
(this was, after all, only a criticism of Soviet Communists) gave us to
understand that the enormity of Stalin's crimes had been exaggerated
and could provoke all enemies of socialism. We were to avoid anything
that could arouse sympathy for elements that might assume their moment had arrived. Apparently, these elements were prepared to attack
the very foundations of Socialist society and the leading role of the
party under the pretense of criticizing the cult of personality. At the
end of October, the Czechoslovak and Soviet press agencies began

reporting appalling news about Communist functionaries being hanged in Hungary, about insurgents murdering their own families, and about how those who had managed to escape from mutinous Budapest were seeking asylum here or even in capitalist Austria.

Father started listening to independent Hungarian radio broadcasts, and when I came home he would change the station to Vienna, so I could listen to the latest news as well. If you didn't know they were speaking about the same events as the Czech official radio, you would have assumed there were two different Hungarian republics. While the Czech Radio would talk about counterrevolution, the other two would talk about a national uprising; one reported that insurgents had resolved to institute a reign of terror aimed at the people and were determined to do away with socialism, and the other reported that the great majority of Hungarians were enthusiastically greeting the renewal of democracy and freedom. But how could socialism be done away with? Did any kind of socialism ever exist anywhere? Hadn't terror been used here on everyone who refused to submit?

Now armed militiamen stood in front of and inside our office building just to make it clear that no such insurrection would take place here. Our chairwoman read to us a proposed resolution in which she proclaimed, in the name of the entire editorial team, support for the powers of socialism to halt the orgy of Hungarian counterrevolution.

I did not like this resolution and fled the meeting before it was voted on.

The next day the chairwoman drily informed me that she had signed the resolution on my behalf, since I had obviously been in such a hurry that I couldn't wait a few more minutes. She knew I would have signed it and assumed that I held the same opinion as she did concerning the events in Hungary. The end of her sentence sounded rather like a menacing question.

The next day—it was already the beginning of November—our deputy editor in chief left for a general factory meeting, and when he returned he told us that socialism in Hungary was under threat; insurgents had started taking control of more territory. They were murdering party members and were planning to occupy parts of Slovakia that were predominantly Hungarian. The situation was so grave that he had decided to do something about it and thus had enlisted the entire editorial staff into the People's Militia.

I think most of the editors were astounded. I said that this would not do; he hadn't even asked us. He answered that he'd had no doubts concerning our consent, and with that the meeting ended.

Five years earlier I had been accepted as a member of the party. At the time I was convinced that what we were taught about socialism being the most advanced arrangement of society was a fact. Then I began to understand that much of what was happening was the opposite of what was actually reported, and crimes were being concealed behind lofty words. If I had been consistent, I would have left the party the moment the first flagrant trials of political opponents had begun, or at the latest when they had locked up Father. It's true that until then no one had asked anything definite of me, at least nothing I had found unpleasant. I had been able to write my thesis the way I'd wanted; I hadn't been appointed to any party function; I wasn't in charge of anything; I didn't harm anyone, and I hadn't allowed anyone to do it for me. Now, as a devoted comrade, I was supposed to go and stand guard somewhere with an automatic weapon to preserve the status quo, so that those in power would continue to rule. Now I was horrified by the idea that I would be trapped forever in a blue-gray uniform with a red armband, subjected to military discipline and an oath of loyalty from which there would be no way out.

I decided to leave the party and thereby resolve everything. I knew I would face much unpleasantness; I would lose my job, and it would be difficult to find another. But this all seemed more acceptable than promising to the end of my life that I would, with rifle in hand, fight for an ideal I would have no influence on. Much to my surprise, I was relieved.

In the morning, I pocketed my party card with the intention of turning it over to our chairwoman. I arrived just in time for the meeting, where the deputy editor in chief was saying that no collective enlistment in the militia would be accepted. Each of us had to enlist on his or her own. He had also been told that preference was being given to working-class staff members over editors, and some of us might be turned away. Nevertheless, he believed we would all go and try to enlist. Of course I didn't (as far as I know, nobody from the editorial staff did), and I did not return my party card.

A few days later, Soviet troops brutally suppressed the Hungarian revolution. When the news came that Soviet tanks were rolling through the streets of Budapest, the old good and worthy comrades on the editorial board starting hugging and kissing one another as if they'd just learned they had been saved and redeemed forever. Someone opened a bottle of vodka, and the foreign desk editor shouted effusively, *Venceremos!*

The only thing I truly enjoyed was writing. Lounging about the office, ordering and editing articles, seemed like a waste of time.

I had just finished my studies when the Writers' Union, in addition to its well-established journals, was allowed to publish *Květen*, which was supposed to serve primarily as an outlet for the poetry of young authors. In the Czech lands, it was mostly poetry that was considered literature. In the first issue *Květen* published about sixty poems of would-be versifiers. I was not among those who ventured to write verse, but I still tried to write, using the form of the short story. "Blossom" was sentimental and moralistic. I wanted to discredit the belief that today all painful conflicts were disappearing from human relations. I thought up a story of a girl who falls in love with a handsome young scoundrel who abandons her when she gets pregnant. My heroine's eyes are opened in the end. *It is only in books that everything works itself out. Only there are pain and suffering cleared away as a housewife clears away dirt when she's expecting guests.*

At the editorial offices, besides two well-known authors, was a decrepit, obviously long-retired "professor" who was supposed to oversee the grammar and sometimes the stylistic quality of manuscripts.

I brought in "Blossom," which I was justifiably proud of, since it differed from stories that were currently being published. The professor called me in a few days later, and I saw my typed copy on his desk desecrated with dozens of corrections in garish red ink. The number of corrections would have earned me an F in school.

I heard the professor out. My story wasn't bad, but it was sloppily written. I had to rework it and eliminate all the literary clichés.

Offended, I replied that they didn't have to publish my story at all if they didn't want to. The professor said it was up to me and handed me my manuscript.

I came back a week later with the rewritten story and humbly submitted it again.

Although literary theory bored me and I avoided literary discussions, my story satisfied the requirements that my fellow poets and literary critics were to designate only a few weeks later as literature or poetry of the everyday.

Květen was subject to somewhat less supervision because of its small circulation, and a collection of authors, heterogeneous in both their opinions and their ages, gathered there.

Because I had already published several short stories, I was seen as a young prose writer and thus appointed to the editorial board.

It soon got around that I was participating in the publication of a literary monthly.

Despite their similar names, *Květy* and *Květen* offered two different views of the world, and these two magazines were like two islands separated by an ocean. It became obvious that I could not work for both of them for long. This conflict was soon resolved. I wrote and published in *Květen* a lengthy essay titled "Political Profile of Karel Čapek, Czech Writer."

I began the article with a quotation from Čapek's article "What Is Culture?" published in *Přítomnost* in February 1934: "In my opinion, all education has at least one common end: to teach something about the experiences, knowledge, and values humanity has thus far produced and not lose or fall beneath them." I continued:

> What a modest request! Nevertheless, it has recently been compromised. Our education has run wild and our thinking has ossified. We have clipped the wings of our own spirit; we have eradicated from the world of philosophy, literature, and art everything that does not correspond to the compartment in which the world was supposed to fit.

For a while no one noticed the essay, but then a new editor in chief was installed at *Květy*. He called me into his office and had in front of him my Čapek essay. He asked if I'd written it and whether I truly stood behind everything I'd said. When I assured him that otherwise I wouldn't have written it, he asked if I thought that I could remain an editor at *Květy*, and he answered for me that I couldn't. He was ordering me to pack all my belongings that day and never show myself there again.

Thus ended my editorship at *Květy* after less than a year. *Květen* was banned two years later.

Essay: *The Betrayal of the Intellectuals*, p. 475

10

I met my future life companion all but symbolically on a bridge. It was a very hot day, and I was coming back from Smíchov. I saw a former classmate walking toward me, a member of our singing trio, accompanied by a redhead whose pale skin was flushed from the heat. I greeted my classmate and learned that the redhead was named Helena. She was in her first year studying Czech and was also a marvelous singer.

Without even glancing at me, the redhead said she sang only in the University Art Ensemble and that we had met once already. I had already graduated and was accompanying her to the cafeteria, but because there was a long line, I had sneaked my way to the front and forgotten about her. She'd been quite offended.

I recalled no such event. Surely she'd confused me with someone else.

Standing in the oppressive heat was unpleasant, and since I wasn't in any hurry, I offered to walk with them.

At one point, Helena stopped before an ostentatious building and invited us inside to her apartment where we could cool off a little.

She lived on the fifth floor of this magnificent structure from the beginning of the century.

Inside, she brought out a large jug of water sweetened with syrup. We sat at a square black table and talked about the department and our professors. Helena didn't do a lot of talking. I, on the other hand, discoursed expansively on how my longest prose work to date had been published in the magazine *Nový život*, but the censors had confiscated it because I wrote about the student May Day celebration. It was unfortunate I didn't have the text with me or I would have gladly read at least a few passages from it. I thought the story quite compelling and heaped praise on my writing to make it clear that I would someday be a writer, the most admirable vocation I could imagine.

Helena did not look at me once the entire time, at least not when I was looking at her.

When I got home, I realized I wanted to see the redhead again. I rang up my former classmate and asked if she happened to have the telephone number of "that redheaded girl who had invited us for a soft drink." She did, and all I needed now was an excuse to call her.

Fortunately, the lock to my briefcase was missing. It was unlikely that I'd lost it at the redhead's apartment because I hadn't opened it there, but perhaps it was a plausible pretext.

When she answered the phone, she assured me that she hadn't found any lock.

When I finally managed to say that I'd like to see her anyway, I'm sure she assumed that I had simply invented the story about the lock, but she nevertheless admitted it might be possible.

I suggested that since she had hosted me, it was my turn. I pointed out that a trolley went from her place almost directly to my building. I'd wait for her at the stop just in case.

She hesitated before she finally agreed.

I waited impatiently. She arrived a half hour late, explaining that she could never keep track of time.

We met again several times; I even went to see her in Louny, where she spent her holidays with her aunt. We set out on a long trip to Oblík Hill. Right at the foot of the steep hill, a Gypsy woman (there were still no Romani living in Czechoslovakia at the time, only Gypsies) stopped us and said she would tell us our future. I saw that my companion was eager to hear about what lay ahead for us, so I consented. The Gypsy read our palms and foretold a beautiful and happy life together—a little boy and girl, a long journey (an illness, which would turn out okay; in fact, it would make us stronger)—and she finally told us we would be rich. In anticipation of enormous wealth and grateful for two children, I bestowed upon the clairvoyant a whole twenty-five crowns.

On one of our outings along the cliffs of nearby Beroun (on the way we held hands and talked), I wrote Helena a long-winded declaration, perhaps in the belief that my literary skill would win her over forever.

Monday morning, the last of September 1957

Just a single sentence,
A message:
to a hazelnut whose shell is judicious but whose heart yields life,
and the shell, therefore, must burst, and I believe that only a great
love is stronger than the will (Yours) and the shell;
and to the child in muddy slippers on the wet grass bending over
an ear of corn, Your thoughts are like a mountain spring that
cleanses me entirely; I will stay by Your side until night and
rain and wind arrive; I will allow only the stars to come inside;
to stay with you forever;
and to the girl with tender fingers that walk as she does along
unfamiliar paths, at times slightly atremble
(my sweet little fingers) this is more than we can relinquish.
And to the star. The one and only arising above the earth and
mirrored in the empyrean—I want to be the wind
the lamplighter and chase away the clouds that would dare
sail in, the only thing reflected in the sky, your light is reflected
everywhere around me;
and to the woman with hands more gentle than soft evening
music—
the train was moving and you were already sleeping, sometimes
quivering like the seashore as a wave breaks upon it. I want to

be the sea within your strand, a sea of powerful waves and a
silent surface. The sea is enormous and teeming with life; time
and again it returns to its shore and never leaves; it is silent
and strong and ever returns; I want to be the sea within your
strand, to touch you in your sleep like a solitary wave rushing
up to shore, to be the sea within your strand, always returning;
and to your eyes, afraid to see lest they lose the power of speech;
and your heart, which threatens to beat too hard,
    only yesterday I understood You and I love You—let us walk
together along high paths, ever higher where the earth fades
away; but let us stay upon the earth, and it will tremble as the
Gypsy foretold,
And to You—I call You Lenička, such an ordinary word, I call
You my dear, I call You my dear, my dear, my dear, and it's too
little for me because words lack scent, breath, and hands for me
    to touch,
and to love, do not destroy us, make us pure,
and to You— . . . I am afraid to say it lest the words grow com-
monplace,
and to You—gentle, pure, and beautiful;
to You—you have grown into my life, and to tear you out would
bring death, but
I will never do that because we will stay together . . .

I'd gone out with a few girls in school; once I even thought about
getting married when my beloved returned from a study trip to Romania. But then I learned she'd found a boyfriend there—at least for her
time in Romania—and I no longer thought about a wedding.

I would always fall in love, but at the same time I would wonder
whether my love was merely a delusion. This time, however, my new
love instilled no fear.

Helena was different from me. She had no yearning to rescue
anyone, but she was convinced that everyone had an obligation to help

others, behave honorably, and never lie. She was a beautiful singer and loved music—naturally, different from the music I loved. I was enchanted by the Romantics: Beethoven and Dvořák. She preferred the spirituals: Bach and Janáček. She was shy and gentle, whereas I demonstrated my feelings in a flood of words. For her the words *my dear* meant just as much as my protracted declaration.

She was almost six years younger than I was, but she'd certainly read more books and seemed to understand them better.

She had absolutely no enthusiasm for my interest in politics. She recognized only moral authority, something that rarely appeared in contemporary politics.

She wanted me to meet her friends and family because they were a part of her life much more than all the ideas I heaped on her. For her, the family was the most important thing in life, and she frightened me several times when she said she wanted seven children. She adored her parents and was an unusually obedient daughter for her age. She refused to stay out late because her mother would worry, and she didn't want to cause her any concern.

Our amatory relations had gone no farther than kissing on the bank of the Vltava River or on anchored boats by Kampa Island. And before we'd had a chance to actually embrace, I had to leave to attend two months of military training in Domažlice, which would be followed by my obligatory military service.

Helena said the waiting would be unbearable and promised to visit me.

It seemed to me that Domažlice would play some sort of role in our relationship, the import of which, however, was unclear. But one thing was certain: I had to reserve accommodations at least one week in advance.

⚍

At the time, military service was compulsory for all young men if they didn't manage to obtain a so-called blue book. The service lasted two years for most, but we lucky ones who had attended military training in college had to serve only two months. Later, the same graduates had to sign up for six months; for my brother it was two years. Although I was completely unprepared, I began at the rank of sergeant trainee and already had a platoon under my command.

In the train on the way to the recruiting station, I met another former classmate and my friend Jirka, who had been called up at the same time. Right away Jirka started bragging about all the philosophy books he'd brought with him to fill the time we'd be sitting around the parade ground.

As future commanders, we were greeted without the usual hazing. We were issued military uniforms and a bunk in the headquarters. They advised us to prepare for our duties by reading through the rules and regulations and introduced us to a pack of obstinate corporals and lance corporals who were to command the newly established squads. The arrival of the draftees was expected a few days later.

The commander of the company Jirka and I were assigned to was small and shriveled. Before his time as an officer in the People's Army, he had been a cobbler, or, more precisely, a worker in a shoe factory in Zlín. He stuttered a little and expressed more complicated phrases only with difficulty. Fortunately, oratorical skills were not in the job description of commander.

The day before the recruits arrived, all of us future platoon commanders (one was a genuine two-star officer and professional soldier) were called together and informed that it was now our task to transform "these civilians into class-conscious and disciplined soldiers who would vigilantly stand on guard and/or fight for our country."

Shortly after the arrival of the afternoon train, half-drunken young men in civilian clothing began straggling into the garrison. What followed reminded me of my war years: shouting, cursing, and unjustly terrified young men reeling through the hallways wearing boots that were too big and uniforms that didn't fit, driven into the uninviting expanse of the barracks, where bunks with straw mattresses awaited them. The confused bustling about, which we at first attributed to natural fear of a new unfriendly environment, however, had a different cause. The soldiers didn't understand what was required of them. They came from southern Slovakia and were fluent only in Hungarian or an odd mixture of languages spoken by the local Gypsies.

The very first days, we noticed that our squad leaders were getting busy. Their triumphant shouting resounded throughout the barracks. Hardly had the recruits managed to put away the clothing and accessories they'd just been issued when they were driven into the bathrooms to fetch buckets of water. Then, to the incessant bellowing of the seasoned veterans, they scrubbed the hallways, while others worked on the floors and windows in the barracks. One Gypsy was even forced to bring out a ladder and clean the lightbulbs. Jirka and I looked on in a state of bewilderment, but since we were not acquainted with how things were done, we didn't dare interfere. We permitted the squad leaders to act how they saw fit. In their turn, they were satisfied with our passivity, or, rather, our uninterest regarding any kind of military activity, and willingly filled in for us. They taught the recruits how to make their bunks, how to assemble their kit bags, how to leap up immediately upon reveille and go to the courtyard for morning drills, and primarily to keep in mind that military service required continual application. It was with the greatest pleasure that they would sound a nighttime alert and, when they were satisfied with how the frazzled recruits were packing their kit bags, would cancel it.

We witnessed a lot during those first few days. As commanders we were allowed to leave the barracks after our duties were finished and, especially at first, we took advantage of this opportunity to wander about the consolatory environs of the town. But despite the tranquil countryside, and most likely under the influence of having become active members of the army, we agreed that civilization was careening toward a tragic end and would perish, not like the brontosauruses, as a result of some cosmic catastrophe, but by our own self-destruction. The claim that we could survive an atomic explosion by lying down with our feet in the direction of the explosion (something we had to teach the new recruits), protected by our chemical suits, seemed like gallows humor.

Nevertheless, we practiced this and other such tomfoolery, and the recruits really did lie down with their feet facing the supposed explosion, but almost half of them, perhaps out of linguistic ignorance, weariness, or spite, lay down with their heads in the direction of the explosion. These were immediately pronounced dead and in punishment were ordered by the corporals to run around the training grounds in their gas masks.

One afternoon I stayed at the barracks and wrote a long letter to my beloved Helena. I broke the rules regarding military secrecy by describing the nonsensicalness of the training I was undergoing, but most of all I wanted to know when she was coming to see me, and I assured her how sad I was and how much I was looking forward to her visit.

When I'd finished the letter, I left the activities room and saw a Gypsy whose squad leader had decided to pick on him. He was kneeling in the hallway and scrubbing the floor with a toothbrush. I ordered him to stop immediately and return to his quarters. Then I told his astonished tormentor I would brook no degradation of human dignity or even the assigning of senseless tasks. I could have disciplined him myself, but I decided to lodge a complaint with the company commander, who would punish him more severely.

So I complained to our cobbler. He was somewhat taken aback and informed me that this was how the recruits were usually treated. He admitted, however, that scrubbing the floor with a toothbrush was ineffective, was unhygienic, and did not contribute to improving the combat readiness of our army. He promised to attend the next education seminar and get it through their fucking heads.

He did actually come and speak to us. Because I still knew shorthand at the time, I transcribed his speech word for word owing to its illustrative nature.

We are living in the phase, comrade soldiers, when the general crisis of capitalism is deepening, when a third world war is the best fact, or rather the third phase, which is characterized by the emergence of socialism. This third phase to this day. We see on the one hand the decline of the revolutionary wave, we see the influence of the global gendarme, the United States, but a further aspect of this is our progressive worldwide body. And this is characterized by the Twentieth Congress of the Soviet Union. This is a characteristic of the era, that is, the influence of revisionism and the danger from the left and the right. But this final phase is different in that the world Socialist body has become the agent of history. Of course there are problems, for instance, in Africa, where we cannot say ahead of time how or which agent or chieftain will develop, but we have a moral duty with respect to it because people are still chewing away at each other over there, comrade solders. But we overdo it, even though that onus is upon us, and therefore such conversations must be undertaken, where the comrade president meets with African chieftains.

Then the commander posed a combat control question: Who was our president?

After a lengthy silence someone suggested Admiral Horthy; someone else came up with Jozef Tiso. I knew how these strange, rarely encountered words unsettled our commander. He looked at us trainees and all of a sudden asked me to tell the soldiers who their president and commander in chief was.

Since time immemorial, military service has combined drills, stupidity, and the unlimited suppression of any manifestation of intellectual ability, individuality, and freedom. The combination of this tradition with Russian brainlessness and Communist illiteracy, however, resulted in something that exceeded all imagination, not to mention common sense.

I conferred with the other trainees. We then summoned the squad leaders under our command and informed them that if we saw any kind of hazing, we would revoke their passes as punishment. The corporals took offense and stopped attending to military discipline, which immediately declined, as did the battle preparedness of our company. Our company, however, was to be sacrificed in the event of war anyway.

———

Father tried in vain to become legally rehabilitated. He secured the testimony of the foremost experts, who confirmed that if the motors had any flaws, the cause was not in the design but rather in the construction or in the negligent way they had been assembled. Witnesses who had testified against him were prepared to now testify that their confessions had been forced. The regional court in Uherské Hradiště, however, confirmed the original judgment with a remarkable explanation:

> While the witnesses are now trying to characterize the activity of engineer Klíma in an entirely different way, the court considering the proposal to resume the legal action is not prepared to admit their new confessions. It is possible to explain the change to engineer Klíma's advantage, in which the witnesses characterize him as properly looking after the enterprise of which he was the director, by the fact that witnesses, as experience has demonstrated, fashion their testimony in such a way as to be most favorable to the culprit after the passage of a longer period of time.

Father once again entered an appeal, and after four years the Supreme Court repealed the verdict saying that Father's guilt was *not indubitable* and returned the case to the regional court. The regional court, however, noted only that *as a result of the president's amnesty of January 12, 1957, the criminal proceedings have been halted.* Thus his innocence was not confirmed; his guilt had merely been pardoned.

Father felt humiliated by the verdict. His honor had not been vindicated, even though it must have been obvious to any court. He decided to seek rehabilitation in a different way: He started clamoring to be readmitted to the Communist Party, which had expelled him immediately upon his arrest.

Since he considered me a better writer, he had me read over the petitions he had sent to various party offices. In my opinion, he was much too submissive in emphasizing his class consciousness and refuting the ridiculous accusations that he was in touch with Trotsky-ites or that he had studied at a German technical school instead of a Czech one. In his defense, he wrote that his scientific work had always held first place for him; nevertheless, he wrote, *As a member of the party, I always fulfilled my party duties conscientiously and to the letter, and I believe I passed muster among my colleagues who always believed in me entirely.*

I should have talked him out of these letters. Why should he beseech those who were in charge when he had been arrested? But it didn't seem appropriate for me to tell him what to do. Besides, I was too occupied with my own affairs to concern myself with what was fettering his mind and guiding his actions.

When I was fired from *Květy*, I didn't know how I was going to support myself. Was I a reporter, a journalist, a literary critic, or perhaps a budding writer?

I still hadn't produced a book, but I had published around ten short stories, several of which had obviously been influenced by Hemingway.

I offered the collection of stories to *Mladá fronta*, but I was in-formed that even if the editors accepted the book, it would not come out for at least two years. Shortly thereafter I received an unexpected letter from the people at the Literary Fund. They had learned that I was preparing a book of short stories. To allow me to complete it in peace, they were offering me a six-month stipend equal to what I had earned at Květy. This fund was to be used exclusively for the comple-tion of the book, and they also pointed out that the stipend could not be extended. At the end of the letter, however, they betrayed their true intentions in a thoroughly unofficial manner: *Please accept our offer as it is intended—as an attempt to assist you in your current situation.*

I didn't think too much about this unexpectedly accommodating and generous organization. On the other hand, when I mentioned this marvelous offer at home, my twenty-year-old brother noted drily, "They're trying to buy you off."

The book I almost had ready was of course too thin—I needed one more story. I decided to set off on an assignment in the hope that fate would offer a marvelous subject. Several ideas came to mind, but in the end, I set out for the Most region northwest of Prague. I descended the Victorious February mine shaft and paid a visit to a chemical factory that was awesome in its enormousness. I even had time to look at the house whose foundations I had helped lay seven years earlier. I also learned that as winter approached one *finds only smoke, fog, dirt, waste dumps, and smoldering mine shafts.* The air finally got to me; I came down with the flu, and when my temperature topped forty degrees Celsius, I called home not knowing what to do.

Father had to go to work but he said that right away he would send Jenda, who would at least get some driving practice. He had just received his license. He would arrive in two hours and bring me some blankets that mother told me to wrap myself in. I waited. A fog fell so thick that the car trip might take double the time.

After more than three hours, I was called to the telephone, and Father, in a somewhat agitated voice, informed me that my brother had had an accident. The car was ready for the scrap heap, but Jenda had by some miracle come through without a scratch.

I arrived home on the bus wrapped in borrowed blankets.

I quickly recovered from the flu and set out on another reporting assignment. I went to the Plzeň region, where the University Art Ensemble, of which Helena was a member, was having an assembly at the Žinkovy

Chateau. Here I met several of her friends, among them the excellent graphic artist Mirek Klomínek. We started talking, and when I told him about my plan for a reportage expedition, he asked if I needed someone to create a pictorial accompaniment to my writing.

Right there on the spot we agreed to travel to eastern Slovakia, to the strip of land that lay between the borders of Poland, Hungary, and the Soviet Union (not long ago it had been Carpathian Ruthenia and inhabited by Ruthenians, but today it is called Ukraine and populated by Ukrainians). I offered to write several reports for *Literární noviny* about this most remote part of our republic. So far nobody had written about these parts of the republic, and no one knew much about them, so my offer was gratefully accepted.

Mirek Klomínek was not only a talented artist and good singer but also an athlete with a sense of adventure. When we laid out all the maps of the area we could get our hands on, we saw that the railway line ended in Stakčin. From there we could identify only small, often unpaved roads. Some villages, according to the maps, were accessible only by field paths. It seemed highly improbable that buses ran in this area. Neither of us owned a motorcycle (not to mention a car), so we decided to use our default means of transportation—bicycles.

At the beginning of the summer of 1958, Mirek and I loaded our backpacks and boarded a train that would spirit us to the final station before the border with the Soviet Union.

Královský Chlmec was not a very interesting town. Low, squat buildings stretched far and wide. The people spoke mostly Hungarian, and the capital, from where we had come, was for them almost another country, which, owing to an accidental series of historical circumstances, now ruled over them. We didn't linger here, and after a couple of hours set off northward on our bicycles. From the first day of our journey I remember only one adventure. On a vast plain we took refuge from the taxing heat in a wine cellar. About two hours later we went back and mounted our bikes, but after a few minutes, worn out by the heat and drunk on wine, we lay down on the scorching ground. I must have fallen asleep for a little while because I was suddenly awakened by a curious thundering and the feeling that the earth below me was shuddering. I looked around and saw a herd of cattle approaching in a cloud of fine dust. It was something out of an American western, and I realized at once we were in fact in a foreign country.

Slowly but surely we made our way across this exotic plain with the Laborec River flowing above our heads, or so it seemed, restrained by several-meter-tall embankments. Then we boarded a motor coach along with our bicycles and made it all the way to Snina.

The most pitiful and backward region in the whole republic was ruled from Snina. The people here spoke a local dialect resembling a combination of Slovak and Ruthenian. The first few days we more or less guessed at the meaning of what we heard. We visited local functionaries (who mostly spoke Slovak) and received many recommendations about people to meet.

The maps had not lied—the asphalt roads soon came to an end, and all that remained were narrow and worn stony paths. Every few kilometers we had to patch up a punctured wheel.

Then we set off for Ulič Valley. I had expected a romantic trip, I had expected poverty. But in my wildest dreams I could not have imagined all the things we stumbled upon here. In this still untouched countryside we chanced upon tiny cottages with minuscule windows, walls of unfired bricks, often just trampled dirt instead of a floor, and animals sometimes living together with people—though there were rarely any animals except chickens. Once we came upon a small wooden chapel on a hilltop, something out of a fairy tale. Inside were cheap icons, but when the worshippers (primarily women) gathered, we heard Eastern hymns so marvelous, so untamed and wild, that they knocked us off our feet. The women wore plain black dresses and skirts. And everywhere we came across the crippled and mentally ill. The former were victims of the war that had passed through here with all its cruelty fourteen years earlier. The latter were victims of moonshine.

Most of the villages had no shops, or if there were shops, there was nothing to buy. The people lived on what they grew, and every now and then would purchase salt, sugar, yeast (as much as was needed to distill moonshine), and denatured alcohol (which could also be imbibed). Because there were no taverns along the way, we ate out of tin cans and slept wherever we could thanks to the hospitality of the villagers, usually somewhere in the kitchen—one on a bench, the other on the floor.

The nearest doctor was in Snina. Sometimes a medic who had learned to treat battle wounds during the war could be found in a village—this skill came in handy because unexploded mines and other munitions lay scattered in the woods. Midwives, herbalists, and exorcists made up for the lack of doctors.

Soon I saw how advantageous it was for my work that I had taken along an artist instead of a photographer. The ability to quickly draw a house, a cow, or a figure of the owner aroused admiration and wonder and was an excellent conversation starter. I listened to and recorded a great number of stories, legends, and superstitions; I heard epic, often tragic tales from the war.

I also discovered something else one found only in such backward regions: how an old and venerable culture—habits and a way of life, costumes, songs, and rituals—quickly crumbles and disappears. A new culture of pop music, kitsch, transistor radios, nylon, and ready-made clothing was making its way into these regions. It was brought primarily by young men who had gone off for their two years of military training somewhere in the western part of the republic (it was a rule of the military authorities to place the recruits as far away from their homes as possible) and also by those who had left the village for work, and when they returned, they saw everything as unacceptably backward and unsophisticated. The new era, of course, penetrated these parts wearing comradely vestments. One goal was to establish agricultural cooperatives. I heard stories of agitators placing upon the table their strongest argument—a pistol—when trying to convince farmers to join.

Helena and I got married, and at twenty-seven I finally left home. (My father thought it was high time, my brother rejoiced because now he could have his own room, and Mother was worried I'd miss living there.)

Although I truly loved Helena, I was not in a very celebratory mood. I was worried about how I would hold up in my role as husband, how I would fulfill this new obligation that I considered inviolable.

On our honeymoon, we took a small plane to Poprad in the High Tatra Mountains, but on the way back (and for a long time Helena did not forgive me for this) I sent Helena home by train, while I took off in the opposite direction for Trebišov, where Mirek and my bicycle were waiting for me. *Literární noviny* was planning to publish our reportage from eastern Slovakia in installments, and I wanted to undertake another trip to the Ulič Valley.

Along with a life companion, I had acquired some new relatives. My in-laws were very quiet and kind people. They welcomed me as their own and generously allowed us the use of one of three rooms in their large apartment. (At the time, apartments were impossible to come by.)

My mother-in-law had likewise been in Terezín during the war, but only for three months—her husband had not yielded to the pressure of the Nazi authorities to divorce his Jewish wife. Something unimaginable had happened there, something that had nearly cost her her life but had saved the life of her sister.

During the final days of the war, as well as maintaining the existence of the Terezín ghetto, the Nazis started bringing in prisoners from other camps, which they had to hastily clean out before the approaching allied armies arrived. I remember the new prisoners well: men and women wearing light blue striped prison uniforms who had been in the worst camps. They had been forced to travel a great distance by foot or by train crammed into boxcars, where they were locked up without food or water. Then they were unloaded, dead or dying, and left to sit for hours on the grass near the rail tracks.

My mother-in-law knew that her sister had been imprisoned in Auschwitz, and even though it would be almost impossible to find her, she set off looking. (We had also tried looking for Father at the time.) A miracle occurred—she found her sister: emaciated, at death's door, half unconscious, and burning up with spotted fever. She loaded her on her back and brought her to the overcrowded camp hospital, where she visited her until she herself became infected. It was already the end of the war, and doctors were coming from Prague to help save the sick. After many months, both sisters recovered.

I met Aunt Andulka thirteen years after these events. She was an exceptionally elegant and cultured lady who had mastered several languages. From our very first meeting, she came to hold for me a special significance. She mentioned a book by Isaac Deutscher that might interest me, concerning the battles between Stalin and Trotsky, that is, the brutal and bloody way Stalin achieved power.

Of course the book was in English, and at the time my knowledge of that language was hardly good enough for the most primitive conversation. My new aunt offered to translate for me, and so I would visit her small flat in Pankrác carrying a thick notebook in which I would copy all the important passages. This is how I first became acquainted in detail with Stalin's diabolical dictatorship. For the first time I read about the monstrous show trials, Stalin's betrayal of his former friends, his collusion with his recent enemies to achieve absolute power.

This bloody tale liberated me from my illusions concerning what had actually happened in the "first Socialist country" and helped me to see what I had been afraid to admit until then. I finally realized that in a society in which all means of expressing disagreement are suppressed and every word of doubt is considered grounds for prosecution and subsequent execution, only the despotism of the leader comes to power.

At the beginning of the new year, my father showed me, as if embarrassed, a piece of paper with the heading:

**Communist Party of Czechoslovakia
Central Committee**

Notice to appear on Wednesday, January 14, 1959, at 8:30 a.m.
at the Committee of Party Control of the Central Committee of
the Communist Party of Czechoslovakia, Prague, Příkopy #35
to Comrade Hasík, who will inform you of the decision by the
Secretariat of the Central Committee of the Communist Party of
Czechoslovakia regarding your membership in the party.

Because the date had already passed, I asked my father how it
had turned out.

He told me to turn over the paper.

On the other side of the austere invitation—or, rather order—
Father had written in his large and clear handwriting:

I was informed that upon my return from prison, I had participated
in few political rallies, and therefore the Secretariat forbade the
renewal of my membership. I responded by pointing out that I
had dedicated myself assiduously to my scientific work, which was
certainly more important for society than any May Day agitprop
activities.

At first I wanted to say that everything had actually turned out
fine, but then I gathered that he saw this rejection as a continuation of
the injustice that was being perpetrated upon him. So I merely said,
"They certainly gave you an idiotic excuse."

Essay: *On Propaganda,* p. 481

11

After the bloody suppression of the Hungarian Revolution, the leadership of the party, of which I was still a member, decided once again to silence even minor hints of criticism and issued an order to "change" the editorship of the Československý spisovatel publishing house. The purge, which fortunately this time was not a bloody one, replaced the more enlightened editorial party members with less enlightened and more obedient ones. I was still far removed from the activity of writers or even party circles and thus heard almost nothing about the changes.

However, the new editor in chief, Jan Pilař, knew about me from *Literární noviny*, which he had directed up until then. He had treated me kindly and even managed to secure me a special fee for my eastern Slovak reportage. Now he called me into his office and told me the publishing house had great plans. He wanted to initiate a series devoted exclusively to prose and reportage dealing with contemporary matters and call it Life Around Us. He was intent on including my little book about eastern Slovakia and asked if I'd like to be in charge of the series.

Working as an editor for a publishing house was not a job that enticed me. It struck me as less challenging than writing reportage, but I had no other offers. I could imagine what was written in my cadre file after I'd been fired from *Květy*, and I couldn't really expect another magazine or newspaper to take me on. So I accepted the offer.

The offices of Československý spisovatel were located in the very center of Prague in a marvelous art nouveau building. It was listed as a national monument, and this designation certainly helped preserve its splendid façade. Inside, however, it had been disfigured by partitions and fittings. I was placed in a tiny, dimly lit room that served as a passageway with a window looking out onto a gallery. The proofreaders in the staff room behind me had it better than I did simply because no one could walk through their room.

The editorial staff was divided into several sections. One was in charge of poetry, another of specialized literature. I came under prose. I was certainly not a good editor for I did not enjoy advising authors how to write. (The author should surely know this himself; otherwise what kind of author was he?) But dispensing this sort of advice was one of an editor's primary duties. He was responsible for the quality and the content of the book, perhaps even more than the author himself. I was somewhat better as a copyreader. Sometimes I could recognize talent, even if it was buried beneath a mass of raw text. Soon the Secretariat started overwhelming me with manuscripts from unknown hacks. All this reading seemed like a waste of time, but later I came to see that it was not without its advantages. For the rest of my life I harbored within me a revulsion for all clichés and hackneyed phrases that bad authors and sometimes even otherwise good journalists employ.

Every now and then a truly excellent text would materialize. Once I was presented with a slender partial manuscript by someone named Alexandr Klimentiev. This story, entirely devoid of Socialist rhetoric, was titled *Marie* and dealt with a deceived and despairing wife. It was written with unusual feeling for both language and narrative. I found the manuscript so engaging that even before anyone else had read it, I took off to see the author to tell him how much I admired his story. Upon the recommendation of the publishing house, Klimentiev (who was only two years older than I was) received a stipend from the Literary Fund in order to complete the novel. He published it under his Bohemized name, Alexandr Kliment, and *Marie* became one of the most successful prose pieces of the period. I also managed to track down Ludvík Vaculík, the author of a pedagogical diary I had read several years earlier. He too received a stipend, and from his slender bundle of notes emerged the extensive novel *A Busy House*, one of the works inaugurating the new wave in Czech prose.

Another book of the new wave, Ladislav Fuks's world-famous *Mr. Theodore Mundstock*, had a rather bizarre genesis, however.

Several copyreaders had to read each book, and disagreements often arose concerning their quality. In this case, everyone agreed it was an extraordinary manuscript, perhaps a bit morbid, but the war, still in recent memory, was a morbid subject. As one of the copyreaders, I recommended the book for publication and gave it no more thought. About a year later, one of my colleagues came to see me. She'd brought with her Fuks's manuscript, which looked as if it had swelled to almost twice its original size. She told me she'd received the book to edit, but the author was driving her crazy. Any suggestion Fuks was given, he immediately complied with, and with such verve that the story was gradually losing all sense. I'd been the first to recommend the book, so perhaps I could speak with the author and advise him what to do with the manuscript. I thumbed through the pages and saw that the story did indeed fall apart. Some passages were digressive and meandering. I called the author and asked if he could find a moment to stop by the publisher's office. He turned up and, even before I could open my mouth, started overwhelming me with thanks and assured me how much he respected me. He had read both my books and hoped I would forgive his presumptuousness in telling me they were simply brilliant. He then made an enthusiastic gesture, and I was afraid he was going to embrace and start kissing me. I thanked him for his praise and asked if he still had the original version of his novel. He said he did but was now ashamed of it. I asked if he could lend it to me. When I reread the text, it seemed so good that nothing had to be changed. I invited the author in again and told him that the original text was excellent. As a sort of apology for all the fiddle-faddle he'd gone through, I added that, of course, there were a few minor things that could be expressed better; for example the figurative phrase "rose-colored dreams" seemed to me a little clichéd. It would be enough to cross out "rose-colored" and replace it perhaps with something like "nice" or "comforting." Or, on the other hand, he could illuminate or expand upon "rose-colored." Enthusiastic assent gleamed in the author's eyes, and I hastily told him not to revise a thing, for goodness' sake, just to read the text through one more time, and then we'd send it straight to the printer.

About two weeks later, Fuks brought his manuscript in and proudly showed me the changes he'd made. They concerned the rose-colored dreams. He'd added two paragraphs, the first of which read:

> He imagined that the boy had a beautiful, bright future in front of him, which was always connected with an enchanting image of fragile rose-colored china—everything was bathed in a curious fairy-tale rosy color. . . . Three years ago the Germans, however, had with a single kick smashed everything as if they'd all been empty ridiculous fantasies, porcelain figures, and then he stopped going to see the Sterns. But here the image would appear before him, swathing him in the beauty, splendor, and rosiness he had felt three years ago.

In another paragraph, one of the characters, named Frýda, performs a puppet theater version of *Sleeping Beauty* for the hero, where everything is rose-colored—the dresses, the props, not to mention the roses surrounding Sleeping Beauty. There was something gruesome in the way the author was willing to destroy his own text, and it occurred to me that his hero might even be willing to inhale coal fumes if someone thought it necessary. I asked him as emphatically as I could to cross out both passages immediately. Mr. Fuks insisted on keeping them because they seemed to him appropriate. I think he finally crossed out the *Sleeping Beauty* scene (I didn't read the novel a third time, and a colleague edited the final version), but the passage about rosiness in this extraordinary work I undoubtedly have on my conscience.

My wife became pregnant less than a year after the wedding. We both looked forward to the child, but the only problem was that Helena was just finishing her degree.

The topic she had chosen for her dissertation (perhaps I had recommended it or she had chosen it because of me) was an analysis of literature about life in concentration camps. I read the books along with her so that we could discuss them.

Soon after the war, authors spewed out their jaw-dropping experiences, often artlessly but in great detail. It amounted to a sort of overview of torture, suffering, boundless cruelty, and attempts to resist by force.

They wrote about doctors who submerged prisoners in icy water until they nearly died; guards who tossed prisoners into stone quarries thirty meters below; mass executions where prisoners were forced to strip naked, climb down into a pit, which they had just been forced to dig, and lie down on still warm and bloody bodies that had been shot before them. They wrote about trucks and uniformed murderers who pumped exhaust fumes into the enclosed truck bed in which they had locked their victims. They wrote about starving to death, about people (called Mussulmen) who weren't even people any longer, just skeletons slouching toward an early death. It was utterly inappropriate reading for such a delicate being as Helena and even more inappropriate for a pregnant woman, but such was life.

This dismal reading along with the fact we were expecting a child renewed my conviction that I had to do everything I could so that those I loved would never have to experience anything like this. I wrote several utopian or perhaps horror stories in which I tried to give shape to my idea of the impersonality of modern warfare as well as of contemporary relationships, which was affecting mankind and could transform us into instruments capable of almost anything. I called one of the stories "Fairy Tale Machine." This was about a family who buy a robot to look after their daughter in the place of Grandma. It was supposed not only to look after the child but also to tell her fairy tales.

The robot did actually keep an eye on the child and tell her stories, but one day it broke down and kept repeating the same sentence about a burning stove over and over. The girl was seized with fear. She didn't know where to hide from the inhuman voice emanating from the machine. The robot was programmed not to let her leave the room. The story ended with Grandma coming home, turning off the robot, and consoling the child.

The story was published in the monthly *Nový život*. Several weeks later I received a letter typed on letterhead belonging to *Bratři v triku* and signed by someone named Mojžíš (Moses). Jiří Trnka had apparently liked my story and was wondering if we could meet.

To me, this was the highest honor. The famous artist and designer wanted to meet me; perhaps he even wanted to do something with my story.

Jiří Trnka received me in his film studio. Marvelous puppets were hanging all over the place, most from *A Midsummer Night's Dream* along with the Good Soldier Švejk and Prince Bajaja. In the background on a little table was the scenery, and the animator was manipulating a puppet.

Trnka was sitting on a high chair (or perhaps my respect for him placed him so high in my memory) and said the basic idea of my story had intrigued him. I had said, figuratively and urgently, that no robot could take the place of a person. To have a machine supply the care for a child symbolized our contemporary degeneracy in a powerful way. "Many people even believe that machines will be our salvation, but I look upon all this with fear. You know," he continued, "today everyone is busy with politics, but this is greater than they are, it's greater than all systems. It threatens to deprive us of our humanity. I sense this fear in your story. We entrust everything into the hands of machines. They will think for us, watch over us, amuse us; they'll write books and draw. And this fiddly job?" He pointed at the animator. "A machine will be able to do it a hundred times faster and better. But what's the result? We do it to express our feelings, our fears, or ourselves. What or whom will a machine express?"

He asked me to try to turn the story (originally only two pages) into a screenplay.

I worked on it as well as I could, took it to the director, listened to his comments, and continued writing. Then Mr. Trnka sent word that the screenplay was suitable, and he would see what he could do with it. Several months went by, and I stopped thinking about my Machine and, as far as I remember, I was certain Mr. Trnka had too. Then one day I received a letter from the Brothers in T-Shirts inviting me to a screening of *The Cybernetic Grandmother*. As far as the details go, not much was left of my screenplay. The story had been improved with a lot of new ideas and was longer than I thought it would be, but not only had Mr. Trnka preserved the basic idea; he had developed it in a wonderful way.

That was the last time I saw him alive. He asked me if I was satisfied and if I was bothered by the fact he'd changed the title. I said the film was wonderful and compelling, and as far as the title was concerned, he was the primary author, and the only thing that was important was that the title satisfy him.

Our son was born not long after, on a chilly January day. I wasn't used to drinking to anything, not even the birth of a son, but when he was brought to me in the maternity ward, my joy knew no bounds. At home waited not only all our relatives but also an old-fashioned white wicker baby carriage, a gift from the Vaculíks, who told us their three sons had spent their first years in this friendly abode.

<hr/>

Shortly after my reports from eastern Slovakia were published in book form, a screenwriter from Barrandov Studios, Ivan Urban, wrote to tell me he found them fascinating and asked if I'd like to write a film narrative about those exotic surroundings.

At first I thought he had in mind a documentary film, but documentaries did not enjoy much popularity at the time, and Mr. Urban explained that a "suspenseful" story would be much more effective.

We got together many times. He was a friendly and pleasant man, a talented dramaturge, a witty screenwriter, and a wonderful storyteller. He told me the story of Hitchcock's *Psycho* in such great detail and so suggestively that when I saw the film years later I was almost disappointed.

I gradually came up with a story about a land surveyor whose beloved dies in a concentration camp. He cannot remain in the region where he met her, or even continue his usual work, so he leaves for the other end of the republic, the lowlands along the Laborec River. The people here live in unimaginable poverty. He works at various jobs, lives in different lodgings, drinks, surveys land for a hospital, and sees how floods often destroy the already miserable crops. He decides to design a series of dams to prevent the flooding. I wove into the story the balladic fortunes of the local residents and postwar life in a dilapidated country.

Over two months I put together the first version. The following month we composed the second version, but this one Urban gave back to me too. Apparently some of the characters were too indistinct, the establishment of the co-op was too drastic, and the way the countryside developed wasn't emphasized enough.

My screenplay wasn't approved even the third time around, and I decided to give up my efforts at film and try to write a novel instead.

I announced my intention at work, and my still nonexistent novel made its way into the publishing schedule. I had until September 30, 1962, to turn it in.

My editing work, however, demanded a lot of attention. I had no time for any sort of concentrated writing and no quiet environment in which to work. When I came home in the evening, I looked forward to playing with little Michal and hearing from my wife or mother-in-law what progress he'd made.

I usually wrote late at night for two or three hours and went to bed after midnight. Unfortunately, the windows of our Smíchov flat looked out on the street, where heavy trucks started rumbling through at five in the morning. The house seemed to shake to its very foundations, and I couldn't fall back asleep. I went around in a continual state of fatigue.

I was convinced at the end of spring that I'd never write the novel under these conditions and went to share my fears with my supervisor. To my great surprise, he was happy to offer me an unpaid vacation (not until later did I realize he was only too glad to get me out of the office for a while). He just wanted to know if I could finish the novel on time. I thought this would be no problem under such wonderful circumstances.

The hero of my novel was still the land surveyor, and even though I had no intention of writing much about his job, my conscience bothered me because I hadn't the slightest idea about land surveying. I happened to mention this to a colleague, who laughed and said her husband, if he could write, certainly wouldn't have such problems. He was a land surveyor. If I had any questions, all I had to do was ask.

Her husband was indeed willing to help me out and said he would be surveying somewhere near Ledeč nad Sázavou on June 1. I could join him if I wanted. At least I would see with my own eyes how simple the job was.

My unpaid vacation was to begin on June 1, and I thought it would be a wonderful way to start work on my book.

He piled me into his all-terrain vehicle along with his theodolite, his surveying poles, and his assistant, and on the way kept assuring me his job was nothing mysterious. Kafka certainly knew no more about land surveying than that it required assistants, and look what a wonderful novel he had written. We arrived at a meadow, where he unpacked his equipment and we could begin. It was a beautiful sunny late spring day, and the meadow was in furious bloom. The air was filled with scents and clouds of pollen. He set up his theodolite and sent his assistant where he needed her, then he called me over to his side. I suddenly began to sneeze. I sneezed almost constantly the whole time, but I pretended that it was my usual expression of enthusiastic interest—they of course couldn't keep themselves from laughing. After he'd explained how the measuring apparatuses worked, he sent me with a surveyor's pole to a corner of the plot. I tried to stop sneezing just for a moment so the pole I was holding would stop wobbling. The friendly land surveyor waved to me with his hands to take a few steps back. I heard something that sounded like cracking rotten wood, but it was too late: I plunged into a cesspool up to my waist, still clutching the surveyor's pole.

When I finally scrambled out, the engineer and his assistant couldn't hold back their laughter.

My trousers were soaked through with brownish liquid manure and stank so horribly that I was no longer fit for any activity among people. I ran into town, crept into the river with my pants, and rinsed them for a long while, but it was no use. In a clothing store, people stepped aside as I approached. I had enough money for only the cheapest shorts. My wife washed my pants at home, then I took them to the cleaners, and finally we pronounced them unusable.

My experience was also unusable because my hero was supposed to be capable of managing complicated situations, and it would be quite unbecoming of him to fall into a cesspool.

<hr/>

Michal was three years old, and we were still living with Helena's parents. The wait for an apartment "allocation" in Prague was around fifteen years. If you joined the co-op and had around thirty thousand crowns (my total salary for almost two years), you might be able to get an apartment four or five years earlier. Another way to get an apartment was through an exchange, but the number of people who wanted to exchange one large flat for two smaller ones was much greater than vice versa.

Because I was on a special (creative) vacation to finish my novel, I had more time to play with Michal. He was at a tender age and unlike me was manually dexterous. He could build elaborate structures out of blocks, and although he sometimes received toys that were too complicated for his age, such as Lego or Merkur construction toys, he always worked with them tenaciously. We often sat for hours fashioning buildings and simple gadgets. Every evening Michal wanted to hear a fairy tale, an oral story rather than a written one if possible.

I invented never-ending tales whose heroes were an awkward and clumsy little puppy, a wise and skillful kitten, and a good-natured horse named Vašek upon whom the pair traveled around the world. The fairy tale continued for a number of years, comprising several thousand installments (not only did my daughter experience them, but also my oldest granddaughter; if I'd written them down, they would have filled more volumes than the celebrated Harry Potter series). Much to my surprise, I managed to think up ever new and usually humorous situations.

The Smíchov Embankment where we lived was ostentatious, but it was not an ideal environment for children. On Sundays, however, we would hike up Petřín Hill. I would take a ball, which we would kick from goal to goal along the way. I kept saying I was making a soccer player out of Michal, but I didn't mean it seriously. I just loved watching the little fellow try to kick the ball. Helena, however, was not keen on the prospect of her son growing up to be a soccer player and tried to talk me out of my plans.

Only in hindsight does one come to understand that the time spent with one's children is unique and unrepeatable—one of the most powerful experiences life has to offer. But this time of life is often overshadowed by many other interests and obligations—making money, hunting down things (an apartment), debating, celebrating various anniversaries or successes with friends, traveling (at least in our own country, since we couldn't go abroad), and finally reaching the misguided conclusion that our children are actually holding us back, and we look for some sort of replacement for ourselves (grandparents in the best case, some sort of apparatus or contrivance in the worst). Before the invention of the computer, the Internet, and the virtual world, I tried to depict this in "The Fairy Tale Machine" and the screenplay *Cybernetic Grandmother*.

I was no different in my relationship with my offspring and reproached myself for neglecting my novel. The time off I'd been given to finish it was speedily passing by, and I realized I'd never be able to concentrate on my work at home. I started to fear my vacation would run out and I wouldn't have anything to show for it.

———✎———

I decided to ask the Literary Fund if I could spend at least a month in one of its accommodation facilities.

The people at the fund gladly offered me a room in Dobříš Castle.

Living in a castle seemed a little much to me, but I was assured I would have a pleasant and peaceful environment for my work. The rooms were furnished austerely, and the garden, as everyone pointed out, was a wonderful place for contemplation. The staff quoted a certain poet who'd said that the spirit here hovers low over the paths.

So I packed some clothes, a few notebooks containing notes from my eastern Slovak travels, a book of Hemingway's short stories (also in Slovak), a bundle of paper containing the first five chapters of my novel, a packet of clean white paper for the rest of it, and a fountain pen along with a bottle of green ink, and headed for the castle.

The kind-looking custodian welcomed me to Dobříš and showed me the way to my room. She gave me the key and informed me that quiet hours were after 10 p.m.

The castle, which the state had appropriated (as the Nazis had before them) from the Colloredo-Mansfeld dynasty and magnanimously donated to writers, was under the administration of the Literary Fund. Thanks to the continuous income it received (a 2 percent royalty for every book or article published), not only could the castle be maintained in decent condition but some modifications could be undertaken as well. One of them was the transformation of the rooms in the front wing into studies.

The tiny rooms were indeed sparsely furnished: desk, chair, armchair, wardrobe, and bed. My windows looked out on a road that wound sharply uphill from the front of the castle and upon which heavy trucks climbed with clamorous effort.

I quickly unpacked my things, pulled out a sheet of paper, and started writing with the utmost resolve. The cars outside started distracting me, so I closed the windows, but I still couldn't concentrate. I forced myself to read several previous pages of my manuscript to immerse myself in the environment of my hero, but my new alien surroundings would not permit it.

I went downstairs to the porter's lodge and asked the way to the garden.

All I had to do was cross the courtyard and open the glass doors, and I'd find myself in the park.

The doors were already wide open. A French park spread out before me with carefully tended flowerbeds and yellowish gravel paths, terraces, statues, and a fountain from which stone horses were drinking. It was a scene straight out of a movie, something almost unreal during these Socialist times. Several women were sitting on benches taking the sun. I walked for about an hour around the park, collected a few mushrooms, and tried in vain to concentrate on my story. I climbed the steep forested hillside and set off along a narrow path back to the castle. At one point the trees parted, and I caught sight of the magnificent structure of the castle from a different point of view: the red baroque walls appeared like blazing flames among the green vegetation, and I saw several figures crawling slowly along the yellow park paths like large multicolored beetles. I sat down on a boulder and felt as if I were in the middle of a dream. Soon I would awaken and find myself in a barracks, flea-bitten and hungry, fearing what the day would bring.

I walked at a leisurely pace back to the castle, overcame my feeling of not belonging, and entered the dining room. It was still half empty. I knew several of the authors who dined here from the publishing house, but I didn't dare sit down with them. I found the most remote empty table and ordered dinner.

Along the sidewall near the entrance you could not miss a long table at which our most famous authors were sitting. I recognized Jan Drda, then Milan Jariš, on whose concentration camp stories my wife was writing her dissertation. A little later Jan Otčenášek, the author of the prize-winning *Citizen Brych*, appeared, and then Josef Kainar with his pretty wife. When I was leaving I had to walk past their table, and Jan Drda asked me not to rush off but to have a seat. His wife, Alice, told him I played Mariáš and they needed a fourth.

—⟨⟩—

I was getting ready to write my first novel, and I thought I would try to articulate all my opinions on the meaning of life, love, the war, and justice. I was afraid I was not well enough acquainted with life in the provinces where the action of my novel took place, but as I continued writing it came to seem less important. A novel is, after all, an invention associated primarily with an author's thoughts, with his imagination and his ability to create a world of his own, which can, but does not have to, precisely resemble the real world. I was enchanted by the opportunity to fabricate. I made more than two dozen characters come to life.

A person feels nowhere more free, and at the same time more responsible, than in a world of his own creation. Suddenly I stopped paying attention to what they'd tried to pound into our heads at school, and dismissed the idea that the hero had to be a typical representative of his environment. Even if he was entirely atypical, he could live if I managed to breathe life into him.

Immeasurable poverty and the constant threat of flooding afflicted the countryside. The period of my novel was wartime. It had deprived some of their lives and others of their property. Others were weighed down with guilt or, on the contrary, well-deserved admiration. Then began a period that promised a happy and unfettered life but that actually brought further suffering—all this offered a multitude of extreme and sweeping plots and entanglements. I was learning that people's fortunes, if described in the key moments of their lives, say more about life, about its values, erroneous faiths, and illusions, than lengthy meditations. I had my engineer join the Communist Party. I chose such a hero not because I had to, but because by depicting his fortunes I could place the repeatedly proclaimed ideals against a reality that was so different.

I spent ten entire days cut off from people and wrote about eighty pages. I concluded with a lament:

> It is probably easier to kill everyone, enclose the country with barbed wire; anything is easier than giving people freedom. . . . We could imagine it all too easily, we discovered the ideal and believed we had found the path to human happiness. But how many times have humans discovered what they believed to be the ideal? And how many times have they managed to make it a reality?

Because the most significant parts of my novel took place in the '50s, I gave it the somewhat symbolic title *Hour of Silence*.

<hr />

The post-February government mercilessly forbade authors to publish if they did not support the regime. The Czechoslovak government tried to follow the Soviet model and replaced their work with the production of new working-class authors. Nothing of interest, however, came from it. Thus those in charge of culture (as well as everything else) decided to give new and young writers a chance. Several literary newcomers and their works joined the ranks of official authors, but most of them were against the dogmatism that raged about Socialist themes. Suddenly manuscripts began to appear with nonpolitical prose or even prose that was critical of society. Surprisingly, the overseeing offices allowed their publication (even though Josef Škvorecký's novel *The Cowards* provoked furious criticism among the "old and loyal" comrades).

I had only one publishing idea. Until now, perhaps for financial reasons, prose works were not published in book form unless they were at least four signatures long. Years might pass before a short story collection reached the required length. Waiting, however, was dangerous. What could come out this year might be banned the next. I suggested a new series of smaller dimensions, so that a book of perhaps only three stories or a shorter novella could be published. Most of the editors, finally even Pilař, liked my idea. We decided to call the series the Little Library of the World Around Us and soon succeeded in publishing several texts that became harbingers, or even the basis, of the new wave of Czech prose. (Three Kundera short stories under the title *Laughable Loves*; Bohumil Hrabal's ingenious single-sentence-long *Dancing Lessons for the Advanced in Age*; one of Škvorecký's best prose pieces, *Emöke*; and some wonderful pieces by Alexander Kliment, Milan Uhde, and Jan Trefulka.)

At the time, the beginning of the 1960s, when party control was still in place, we were already receiving information about artistic developments beyond our borders. In literature, it was the wonderful review *Světová literatura* that saw to this. It published the first translations of the French nouveau roman and the works of the foremost authors from around the world. We could read the first examples of magic realism and acquaint ourselves with theater of the absurd.

Experimental texts began to appear, at least in manuscript form, along with their passionate advocates as well as their detractors.

While working at the publishing house, I got to know most of the prose authors from several generations and their opinions about art, which then, unlike those in very recent times, differed sharply. I felt no need to profess allegiance to a certain group or literary trend. If anything brought me together with some friends, it was our opinions on politics rather than any literary credos or formal approaches.

If someone is genuinely endeavoring to create something, he determines what he wants to say and seeks out his own rules, his own arrangement. If he is unable to do this, nothing will come of it. A writer has at his disposal the words of his language, his own experience, and his fantasy. He must possess the ability to perceive the delicate fabric of the work he is trying to usher into existence. External injunctions are worth nothing or are even harmful. It is true that almost every artist who lays hold of a trendy formula and manages to exploit it can not only create an artifact but also achieve recognition or even fame. Fashionable formulas offer success to average and uncreative individuals and even swindlers. According to the example of great artists or the latest exclamations of theoreticians, they line up letters or cobble together a story; pile up tin cans, tiles, or stones; or douse a canvas with paint. Why not? In all branches of human activity, the average has always prevailed over genuine creativity or even genius, and there has never been a dearth of proficient frauds.

—❦—

It was at this time that I was summoned to the secretariat of the Writers' Union and asked if I'd like to go to Poland. According to a mutual exchange agreement between our union and theirs, one of our authors was supposed to go to Poland, for three entire months if possible. My hosts would pay all my expenses, and I'd receive a daily food allowance as well. My task was to write several reports from my trip—something I knew how to do.

I objected that I didn't know Polish.

The secretariat staff told me I could go in three months' time, and in three months one could learn even Turkish.

This I doubted. But one thing I did not doubt was that they had looked for someone interested in going to Poland but hadn't found anyone. Had it been a trip to France or Italy . . .

I couldn't just get up and leave work for three months.

But they'd already asked at the publisher's office and obtained approval.

I said I'd have to consult with my family. But just in case (not to waste any time), I immediately purchased a Polish textbook.

I knew little about Polish history and even less about Polish culture. I'd read something by Henryk Sienkiewicz, but his works didn't make any special impression. Adam Mickiewicz's novels *Pan Tadeusz* and *Forefathers' Eve* didn't speak to me. Of contemporary Polish literature I loved two of my peers, Sławomir Mrożek and Jakob Hlasek.

I liked Mrożek's wittiness and biting satire and Hlasek's stories for their special rawness or even crudeness. I'd read something by Bruno Schulz—another interesting author who, like Kafka, had been concealed from us in school, someone with whom I had in common my spinning of dreamlike worlds. I liked *Ashes and Diamonds* by Jerzy Andrzejewski and admired some wonderful Polish films: for example, Jerzy Kawalerowicz's *Night Train* and *Mother Joan of the Angels* and Andrzej Wajda's *Sewer* and *Innocent Sorcerers*.

I knew a little more about Polish politics. I'd followed the developments of the bloody Poznań protests with the naive hope that the new chair of the party, Władysław Gomułka (his comrades had nearly sent him to the gallows a few years earlier), would be able to combine socialism with freedom. Shortly after he was elected, he announced that the current system *oppressed and wronged the character and the conscience of the people. In this system, human honor has been spat upon. . . .* whereas now the *silent, enslaved minds were beginning to wake from the stupor caused by the poison smoke of lies, falsehoods, and sanctimoniousness. We have finished with this system or we are finishing with it once and for all.* Such a public condemnation of our regime was unthinkable.

But the most important thing for me was that at the moment I did not have a topic to write about. Perhaps I would stumble across it on the journey.

I decided to accept the invitation. I convinced my friend Mirek Klomínek to go with me to draw some accompanying pictures, and I would try to get him the same invitation I had.

In the end he didn't get it, but the Polish Writers' Union was willing to pay a month's accommodation for the two of us. Fortunately, my food allowance was sufficient for both of us to travel by train or bus and dine in cheap canteens.

Before the departure I devoted my spare time to learning Polish. I took a subscription to the Polish newspaper *Polityka*, which published socioscientific essays that would never be allowed in Czechoslovakia, and from the Polish Cultural Center I acquired some original stories by Sławomir Mrożek. I discovered that Polish was not that difficult for someone who knew Czech, Slovak, and Russian; had heard a bit of Bulgarian; and had moreover studied Old Church Slavonic. Also, Polish seemed, at least at first glance, to resemble old Czech most of all. When we finally departed, I was certain I would be able to manage any necessary conversation.

Klomínek and I traveled across Poland, from the south to the north and back again. We stayed in Warsaw, Rzeszów, Gdańsk, Gdynia, and even Łódź.

I soon learned that Poland was afflicted with an even worse scarcity of goods than we were, but at the same time there was a small but enterprising private trade that offered a selection of materials that were in short supply, especially fashionable (and almost certainly smuggled) goods. This was already a sign of a more unfettered society. More important, however, at least to me, was the greater freedom of the press and the availability of foreign books. I spent a half day in the frightful Palace of Culture, where foreign books were stored in the basement. There were hundreds of books in German, English, and of course Russian and sociological and political studies that were patently non-Marxist, which was the main thing. Such bookstores did not exist in Czechoslovakia. I knew that here I would spend all my remaining money. The only thing I hesitated over was what language to buy them in. Finally I chose, probably sensibly, English.

Klomínek and I returned to Prague, where I stayed for a brief visit, but then I went back to Poland—this time alone. I had decided to visit Auschwitz, but I did not dare write about this place where so many of my loved ones and millions of others I hadn't known had been murdered.

In this desolate wasteland teeming with the remnants of its previous horrors, I was oppressed by an awareness of something I had already begun to forget: Everything I had heard and read had actually occurred. I saw the gas chambers and thought again of the thousands of people who had been brought here to be slaughtered.

In Kraków, I wrote a long letter to Helena, not about what I'd seen but to tell her I loved her. I also bought a bundle of postcards with all kinds of animals on them: a hippopotamus, a lion, a parrot, a crocodile, even a cuckoo clock. Every evening I wrote a short fairy tale on one of the postcards and sent it to Michal. It was probably the first correspondence he ever received in his life.

I attended the theater as well. I remember a play by Tadeusz Różewicz called *Our Small Stabilization*. It came highly recommended, but I was disappointed because it so blatantly hovered between Ionesco and Beckett.

I visited a few painters, theater people, and writers of my generation. All of them lived in small apartments suffused with tobacco smoke (destroyed by the war, Poland had an even worse housing situation than we did).

We held opinions that were similar on politics, less so on literature. Compared with them, I was a conservative. I believed that literature had a mission and thus a responsibility. I also didn't feel the need to get drunk and disdain the world and human narrow-mindedness. It seemed to me that here—certainly owing in part to the greater political freedom—artists were reveling in fashionable trends that their colleagues professed in countries wearied by freedom.

I managed to cajole a short interview out of Mrożek in Warsaw; I didn't get to meet Hlasek, who had fled to Israel, where he continued to drink himself to death.

I don't like it when people make generalizations about nations or ethnicities, claiming that Germans are disciplined, Czechs have a sense of humor, the English are tight-laced, the Russians are drunkards, Jews are businessmen, and Gypsies are thieves. I did not attempt any such generalizations about the Poles even though I noticed that most of them went to church, and I ran into monks and nuns everywhere I went. The Poles also like to talk about their glorious past. Their heroism of both recent and ancient times is shrouded in an almost mystical reverence, as if they are trying to convince themselves that being a Pole is a calling.

And it was precisely these topics that were argued about passionately in the newspapers and in private. In a slender booklet I wrote about my trip, in which I combined reportage, conversations, feuilletons, and essays, I quoted an advertising billboard that somewhat suggested this:

THE SCRIPTURES EXIST IN 830 LANGUAGES

AND DIALECTS OF THE WORLD.

THIS INSTITUTION WAS FOUNDED IN 1840.

IN POLAND IT HAS EXISTED SINCE 1816.

———

Helena noticed me trying to decipher the book about socialism and democracy with the help of an English dictionary and said this simply would not do. A few days later a little man appeared at our door and introduced himself as Vlček, previously Wolf. He told me that upon the wish of my dear wife he would perfect my knowledge of English. From then on he came twice a week and induced me to speak the language of Shakespeare and Dickens. He had an odd teaching method. The only available books in English at the time were published in the Soviet Union. Besides the history of the Communist Party, the works of Karl Marx, and the life of Lenin translated from Russian, it was possible to find brief retellings of classic novels such as *Robinson Crusoe* and *Gulliver's Travels*. These books were used for the study of English in Soviet schools. For the youngest students they published fairy tales. I had to buy every volume available, and during each lesson I would retell one of the stories. Mr. Wolf listened in silence (and probably in pain) and then pointed out my grossest grammatical errors by saying that English really had no obligatory grammar. He explained something about a strict sequence of tenses and forbade me to use the conjunction "if" in the future tense.

Later, when the political situation in Czechoslovakia was becoming more interesting, he started speaking about politics with me and would ask if I thought we'd ever slip out of our Soviet shackles.

Sometimes when my English retarded the conversation, he allowed me to speak in Czech. It didn't occur to me that he could have been sending someone reports about my opinions, but I was definitely grateful for the lessons several years later when I had to teach in English for an entire semester at an American university. This was just after the Soviet occupation, and he had disappeared somewhere out in the world. I never heard from him again.

At the same time I plunged into English, my friend Ludvík Vaculík excitedly informed me that an American astronomer by the name of Schmidt had discovered a quasar. A quasar, he explained, was an extremely distant body radiating an enormous amount of energy. According to Vaculík, this was a revolutionary discovery, and he expected that more such celestial bodies would be discovered. The universe was loaded with energy as well as the mysterious antimatter.

It was 1963.

This year was revolutionary for Czech culture as well. This is when Miloš Forman's *Black Peter* and *The Audition* were premiered, as well as Věra Chytilová's *Bagful of Fleas*. Bohumil Hrabal's *Pearls at the Bottom* came out, along with Fuks's *Mr. Theodore Mundstock* and Vladimír Holan's *Mozartiana*. While Stanislavsky was still the highest authority in the permanent repertory of so-called stone theaters, viewers were avidly attending the Semafor Theater. Theater Na zábradlí brought out Václav Havel's *The Garden Party*, a wonderful parody of the emptiness and vapidity of official thinking and speech. My *Hour of Silence* was published that year as well.

Some of the above authors, including myself, were members of the Communist Party. Others (at least in thought) were its opponents (like Hrabal, Havel, and Holan), and their words had until recently not been allowed to be published or performed.

At the same time—at least at the very top of the power structure— very little had changed. There was change, however, taking place below—primarily among those educated in the humanities—in individual artist unions, universities, and the Academy of Sciences. Of all the legal organizations, the Writers' Union resisted and provoked the government the most, even though it had arisen from the will, or more precisely the despotism, of Communist power. The Communists had broken up the original writers' organization, Syndicate, and replaced it with the Writers' Union, composed primarily of party members who in the beginning served it loyally. Now the ruling power tried to distance itself from all writers' gatherings as much as it could. Nevertheless, after seven years, the union met for only its third congress. (The congress was important for me because I could participate. I had heard almost nothing about the shameful inception of the union; those whom I met and who had participated in its beginnings usually didn't talk about it.)

Scores of writers came together, many of whom I'd never heard before. Most of the contributions were provided by famous authors, and almost all of them dealt with the past. It even seemed that, whereas the recent past had been criminal, today those crimes were being atoned for and freedom was just around the corner. The speakers kept repeating that the dogmatism in the official Communist approach to literature was responsible for the breakdown of creative activity. Others kept returning to some personal wrongs they'd suffered. The former editor in chief of *Květen*, Jiří Šotola, criticized *Literární noviny* for working with an overly narrow group of writers.

At the congress, I was one of twenty-three "novices" (most of them were as young as I was) who had been elected to the central committee of the union.

It was a monumental gathering, but the greatest event of that year was the birth of our daughter, Hana, beautiful and long-haired even as a baby.

My wife, who invariably comes up with nicknames for everyone, at first called her Františka and later Nanda.

The new leadership of the union decided to reshape the content of *Literární noviny*. Until then the editor in chief was more of a Communist functionary than a writer and journalist, and he personified the dogmatic thinking that had been much criticized.

At the end of the year the first quasar was discovered, a meeting took place during which it was decided to recommend that the editor in chief take a working vacation. It was difficult, however, to find a replacement. Finally we offered the position (perhaps somewhat mischievously) to Šotola, who had been critical of the newspaper. Let him try to run it, we thought. He accepted the position and asked if I would join him as perhaps his deputy. I don't know why he chose me. We knew each other a little from *Květen*, and he obviously assumed that I had at least a little journalism experience. He was also worried about how he would be received. He knew that I contributed to the paper and that my wife worked there, so perhaps he hoped that he would be well received.

Our editorial offices occupied two floors of a building on the corner of Betlémská Street and the embankment. From the street came the constant ringing of the tram and the roar of automobiles. Several windows had an unequaled view of the river, the Little Quarter, and the castle from which, of course, the proletarian president looked down on our journal with growing ill will.

Apparently so that I would not become conceited or feel like one of the worthies, I at first didn't get a desk. (I sat across from my wife at hers.) Then, just as at my last place of employment, I was placed in a dark, but quiet, passageway with a forlorn view of a wall of the building next door.

This new job was unlike my start at the publishing house; here I had some idea of the work. *Literární noviny* arose as the traitorous heir of *Lidové noviny* (which had been renamed *Svobodné noviny* after the war). Although nothing remained of its prewar freethinking spirit, it had taken over the format and rotary printer despite the fact that it had become a weekly.

A slightly idealized image of the prewar *Lidové noviny* became fixed in my mind, a journal that masterfully combined all journalistic and literary genres. On the first page it would print a poem and a column, usually by writers rather than journalists. The first page would also have the beginning of a feuilleton and an installment of a novel. Alongside the daily news, *Lidové noviny* would run a column of criticism along with reportage, national and foreign political commentary, articles about the economy, and even a small sports section. The foremost writers and specialists contributed to the newspaper. For a moment I forgot I was living under completely different conditions and believed we would succeed in relaunching *Literární noviny* in that form and at that level. We would create a marvelous journal difficult to compete with in Czechoslovakia.

Essay: *Dogmatists and Fanatics*, p. 491

12

At a meeting of the General Assembly of the Central Committee of the Communist Party, a resolution was passed concerning ideological work. As usual they were trying to resuscitate old phrases with new words. I never read party resolutions of this type—probably, neither did most people. This time, however, someone decided that it would be necessary to explain the significance of the resolution to members of the party throughout the country, and hundreds of activists were supposed to go out into the "field" at the beginning of 1964. As a young writer (that is, a worker on the "ideological front" in the eyes of party functionaries), I now had to take my turn. This time they sent me, not to eastern Slovakia, a place I at least knew something about, but to Moravia.

They put up the entire group of agitators in the Grand Hotel, one of Brno's most luxurious hotels.

Our group was led by Prebsl, the secretary of the ideological department of the Central Committee. He was a worker by trade—apparently he'd been trained as a stove fitter—which is why he held the position he did. I came to understand that it was party policy that the less someone understood what he was in charge of, the more obediently he carried out the instructions of his superiors.

We gathered in Prebsl's apartment, where he handed out our agitprop brochures, which we were to read immediately, because the first meetings were to take place that very evening, and we would always be working with two local functionaries. He distributed our food allowances—nine hundred crowns for the week—and expressed his conviction that we would not let him down.

I opened the brochure when I got back to my room and read that in Czechoslovakia, *new societal conditions are supporting and stimulating an unprecedented development of culture, imprinting Socialist features onto its face, creating the conditions for the broad development of culture and the overall advancement of the cultural level. All cultural politics in Czechoslovakia, the development of culture, education, and enlightenment, are being led by the spirit of scientific worldwide Marxism-Leninism in close conjunction with the life and work of the people.*

I couldn't imagine repeating such gibberish, in which conditions were creating conditions and culture possessed a face with features. Most likely I would say it was necessary to correct previous crimes and that much of what was now taking place was problematic. Whoever did not want to admit this should not hold office. I tossed the brochure into the trash and devoted myself to reading some short stories by Heinrich Böll.

At about 7 p.m. my provisional superior knocked on my door and delivered some news he found depressing: The meetings planned for this evening were not going to take place. Owing to an unfortunate error, the meetings would not be taking place for another three weeks, and we, of course, would no longer be here. He went on to inform me of the schedule for the rest of the week. Today, Monday, was a free day. For Tuesday, a meeting had been scheduled at the Integrated Agricultural Co-Op in the Blansko District. Wednesday, a meeting at the Industrial Construction Company of Gottwald; Thursday was a free day for the same reasons as today. Friday there were three meetings scheduled at the Integrated Agricultural Co-Op in Jihlavsko. On Saturday and Sunday we would probably not have any work again. Then he asked if I played Mariáš.

The next day those who knew Mariáš started playing right after lunch. The others took off somewhere, most likely to chase women. The boss brought in a few bottles of beer, and because his cards were going well he was in a good mood.

Toward evening, a frost descended on the city. Two cars were waiting for us in front of the hotel, and we were all dressed in sweaters and winter coats ready to take off wherever we were summoned. But there was no place to take off to because the meeting in Blansko also had been canceled. Our stove fitter grew angry, cursed the local functionaries, and considered how he would put this into his activity report. I started to realize that this was the way these things usually went—groups of functionaries travel across the country pretending to work. For this they are paid and receive an ample food allowance, but in reality they're simply enjoying some time off, chasing women, or, at the very least, playing cards. Every now and then they write a report in which they praise their own activities. Anything could be put into these reports. Those who are supposed to read them never do because they themselves are out either chasing women or playing cards.

———

Shortly thereafter, the members of the Writers' Committee were invited to meet with President Novotný. I'd met several high functionaries before and was always surprised at the immodesty with which they voiced their platitudes and catchphrases. What kind of man stood at the head of the entire country and determined almost everything? What could he actually determine in a country so dependent on the Soviet Union?

The meeting took place in a large boardroom on the second floor of the Central Committee of the party and was supposed to start at three in the afternoon.

The president arrived exactly on time. He went around the entire room and shook everyone's hand in turn. Then he sat down and placed in front of him a bundle of white paper along with four perfectly sharpened pencils (three of them were for some reason red) and said he would not speak for long. He'd come primarily to hear the opinions of the workers of the soul and the pen. Despite this promise or resolution, his oration was a lengthy one. I had to admit that he spoke quite fluently and engagingly and without any notes. But his speech wallowed in a general deluge of figures, statistics, and economic results along with anecdotes that seemed to come from real life. The anecdotes were obviously meant to illustrate that his life was just like everyone else's. For example, once he was riding the tram with his son and overheard two men exchanging information about him and his speech at a session of the presidium. So you see, comrades, this was something that was supposed to be secret! A moment later he pulled out another anecdote. He and his wife had gone to a shop on Wenceslaus Square to buy a watch, and he was shocked to discover that the prices of some watches were reduced. How could the economy and commerce continue to function if some goods were sold at a low price and others at a needlessly high one? He wandered from topic to topic and even touched upon the problem of churchgoers. Personally he was for tolerance. He knew, for example, the chair of a cooperative who was a member of the People's Party. An outstanding worker with excellent results. He sends his children to church and stops by himself as well. And why wouldn't he, comrades, since he's a believer? But he no longer, he informed us triumphantly, prays every evening.

Was this naive, stupid, or shameless? Most likely all three.

He also returned to the topic of the executed members of the Communist Party and assured us that Slánský—he'd known him personally—had been a genuine fiend who had on his conscience a number of villainous blunders and the arrest and persecution of innocent people. He said he would never agree to the rehabilitation of Slánský's name and raised his finger as if threatening anyone who would try.

I noticed with amazement that when he spoke about the deficiencies in the running of the country, he—the man who stood at the peak of power—used the plural "we" or "they," or he talked about something as if it had appeared out of nowhere. Why had they nationalized the newsdealers and pubs and not returned them to those who worked there? Why couldn't we have private beekeepers or bell manufacturers, he asked, somewhat affronted and taken aback, as if it were "we" and not "he" who decided such matters.

It occurred to me several times that his speech touched upon some of his own personal issues. He found himself in an important position that separated him from others and therefore tried hard to give the impression of a common, ordinary, and, primarily, concerned citizen. He was trying to earn a little appreciation from people whom he perhaps subconsciously respected and at the same time feared because they possessed something he didn't: an education and the art of public speaking. He was also aware (even though he refused to admit it) that he had been present when many judicial murders had taken place and therefore claimed—perhaps he'd even convinced himself—that genuine criminals had been executed, and deservedly so.

At one point when he was discussing the future he suddenly dropped the "we" (we the party, we its presidium) and switched to the singular: "My politics is one of reason and peace and the gradual path to the prosperity of all."

I recounted my meeting with Novotný to everyone at the editorial offices and paused over the fact that he had invited writers but hadn't mentioned a word about literature.

"Be glad!" someone remarked, and everyone broke out laughing.

Jean Paul Sartre and his companion Simone de Beauvoir visited Prague. Our meeting with them took place at Dobříš Castle. At the time, Sartre was one of the most famous philosophers in the world (shortly thereafter he was honored with the Nobel Prize, which he refused to accept, claiming he wanted to remain absolutely independent). His notebooks on existentialism (along with Camus's *The Stranger*) thrilled me and perhaps, at least a little later, influenced my own perception of the world.

People usually idealize their models, including their appearance. Sartre was anything but imposing: a small, cross-eyed, unattractive little man whose features lit up only when he spoke.

To my embarrassment and shame, and despite the fact that I'd tortured myself with six years of Latin and tried to teach myself a little Spanish and Italian, I didn't know a word of French. I could communicate to the famous philosopher only through a translator that I admired existentialist philosophy, especially his. Sartre was used to such expressions of admiration and had a prepared response: He'd written all that so long ago that he felt the need to polemicize with himself.

During the meeting with him I wrote down and underlined one of his assertions: The hero who, despite all of his horrific experiences, remains a Socialist seems to me especially human. And he elaborated that he was referring to those who had lived through Stalin's prisons but had nevertheless remained Communists with their convictions fortified. He added that the West no longer had anything to offer mankind. The only great topic for a novel of the twentieth century was man and socialism.

My colleague Milan Kundera then tactfully asked (or perhaps objected) that perhaps we might consider the entire Socialist attempt a dead end, an aimless turn of history.

Sartre, however, maintained his claim. Socialism, whether or not it had a future, was leaving its mark on an entire era. Perhaps it was a hell, but even hell could serve as a grand literary theme. A disappointed faith, death at the hands of one's own comrades—wasn't that the most modern embodiment of tragedy?

Certainly, I didn't say this aloud, but hell was indeed a wonderful theme, especially if you didn't have to live in it.

Otherwise the French thinker was thrilled (or at least for decency's sake he pretended to be thrilled) that the Socialist state had bestowed such a beautiful castle upon its writers. But he could not have perceived that the same prominent writers were living here whom I'd seen a year ago. It was they who applauded Sartre's contention that socialism offered a grand subject for a magnificent contemporary novel.

It occurred to me that even they, without realizing it, were one of these grand subjects—not for a novel, but for an absurd comedy.

Several days later I started writing a play I called *The Castle*.

The play was about a group of notable personages residing in a luxurious castle entirely cut off from all hardships and worries. They hold empty conversations about the people they serve and the work they do, although it is clear they do nothing at all. I wanted to write, not about a castle of writers, but instead about an elect class of almighty, yet otherwise feckless, notables, who rule in the name of the people. One of the heroes, Aleš, was a writer, another was a philosopher, a third a biologist, a fourth a commissioner in charge of demolishing the statue of Stalin; the fifth man's occupation is unknown, but he's apparently a worthy functionary.

I thought the beginning of the play quite imaginative. Behind the closed curtain the audience hears the horrifying scream of a man being put to death, and when the curtain opens, all the residents of the castle come onstage, and the dead man is lying on a table. It appears to be a murder, and at first each character provides his or her own alibi and at the same time calls into question the alibis of the others. At this moment an unknown young man enters the room and politely introduces himself.

Because I was afraid of being accused of stealing the name of Franz Kafka's novel, or even of not knowing the novel, I gave the new arrival the name of Josef Kán and went on to note he was a land surveyor.

The castle inhabitants immediately unite against the newcomer, who has been sent, as he tells them, to continue his work in peace and quiet. Now everyone starts talking about the dead man as if he'd been their friend and had been felled by a heart attack.

The writer Aleš explains to him:

We welcome you among us. We are well aware that none of us is here of his own free will. This castle was once a stronghold of the most confirmed enemies and exploiters of the people. Today it has become the sole property of the people. It was their decision to send us here, a decision by the people, for the people, and it is our sacred duty to repay their faith in us a hundredfold. And you are certainly wondering how we will repay it. Josef, this place used to be a place of drunken brawls and unbridled debauchery, such as only the ruling class is capable of. We must convert it into a place of honor, a chapel of truth.

Of course the corpse must be removed, but because the castle is inhabited by respected personages, they induce a doctor they've summoned to certify that the cause of death was a heart attack. The doctor is only too glad to comply, but at the same time he tells them that conditions have changed somewhat, and a sort of commission will have to confirm the death certificate.

Never had writing pulled me into its story line so much as when I was working on this clearly metaphorical drama. I couldn't tear myself away from it, and I carried the manuscript with me to the office, and there, in the middle of visits, meetings with authors, and telephone calls, I composed dialogues, which I believed mirrored the entire absurdity of the reality in which we were all living. *The Castle* gradually turned into the epitome of that absurdity—a metaphor for the ruling and untouchable party.

Conditions had indeed somewhat changed. To the surprise and displeasure of the inhabitants, a polite but uncompromising investigator appears as a bearer of justice. To the ongoing protests of the notables, he gradually discovers that a murder has in fact taken place at the castle. Furthermore, Josef Kán turns out to be an important witness, and it is confirmed that everyone was in the room when the victim shouted.

The investigator conducts a reenactment of the crime, which confirms that all of those present participated in the murder. The bearer of justice concludes:

My gracious lady and fellow citizens! I have come here among you because one of your colleagues has departed under somewhat unaccountable circumstances. Would you please all rise. Thank you. I would like to announce that all of the somewhat unaccountable circumstances have been carefully considered during the detailed conversations and are now explained. There is no doubt that grievous errors have occurred here. I hope that my findings will not be understood as an attempt to besmirch the essentially flawless reputation of the castle. Thank you. Respected friends, please accept my most sincere thanks for the willingness and love with which you have welcomed me to these famous and historical places and devoted to me so much of your precious time. I can assure you that no one will interrupt your important and beneficial work from now on.

The ending seemed to me entirely logical. The play must end the way it began: with another murder. Also, it was clear who the victim should be. The murderers, who were the unpunishable notables, could not let the one who testified against them live.

I wrote the play in less than three weeks. I thought I'd managed to express everything I believed to be important. At the same time I was certain that no theater would be allowed to stage it—the parallel between what my investigator said about the castle murder and what was said about the political murders by everyone on the party commission was too obvious. It had been determined that the crimes had been a regrettable breach of the law, but those who had participated in them either were still in power or had been demoted to less important positions. Certainly no one had been called to account. I was so convinced that my play had no chance of being performed that I didn't even type up my manuscript; I just read it to a few friends. They also didn't believe the play had a chance of being staged. The only thing that would happen was that I'd finally be kicked out of the party; nevertheless, they kept insisting that I offer it to the Vinohrady Theater.

I continued to think it would be a waste of time to type out the play (I typed with only two fingers and usually had to retype each page several times), so I dictated the text into a tape recorder and took the tape to the theater.

Much to my surprise, a few days later I was informed that the theater company liked the play. They found the topic very compelling and would try to produce it. Let others ban the play if it bothered them; that would be their business. They weren't going to ban it themselves.

But the authorities did not ban it. The premier took place on October 25, 1964. I do not suffer from stage fright, and even at the premier I felt only curiosity or perhaps anticipation concerning the audience's reception and appreciation of my representation of arbitrary power and its homicidal dignitaries. At the time, viewers were already used to the language of allegory, metaphors, and hidden allusions. They understood everything and interrupted the play many times with applause.

Our joy, however, was premature. That very week the municipal council of the Communist Party complained that the theater had performed a play antagonistic to socialism. Because the play had already been approved, it was not prohibited immediately, but any sort of advertising was forbidden (the council did not understand that such a prohibition was the best kind of advertisement, and the play was always sold out). Then they decreed that the play could be performed only once a month, and after a few months it was to be removed from the repertory.

Nevertheless, the attempts to escape the mendacious ideology multiplied, as new theater and radio plays appeared by Václav Havel, Milan Uhde, and Josef Topol, along with the films of the young directors Věra Chytilová, Miloš Forman, Jan Němec, and Antonín Máša. We began to fall prey to the illusion that despite the conditions in which we were forced to live, it was possible to achieve at least a certain measure of freedom.

————⁂————

The reception of *The Castle* and the effortlessness with which I wrote it impelled me to write another play.

Again I tried to think up an effective metaphor that would help me speak about our current problems. I imagined a detective story that included several murders. But this time my effortlessness abandoned me. I wrote sixty pages in nine months and completely altered the play at least as many times, even the title. Finally I settled on *The Master*.

The play was set, like all good detective stories, in a secluded mountain villa. Unexpectedly and for no apparent reason, a master coffin maker arrives—although no one has died—claiming he's been summoned there by telephone.

A corpse is soon discovered. An old man, the owner of the villa, has just died in his room. Furthermore, his dumbfounded relatives learn that he was apparently poisoned. The plot gradually unfolds. Of the four remaining residents, one of them is clearly the murderer. The coffin maker, who envisages a fanciful desert representing a blissful place everyone desires to reach, participates in the investigation. He interrogates, advises, accuses, and consoles. Then another murder takes place. Except for one woman, all the inhabitants of the villa die one by one at the murderer's hands. Finally the surviving member of the family accuses the coffin maker. She wants to shoot him, but in the end cannot take the murderer's life.

The play ends with the monologue of the murderer, the coffin maker. First he addresses the woman who uncovered him but could not kill him:

Sometimes when I'm treated with such appalling words of incomprehension, accused of such deeds, I become afraid: What if they do not understand my words and are seized with horror? Have I chosen the wrong time to come? . . . But yet I can see it! Transparent and aflutter! The sand, the dusky boulders rising to the heavens. I can discern the bells of the caravans, the distant roar of tigers, the bleat of antelope. And a sandy bed within a shallow depression waits to receive me. . . . And the stars are already descending until my heart breaks. The desert! My hope. So many times it has been promised—it must exist.

I was convinced that I had found a forceful image for an insane vision that tries to pass off a desert and death as the only salvation. In my opinion, this was where we had all been led, in the name of a redemptive vision and as the only hope for mankind, by those who had defiled themselves with murder. This time no theater would dare produce this image of our present day. It was performed in the United States, but it was printed in Czechoslovakia. In print, there was no danger that people would applaud the concluding speech of the diabolical master.

Our daughter was already two years old when we finally got a co-op apartment and somehow succeeded in exchanging it for a flat in a villa on a street named Nad lesem (Above the Forest). The forest actually began just fifty meters from the building's entrance. My dreams of the forest—from the time I was forced to live in barracks confined within the walls of a fortress—had become a reality. Suddenly instead of clamoring automobiles, we were awakened by the chirping of birds in the garden or a woodpecker that had taken a liking to our lightning rod and immediately upon the break of day started in on it with powerful blows of his beak.

We redesigned our second-floor apartment in the house, which had been built at the end of the 1920s. We turned the kitchen into a dining room and moved the kitchen into a little room originally intended for a maid. We also altered the heating system. I finally had my own study. Because it was impossible to get a proper desk, I bought a brand-new—and, most important, large—tabletop and placed it on a small cabinet on one side, which I'd used to store my shoes, and two pickax shafts on the other. It was far from a stylish desk such as you find in the well-kept studies of famous authors, but I could write well enough on it.

Helena and I liked arranging and fixing up the apartment, but at the same time we both had a lot of work, perhaps too much, and there wasn't time for anything but the most important things.

I think Helena perceived the lack of time we could spend with our loved ones as inflicting more damage than I did. She started writing a series of articles concerning the harm we were doing our children in their upbringing; we were forcing upon them, especially in the cities, an unhealthy way of life. It was bad for children to spend time in different nurseries, preschools, or day-care centers where they were deprived of freedom of movement. She rejected the image that emancipating women from their children was supposed to lead to their greater overall freedom and equality with men. She believed that the contemporary concept of the care of children hinders the free development of the nascent individuals; it deprives them of movement, does not lead to creativity, and, at most, compels children to memorize often useless or dubious knowledge. Thus what we are raising is the *relatively educated and cultivated—artistically disciplined and seemly—average. . . . Our children are not doing badly. They have it **a little** good and **a little** bad. When they grow up they will be **a little** kind. To us too.*

Her articles aroused extraordinary interest among readers and were subsequently published in book form.

I was still perceived as a novice at the editorial offices, and I never got close to any of the older editors. My closest friends remained Ludvík Vaculík and Saša Kliment, who had both joined the editorial board. They were a little older, but because I had helped them publish their first books, they considered me more experienced or at least more worldly-wise in the area of literature, a place in which neither of them felt very comfortable. Our family became such good friends with Ludvík's that we sometimes went on trips together. After I bought a car with the proceeds from my book advance, we took off on our first journey together, eight of us crammed into the little Renault. To demonstrate what a wonderful, although in truth quite inexperienced, driver I was, I almost collided with an oncoming car as I was overtaking another.

In Prague, Ludvík, Saša, and I mostly talked about politics (in this land of socialism, everything became a political topic) and speculated about what we could and should discuss or, as Ludvík would say, have our word about the situation. In our opinion it was not very satisfactory.

No one who had preserved even a little sense of reality could accept without shame the fact that we were living under a regime based on injustice and violence.

Saša and I, along with a historian who contributed to *Literární noviny*, were once invited to a radio talk show to discuss life values. The discussion was too abstract and wasn't very successful, but Saša pronounced one brief sentence that made the discussion worthwhile and that the censor surprisingly allowed: "I admit that every day I wake up with a feeling of shame."

Essay· *Weary Dictators and Rebels*, p. 496

13

Sometime in the middle of the 1960s, a dark BMW stopped in front of the house we had recently moved to. A short, burly young man stepped out and a moment later was buzzing at our door. He informed me, in good Czech, that his name was Ehrenfried Pospisil and he'd just come from Hannover—he was translating my *Castle*. He was quite talkative, and I soon learned he'd been transferred from the Sudetenland, entirely unjustly, since his native language was Czech. He was not sorry, however; what would have become of him had he stayed in Most or Chomutov? Could I imagine the horror? Not only were houses and churches disintegrating, but pubs as well, whereas in Hannover he was the owner of a prospering fur dealership. Of course, he mostly concerned himself with art. Each morning he stopped by his workshop for a couple of minutes, assigned tasks, and worked up a design, and then he could devote himself to his creative profession, which right now happened to be my *Castle*. Afterward his wife would look over the text to make sure it read well. She was an actress, and I wouldn't have to worry in the least. He even suggested his translation would be better than the original and gave a loud cackle to inform me that although he was genuinely of this opinion, I wasn't to take it altogether seriously.

I had no experience with translations, but the vocation of a furrier did not strike me as the best preparation for a translator. I did admit, however, that Mark Twain had been a riverboat pilot, Jack London had been a gold prospector, and Edison hadn't even had any schooling. Perhaps the Hannover furrier would turn out to be an ingenious translator.

Then another German paid me a visit, this one thin and possessing the face of a brooding philosopher, Mr. Eric Spiess. He directed the theater division of a large music-publishing house, Bärenreiter, and informed me his firm was representing my play in Germany, just as it was representing Pavel Kohout's plays. He told me that the premiere of *The Castle* would take place in January in the famous Düsseldorfer Schauspielhaus. He assumed I'd heard of his stage director, Karl Heinz Stroux. I pretended I had.

Mr. Spiess praised my play, and I put his praise down to politeness. Nevertheless, neither the play nor the translation could be completely bad if it had pleased the famed stage director.

The German theater had decided to adopt the Czech production. Soon thereafter I received an official invitation and started to believe that my play would actually be performed on a stage somewhere in Germany.

Except for sojourns in countries proclaiming themselves Socialist, I had never in my thirty-three years been abroad. Now, at the insistence of my wife, I bought new shoes and a white shirt, packed my best suit, said goodbye to my family, and on a moderately cold January day boarded a train for Frankfurt.

The moment the train arrived at the sleek train station in Schirnding, I thought I had suddenly entered another world. There were no border guards with dogs or battered houses, just a vendor scampering along the platform offering beer and Coca-Cola.

I continued on to Düsseldorf, where I was welcomed by my translator and Mr. Spiess, who then drove me to my hotel, which to me seemed ridiculously opulent. I was in Germany. Instead of a gas chamber, I was led into a room with leather armchairs, a minibar, and a television set. Six towels were hung in the bathroom, and on a little table stood a vase with a large bouquet of flowers; next to the vase, a bottle of Riesling. A newspaper lay on the bed with an article highlighted in red about a young Czech writer who was attending the premiere of his play, *The Castle,* and so on.

The next day I walked around the city a little, looking into bookshop windows. I was amazed by the number of periodicals sold at the news kiosk. For a while I watched a young artist drawing on the sidewalk a picture of a woman and a guitar. On the same sidewalk he'd written, in beautiful calligraphic script and in different languages: *Studentschüler auf Studienreise durch Europa, Student of art on a study trip through Europe, Beaux Arts.* He had a small box inscribed with *Danke, Thanks, Gracias, Merci.*

I asked him where he was from. He was from Italy and said he was traveling around, painting, drawing, and visiting galleries. I was truly in another world.

The premiere went over well, but in a few places that had been interrupted with applause or laughter in Prague, here everybody was silent. Instead, the viewers laughed at entirely different points in the play. They lacked knowledge of the actual circumstances and didn't understand the allusions. Mr. Spiess comforted me during the intermission: In Germany we applaud during a play only when someone gets kicked in the butt, he told me. (I considered this a mere witticism, but two days later I attended the premiere of Brecht's *Mr. Puntila and His Man Matti.* At one point Mr. Puntila kicks his servant, who flies to the other end of the stage, and the audience did indeed break out in applause.)

When my play ended, the audience clapped for quite a long time. This was certainly also due to the fact that the curtain whipped about in such quick intervals that they didn't have a chance to get up from their seats.

Mr. Stroux invited me to a celebratory dinner, and everyone assured me my play had been a tremendous success, but surprisingly I felt no need for success.

When I was finally alone in my overly luxurious hotel room with a television set and six towels, I realized that it wasn't fame I longed for. I wanted to say something to people at home about what I was feeling and going through with them. If I lived here, I'd probably feel something completely different and therefore write about completely different things that would make an impression on Germans. Perhaps I was mistaken. As long as a person expresses something powerfully, he should be able to make an impact on people anywhere in the world. But I couldn't believe someone like me was capable of something like that.

There were probably twenty reviews of *The Castle*, most of them positive, but also cold and unemotional. They compared my play to Mrożek's marvelous *Tango* and Kafka's *Castle*, something my play had nothing in common with except the title and the name of the protagonist. All the same, I had baffled the German critics (for whom Franz Kafka was usually the only source of knowledge of Czech literature). If my play shared anything with Kafka's writing it was the attempt to seek out allegorical images. But Kafka, as I learned later when I was writing about him, spoke allegorically because his shyness forced him to conceal the fact that he was writing about his own most intimate experiences and feelings. I sought out allegory because without it, *The Castle* would never have gotten past the censors. If anyone influenced my writing, at least formally, it was not Kafka but Friedrich Dürrenmatt.

As it turned out, my *Castle* was somewhat haunted by misfortune. It went well in the famous Düsseldorf theater, but at the American premiere in Ann Arbor, one of the few stages with a permanent professional company, it had its first catastrophe (which I'll tell you about a little later).

At the Swedish premiere, the avant-garde director decided to improve the play by shifting around the individual scenes in order to demonstrate that the author actually didn't know what he'd written, and that only the director could give the play a meaningful form.

However, *The Castle* suffered its greatest calamity in England, where the famous Royal Shakespeare Theatre was getting ready to perform it. The director, Mr. Williams, even came to see me in Prague to go through the production details. Then I received an invitation to the premiere along with a printed program that boasted an all-star cast. But the premiere never took place. A week before it was to be performed, the board of directors met and discovered the unsatisfactory financial situation of the theater and replaced *The Castle* with a Shakespeare comedy. The director informed me of the situation by telephone and with a great many apologies. With respect to earning capacity and artistic value, the board had certainly acted wisely, but *The Castle* had indeed been unlucky. If only the board had waited a week longer for their meeting.

During the interwar period, but actually near the end of the Austrian-Hungarian Empire when there was an exaggerated interest in literature and freedom of the press (which was only somewhat limited) in the Czech lands, dozens of literary trends and groups began to emerge, primarily due to critics and theoreticians. We had circles of decadents, symbolists, vitalists, impressionists, dadaists, ruralists, and Catholic authors. Vitězslav Nezval professed poetism and later surrealism; Karel Čapek and some of his close friends were considered by some as adherents of pragmatism.

After the February takeover, the only permissible artistic trend was socialist realism, and authors were differentiated, at most, by age, place of residence (there were Brno authors and critics and Ostrava authors, as well as western Bohemians), and the literary journals they subscribed to. Two journals were the most pronounced in their views: in the second half of the 1950s, *Květen*, with its poetry of the everyday; and beginning in 1964 until its involuntary demise, *Tvář*. Both were originally intended for young authors just starting out, but the moment they began to unduly resist the current ideological norms, their publications were discontinued upon the orders of the party authorities.

The midsixties, which saw the beginning of *Tvář*, of course had a drastically different atmosphere from the midfifties, when *Květen* began. At *Květen* we tried to write without the ever-present ideological agitation. We sought to focus on ordinary people and ordinary affairs. For the most part, the authors were members of the Communist Party; all the editors were Communists as well; and only with difficulty could we attempt to polemicize openly with the official ideology.

After 1948, authors who had never accepted the Communist Party began to gather at *Tvář*. They had no need to correct their own errors (not to mention crimes). Along with the remarkable Christian philosophers, several gifted young poets published here, as well as, significantly, critics Bohumil Doležal and Jan Lopatka (they had already published in *Květen*). With an erudition remarkable for their age, these writers subjected to criticism almost all contemporary literary authorities and meritorious writers. They saw that much of what passed for independent literary production was merely old ideas better articulated.

Again, the Writers' Union was the publisher of *Tvář*, and many authors accustomed to admiration and praise—or minor political reproaches, which elevated them in their own eyes—were aggrieved by the criticisms now issuing from *Tvář*. It was something other than critical essays on literature that troubled the party ideologues. At *Tvář*, it was as if Marxist ideology did not exist. Its authors had no intention of trying to reform Marxism with quotes by a younger Marx; they didn't want to try to restore socialism by recalling the ideas of Lenin. They simply didn't take this ideological rubbish into consideration. Their great philosophers were Heidegger, Teilhard de Chardin, the Czech philosopher Jan Patočka, and, of course, the darling of all rebels and exiles, Ladislav Klíma. *Tvář* wasn't even as provocative as *Literární noviny*. It was just that *Tvář* ignored the guidelines that the wearied dictatorship kept demanding.

Tvář was discussed at almost every meeting of the central committee of the Writers' Union, but the topics of conversation were individual articles or sentences. No one tried to attack or even mention its independent and nonconformist spirit.

Finally, upon an initiative "from above" (that is, from the ideological department of the Central Committee of the Communist Party), our union committee met in Bratislava to discuss the continued existence of the ideologically cantankerous journal.

Every meeting of the union's central committee (as was the case with all legal organizations) was preceded by a meeting of the Communist members. As I've already mentioned, this was practically the entire committee. Because every resolution accepted at the meeting was binding for the Communists, the meeting of the writers' central committee was just a formality. Everything of significance had already been discussed and decided, but it wasn't until this formal meeting that minutes were taken. In this way, the Communist Party was continuing the methods it had employed when it was seeking to gain power. Everything of real significance was supposed to happen in secret, not before the eyes of the public.

At this time, however, the party organization in the Writers' Union was fractured and did not look anything like what it was supposed to be, that is, a collection of subordinates obediently endorsing the party's orders.

Of all the meetings I have experienced, and often suffered through, this one in particular stuck in my memory. It was led by the chairman of the Central Committee's ideological department, Pavel Auersperg. Those present were other subordinates in his department. The principal party ideologue explained that the journal *Tvář* was a disgrace to the good name of Czech writers. We were all proud to have among our ranks genuine creators and a number of authors dedicated to the party, but which of these great writers had ever appeared in *Tvář*, except as an object of uncritical attack and perfidy? The journal had begun as a tribune for young authors. Who of our young and talented writers had appeared here? Only scum, both homegrown and translated. What did the verses of the aging Vladimír Holan have to say to us? He had the recalcitrant journal in front of him and began to read.

> *Dungeon after dungeon grows*
> *And almost all of us are imprisoned*
> *perishing within as if God willed*
> *to be in us only without us . . .*

What did young writers have in common with Gerard Manley Hopkins, who had died three quarters of a century ago, the sixty-year-old Witold Gombrowicz, Georg Trakl, or Pierre Teilhard de Chardin? What about Ladislav Klíma, who was even passed off as an example worthy of being followed? In an enthusiastic paean to the idealistic philosopher, young readers will learn that he was reading again, that he lived on raw horsemeat and pure grain alcohol, and that he had once, as he himself writes, *stole a bitten-into mouse from a cat and gobbled it down, just as it was, with the fur and bones—as if I were eating a dumpling.* A wonderful example for our young writers.

Why was it precisely these authors who were appearing in the journal? Because they were decadents and thus ideological opponents of any sort of progress; they had nothing in common with our efforts to build a Socialist society.

A debate followed. To the surprise of the party functionaries, many of the discussants—such as Milan Jungmann, Kundera, Kohout, Karel Kosík, and Jaroslav Putík—praised *Tvář* for introducing new topics and new names, and, of course, even young authors (one could name dozens of them). The critical section, which formed a significant part of the journal, was certainly one-sided, but it decidedly expressed the opinion of part of the young generation. Of course there were also plenty of discussants endorsing the opinion of the party ideologues, and during the break they warned those of us who were defending *Tvář* that this was a serious matter; if we did not retreat, we could count on provoking those who determined literary matters.

The debate over *Tvář* lasted well into the night, and at one point the telephone rang. Auersperg picked up the receiver, and at once all the arrogance vanished from both his face and his demeanor. With almost servile deference, he sank into some sort of vassallike bow and then answered as loudly as he could, "Yes, Comrade President, the discussion is still under way. I will definitely pass it on. I'm certain your concern will encourage them."

He hung up and passed on the greetings of President Novotný, who was greatly interested in ensuring that Socialist literature received the utmost support, both material and ideological. Then, still with an expression of deference and devotion, he added that the comrades in the central committee of the union will certainly appreciate the president's concern and will not gamble with his goodwill.

This performance had obviously been prearranged; the players sought to stage a scene combining promises with hidden threats.

Around midnight, when everything had finally been said, we requested a vote on whether *Tvář* should be halted or allowed to continue.

The vote was close, but we who voted to preserve the journal prevailed. We enjoyed our feeling of victory for only a few minutes, however. The envoy of the party leadership informed us that the Central Committee of the Party had already decided the matter. *Tvář* would no longer be published. It was up to us to plausibly account for its demise, and for us, as members of the party, this decision was binding.

During the following meeting of the now legitimate central committee, some of us knuckled under; others either abstained or even, despite the warnings, voted against the ruling.

Thus *Tvář* was closed as an unprofitable enterprise.

Before the Six-Day War, Helena and I were invited to Israel by an organization of Czech-Israeli friendship. Although at that time the relationship between Czechoslovakia and Israel was a cautious one, it wasn't unfriendly, and because the invitation had come from an organization that behaved amicably to the Communist regime, our trip was approved.

I was somewhat surprised. Why had they chosen to invite me? I'd never written anything about Israel, and I wasn't very interested in the problems of the Jewish state. In this I was probably influenced by my mother; it seemed a mistake to let some Nazi rules tell me how to see myself. Despite my time in Terezín, I had only indistinct ideas about Judaism. I didn't speak a word of Hebrew (with the exception of the greeting *shalom*); I had not the slightest knowledge of the Talmud or even the prescriptions adhered to by believers.

Helena, on the other hand, was excited. She had some distant relatives in Israel, as well as her first love, and she harbored an affectionate admiration for the country. (Later I learned that it was she who had arranged the invitation.) I was most interested in Israel's agricultural communes, which my wife had enthusiastically told me about several times. I learned that they were the only communes in existence and perhaps even prospered in the middle of a free and democratic society.

In Haifa, overwhelmed with the scent of thousands of blossoming orange trees, we left for the kibbutz Artz, which would be our home for nearly a month.

The kibbutz was pleasant and bright, the houses small but modern. The common kitchen was amazing in its spaciousness and quantity of food. Each person could take as much as he wanted, but because the food mostly consisted of chicken, overeating seemed to have fallen by the wayside after a while.

We were treated kindly by one and all, as if we were their close relatives. They praised our republic, which had sold them weapons when they were fighting to establish their state.

I was still curious about the possibility of realizing the Communist vision of a society of comrades. I wanted to know what life and work looked like in a commune nobody was compelled to join. So I talked to a lot of kibbutzniks and took note of the different fortunes and opinions. They were usually educated, but they had chosen the kibbutz as a place for their life and work, even with its Communist precepts. For many it had been at first a provisional emergency solution—they'd come to a country where it was not easy to find a job. They were often fugitives or illegal immigrants without any belongings. The kibbutz had offered them first aid: housing, food, the most necessary clothing, and health care. In return it demanded work, for which they received an insignificant amount of pocket change. The new arrivals, however, shared all the privileges and responsibilities of the other members and were subjected to the same regulations. The most drastic (and unnatural) of these rules seemed to me the handing over of offspring, immediately after birth, to a nursery where their mothers would visit to feed them. The children were not allowed to live with their parents; only during their free time could they visit together. All important decisions were made at meetings of the commune. The standard of living for each of the members depended on the overall results as well as the strict following of communistic principles, which were voluntarily embraced. These principles were so severe and rigid that they often struck me as absurd. Each member had to fulfill certain duties, which could not be avoided. For example, members took turns working in the kitchen, the laundry, or another communal facility. If any of the members found themselves beyond the environs of the commune, for example, if they had been elected as a representative or worked in one of the academic institutions, they not only had to deposit all their income into the mutual treasury (the kibbutz then paid their room and board outside the commune) but also had to come back every now and then to carry out their regular duties in the kitchen or laundry.

I was interested in how this fundamentally spartan or semimilitary way of life could prosper in a free society

The communes arose during the time when a haze of idealism wafted above Europe. The members of our kibbutz belonged to, or were adherents of, the leftist Mapam (united workers) Party, which supported their endeavors. I could understand that the people who had founded the communes were grateful to their principles for help in their own difficult beginnings and had remained loyal to the Communist ideas. But what about their children? What if someone didn't feel like staying in the commune? Even after dozens of years of work, they owned almost nothing except a few shirts and a pair of shoes.

I was assured that each person was allowed to decide for himself, keeping in mind, however, that he might have to start all over again no matter what his age. The kibbutz, on the other hand, had over the years allowed him to acquire new and useful knowledge free of charge. Even the young were allowed to leave.

Never before had I realized how powerfully illusory and utopian was the Communist ideal here, where in a free society people chose to serve a collectivist goal; they suppressed their individual needs and were trying to create a completely new and, from the point of view of others, unnatural or, more precisely, precivilized type of human relations.

Upon returning home, I wrote a lengthy article about kibbutzim, in which I expressed my doubts about the utopian idea of communes and Communist ideals. (To my surprise, it was noticed in Israel and translated.) I expected that my impugning of Communist education and the ideal itself would provoke some sort of reaction, but nothing happened.

⚬⚬⚬

Soon thereafter, I took another trip into the freer world, to a country that seemed to me the embodiment of democracy.

It was impossible to go abroad to the West without an exit visa and an allowance of a limited amount of hard currency (which was in short supply for most writers).

Sometimes editors at *Literární noviny* received both. My stay in Germany, connected with the premiere of *The Castle*, was paid for by the Düsseldorf theater, so I could manage without the hard currency. My trip with my wife to Israel was upon the invitation of our hosts and also free of charge for our offices. Now our editorial offices were offering me an allowance of hard currency to go on some sort of study trip. Because I'd already been to Germany and because the only foreign language I could make myself understood in was English, I decided to go to Britain. I also had a personal reason for this trip. In England, if he was still alive, lived Isaac Deutscher, the man whose book on Stalin's struggle with Trotsky revealed to me more about the foundation of the Stalinist regime than any other book.

My well-traveled colleagues offered me many pieces of advice for the trip. I received the address of a particularly inexpensive Paris hotel bearing the exalted name Bonaparte as well as the addresses of some Czechs in Birmingham in case I happened to wander into that city. My wife had a friend named Janet in London, and when she'd written to her, Janet offered to let me stay at her house. She would ensure I saw the most important things in England.

In Prague I purchased, besides maps and guidebooks, all the train tickets I would need to Paris, London, and Birmingham, and from there—most likely because I'd seen it on the map rather than from any personal reason—to Inverness, which was the northernmost station I could get to. I'd always wanted to see Scotland—it was supposed to be exceedingly beautiful and romantic, and ancient monsters dwelled in the deep lakes. Besides that, I loved Scottish folk songs.

The Hôtel Bonaparte was indeed inexpensive, and the cheapest room, which I requested, was a small black hole with a window opening onto a murky airshaft. The air in my hole had probably traveled here all the way from the Sahara. I bought an unbelievably cheap bottle of wine at a little shop next to the hotel (even so, it was an additional expense; I'd brought bread and a can of liver pâté from home), and when I'd washed down my food with a liter of wine I even managed to fall asleep.

In the morning, aware that I wouldn't be able to communicate with anyone, I set off to the Louvre with my map. I didn't have money for a bus or taxi, so for three days I covered on foot dozens of kilometers on the boulevards and in museums and galleries. And because I had no sense of proportion and didn't realize that it was better to examine five pictures thoroughly than several hundred on the run, only a confused welter of experiences remain in my mind about the trip.

On the morning of the fourth day I headed for the train station, where I was astounded and overwhelmed by the number of platforms. Although I found the information counter, I couldn't find anyone who understood English or German, so I ran back down to the hall in a panic, thinking I'd never make it out of Paris. I went from platform to platform looking for the train to Calais.

A few minutes before departure I found it, much relieved. I took a seat in a compartment occupied by several Englishmen.

Soon after the train departed, a pair of uniformed men entered the compartment, said something in French, and all the Englishmen presented their passports. I assumed this was the border control (the train wasn't stopping until Calais), and so I handed my passport to one of the uniformed men. Whereas the Englishmen got back their passports with a simple "*Merci*," I was treated to a flurry of explanations or more likely questions. I had no idea what they were saying, and they didn't understand me either. For a while we exchanged inquiries. The Englishmen were listening and certainly would have tried to help had their linguistic knowledge been any better than mine. The uniformed men then left with my passport, and after about an hour I started to fear I'd never see them or my passport again and I'd remain forever in this country where I understood not a word. My fellow passengers nodded their heads in apparent sympathy with my misgivings. They agreed that the behavior of the border guards was indeed odd.

When we arrived in Calais, the uniformed men reappeared, returned my passport, and treated me to another long explanation. I didn't know if everything was all right or if I was being expelled from France or wasn't allowed to leave. The most likely explanation was that they had seen in me a citizen coming from a country of the Soviet Bloc; I had squirmed out of a dark hole encircled with barbed wire, a place from which nothing good could come. I was in all respects suspicious, and they had to check to see how much damage I could cause.

With that unpleasant experience behind me, I soon learned that the English Channel was rougher than the Mediterranean Sea; nevertheless, the trip went smoothly, and I peered at the approaching land. When we'd almost made port, there was an announcement, this time in English, but in sailor talk and, moreover, from a raspy loudspeaker. Once again I understood nothing.

The others got up and started disembarking, so I joined them.

The sailors ordered us into a single group and then ringed a long rope around us.

No one else seemed upset or frightened, just me, who had come from a country in which you could never be certain what awaited you. Also in mind were my experiences from the concentration camp. I was afraid and it occurred to me that all it would take was a light machine gun, or perhaps just a rifle, and none of us could hope to escape.

Even though it was merely an idea, a paranoid fantasy, however excusable in view of my own experiences, the feeling of standing in a group hemmed in by a rope stayed with me, and I never forgot it.

Everything proceeded, though, without the expected terror. At the London station, the pleasant and energetic Janet was waiting for me. She had prepared a bed in her study and an almost hour-by-hour schedule for my time in London. When I mentioned Isaac Deutscher, she said she knew the name and as far as she was aware he was still alive. She would try to set up a meeting for me.

I spent a week in London visiting various galleries and the British Museum. Janet took me to some sort of court hearing so I could see the judges wearing their wigs, to Buckingham Palace to watch the changing of the guard, to the City of London to see the capitalists in their top hats, and to Soho so I could have a good time where Londoners had a good time. She also bought me a ticket to the Royal Shakespeare Theatre, where at one time my *Castle* was supposed to have been performed. Shakespeare's *Much Ado About Nothing* was on the program and I was amazed that people wore sweaters in this sanctuary of the greatest dramatist who had ever lived. They tossed their coats over the backs of their chairs and even smoked as if they were in a beer joint.

At first London enchanted me. I fell in love with the double-decker buses and spent hours on a corner in Hyde Park listening to the fiery and rebellious orators. An institution not restricted by anything or anyone seemed to me the embodiment of freedom. Only later did I realize that in a free country there was no need of such rostrums, and therefore they were used mostly by crazy people, freakish messiahs, experts who knew the only correct path, or diseased gasbags.

From London I traveled to Inverness, where I chanced upon a bagpipe festival. To my surprise, besides the beauty of the wild countryside, only one, somewhat mystical moment has stayed with me. I was climbing a hill toward a little village beyond Inverness, and all at once from the window of a cottage I heard a female voice singing a beautiful Scottish ballad. The singer was nowhere to be seen, and it was entirely possible that the voice was issuing from a radio or a record player. But I stood there in stupefaction, leaning against a wall, listening and gazing out into the horizon and the mountains bordering it. Suddenly a white house emerged for a moment on the ridge of the mountain as if from a mist. The house seemed to light up and then vanish. It seemed to me miraculous.

When I returned to London, Janet proudly announced that she'd discovered the address of Isaac Deutscher and had set up a meeting with me for the next day at four in the afternoon.

The following day I bought an egregiously expensive (at least for me) bouquet of flowers and set off to see Mr. Deutscher. He was a small, bald sixty-year-old man with lively eyes and sporting a beard like his beloved Lev Davidovich Trotsky. He studied me carefully at the door, most likely making sure I didn't have an ax or ice pick hidden somewhere under my coat, and then led me to his study. I remember this study very well. It was an enormous room, tall, with thousands of books lining the walls.

Much to my relief, Mr. Deutscher spoke Polish (my Polish was still better than my English), and I could easily convey to him the enormous influence his book had had on me. I told him that our country was still being governed by an only somewhat less tyrannical Soviet regime and tried to explain how horrible it was for me when I realized that I had barely survived one bloody dictatorship only to begin serving another. Just like *Literární noviny*, where I worked, I was trying with my limited possibilities to do everything I could to push for a renewal

of democracy in Czechoslovakia. Because as soon as democracy is suppressed, I opined, tyranny takes its place.

I think he listened to me with solicitude. He said he'd been following developments primarily in Poland, but also in the other countries
of the Soviet Bloc. He knew of our newspaper; reading in Czech didn't
cause him any great problems. He said he understood our disenchant-
ment with the postrevolutionary developments in our countries, but he
believed that the Stalinist bureaucratic deformation of socialism could
not survive for long. What must survive, however, what we must guard
and try to preserve, is the idea of socialism and its undeniable advantages
over capitalism. Stalin was a tyrant, but we cannot compare him to Hitler.
Hitler represented a blind alley of history. Stalin was a criminal who had
veered from the path, but the path still represented hope for humanity.
My radicalism, he warned me, could lead to an entirely different place
from where I want to go. Surely I wouldn't want to have a hand in the
workers' becoming once again an object of exploitation. It was necessary to genuinely return the government to the hands of the people, and
bourgeois government the Czechs and Slovaks had experienced before
the war would never do that. Our slogan should be: Never return to the
old democracies but do return to the regenerated Soviets of the people's
representatives.

He was recommending this to me, someone who had come from
a country where we had to argue with the censor over every semi-
intelligent article, while he was living in a country where he himself
enjoyed all the freedoms offered by a system he referred to as a bourgeois democracy.

Even though our newspaper was acting rebelliously, we could in no
way extricate ourselves from the Soviet system. It had its maximum
allotment of paper; it was distributed by the Postal News Service—the
only organization set up for this. Because *Literární noviny* was a legal
periodical, the editor in chief received daily news reports from the

Czech News Agency, even reports to which only a privileged minority of party members and journalists had access. These reports, copied on red paper, usually contained editorials from the otherwise consistently jammed Radio Free Europe or translations of articles, published in the main West European or American newspapers and magazines, which concerned the countries of the Soviet Bloc. Even some foreign journals were mailed directly to the editorial offices (they were naturally not available for purchase anywhere). We were allowed access to this material to better polemicize with "enemy propaganda." We decided against polemicizing, but for us all of this "red news" was an important source of information and knowledge.

But our most vital source of information was of course the reality we were living in. *Literární noviny* began publishing more reportage treating contemporary everyday difficulties. Personally, I rarely contributed to the paper, but because I was in charge of the opinion pages, I sought out the most qualified specialists.

The editorial office kept growing, doubtless owing to the Socialist economy and the increasing interest in *Literární noviny*, which was reaching a circulation of about a hundred thousand.

A large group of contributors gradually became concentrated around the newspaper. Among them were philosophers, sociologists, economists, historians, and young lawyers. Because we were a newspaper of writers, we had to attend to the level of language, which often demanded significant editing, and several, later important, authors of academic articles and books recalled how *Literární noviny* had taught them to write more "humanly." We also had to publish prose, poetry, and articles that were not so much to our taste, but we couldn't refuse them either because they were written by members of the Writers' Union, that is, our publishers, or because otherwise we would be accused of censoring opinions we didn't agree with.

Writing or procuring a good article, however, was only the first step in the editorial process. The second was securing permission for its publication. The more compelling the topic, the more original and nonconformist its conclusions, the less likely it was that the supervisors would approve it.

We became accustomed to preparing several such articles for a single issue; thus it was more likely that one would get through. We also agreed with the authors ahead of time which sentences or paragraphs were possible to delete so that we could make a deal with the censor. Because the censor wanted to see only the printed page, whoever was working in the typesetting room would run with the page to the editors' driver, Mr. Houdek, who was always parked as close as possible to the printers. Then we waited to see if the page would be approved. One of my diary entries (from May 1967) describes it best:

> In the afternoon it was my turn in the typesetting room. When I'm on duty here (at least so it seems to me) the censor raises more hell than usual. They stopped a gloss of academic titles (why this, for God's sake?). The lead article about the coldheartedness of people and dehumanizing bureaucratic relations. Excellent reportage about the housing situation—no generalizations, just facts and figures, unless insisting that people are entitled to a place to live is a dangerous generalization. Then they removed a report on prostitution. Also excellently written. The typesetter said: as if we had prostitution. And laughed. He said he had to read it—he liked reading things that wouldn't make it past the censor because they were actually about something.
>
> Production dragged on and on. The issue is going to be so dreadful I could scream. Mrs. H. complains she'll be here until at least eight, another fourteen-hour day. She's had enough. The proofreader is moaning because he has the flu. He wanted to stay home, but the doctor refused to allow it. If only it wasn't taking so long; he's getting feverish. The typesetter had to finish up because his train leaves at six. The new typesetter is more patient—don't worry, we'll make it, he assures me.

We drove to the inspector just before eight. As on every Thursday he curses the day he became a driver. He was supposed to have stayed at Walter, where he'd been a clerk until 1945. Usually he doesn't curse the institution of censorship, he only curses himself for allowing himself to be dragged into a job that makes his life so difficult. He stopped in front of the dreary building and took off about fifteen minutes later with another man, who had shaken his hand cordially. "Who was that?" I ask later. He said it was our censor. "Why do you greet him so warmly?"

"Please," he says, "if I wasn't friends with the censor, we'd never be able to publish."

So that's why we're still being published.

Usually their objections were not expressed directly. Instead they would say things like society was not yet ripe for such opinions expressed in a certain article or that the article might be true, but it wasn't the whole truth, and because it wasn't the whole truth (since the concept of whole truth is ridiculous), they had confiscated the article. At other times they would say the party was currently giving priority to other issues.

Arguments with press control became more frequent as well as more serious. Everything came to a head at the beginning of July 1967 and the Six-Day War. The official Czech reaction to the war, like the Soviet reaction, was severe and one-sided. The Czechs and Soviets broke off all diplomatic ties with Israel as the aggressor and launched a hateful press campaign. The unconditional bias of the official propaganda, which did not take into consideration the fact that the Arab states had been preparing for a war in which the Israeli state was to be "wiped off the map," led us to organize a discussion of several writers. We all tried to speak as dispassionately as possible about the causes of the war and about Israeli politics in general, that is, at variance with government policy, both ours and that of the Soviet

Union. The transcript of the meeting, which we wanted to publish, was confiscated, and the news office warned that it was beyond what could be tolerated.

This happened right before the Fourth Congress of the Union of Writers.

―∞―

The congresses of all organizations were supposed to be a display of loyalty to the Communist Party. The ideological department, which was intended to oversee the Writers' Union, was aware that writers had been lately behaving ever more recalcitrantly (irresponsibly, in their conception) and therefore insisted on postponing the congress in order to buy time and try to figure out who might disrupt this manifestation of loyalty. With the help of state security forces, they designated two groups of writers as the most dangerous: the first were nonparty writers who had contributed to the recently banned *Tvář*, including Václav Havel, Antonín Brousek, Věra Linhartová, and Jiří Gruša. The other group were writers of *Literární noviny*, primarily Milan Jungmann, A. J. Liehm, Ludvík Vaculík, and myself. A proclamation, delivered to parliament by Deputy Jaroslav Pružinec several weeks before the congress attests to the concept of art that prevailed among party officials. The target of their attack was the movies of young filmmakers, primarily the wonderful *Daisies* by Věra Chytilová along with other remarkable films by Jan Němec, Antonín Máša, and Juraj Herz. The proclamation applied, however, to art in general.

> Respected members of the National Assembly, I would like to present an interpellation in the name of twenty-one members of Parliament in which we would like to demonstrate how resources required by the state budget are being squandered. . . . This regards two films we have seen, which, according to *Literární noviny*, . . . "demonstrate the fundamental path of our cultural life." We are convinced (however) that no honorable worker, farmer,

or intellectual would want to or could tread this path, because
the two films, *Daisies* and *A Report on the Party and the Guests*,
filmed at the Czechoslovak film studios Barrandov, have nothing in common with our republic and the ideals of communism.

We therefore request the Minister of Culture and Information,
Comrade Hoffman, the Cultural Commission of the National
Assembly and the People's Central Auditing Commission, and the
National Assembly as a whole to deal radically with this situation
and adopt the appropriate measures against those who were involved in these films and especially against those who were willing
to finance this refuse. We ask the directors Němec and Chytilová
what sort of enlightenment—occupational, political, diversional,
or otherwise—this trash brings to people working in factories
and fields, on engineering projects, and at other workplaces. We
ask these "cultural workers" how long do they plan to offend the
lives of all honorable workers, how long will they continue to
trample upon Socialist achievements, how long do they plan to
dally with the nerves of workers and farmers? What kind of democracy are you trying to achieve? Why do you think our Border
Guard carries out its combat duties keeping enemies out of our
country, while we, Comrade Minister of National Defense and
Minister of Finance, pay a small fortune to our internal enemies,
allowing them to trample upon, Comrade Minister of Food and
Agriculture, the fruits of our labor?

The denunciation mentioned two more films and ended with the
appeal: *We demand these film be withdrawn from our cinemas!*
This unbelievably reactionary attack (today it seems almost like
a parody) roused most of us to action. Fourteen film directors signed
an indignant protest, ending with the words:

Artistic freedom is indivisible. If one of us is subject to restrictions, we are all subject to restrictions. Therefore we categorically

reject Deputy Pružinec's proclamation and point out the danger
of threatening fundamental civil rights and freedoms, an essential
part of which is the freedom of speech.

Then we waited to see how other writers would react to such opinions
at the congress.

I'll try to give at least a general outline of our opinions in those
days. We had no doubt that the Communist regime ruling the Soviet
Union, and other countries that had accepted its political system, had
nothing in common with socialism or democracy. It was in no way any
sort of rule of the people. It had committed serious crimes, admitted
to only a small number of them, and apologized for even fewer. Those
responsible for the crimes had gone unpunished, and some were still
governing us. The dictatorship, also known as the cult of personality,
persisted in a somewhat more sophisticated form, and there was no
guarantee that past crimes would not be repeated in the future. We were
exasperated by the mendacious propaganda, the manipulated elections
"by acclamation," with an absurd 99 percent of the votes going to candidates proposed directly by the party. At the same time, however, we
were still not convinced that socialism was an unrealizable utopia. We
knew that the nationalization of private property had been not only
unjust and violent but also senseless and was the reason why almost
nothing in the country functioned the way it did in democratic countries. Nevertheless, it didn't occur to any of us that everything should
be returned to the hands of private banks, mines, and the largest in-
dustries. (In many traditionally democratic countries, large enterprises
had become the property of the state.)

We wanted to do everything we could to help renew basic freedoms in the country. We wanted political parties to stop being just
formal organizations that were trying to hide the totalitarian character
of the regime from the uninitiated. We knew that the Communist
Party, which had its eternal rule enshrined in the constitution, controlled all organizations and placed its own members in positions of

authority. From our experiences as journalists, however, we also knew that the Communist Party was united only superficially; in reality its members held quite disparate points of view. Many were dissatisfied with developments in the country and disdained contemporary politicians. As a result of the experiences of recent years, they were afraid to express their opinions, but they still wanted more freedom: freedom of thought, freedom to travel, genuinely free elections, and a judiciary not beholden to power.

At the time, few thought a complete transformation of the political system was possible. We ourselves didn't think so.

I was intending to defend *Literární noviny* at the congress. Some colleagues were trying to accuse us of serving only a narrow and limited group of writers. In the second, more substantive part of my contribution, I wanted to talk about censorship and had collected examples of the censor's interventions. The day before the meeting, a lawyer brought me some interesting information from one of our contributors. He'd noticed that the National Assembly had approved a new press law legalizing censorship and defining its field of activity without realizing that the law would go into effect on the one-hundredth anniversary of the enactment of a law whereby the "corrupt" Austro-Hungarian monarchy guaranteed freedom of the press when the Czechs had been the monarchy's vassals. This one-hundred-year-old law was much more liberal than the one to be enacted.

On June 27, 1967, the congress convened in the festively decorated Vinohrady House of Railway Workers in Prague.

Obligatory invitations had been sent out to a good-sized party delegation led by a member of the presidium of the Central Committee of the party. A minister and other party bureaucrats were in the delegation, which was supposed to keep an eye on the activities of artists. The delegation, as was appropriate (or inappropriate), was greeted by the applause of at least a few writers.

Milan Kundera was the first to speak. He avoided direct criticism of the current political conditions but emphasized that the primary role of the union was to facilitate the free exchange of different opinions. He recalled the famous passage attributed to Voltaire: "I do not agree with what you are saying, but I will defend to the death your right to say it." Then he talked about the great sweep of Czech art, especially literature and film, and emphasized, *If our art has blossomed, it is because intellectual freedom has increased. The fate of Czech literature is vitally dependent, just now, on the degree of intellectual freedom that exists.* Then he moved on to Věra Chytilová's *Daisies*, one of the films attacked by Pružinec. The film concerned vandalism, claimed Kundera, and he used the film as a pretext to discuss the subject.

> Who are the vandals today? Not your illiterate peasant setting fire to the hated landlord's mansion in a fit of rage. The vandals I see around me these days are well-off educated people, satisfied with themselves and bearing no particular grudge. The vandal is a man proud of his mediocrity, very much at ease with himself and ready to insist on his democratic rights. In his pride and his mediocrity he imagines that one of his inalienable privileges is to transform the world after his own image, and since the most important things in this world are the innumerable things that transcend his vision, he adjusts the world to his own image by destroying it.

Everyone (even the party delegation) understood that this definition of vandalism, still valid today, was a criticism of the current party's attitude to literature, art, and independent thought.

Saša Kliment then spoke about censorship and the freedom necessary to create. *I understand plenty, but not, however, necessity as freedom.* He was referring to Marx's assertion that freedom is the recognition of necessity, *especially when those things that enter our lives as necessary, inevitable, and essential are in fact only at the discretion of the people. . . . Ever since literature began, administrative and psychological pressure has been, to a greater or lesser degree, exerted on the author in order that he conform to the present needs of society. . . . Whereas, however, the needs of society are represented by a collective ideal of the group, the writer always expresses his own independent and personal viewpoint. . . . Thus the writer's word has been, and always will be, uncomfortable; he will always be more likely to jab his finger in the wounds of society than try to bandage them. . . . The relationship between the individual conscience of the writer and his work and official doctrine, therefore, will always be strained. . . . Culture, however, is a public affair, and the writer, even though he creates in isolation, can exist physically and intellectually only in dialogue.* He then demanded that literature be allowed to assume an independent and free position. *Because the current practice of censorship is incompatible with the constitution of the republic, with the union's articles of association, and primarily with the personal conscience of every writer, I move that it be abolished . . . and that our congress present a concrete proposal to the National Assembly.*

Here his address was interrupted by applause, but what exasperated the party delegation even more was his next, quite legitimate, demand:

> I recommend that the secretariat undertake effective action to ensure that members of the union be kept better informed. It is astounding that we must learn about many things that have a direct bearing on literature from *Le Monde* or West German radio broadcasts. I have in mind specifically A. I. Solzhenitsyn's letter to the Fourth Congress of the Union of Soviet Writers.

Here Pavel Kohout announced that he had the text of the letter with him and, if the congress wished, he would read it aloud. The writers voted and, with a single exception, requested that it be read.

The reading of the letter, so deeply critical of the Soviet regime, obviously alarmed, or rather enraged, the party delegation, which demonstratively left the meeting, at least for that day.

The next day Antonín Liehm, an editor of *Literární noviny*, read another critical speech. The subject of his analysis was official cultural policies. *The protection of state interests*, something politicians typically referred to with respect to culture, *must be clearly delineated and defined and can never be concealed by blanket proclamations or laws, which are being generated more and more arbitrarily.* Then Liehm formulated a program demanding *the freedom of culture unrestricted by anything other than criminal prosecution, and that the state undertake to be the tangible guarantor of such an emerging culture and that it do everything in its power to ensure that the culture of the nation, in all respects, will become the property of the widest strata of the nation.*

My account of *Literární noviny* and primarily my criticism of the current press law, which fully legalized prior restraint, infuriated the party delegation.

> I was talking the other day with a party official who insisted that the law was a good one. When I disagreed, he was amazed, saying that it had to be incomparably better than the previous situation, when we'd had no press law at all. This opinion is not unique. It assumes, of course, that we view our entire history as beginning in 1948. . . . But our history goes farther back. Permit me to quote: "Everyone has the right to express his opinion freely in work, letter, print, or pictorial representation. The press may not be subject to censorship."

To the delight of the audience, I pointed out that *this quotation came from an imperial patent issued for the Bohemian Crown Lands under No. 151 of the Imperial Statute Book.* Censorship had been restored for a brief time under the absolutism of Alexander Bach, but it did not last long, and *under the December constitution of 1867, press freedom was guaranteed, and censorship and the licensing system were abolished.* I added that those who had issued the latest *law did not lack a certain sense of absurd humor* when they passed censorship regulations, which, as an outrageous holdover from Bachian absolutism, had been abolished exactly one hundred years ago. I concluded with a number of proposals, which were immediately judged by party organs as provocative. I demanded that the union protest with all vehemence *any abuse of power by an administrative body . . . and that the congress should express its disagreement with the literal wording of the law that, among other things, instituted precensorship, which had been outdated for decades.*

Ludvík Vaculík—unknown to most of those present—offered something never before heard in a public forum the entire time the Communists had been in power, namely, an analysis and condemnation of the totalitarian nature of the regime.

Vaculík began with the concept of the citizen and the manner in which he exerts his influence on the powers that be.

> The preservation of such a formal system of democracy [in other words, the level of the democratic institution] does not bring an especially solid government along with it; it merely brings the conviction that the next government might be better. So the government falls, but the citizen is renewed. On the other hand, when a government reigns continually and stands for a long time, it is the citizen who falls. Where does he fall? I will not oblige our enemies and say he falls on the gallows—this is only a few dozen or hundred citizens. But even friends realize this is plenty, for what follows is the descent of an entire nation into fear, political apathy, and civic resignation. . . . I believe we no longer have citizens in this country.

The introduction alone was sufficient for the entire Writers' Union (not to mention the present author) to be denounced. But Vaculík continued his analysis that power relies exclusively on the most obedient and the most mediocre; everything is controlled by people less competent than those whom they control, and this situation has lasted for twenty years. On the status of art, he said:

> Just as I do not believe that the citizen and the power structure can ever become one, that the ruled and the rulers can come together in song, I also do not believe that art and power structures will ever take pleasure in each other's company. They will not, and they cannot—ever. They are different, incompatible.

Everyone knew that Vaculík was speaking about our contemporary Communist government, but lest anyone be in doubt, he added:

> Are they really masters of everything? What, then, do they leave in the hands of others than their own? Nothing? Then we needn't be here. Let them say, let it be completely perceptible by all: Essentially, a handful of people seeks to decide on the existence or nonexistence of everything, of what is to be done, of what is to be thought, and what is to be desired. This reveals the position of culture in our land; it is an image of the nature of our culture. This politics of nonculture . . . is creating a focal point for struggles for freedom, and it is always being talked about; it does not understand that freedom exists only when it does not have to be discussed. . . . [All of this imperils the one thing worthy of passion:] the dream of a government that is identified with the citizen, and of the citizen who rules almost by himself.

In conclusion, Vaculík voiced that famous appraisal of Communist rule:

> It is obvious that in twenty years no human problem has been solved in this country—from such fundamental necessities as housing, schools, or a flourishing economy to more insubstantial

necessities that nondemocratic regimes cannot satisfy, such as a sense of one's value in society, the subordination of political decision making to ethical criteria, . . . the necessity of trust among people, and the enhancement of education on a mass scale.

When Vaculík finished speaking, the hall erupted in enthusiastic applause, and I think most of us, for a moment at least, experienced enormous and liberating relief that this was precisely what we felt ourselves but were unable, or lacked the courage, to put into words.

For their part, the party delegates did not even wait for the ovation to end but rose and demonstratively stormed out. The leader of the party delegation said—but only the next day—that not even the most primitive anticommunist propaganda would dare voice such an appraisal.

At that moment, it was as if many of my colleagues had woken from a delirium and then descended into gloom.

Yes, we'd had our say, but they held the reins of power. They'd made it clear that we had overstepped a boundary that they had graciously shifted just a bit toward freedom. What would happen now?

All these speeches ended in the apparent and total defeat of everyone who held a different opinion of how the country might be ruled.

Our proposal for a new committee of the Writers' Union was killed by the party bureaucracy, which then filled the committee with people it considered obedient. *Literární noviny* was taken out of the hands of our own union, and the editorial board dismissed. There were rumors that other union journals were under threat. But most likely all that would happen was that prominent writers would be deprived of Dobříš Castle—the horror.

Some of the speeches, of course, could not be published. These included, especially, Vaculík's, so it was copied, and hundreds of copies began to circulate among the populace.

At the same time, it turned out that the regime no longer dared resort to more brutal and repressive measures; no one was arrested or interrogated.

Upon the determination of the presidium of the Central Committee, a disciplinary commission was formed, aimed against the primary persons involved in the writers' revolt who were at the same time members of the Communist party: Kohout, Liehm, Vaculík, and myself.

Because I was almost completely forbidden to speak at the hearing, I subsequently wrote a brief letter in which I defended my views. I wrote that I had sought to understand and find sympathy with everything that went on, from the wrongdoing that took place in establishing the cooperatives to the arrest of my father. I continued:

> I realized that everything could be comprehended (that is, everything could be explained by the occasion and the needs of a given situation), and in this ability to "comprehend" lies an inherent danger for any kind of human, let alone creative, activity. To comprehend something does not mean to resign oneself to it. I am not a politician. As a writer, if I were to resign myself to the existence of censorship, given the way it is today and the way I spoke about it in my contribution to the congress, . . . I would have to be somehow corrupt and internally divided. For one cannot expect me to write counter to my conscience and convictions. How then could I welcome the prior restraint placed upon me?

Of course they ousted us from the party; Pavel Kohout got off with only a reprimand.

They insisted that I report to their palace to be informed of their verdict and hand in my party card, but I had not the slightest desire to set eyes on them again. After receiving two reminders, I replied:

> Dear Comrade,
>
> I am aware via the foreign press of the results of the disciplinary proceedings. It therefore seems to me unnecessary to be made aware of the results yet again. Furthermore, I cannot bring with

me my party card because I have surrendered it to our constitu-
ent organization.

I did not add that I had surrendered it with relief.

Thus, after fourteen years, concluded my membership in the Communist Party. What also ended was my attempt to understand what
had happened. Everything that they had called wrongdoing, error, or
a necessary sacrifice on the path toward Communism, but that caused
the tragic deaths of many people, was merely a necessary, concomitant
phenomenon of the building of a new society. This was the Communist
Party under whose leadership a society was supposed to arise that was
less selfish, more peaceful, and at the same time wealthy.

I admit that not even at this moment did I realize that the party
of which I had been a member represented a nefarious confederacy
that in the name of grand objectives stole the property of society and
destroyed what had taken generations to create. But I did know for
certain that in the name of some sort of future objectives, the party had
deprived the people of freedom, usurped all power, destroyed political
life, falsified history, mocked the act of voting, and transformed a free
country into a colony.

I wasn't much interested in economics and did not ponder whether
a planned economy could actually work or whether the entire concept
of socialism was an unrealizable utopia. But I was certain that without
unencumbered scholarship and free clashes of opinion in which no
subject could be forbidden, no society could evolve. Thus the party that
defended its dogmas and persecuted all who refused to subordinate
themselves to it was leading its society to ruin.

The fact that they had banned me from the party without even
trying to understand what I was saying made me bitter. I was convinced
that everything I had been trying for years to achieve and everything that
I demanded was correct, even necessary, if society was not to fall to ruin.

At the same time I felt free. I was no longer a member of an
organization in which a person was required to submit to the will

and despotism of those who, by whatever means, had worked their way into a leadership. In the party, having one's own opinion, let alone expressing it, was considered a deed for which one was at first sent to the hangman, later sent to prison, and later merely ostracized.

Surprisingly, I did not have any great fear of further punishment, whether I would be allowed to publish anything or whether I would even be able to find a job. I was thirty-six, and it was high time to tread a path that was, as much as possible, not subordinated to anyone who had arrogated to himself the right to define for me what was correct and what was not.

PART II

14

Just after the leadership of the Writers' Union was dissolved, every single one of our editors was fired during the summer of 1967. I had a meeting at the writers' club with a German journalist. (Journalists are always most interested in someone who has something scandalous going on around him.) He wanted to know if there had been an agreement among us before the writers' congress and if I was worried I would be brought before a court or at least banned from publishing.

He was surprised that I didn't think I'd be arrested, nor did I think I would have much trouble finding employment. He said he wished he shared some of my optimism. We said goodbye and parted on the corner by the National Theater. I'm not sure why, but I looked around and noticed a young man wearing jeans and a checkered shirt who seemed to be trying to conceal himself behind a column near the theater's entrance.

I set off along the embankment in the direction of my former editorial offices. When I stopped after a moment and looked around again, the same man, not far away on the opposite sidewalk, also halted. Then he pulled out a camera and began photographing the castle.

I was suddenly curious and started wandering aimlessly through the streets of the Old Town. The man in the checkered shirt disappeared, but I was almost certain he was replaced by someone else, this time by a man wearing a short-sleeved shirt.

I'd never been followed before, or at least not that I'd noticed. Even with all my optimism, I had to admit that I'd suddenly found myself in a different category of people—the dubious and suspicious who are kept under surveillance—enemies of socialism.

Literární noviny continued to be published, but its entire orientation had changed. The new editors came from the military press and departments of the Communist Party; most of them, as it became clear after the Soviet occupation, had thereby ensured themselves a career for the next twenty years. Jan Zelenka was the head of the new editorial board. Under his direction, the newspaper tried to attract contributors from among the ranks of its writers, but most of my colleagues from the misappropriated newspaper refused. A letter written by Milan Kundera to Zelenka exemplifies the prevailing mood among the writers at the time.

> Comrade Zelenka,
>
> A short time ago you stopped me on the street and we spoke for about three minutes. I have recently learned that you referred to this conversation before a large gathering of students from the departments of law, humanities, and journalism; referred to me intimately by my first name (even though we've spoken to each other only twice in our lives); claimed that I regretted my position as I formulated it at the Writers' Congress and elsewhere, and that I am now on the way to grasping my errors; et cetera, et cetera.
>
> I do not intend to ponder how or why you fabricated this self-criticism, but so that it does not happen again, I must inform you that I would not change a word of what I said at the congress; I disagreed then and disagree now with the encroachment upon *Literární noviny* (I announced it publicly, after all). I consider your role in this matter extremely cowardly and yourself a preposterous figure.

While most writers boycotted Zelenka's paper, as they referred to it, those of us who were fired were invited to other journals that had not yet been misappropriated.

It was as if, in a society that had been divided since the end of the war—actually since the beginning of the republic—the dividing line had shifted. Now it was no longer democrats versus followers of the revolutionary dictatorship, Communists versus non-Communists. Instead it was those who were trying to hold on to power versus those who wanted to think and act more freely.

My wife and I met now and then with my friends from the editorial board, who would bring me news of battles raging within the leadership of the Communist Party. Apparently there had been arguments, especially between Slovaks and Czechs. The chairman of the Slovak Communists, Alexander Dubček, had criticized First Secretary Antonín Novotný. In his turn, Novotný had treated the Slovaks with haughty disdain on a trip around Slovakia. It all culminated in the city of Martin on a visit to the oldest and most revered cultural institution, the Slovak Matica, where the Slovaks intended to present Novotný with a copy of the 1918 Pittsburgh Agreement that paved the way for the creation of Czechoslovakia. Novotný refused the gift.

Besides conflicts between Czechs and Slovaks, followers of Novotný and devotees of reform were fighting in the Central Committee. The economist Ota Šik gave a long speech criticizing the fact that a small group of conservatives led by Novotný was ruling the country, and he said economic reforms would fail without political reforms. We tried to figure out what he meant and if such reform was even possible in a country ruled by the Communist Party.

On the last day of the year, we invited a few friends over. A minute before midnight the telephone rang, and an unfamiliar voice introduced himself as Borůvka, Borůvka from the Central Committee of the party, he explained. First he wished me a happy New Year and then he assured me that everything would turn out fine for me and other writers. "Comrade Klíma, please tell your colleagues that everything is about to change completely in the next few days. But we're also counting on your help and support!"

I didn't know how to respond. Was this some kind of joke, or a drunken dialer? The voice on the telephone added, "Read *Rudé právo* and watch the television. You're going to be surprised!"

I didn't subscribe to *Rudé právo*, and we didn't own a television set.

Astonished by this bizarre communication, I told my friends what I'd just heard.

It was typical of the times that no one knew whether to take this seriously or as a practical joke.

On January 5, 1968, the citizens of Czechoslovakia were informed that Antonín Novotný had stepped down as first secretary of the Communist Party. The Central Committee thanked Comrade Novotný and praised the selfless and meritorious work he had performed on behalf of the party and the republic. Alexander Dubček was elected first secretary (unanimously, as usual). Not even those of my friends who had remained party members knew what to make of this new development. But they understood from experience that as long as a party that alone assumed the right to govern existed in the country, every political change must be preceded by a change in the leading positions of the party.

When I was reading Kafka's diaries, I was struck by his entry from August 2, 1914. It was very brief. *Germany has declared war on Russia—Swimming in the afternoon.* I wrote two exclamation points next to it and in the margin penciled: *This concurrence of world events and personal history is an inherent aspect of modern literature.* More exact would have been: an inherent aspect of human life.

At the end of January, the Writers' Union announced that the administrative interference in *Literární noviny* had been politically misguided, and the union should request permission to register the weekly.

At the beginning of February, a member of the Communist Party's Central Committee, Josef Smrkovský (only sixteen years earlier sentenced to life in prison), wrote a letter to *Rudé právo*:

It is necessary to eliminate everything that deformed socialism, everything that corrupted the spirit, everything that inflicted harm on the people and took from them so much of their trust and enthusiasm. We must finalize the rehabilitation of those Communists and others who were innocently sentenced in the political trials. . . . It is up to us Czechs and Slovaks to bravely set out toward uncharted territories and seek our own Czechoslovak Socialist path.

Something like this from a high party functionary would previously have been unthinkable. It was beginning to become apparent that events were occurring that were more significant than the replacement of the first secretary of the ruling party.

On February 20, 1968, our journal was in fact renewed under the name *Literární listy*. All those who had been fired from the editorial board in the summer of 1967 returned to their positions on Betlémská Street with the feeling that justice had for once prevailed, and we started to prepare the first issue.

Around this time, Ludvík Vaculík, A. J. Liehm, Pavel Kohout, and I were invited to the Municipal Council of the Communist Party, where an apology was transmitted to us from the higher-ups. They decided that our punishment had been an improper administrative response to criticism. Our expulsion from the party and Vaculík's reprimand were nullified.

The realization that they were thereby acknowledging the truth of what I had claimed at the congress concerning the suppression of freedom of speech blinded me to such an extent that I accepted their decision without mentioning that I did not want their membership card, that I no longer desired to be responsible to any superior committee or party discipline. (Fortunately, a few weeks later, when I was once again banished from the party, no one asked me for any discipline.)

It was apparent that with the arrival of Alexander Dubček, the Slovak Communists were acquiring much greater influence. We in the editorial office suffered from what most of Czech society suffered—an ignorance of Slovak conditions, Slovak history. We didn't even know most of the Slovak politicians. Since I had written two books about Slovakia, some of my colleagues assumed I knew more about the country, but my books had been about the most eastern part of Slovakia, which was a republic within a republic.

Substantial changes were taking place under Dubček. Censorship was abolished in the spring, and important political organizations were being established: the Club of Engaged Independents and the association K231, which brought together political prisoners sentenced in the show trials at the beginning of the '50s.

Our editor in chief, Milan Jungmann, invited a representative of K231 to our offices. From the chair of this organization, Jaroslav Brodský, I once again heard how little attention the courts, and government offices in general, were giving to reevaluating the trials of those who had been victims of arbitrary despotism even though they had never been Communists. I heard tales about concentration camps in the uranium mines and prisons where priests lived side by side with former democratic politicians and scouts, as well as criminals and swindlers and even the last remnants of Nazis. I was ashamed to confess that much of this was new to me—they wouldn't have believed me anyway and would have considered it merely a pitiful excuse.

The times did indeed seem favorable for serious changes, but what should be the priorities? What was imperative, and what could be put off for a time? What could we allow ourselves without provoking those whom we referred to as conservatives? What was still acceptable in the eyes of the superpower to the east, the superpower that demanded that no one doubt whatever it proclaimed indubitable?

The launch issue of *Literární listy* came out on March 1. The first two issues comprised twelve pages just like the previous instantiation of the paper. With the third issue, however, we increased the number of pages to sixteen, and our circulation rose from the previous 120,000 to 270,000, and a few weeks later to 300,000—an unprecedented number for a literary newspaper. (Even during the big news moments we continued to write about literature and culture in general.)

I was put in charge of the so-called opinion pages. I'm not sure if we were aware, but we should have assumed, that these pages would become the most talked-about section of our newspaper.

It was already apparent that the promised reforms would apply to all spheres of life. I started to realize that a couple of editors from our opinion section were not qualified. I recommended we establish several multimember advisory boards composed of specialists, each for a different sphere of societal life. Thus arose our working groups in which we discussed articles on economics, history, philosophy, sociology, and law. The working groups met at least twice a month; the members worked without pay and mainly brought in their own articles.

At first we considered the essential focus to be the rectifications of recent injustices. It was necessary to rehabilitate the unjustly persecuted or sentenced—professors deprived of their positions during the purges, students forbidden to study, the western resistance, works that were not allowed to be published, ideas that the ruling ideologues had designated as erroneous or unfriendly. This was the past of our First Republic.

Soon, however, other points rose to greater significance. We understood that if we did not succeed in removing, or at least limiting, the rule of a single party and renewing democracy, things could always turn around. The first voices demanding a radical change in the political system came from artists in response to a question published in our paper: *Whence, With Whom, and Whither?*

The philosopher Karel Kosík wrote:

Because the politicians who brought this country to the edge of economic, political, and moral catastrophe still hold powerful and influential positions and are hoping they will survive today's wave

of regeneration, democracy must be vigilant and not forget the
fundamental experience of history: politics is decided by power
and deeds, not words and promises.

My friend Alexandr Kliment went even farther in his response:

Renewing political life means finding the courage for free discussion of all vital matters. Such a discussion cannot take place in a
privileged party circle; it must include all citizens of the republic.
I believe in free elections, a functioning parliamentary opposition, the rehabilitation of public opinion, active neutrality, and
the federalization of a neutral state.

Today these demands seem innocuous and obvious, but they
seemed at the time more like a dreamy, unrealizable fantasy.

———

In the fourth issue of our journal we published an article titled "The Re-
naissance of Power" by one of our foremost lawyers, Vladimír Klokočka.
He began by discussing power in general:

It is possible to misapply political power as well as steal it. . . . The
theft or misapplication of power is still a more advantageous type
of criminality than the theft of property. It brings rule not only
over property but also over people. [The people] must therefore
be protected even from their own representatives and delegates.

One of the most important questions in a modern society is how
to control power and by what means we can ensure this control. Ever
so cautiously, Klokočka moved on to questions of a legal opposition.
The word "opposition" itself must be stripped of its criminal conno-
tations. A healthily functioning society requires opposing opinions.
The fundamental question of power is whether opposing opinions

will become the basis *for organizing interests in the creation of political will, that is, whether opinions will be the foundation for specific political behavior, political action.* The idea of the need for an opposition party was concealed behind this formulation.

In "Freedom and Responsibility," the sociologist Miroslav Jodl distinguished between external and internal freedom. The political system must ensure external freedom in the form of political freedoms, that is, the freedom of expression and of association. He also discussed, although on a theoretical level, the character of contemporary power: *All power tends toward hypertrophy. From this it follows that no power can be allowed to exist for long without control from below. Otherwise power degenerates into license and arbitrariness; it does not recognize any limitations other than those it establishes itself, and it transforms the citizen into a vassal.*

Václav Havel contributed an essay to the same issue titled "On the Theme of an Opposition." Even in a Socialist society, he claimed, an opposition is necessary, and whoever imagines that such an opposition can be substituted for by some sort of unorganized public opinion (for example, the press) is mistaken. Every opposition must have the opportunity to try to hold power. He expressed this aphoristically. *Ultimately, power really listens only to power, and if government is to be improved, we must be able to threaten its existence, not merely its reputation.* Aware that the Communist leadership would allow only unwillingly the founding of new parties, he cautiously proposed the concept of such a new party. Its goal would also be to create democratic socialism, but it would come from the historical and humanitarian traditions of our country. Although it would be a fully legal partner in the battle for power, because it would no longer be built on class bases, its politics would be founded on a historically *new type of coalition cooperation . . . with full political autonomy.*

At the end of April, I wrote an article called "One Program, One Party" and tried to impugn the image of an ineluctable Socialist society. I identified all the praiseworthy aspects of socialism, such as the socialization of the means of production, the payment for work according to merit, and the building of a humanitarian society. Then I asked how much of this had been achieved. The answer was obvious: nothing. The entire project had been a utopian fantasy combined with the ideals, illusions, and one-sided rationalism of the nineteenth century. I characterized the party, which had taken on responsibility for the creation of what it called a Socialist society:

> The party that arose to create a rationally governed society is engendering irrationality and chaos. It proclaims itself a scientific government and at the same time chains down science. It proclaims itself the most just order and at the same time sentences thousands, tens of thousands (in some countries, millions) of people who doubt the justice of this order. It proclaims the equality of the people and at the same time creates a myth of a chosen class; it proclaims a higher form of democracy and at the same time disposes of even imperfect guarantees and institutions of the previous system. It proclaims the greatest freedom and at the same time limits the most fundamental freedoms. . . . It proclaims class consciousness as the primary motivation for work and at the same time builds masses of forced-labor camps. It proclaims itself the embodiment of progress and at the same time quickly turns into an odd community, where side by side stand the remains of the elite, careerists, even sordid hoodlums. It proclaims itself the party of the working class and at the same time deprives workers of rights for which they have fought persistently for hundreds of years. . . . For this party there are only two choices: look truth in the face, no matter how shocking it may be, or continue down a path that cannot lead anywhere but to national catastrophe.

I then admitted that several positive changes had occurred over the past few years.

> One thing, however, has not changed: the theory of the necessity of a single, optimal, societal design and a single avant-garde political

organization that will consistently and without fail discover the truth. After every change, no matter how absurd, the investigators have stood side by side with their rehabilitated victims. After years, the most obvious thing has not taken place: Those whose politics were errant or monstrous have not abandoned power.

At the request of several of our foremost scholars, Ludvík Vaculík composed and published "Two Thousand Words" at the end of June. In what he considered a sort of democratic manifesto, he attempted to characterize the corruption of Communist power and provide some guidelines concerning the means of rectifying the situation. His enumeration of the attributes of Communist power was overwhelming. The Communist Party *transformed a political party and an alliance based on ideas into an organization for exerting power, one that proved highly attractive to power-hungry individuals eager to wield authority, to cowards who took the safe and easy route, and to people with a bad conscience.* Because the party was connected with the state and everything that happened in the country, there was no one to criticize it. *Parliament forgot how to hold proper debates, the government forgot how to govern properly, and managers forgot how to manage properly. . . . Personal and collective honor decayed.* An uncontrollable apparatus ruled the country. It claimed that the working class was in charge, whereas in reality the apparatus itself had become the new suzerain. The manifesto warned people not to be satisfied with what they had gained so far. He recommended that citizens call for the resignation of those who until only recently ruled incompetently, those who *abused their power, damaged public property, and acted dishonorably or brutally. Ways must be found to compel them to resign. To mention a few methods: public criticism, resolutions, demonstrations, demonstrative work brigades, collections to buy presents for them upon their retirement, strikes, and picketing at their front doors. . . . For questions that no one else will look into, let us set up our own civic committees and commissions. There is nothing difficult about this; a few people*

gather together, elect a chairman, keep proper records, publish their findings,
demand solutions, and refuse to be shouted down.

On the day the manifesto was published, Ludvík and I were at
a meeting somewhere in Vysočina—I no longer remember the name
of the town—and because the discussion, as often happened during
that time, went on well into the evening, we spent the night in a small
hotel. The manifesto did indeed elicit disapproval, even among Dubček's
leadership. Vaculík was hunted everywhere, but the manifesto had already seen the light of day. Tens of thousands of Czechoslovak citizens
had signed it, and for all the opponents of change both here and in the
Soviet Union, it became one of the pretexts for the accusation that
counterrevolutionaries were making their way to power.

If Vaculík had published the text merely as his own personal opinion, rather than as a manifesto, it probably wouldn't have been greeted
with such enthusiasm. In the same issue he wrote an article called "The
Liberalization in Semily," in which he quoted a statement by one of the
discussants: *It is necessary to consider the Communist Party as a criminal*
organization . . . and exclude it from public activity no matter how pleasant
its current members make themselves out to be. This was perhaps the most
critical political formulation that appeared in the press at that time, yet
I do not recall that it aroused any reaction.

⁕

Editorial Board of *Literární Listy:*

I align myself with the great number of those who express complete agreement with the article "Two Thousand Words." I cannot
refuse to join you despite the fact that I cannot operate within the
framework of any organization. . . . I enclose two pamphlets (with
the same text) of the fifty or perhaps more I found today (6 July
68) around 5 a.m. on the way from Vysočany to Ohrada. These
pamphlets lay scattered along the right side of the road near the
sidewalk in the grass:

COMRADES!

OUR SOCIALIST HOMELAND IS UNDER SERIOUS
THREAT.

Enemy forces are going on the offensive. . . . They have taken
over the press, radio, and television. With their irresponsible
speeches they are disorienting the public and inhibiting its activity. They are maligning everything we have achieved over the past
twenty years and attempting to dismantle the social amenities
of workers and farmers. . . . The proclamation "Two Thousand
Words" is an open call to counterrevolution. . . . The rabble of traitors and murderers from the K231 Club are preparing a reactionary takeover and preparing to massacre honorable Communists
and patriots. Minister of the Interior Pavel is systematically providing Mr. Brodský a list of names and addresses of members of
the state security forces in order to institute mass terror. . . . Close
ranks and prepare for battle against the enemies of socialism!
People, be vigilant! Be prepared to defend socialism, weapon in
hand. Organize demonstrations with armed units of the people's
militia.

From a letter to *Literární listy*

At the editorial offices we started to realize the danger threatening
from within the disunited but still ruling party, as well as from the
Soviet Union and other Stalinist countries of the Warsaw Pact. We
tried to formulate things more cautiously, and we naively assumed that
someone would take note of our more moderate tone. It soon turned
out, however, that everything had already been decided.

Never before or since have I lived with such haste or intensity.

Even though we wrote about the necessity of an opposition party,
these were merely theoretical considerations. An opposition party never
arose, and if we had been even a little honest with ourselves, we might
have suspected that the ruling party would never have allowed it. Certainly most of our readers suspected as much. Some even started to

consider our paper as such an opposition party, or at least the voice of one.

Readers came to our offices offering advice on what to write about or to tell us their stories. But we had only sixteen pages, two of which were devoted to advertisements and cultural events. The critical and foreign sections demanded at least half the remaining space.

Although we hired several more editors, we didn't have time even to read all the letters we received. When I left the offices on Friday, I would carry them home with me in my briefcase, but I knew I wouldn't have time to look at most of them. Foreign correspondents came to see us, as well. Many of them stopped by the foreign desk. This is how I came to meet Neal Ascherson from the *Observer*. He was interested in everything that was going on and in return invited me to visit his own editorial offices in London.

Vaculík, Pavel Kohout, Jan Procházka, Alexandr Kliment, Jiří Hanzelka, myself, and many other writers were often invited to various meetings and discussion evenings. It was as if a miracle were taking place. The silent crowd of people was suddenly transformed into citizens eager to communicate their opinions and suggestions. Most of all they asked us what they should be doing, what we thought about the situation, and how everything would turn out.

But we knew nothing more than they did.

When troops of the Warsaw Pact started traveling around our country in July pretending they were merely extending their planned maneuvers, I wrote an article in which I challenged our government to make it clear that if we were attacked, we would defend ourselves. (As early as the beginning of May we published such a challenge, in which my colleague Jiří Lederer quoted from *Le Monde*: "General Yepishev, chief of the Main Political Directorate of the Soviet Army, announced that the army of the USSR was prepared to fulfill its duty if he received a request from a group of loyal Communists to come to the aid of socialism in Czechoslovakia.")

Milan Jungmann called me into his office and said my article might incense our Soviet comrades even more. They were already incensed, I objected. But if they knew we were willing to take up arms, perhaps they were hesitating, if only in view of the international repercussions a war in Central Europe would have. To capitulate ahead of time had turned out to be a serious tactical mistake in 1938 when we surrendered to Hitler without a fight.

Finally I agreed that we would go to the Central Committee of the party and consult with them.

Most of the functionaries had already been replaced in the ideological department. I was received by Milan Hübl, who was also a member of our working group of historians. He said he'd read my article with interest. Afterward he rose, brought out a large map of Europe, and ran his finger along our borders. Here the border with the Soviet Union continues with the border with Poland, then the German Democratic Republic, where Soviet units remain until today. Then a small border with Bavaria and neutral Austria, and then János Kadár's Hungary. "And you want to take up arms?" he asked. "As far as international repercussions go, have no illusions in that regard. The Americans will submit a note of protest; the French will submit a polite query that will make its way to a meeting of the UN Security Council, where every resolution will be vetoed by the Soviets. Furthermore"—he continued his deductions—"the Soviets are just waiting for something like this so they can substantiate our betrayal because to take up arms against the Soviet army would mean betrayal. The manifesto 'Two Thousand Words' was enough for them to allege that socialism was under threat in Czechoslovakia."

It was difficult to decide who was right, but I pulled the article.

———

About a week later two students appeared at our offices asking to speak with someone in charge. They were brought to our department, where Saša Kliment and I happened to be. The students feverishly told us they had positive information about a provocation being prepared by Soviet agents who were calling for a demonstration on the Old Town Square in the name of some new organization (I don't recall the name). They were going to call for our exit from the Warsaw Pact and for a proclamation of neutrality. They had invited correspondents and journalists from the Soviet Union as well as the West. The students asked us to do something because the outcome of such a demonstration was certainly clear.

The students left, and Saša and I argued about what to do. As if we could prevent any sort of demonstration. The police were the only ones who could do anything like that. Finally we went to see the new minister of the interior, Josef Pavel.

It was a strange time when two editors from a literary newspaper could set off for the Ministry of the Interior, introduce themselves at the porter's lodge saying they had to speak immediately with the minister, and a few minutes later enter the minister's enormous office.

The minister seemed out of place in the expanse of the room, even symbolically small. We relayed to him what the students had told us. The minister didn't seem at all surprised (it later occurred to me that he'd certainly known about the planned provocation before we had) and said, "Gentlemen, if we started forbidding people to gather, we'd be behaving just like those who had forbidden us before them." But he promised to take it under consideration and consult with his deputies. With that we were dismissed.

The police actually did prevent the demonstration, but those who had prepared the provocation could go off and organize another one at any time. There was no doubt about that.

Essay: *Dreams and Reality*, p. 503

15

It was sometime in April of that cataclysmic Prague Spring when Helena and I went to a party at Karol Sidon's. There were many other guests in his home, most of them unfamiliar to me. As usual during this period, politics was the primary topic of conversation. However, I noticed a girl there—perfectly made up and beautiful—who was unquestionably bored. She hadn't said a word the entire time and then proceeded into another room. I set off after her.

She was sitting on the floor paging through some illustrated magazines. I introduced myself. She said her name was Olga and added that she'd heard of me.

We talked about acquaintances, and then she started to tell me about a trip to Italy the previous year and described the dazzling sun and marvelous countryside, the wonderful and subtle wines, and the delightful slender and suntanned lads who, unlike Czechs, hardly set eyes on a girl before they try to make a move. She became quite animated as she recounted her sojourn. She had a melodic voice and spoke passionately about something in which I had no interest. I also learned she was finishing her studies in applied arts and was not married. The tall boy sitting in the next room getting drunk on crappy wine belonged to her. I understood from her stories that there were several more boys who belonged to her. I can't explain why—most likely simply because she was appealing—I suggested we get together sometime. After a moment of hesitation and on the condition that we would talk about something other than what everyone was always talking about, she agreed.

We ended up meeting on several occasions. Unlike her, I didn't have a lot of time. Usually we would drive outside Prague, stop somewhere, and kiss in the car. She would weave her tales of foreign lands; sometimes she would pretend to listen to what I was saying, but she obviously wasn't paying any attention. She tried to conceal this fact by repeating my last sentence in a slightly bored tone: You really think you can change anything? Do you really want to see me again?

I knew our relationship would soon come to an end. I couldn't imagine abandoning my wife and children, but at the same time I couldn't tear myself away from this strange new lover.

Until then I had never been unfaithful to my wife; now I was trying to justify my actions. A year earlier, Helena participated in a Quakers' seminar at Lake Balaton and fell in love with one of the student leaders. When she told me about it, she explained that he had saved her life. She had swum too far out and had lost her strength. He swam out to her and held on to her side until they made it back to the shallows. Later, she was so moved when he told her about his childhood and that his father, a Communist, had been locked up. She wanted to help him somehow. It was only a brief fling, she explained to me, and added that when we had met, I had already been with several girls while she hadn't had anybody.

I could offer no reasonable justification for what I was doing, except perhaps the fact that this girl, thirteen years my junior, was different in every respect from all the other women I knew. I was impressed by the ease with which she accepted the world as a place intended for distant journeys, lovemaking, and sojourns in pleasant places (best of all where a willing servant brought you food and drink).

I understood I was only one of many. I could be replaced at any time, or I could leave anytime and would be immediately forgotten. That's how things worked in her world—something I, perhaps prematurely, criticized about her generation. Also, and unlike my wife, she was not interested in anything that interested me.

This apparently cynical girl painted surprisingly well and as a graphic artist had a sense for detail even in her stories. I learned that as a child she'd longed to have a puppy. When her parents refused to grant her wish, she took an old shoe box, painted it, and dragged it around on a string behind her and talked to it like a real dog. She also confided in me that she had her own image of God—he was an agreeable, stout old man whom she prayed to when she was sad. I realized that all of these stories were meant to hide some kind of internal wound, perhaps an insufficiency of love during childhood. Perhaps she needed to raise her self-esteem and therefore sought out ever new declarations of love from different men.

Once I invited her to a match of the Davis Cup, and, to my surprise, she accepted. She brought along with her, however, a Dutch student whom she described as exceedingly sweet and beautifully naive. So right now she was in love with him. While I was trying to follow the action on the court, she was softly chitchatting with him and kissing him.

—∞∞—

One evening I started writing a one-act play called *Klára and the Two Gentlemen*, which I finished by morning.

Just like my own lover, Klára longs to be happy, while her married "gentleman" dreads the situation in which he finds himself. I situated the amorous couple in Klára's flat. In one room they are getting ready to make love. In the other, Klára's previous lover, who has recently returned from a Communist concentration camp, is dying. Apparently absurd details and circumstances keep entering the play: A bale of barbed wire is in a linen cupboard, and the dialogue is interrupted by the ringing of a telephone, but no one is ever on the line. At the end, the protagonist, upon the wish of the dying man, barks in the place of a guard dog.

It was Olga's words that I heard in Klára's dialogue, which moved back and forth obsessively between lovemaking and foreign lands.

Because I've always had a tendency to moralize, the lovers' desire for a moment of bliss, when they can forget all their responsibilities and the world around them, never arrives. On the contrary, they part with a feeling of emptiness and silence, within both themselves and their surroundings.

A one-act play seemed too short to offer to a theater; I needed at least one more of the same length, but I didn't have any ideas, nor did I have the time to write anything.

Then at the beginning of August I went into a little oak forest not far from our house in Hodkovičky to see if I could find mushrooms for soup. Right on the edge of the forest, I was startled to see dozens of death cap toadstools. I'd never seen so many in one spot.

This unassuming toadstool always excited my imagination. Whereas all poisons are subject to more or less strict control, the death cap offered every mushroom hunter an abundance of one of the deadliest poisons known. (As our foremost mycologist Albert Pilát writes, just two-hundredths of a milligram of the poison, called amanitin, would kill a mouse in twelve hours. Half a gram would kill a hundred thousand mice, which, as the mycologist calculates, would create a line of mice eighteen kilometers long!)

The possibility of coming into possession of such an effective poison tempts a person at least once—at least in his thoughts—to become a killer.

I do not think the task of literature, even though it is sometimes assumed so, is to concern itself with politics. In my defense, I can only say that in my play I allowed myself to be much more skeptical than I would have in a newspaper article or a speech to people who were longing to hear some good news about a situation that was becoming increasingly strained. The plot of The Sweetshop Myriam was simple. A young couple who are trying to get an apartment are supposed to find an old homeless person and bring him to a renowned sweetshop. With the payment of a small amount of money, the forsaken man would be given some almond cookies that had been poisoned. The manager of the shop would then see to it that the young people received an apartment.

My two heroes, Petr and Julie, need a place to live. When they discover how they can acquire one, Julie hesitates slightly but her boyfriend is appalled and decides he must publicly reveal and thwart the criminal enterprise. One after the other Petr summons a policeman, a lawyer, and a minister of parliament. To his horror, he discovers that everyone not only knows about the crimes but also participates in them. Each of my characters has a good reason for his or her actions. The mushroom hunter who supplies the sweetshop with death caps explains that a person's got to make a living somehow when he has children and is building a house. The manager of the sweetshop claims he does it so that young people can get housing. The policeman himself needs an apartment, and the lawyer says the police stand on the side of the criminals—they not only fail to investigate but directly support the malefactors.

Finally the minister shows up and expresses his shock at what he hears. There is no longer any doubt that everything going on here is a criminal conspiracy. And then, Petr is brought a bowl of poisoned cookies and will be forced to eat them. Julie keeps trying to silence him and leave as quickly as possible before they kill him. Petr, however, is determined not to back down.

> They can kill me. I don't care. Can one live in a place where criminals go unpunished? Where powerful criminals protect murderers, and the others beg for a part of the loot?

To Petr's astonishment, the minister applauds. At the conclusion of the play, which until then seems to be nothing more than black humor, I express my fear that everything that happens in society is only a cunning attempt to preserve felonious power.

The minister explains to Petr why he is applauding:

MINISTER: I am applauding your justice, which spares no one.
       (*Loudly*) Justice that spares no one is necessary. Yes—how
       many times have I tormented myself with this question?
PETR: But I, I am accusing you. You are murderers!
MINISTER: Am I guilty of anything? Sometimes I think, yes, I am
       guilty of a great love for you, my children. That blinded me.
       And you (*to the others*), didn't you come here like lambs?
       Did you not hold out your hands? Did you not declaim your
       thanks? And now these accusations, their sting, strikes me
       here! (*Grabs his heart*)

At the end, when those who have consumed the poison along with
those who are supposed to investigate the murder sing insane songs,
the pastry chef who prepared the poisonous cookies lifts the rebellious
Petr onto his shoulders while the minister proclaims:

But I applaud you nevertheless. (*To Petr*) I applaud your justice
and devotion. I applaud your incorruptible longing for pureness,
which makes no distinctions. We need youth and pureness. We
need those who are able to give precedence to a bed beneath
the arch of a bridge instead of a bed that is considered tainted.
We need those who are able to speak out about crimes so that
evil, which is necessary, does not become a custom. We need
those who do not divide but rather unite. We were united in
the longing to help you find a home. And we were united in the
impact of your angry words. We feel ourselves guilty, for who
is innocent? (*The others applaud.*) And who would not, once in
a while, like to hear that he is not alone in his longing, or even
in his guilt? Young man, we need you on our team! Come to the
sweetshop Myriam every Thursday at eight o'clock and shout out
at the top of your voice. (*He raises his hand to Petr and presses*

it.) Repeat those beautiful, cleansing words you pronounced today. Thank you!

The play ends with a funeral procession for another victim. The criminals who hide behind beautiful words need jesters to help create the impression that we are living in freedom because while crimes are being identified, the criminals are going without punishment and continue their activity.

I offered the play to the journal *Plamen* but the editors turned it down. No theater would stage it. The criminals who soon took power no longer needed their jesters.

———

Literární listy was now actually making a profit, and so it was no problem to hire several more editors. My wife and I could finally take a vacation. As long as I'd known her, Helena longed most of all to better know life in Israel. She put together a group of her colleagues and acquaintances and organized a working trip to the Shomrat kibbutz. She also decided to take along Michal. I didn't feel like going anywhere to work, and I was also enticed by the idea of spending a few days with Olga. Helena couldn't convince me to come along. She departed, and I decided to set off for England, which I had liked on my earlier trip. What's more, Mr. Darling offered me his apartment in Hampstead; he was currently in Prague and I would be spending the whole summer on the Continent (this is how the Britons refer to the less significant part of Europe). So I would have the flat all to myself. He entrusted his keys to me along with the name and address of his neighbor with whom I could leave the keys when I left.

Somewhat abashed, I suggested to Olga a trip to Britain. She didn't understand why I hadn't chosen Italy, since I could go wherever I wanted, but she admitted that she'd never been to Britain and could stand a couple of days there.

Before I left, I went to say goodbye to my parents, and Father wanted to know why I was taking a vacation right now of all times. I explained that I was tired and needed to be somewhere far away and not think about politics and not attend meetings every night with my fellow citizens.

Father said he understood, but in fact he assumed that I actually wanted to be out of the reach of the Soviet police when the Russians invaded. He suggested I take the car and as many things along with me as I could. My mother led me into the bedroom and almost in a whisper complained that ever since Father had been locked up, he was always expecting the worst. I shouldn't let him ruin my vacation. Then, counter to what she had just said, she softly asked me to be careful what I wrote about and not to see friends such as Vaculík and Kohout. I had to realize that people, and definitely the Soviets, were looking at them and at me in completely different ways.

Even though Father's prediction somewhat shocked me, I did not follow his advice. Although I did go by car, I took only enough belongings for a two-week trip.

Our daughter, Hana, who was five years old at the time, was staying with Helena's parents nearby, and when I went to say goodbye to her, I was weighed down by unease. Father's prediction was certainly possible, if not probable, and to leave a child at this time seemed like a betrayal. But I persuaded myself nothing would happen. After all, just a few days ago the Soviet leaders had agreed with our leaders that everything would be resolved peacefully and amicably

When I'd first visited London about a year earlier, I had been alone and was therefore master of my own plans. Now I had Olga with me (she didn't speak any English), and I felt a responsibility to show her a good time. I assumed she'd be interested in seeing some galleries, so I took her to the famous Tate, but she seemed bored by it. It wasn't that she minded walking among all those paintings; it was more that my presence was somehow a nuisance. I was a man from another world, with other interests and other desires, who assumed he had a greater claim to her than anyone else she might choose.

Just as we left the gallery, she noticed a group of beatniks sitting on the sidewalk drinking beer and smoking what I guessed was

marijuana. I saw that Olga wanted only one thing: for me to leave
her alone so she could sit with them, go off somewhere, and spend
an interesting night.

The next day it rained, so we took refuge in a cheap Irish pub where
some fellow in a sailor shirt was playing an accordion, and my perfectly
made-up conductress started recalling beautiful, sunny Italy and asked
if we couldn't leave here and travel to the south. The day after that I
gave her part of the money I'd scrounged for the trip and suggested she
spend the day however she liked. I asked if she would be able to communicate without me. She assured me that she would speak in Italian
or with her hands. Then she kissed me and said, "Klíma, I think I'm
starting to fall in love with you," and promised to be back by evening.
I used this time to visit Janet, whom I had stayed with on my previous
visit, and passed on to her a gift from Helena. Then I walked around
the streets. I called Neal Ascherson at the *Observer* and reminded him
that we had met in our offices and he had invited me to look him up
when I was next in London.

We met at a small bar. Neal seemed worried: According to the
latest news, armored brigades were gathering on the Czechoslovak
borders, not only with the Soviet Union but with Poland and Hungary
as well. I asked if he thought it might come to military intervention.
Yes, this is what he feared.

I wanted to know what the Western powers would do.

He thought for a moment and then said: Nothing.

I asked what we should do.

Nothing, he said. You're not an island. If we did not live on an
island, we would never have been able to defend ourselves against
Hitler.

———∞———

My sweetheart showed up that evening with a large box. She brought
with her two slightly tipsy young men who were around her age and
wore tattered jeans. She kissed them and told me they had invited

her to their place for the night, but she'd refused because she was here with me and loved me because I'd brought her here, to this city full of fabulous boys from all over the world. Then she pulled from the box a pair of leather boots and put them on to show them off. She said she wanted to make love to me in these boots.

Suddenly I felt I was taking part in some stupid comedy I myself had written. I longed to see my wife and children. While this unfamiliar boot-shod girl was falling asleep at my side, I wanted only to be at home with my family.

The next morning I was awakened by the telephone. It was Mr. Darling, and in a voice that was both precipitous and somber he advised me to be careful if I wanted to return home. It would be best not to make any statement right now. When he realized I had no idea what he was talking about, he asked in astonishment: "You don't know? Soviet troops invaded your country last night."

Then he said I could stay in his apartment for at least a month, and I should use the telephone as much as I needed. I managed only to stutter some thanks, and he added that he was sorry—very, very sorry.

I had no idea what to do. I was here with a girl who, although I had been making love to her, was a stranger to me.

She took the news about what had happened at home quite calmly. I said that was the end of freedom, and she repeated after me, "So you think that's the end of all freedom?" And then she objected with unexpected judiciousness: "But that depends on the people." She asked if we were going to return and added that I had my family there, and she had her boyfriend, parents, and brother, and everything.

I wanted to leave, but I needed to know more about what was going on at home, if there was shooting in the streets, if those who had said or written too much were being locked up.

Meanwhile, just as she did every morning, Olga made herself up perfectly, and when I expressed surprise that she could devote herself to something like that at a time like this, she said we didn't know when we were going back, so she would have to start searching for work, and

My father and mother, before I was born.

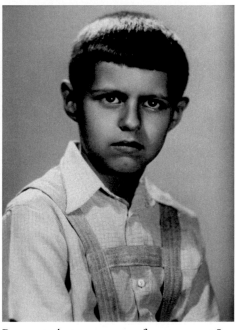

Passport photo, age seven, for a passport I never used.

In the army, 1953.

During one of my reportage expeditions, here with Mirek Červenka in the Soviet Union, 1956.

Family wedding photo, from the right: father, mother-in-law, grandmother, Jan, Helena, myself, mother, father-in-law, sister-in-law.

Helena and me with my brother Jan in London, en route to the United States.

As a visiting professor at the University of Michigan in Ann Arbor.

© Michal Klíma

© Petr Kliment

Tuning in and listening to Svobodná
Evropa [Radio Free Europe] with Helena.

Working as an orderly, early 1970s.

A get-together in Broumar; Milan Uhde reads aloud. To his right, Honza
Trefulka; to his left, Milan Jungmann and myself, June 1984.

With Milan Kundera, 1973.

Michal and Arthur Miller at our place in Hodkovičky.

Meeting with Philip Roth during one of his visits.

vel Kohout and *Václav* Havel at the beginning of the 1970s in Hrádeček.

From left: Zdeněk Kotrlý, Miroslav Kusý, Milan Uhde, Šimečka Junior, Václav Havel, Miroslav Zikmund, myself, Milan Šimečka, Eda Kriseová, Petr Kabeš, Karel Pecka, Milan Jungmann, Jan Trefulka, Iva Kotrlá, Lenka Procházková, Zdeněk Urbánek, Ludvík Vaculík, at the beginning of the 1980s.

As a public speaker at the end of 1989.

for that she had to look nice. Then we drank some tea, and she left, saying she'd be back in the evening.

All day I floundered about with a sick feeling in my stomach. I tried to call Helena in Israel but couldn't get through to her kibbutz, so I sent her a telegram with my phone number. Then I called our editorial offices, but apparently no one was there. Maybe they'd all been taken to be tortured somewhere. Finally I got through to my parents. With his typical matter-of-factness, Father told me there was only a little shooting going on. For now the radio station was transmitting freely. Dubček along with several other politicians had been spirited off to Moscow, but otherwise he didn't know of anyone being arrested or locked up. At least they weren't talking about it on the radio, but for now I should definitely be glad, he said, that I was where I was. Then I called my mother-in-law, who assured me everything was completely calm in Hodkovičky, no tanks or soldiers. Then she put Hana on the line, who said, "Hi, Father, I miss you. When are you coming home?" "As soon as I can," I answered.

Suddenly I was seized with a feverish energy, which only concealed my feeling of helplessness.

I ran out into the street in a vain attempt to escape reality. Behind the windshield wiper of my car I saw a note. To my amazement, it was from my colleague Igor Hájek, who worked at the foreign desk of our paper. He'd been in London several days, but had no idea where to find me until he saw my car. He was staying not far from here and included the address. He added: *I've got a transistor radio and can get Prague. Come.*

I can still see the small room crammed with furniture. Everything was immaculate, and in the middle of the room a wire stretched from wall to wall, compensating for, or rather amplifying, the antenna. There we were, two men from a Prague newspaper that had once again been silenced. Against all odds we had met in this city of several million and were sitting by a small radio receiver that was, with variable signal strength and intermittent comprehensibility, informing us about what was happening in the streets of Prague: Tanks were headed toward the radio station, and there were the first dead.

I asked him if we should go back right away, and he in turn asked if I was crazy.

The next morning Olga carefully made herself up once again, and as she was preparing to go out the door told me not to worry about her. She would take care of herself. I set off for our embassy.

For the time being they had no special instructions from Czechoslovakia and were just copying important documents. On the night of August 21, the president of the republic announced very briefly: *Troops from the USSR, PRP, PRB, NDR, and HPR invaded the territory of our country. This occurred without the agreement of the institutional organs of our state which, however, must quickly resolve the situation and achieve the removal of foreign troops in accordance with its responsibility to the people of our nation.* And he added that *for us there is no way back.* The next announcement was issued by the presidium of the Communist Party, which considered the act of military intervention to be *not only inimical to all principles of the relationships among Socialist countries, but a repudiation of the fundamental standards of international law.*

The foreign minister, Jiří Hájek, flew back from Yugoslavia, where he'd been vacationing, and quickly went to the Security Council, where he apparently spoke with greater fervor and rejected the Soviet claim that the troops had invaded upon the invitation of our officials.

No such request was ever issued. I speak with emotion, sadness, and sorrow of the tragic occupation of my country for which the governments of Socialist countries are responsible, who, without regard for fundamental mutual relationships, without regard to the contractually established bilateral and multilateral obligations, resorted to force and occupied militarily the territory of Czechoslovakia on the night of the 20th to the 21st of August. This is an act of force that cannot be justified in any way.

This unexpectedly candid condemnation of aggression, by a minister who at other times and at similar meetings always obediently supported the Soviet position, had a galvanizing effect.

I asked at the embassy if they had any new information. They didn't. Our delegation was at a meeting in Moscow, which was most likely involuntary. The people were expressing their support of the government so spontaneously that the Soviets had obviously been caught off guard. I was told to come back tomorrow when they might have more information. (The Western powers behaved precisely the way my English colleague Neal had anticipated.)

Back in my transient home, where I didn't feel at home in the least, I once again tried to call my wife. Finally I heard her voice. She wanted to know what I was planning to do. Our daughter and parents were in Prague; we had to return. She said she was in charge of the whole group and was responsible for their care. Some were hesitating; others had already refused to go back. She would stay for a few days until things cleared up. Then she added, "The Israelis are surprised we didn't fight back, but otherwise they've been wonderful. They offered everyone asylum and understood that no one felt like working on the kibbutz right now." I asked what Michal was doing, and Helena said he was playing with the other children. I promised to call again, and when I hung up I realized we hadn't shared any kind words between us, not even that we would stand by each other or that we loved one another.

All Czechs and Slovaks in England who hadn't yet found work were entitled to collect unemployment compensation. Olga managed to find a job as a waitress in some sort of exclusive club. When I asked her how that was possible, since she didn't know English, she said she already understood a little and was learning quickly. She also said the club was at the other end of the city and had offered her free lodging. If I didn't mind, she'd move in right away.

So the next morning we said goodbye. She gave me her new address, kissed me, and said, "I just hope you won't leave me here when you go back."

Janet called and told me to stop by. We would go together to the appropriate offices so I could receive my unemployment benefits. I objected that I still had money left, and it was embarrassing to collect unemployment when I was able to work. Besides, I wanted to go home. But Janet took me anyway to some social office, where I filled out several forms and questionnaires, and to my amazement I was immediately given four hundred pounds and told to return in a week. This was very generous of the British government, but I still felt like a beggar rather than an exile, and I decided I wouldn't collect more money. Since I was delayed here, I would have to earn it. But what did I know how to do except write or edit books and articles? And my English wasn't good enough.

It occurred to me to go to the Royal Shakespeare Theatre, where my *Castle* was to have been produced, and ask if they could stage the play now, since it had acquired a new topicality. I was received by the theater's director, an older gentleman who politely asked about my situation. In a sudden outburst of emotion, I tried to explain what had happened, why foreign troops had invaded our country. I also told him that my wife and son were at present in Israel, while my young daughter had remained in Prague. I couldn't imagine what was going to happen next or if we'd ever see each other again. Because of the tension of the last few days, my nerves were shot; all at once I couldn't go on and almost broke down in tears.

The director nodded sympathetically and told me the theater schedule had been planned a year in advance. He could perhaps consider *Castle*, but he had something better in mind. What if I wrote a new play about what I was now going through? We could make a contract on the spot, and he'd write out a check right there as an advance. Then he wished me all the best for both myself and my family.

I left with a check for fifty pounds and once again felt like a panhandler. (I never cashed the check and several weeks later, back in Prague, I put it into an envelope and returned it with many thanks and a feeling of relief.)

⸺∞⸺

Neal called. He was going to Prague for a few days and wondered if I wanted him to bring anything or to pass on any messages—as if it were obvious I wouldn't be back for a long time. I didn't know what to say. I gave him the address of Helena's parents and asked him to send them my love and find out how they were doing and what sort of danger they were expecting. An English rain was falling outside, and I realized I didn't have an overcoat, and if I was going to defer my return for a while, it would be difficult to get one here. He assured me he would bring back my coat.

A day or two later a man called, introducing himself as Karel Baum. He spoke perfect Czech and said he'd learned about me from Ruth Willard, my American translator, who was also his relative. He informed me that she was in negotiations with a theater in Ann Arbor to produce my *Castle*. But he was calling primarily to find out what my plans were for the immediate future.

I explained that I wanted to go back home; I was just waiting for my wife to return from Israel.

"That's a praiseworthy resolution," he said, "but you must realize that occupation is occupation, and the first people to be taken away would be the Jews and the intelligentsia." In the meantime, he suggested, I could live with them. As their guest, of course. He could imagine my situation. He'd experienced something similar when fleeing Hitler. He asked for my current address and was pleased to learn it was around the corner. Without even waiting for a response, he said he'd be over in half an hour to help me carry my things.

So I moved into his home in Hampstead Heath. I was put in the guest room with a bookcase. I remember only one of the books, *Mission to Moscow* by Joseph E. Davies, the American ambassador to Moscow from 1936 to 1938. The book mentioned the political trials that took

place during that time in Moscow, and although the ambassador had
his doubts, it didn't seem possible to him that it had all been staged.
Not very encouraging reading for someone who was resolved to return
to a country occupied by the Soviet army.

When I called Helena again, I mentioned that I had moved and
asked her what she thought we should do. She said that in situations
like this it was up to the man to decide. She and several members of
her group were staying in the kibbutz, but others had made up their
minds not to go back. A notary had prepared for her free of charge all
the papers necessary to get our daughter permission to leave Czechoslovakia. And a distant relative in Israel who was a pilot promised he
would get Nanda out, legally or otherwise.

I went to the embassy and learned they were organizing a meeting of Czechoslovak citizens, especially students, of whom there were
several hundred in London. The participants were certainly going to
ask what they should do—stay or go back. Did I want to say anything
to them?

The meeting took place the next day in a hall. More than two
hundred people showed up. The speakers, even a handful who had
experienced the occupation at home, took turns. According to some,
nothing essentially had changed, and the reform policies would continue. The Soviet troops had withdrawn to some military areas and
had obviously received orders not to interfere in anything. According
to others, the occupiers were firing wildly into the crowds. They did
not recommend going back.

Then I was given an opportunity to speak. I, who could judge
everything that had been happening only from afar. On the other hand,
I belonged to the editorial board of a newspaper that embodied what
the occupiers had come to suppress and silence for good. I said I could
not give advice to anyone; each was responsible for his own decision, for
his own life. At home we had begun a struggle to reinstate fundamental freedoms, and this struggle would continue even though an entire
army had been dispatched to suppress it. And that in precisely this

situation every decent person would be needed, everyone who wants, despite what has happened, to live in a free country. I ended by saying that I had friends at home fighting for this, and I thought it would be a betrayal if I did not return.

I don't know what effect my speech had. But years later in a tram, a young man approached me and said, "You don't know me, but after your speech in London I decided to come back." That's all he said, and I didn't ask if he was reproaching or thanking me.

Even though only fourteen days had passed since that night of August 21, I felt time was passing unbearably slowly. I sat in the Baums' guest room and read the documents that the appallingly naive Mr. Davies had been sending to Washington. I also read the *Daily Telegraph*, which kept putting news from Czechoslovakia on the front page. But I could not rid myself of the feeling that I was living here like a sponger who only took and had nothing to offer.

I at least bought a few sheets of paper and started to write. My host offered me the use of his typewriter (it was lacking diacritical marks, but had the *é* and *á*). I hoped to write the drama for which I'd received the generous advance, though in my state of mind, I couldn't create more than an exceedingly transparent metaphor for what had happened at home.

A Bridegroom for Marcela was an extended dark anecdote, just long enough for a one-act play. The hero, whom I named Kliment, is called to an office and informed by an official that he would be glad to approve his request to marry a certain Marcela. Kliment is amazed because he knows the girl only by sight. At first confidently but then more and more desperately, he tries to explain that there's been some misunderstanding. The official stands his ground and tells Kliment that he is simply helping him achieve happiness. It turns out that the truth has no relation to the actual facts, but rather relates to what the official claims. While trying to convince Kliment, the official employs everything the hero objects to and provides false witnesses. Finally he alleges that the girl is expecting a child by Kliment. The play ends with brutal coercion, and the hero breaks down and dies.

His two torturers lift up the corpse, and the official says, almost with sadness, *You see, Mr. Kliment, you could have been happy if you'd only wanted to. . . . Sometimes I wonder if we're doing all this in vain. People simply do not want to be happy. . . . But this does not relieve us of the responsibility to serve them.*

Before I had time to take the play to the Royal Shakespeare Theatre, Neal returned from Prague. He had brought me my green Hubertus overcoat and told me all of my friends and loved ones, including my daughter, were safe. He added that in his opinion there was no threat of danger in the near future. They were not locking anyone up, and the same politicians who had led the renewal process were still in charge of the country and the party. During the first days, the Soviets had shot a few dozen people, but it had apparently not been upon any order from higher up. Considering it had been a violent invasion by an army of a hundred thousand, the number of victims was insignificant. Some Prague citizens had shown Neal bullet holes in the walls of the National Museum and the radio station as well as many placards and inscriptions, which of course he didn't understand. They were all apparently demanding that the Russians leave immediately, and often they invoked Lenin, which seemed to him somewhat illogical.

When I asked him if he thought the Soviets would really withdraw, he smiled and said, Armies of superpowers obtain territory to stay there, not to abandon it again. You'll have to reconcile yourself to this.

I thanked him for everything and said I was going back.

When I called Helena, she said we should have returned a long time ago. She suggested we meet in Vienna and gave me the name of a hotel where she hoped we could go over everything in peace.

As soon as I'd made the decision, I was relieved. I wouldn't have to hand over my play, which I thought the director would find difficult to stage in the theater bearing the name of the great dramatist.

I still had to say goodbye to Janet and my colleague Hájek, who was still refusing to return. I also had to go see Olga, since I'd promised not to abandon her.

She was living in a tiny room at the bottom of a few steps, and if the window was open, anyone could crawl in from the street. We kissed, and she told me what it was like working as a waitress in a restaurant where only bankers smoked and drank whiskey and soda. They behaved quite genially, but they were more interested in the stock market reports than in her. Then she embraced me and said she'd missed me and hadn't made love to anyone during these three whole weeks.

In the middle of September we set off on our return trip.

I was out of money, so we dozed for a while in the car. At daybreak we drove along a completely empty highway somewhere in eastern France. After a couple of weeks on an island, I was hurtling along on the left side of the road, and owing only to the presence of mind of an oncoming French driver we were not killed in a collision.

I arrived in Vienna alone. Olga had gotten out in Nuremburg and taken the train home. I met my wife at the reception desk of the hotel. Michal was rejoicing over our reunion and was eager to see his sister, grandmother, grandfather, and classmates. Helena introduced me to a young man named Jirka who was also returning from Israel to his home in Brno. He was certain I remembered him. He was one of the student leaders who'd been thrown out of school for political activity a couple of years ago. We had written about him in our newspaper. But I didn't remember him.

Jirka had an interesting face, very serious but at the same time kindly, with something obstinate in his expression. Of course, I offered to take him to Brno.

Our hotel room was large. Besides an extra bed for our son, there was an enormous double bed. Helena and I lay beside each other almost as if in embarrassment. I embraced her and said I was exhausted. She said she was tired too and stretched out beside me, and we both fell fast asleep.

The next morning we got into the car and set off for our homeland. Michal, usually not very talkative, saw that the adults for some reason didn't feel like talking and started telling me about the kibbutz school, various farmwork he'd participated in, and how everyone was devastated on learning what the Russians had done.

At the border we noticed many more cars leaving the republic than returning to it. The border guards were pleasant, almost friendly; they stamped our passports and wished us a pleasant journey.

At home, it was as if the fatigue and tension fell away. I took my daughter into my arms, listened to how good she had been and how much she had missed us. She had even drawn a picture in which we were all there together and in color.

No one was home at my parents' house. My brother and his girl-friend were in Vienna and were hoping to get to England. Mother and Father had gone to Switzerland. They'd left me a message that Father had been offered a good position in a Swiss electrical engineering plant called Brown, Boveri—only for two months, but the contract would probably be extended.

I called my friends, who promised to come by straightaway. Over the next few days I heard almost identical stories. The invaders had occupied the radio station, but the broadcasters started transmitting from hidden sites and from transmitters that had been prepared in case of war or other such crises. I learned how my colleagues had printed a special edition of our newspaper and distributed it right beneath the eyes of the Soviet soldiers, who understood nothing. Our editorial of-fices, where the occupiers had first burst in, were now vacant, and it was up to us to decide whether or not to renew publishing the newspaper our readers were so keenly awaiting.

For a moment I succumbed to misplaced hopes. At once I was ashamed that I had hesitated for almost a month before coming back, while my friends had been resisting the occupiers as much as they could.

A few days after our return, after the children had gone to bed, Helena said she had something to tell me. It had been such a difficult time, I was so far away, and when she called me it seemed I was even farther away. She needed someone to come to her aid, someone to lean on, someone to draw comfort and strength from. And Jirka, the student we took to Brno, had tried to help her as much as he could. Now that we were back together, she didn't know what to do—at least she was telling me about it. One has to live in truth no matter how painful it might be.

I too confessed with whom I'd been in London.

We offered each other no reproaches. We both started to perceive that a time was drawing near when the only certainty (if there was such a thing in life) would be our loved ones. We put aside our infidelities, at least from our conversations. Despite all the dejection we were experiencing, we were both glad to be home.

Life, which I had been watching from afar, quickly pulled us back into its quotidian embrace.

The Writers' Union had decided to reestablish the weekly under the new name *Listy*. I returned to my office and for the first issue wrote a prefatory column, which I named after Viktor Dyk's famous poem, "If You Leave Me."

I wrote about my feelings over the course of those emotion-filled postoccupation days while I was abroad. I wrote about what the word "homeland" meant to me.

To hear! Unable to give ear to my native language, to words that opened the world from the depths of the first darkness?

. . . Of course you can speak any language, you can order dinner and debate politics or the overcrowding of cities in English or Spanish, but can you express your love, can you do this in a language that is not your own?

And I said to myself: My lover, my little duckling, my little doe, my little fawn, my sweetheart, snowdrop of spring daybreak, little skirt full of tenderness, princess of my wakefulness, my petite starry-eyed dove, my graceful goddess, my love, is it possible you are no longer mine? Is it possible that I will abandon you, that I will renounce you, the only one who can thrill me with tenderness? . . . Then I realized: What a terrible world it is in which you can choose between a homeland that promises suffering and the suffering that afflicts those who choose to renounce their homeland. And I said to myself: The only human prerogative is the right to choose, even if it is between two sorrows. I do not know which is greater, but I know that in the first case I will not remain alone, I will remain in it and with you, my friends.

The column was overwrought, even sentimental, but it was understandable given a time of such intensified feelings. Perhaps this was the reason that, of all my articles, this one had the greatest response among readers. I received letters from people telling me that they had clipped out the column and sent it to loved ones abroad who were hesitating to return. Perhaps I convinced a few to come back. Later I felt this as a commitment, a choice I had to validate through my own behavior.

Many of my friends, however, opted for emigration. Six from our offices left immediately after the occupation. Igor Hájek, with whom I had listened to Prague radio in London, remained in Britain as well.

Although most of the politicians who had garnered popularity and trust retained their positions and enjoyed the support of the citizens, I noticed the atmosphere in the country changing day by day, and I had no illusions that anything would halt this progression. An army of a hundred thousand soldiers from a totalitarian power did not invade our country in order to help build a democratic regime. We also had no doubts that those who had until recently held power and then lost it in the spring must come back to life after the occupation; it was only a question of how soon.

My friends and I discussed what could still be preserved. On the last day of October we met at the Writers' Club, and beneath the banner "Prague Writers," we adopted a resolution. We announced support of the politics of the Prague Spring, which had chosen *a trajectory on the basis of socialism* and protested the fact that this period was beginning to be referred to as the advent of counterrevolution. The resolution warned against a politics of compromise: *The real tragedy of Czechoslovakia would come to pass if compromises overwhelmed the genuine import of our battle and only the name of the democratic process remained.* The text pointed out that censorship was already being reinstated; people who had earned the trust of the citizens were leaving government and were being replaced by *those who have squandered their moral credit.* The prepared economic reforms were not being instituted. It is unacceptable *to reconcile oneself with the idea that the presence of foreign troops on our territory has been legalized with no time limitation.*

The resolution ended with an impassioned appeal to Jan Hus. *We recall that if anyone, after many years, had preserved the character and resolve of the Czech nation and saved it from ruin, it was the man who said: I do not recant.*

We printed the text in the first issue of *Listy*; in the same issue was a less eloquent but bitingly ironic poem by Václav Havel:

> *WE DO NOT DECLARE!*
> *WE DEMAND!*
> *WE STAND!*
> *WE WILL NOT RELENT!*
> *WE CHALLENGE!*
> *WE PROMISE!*
> *WE DO NOT BETRAY!*
> *WE REFUSE!*

WE WILL NOT PERMIT!
WE DENY!
WE CONDEMN!
WE WILL ENDURE!
WE WILL NOT DISAPPOINT!
WE WILL NOT RELENT!
WE WILL NOT ACCEPT!
Hm . . .

⸺ ✎ ⸺

At the beginning of November 1968, I received a registered letter from the Mendelssohn Theatre in Ann Arbor. The director would be staging my play *The Castle* on December 3 and would be very pleased if I could take part in the premiere; my travel and accommodations, of course, would be reimbursed.

The prospect of spending several days in America and escaping the depressing environment of an occupied country thrilled me. Surprisingly, it was easier to get an exit permit from the Czech offices at that time than to obtain an American visa. The Americans, more or less since the period of McCarthyism, were displaying (and justifiably so) a significant amount of distrust toward anyone who had been in the Communist Party. Nevertheless, I managed to secure a visa without great difficulty. The relevant offices apparently did not suspect me of working as an agent of the Czech Secret Service.

On the last day of November, I boarded a plane with a feeling of wonder at what fate had prepared for me and set out on my overseas journey.

At the New York City airport, my translator, Mrs. Ruthka, a kindly and demure woman, was waiting for me. She drove me to her large home in Roslyn Heights, where she and her family lived: her diminutive husband, a somewhat eccentric son—a mathematical genius—a quiet daughter, and a lazy, shaggy mongrel with the philosophical name Plato.

Mrs. Ruthka confided to me that my *Castle* was her first attempt at translation. She had never presumed to undertake anything like this, and then she started asking me about various linguistic subtleties that she'd discovered in my play. I was taken aback by her questions because the premiere was in three days, and I assumed it was too late for textual alterations. The next day we walked around New York, a city that seemed to have been relocated here from some utopian vision. Then we both got on a plane to Detroit.

At the airport I was welcomed like a genuine author (till then I was astonished that anyone would take me seriously as a writer). Waiting for me were the head of the theater and the director, a small, slightly rotund Jewish woman, Mrs. Marcella Cisney, who hailed from one of the Baltic countries, which at the time enjoyed the inauspicious privilege of belonging to the Soviet Union.

I learned that the university theater in Ann Arbor was one of the few American theaters that had a permanent ensemble. The company considered *The Castle* a remarkable comedy (they spoke about my play with polite exaggeration), and they were delighted that they would be the first to produce it in America. Nevertheless, the director wanted to go over a few passages where she had some recommendations to pare down the dialogue.

We checked in at the hotel, and the translator and I set off for the theater, which surprised me with its conservative stateliness. And while the actors were getting ready to rehearse, the director brought the script to go over her proposed deletions.

It slowly dawned on us what had happened. My pleasant and inexperienced translator had thought that in several places the allusions would be incomprehensible to an American audience and had added explanatory lines, which threw off the tempo of the play as well as the style and speech of the characters.

When we came to the fifth such interpolation, the director could hold back no longer and started screaming at poor Mrs. Ruthka until she burst out crying, and I tried to calm down both of them. They would simply leave out these insertions; the actors could certainly manage that by the premiere.

None of us suspected what still awaited *The Castle*.

The actor, with the beautifully literary name Henderson Forsythe, who was supposed to play the scientist Emil was struck with a heart attack on the very day of the opening. None of the available actors dared try to learn the role in the few remaining hours, and so it was played by the stage manager, who walked about the stage with the director's script and simply read the lines. I sat in the audience, sweating in terror. I thought the play was ruined and wanted to flee the theater.

The audience, however, considered this stage improvisation an unusual variation and gave the young unknown writer from a country just occupied by the Soviet Union lengthy applause, whether out of commiseration or politeness.

After the play there was a small reception. The actors praised the director and the play, while I praised the actors and the director, and then we all sent a telegram to Mr. Forsythe at the hospital. The director had already forgiven my translator for her additions; she even praised Mrs. Ruthka and said that otherwise the translation read well. She also praised the university, claiming it was one of the best public universities in the country, especially the law and medical schools, which were world famous. Then the chair of the Slavic department congratulated me and asked, as if in passing, if I'd be interested in teaching Czech language and literature next year. I was so taken aback by his offer that I didn't know what to say. I'd never taught Czech language and literature in my life, but he must have assumed, or most likely he had no idea, that I'd studied these two areas. He noticed my perplexity and said of course I didn't have to answer right away; I could let him know my decision before I left.

A little while later, Professor Ladislav Matějka, who had fled Prague twenty years earlier and was now teaching in the Slavic department, stopped by. I told him about the offer I'd been given, and he asked, "Did you discuss the salary? My friend," he instructed me, "you cannot reply if you don't know the salary." Then he added that the department must offer me at least twelve hundred dollars a month.

He also told me that now, because of everything that was happening, students were expressing extraordinary interest in Czech. I would definitely have plenty of grateful students. As far as teaching the language was concerned, I wouldn't have to bother myself too much; it would just be some language exercises, since Czech was an elective course.

Then a man appeared who informed me that Henry Ford had also been at the performance, but unfortunately he couldn't attend the reception. He would consider it an honor, however, if the three ladies and I (the third lady was my aunt Ilonka, who had come from Toronto) could join him for lunch tomorrow at his Detroit office.

The next day an extremely well-dressed secretary, or perhaps a bodyguard, led us to a door with a glass panel bearing the inscription HENRY FORD III.

Mr. Henry Ford the Third took us out onto a small terrace with a beautiful view of the ugly city. He spoke politely about my play, asked about conditions in our country, and then said what a shame it was that our market had been closed for so many years. Of course, this had little effect on him because our market wasn't very significant; instead we were harming ourselves because without competition the production of any sort of artifact of human labor starts to lag behind significantly. When we'd finished eating and were drinking coffee, Mr. Ford asked if we'd be interested in visiting his manufacturing plant. Then he called the man who had escorted us here and bade us farewell.

The most captivating thing for me about our meeting was that for the first time in my life I had met a genuine big-time capitalist. The director, the translator, and my aunt were thrilled. They felt we had been shown a great honor: This rich and powerful man had devoted so much of his precious time to us.

The next day I went to see the departmental chair.

He greeted me and said I must be curious about the conditions of the position. It was proposed that I teach a literary seminar four hours a week along with the same number of language-teaching hours. My pay would be twelve hundred dollars a month. Would this be acceptable?

I said it would be and thanked him.

We shook hands, and he asked if I would be coming with my family. I said I would have to consult with them, but they would almost certainly be coming along.

Back home, when I announced I had accepted an offer to teach at the University of Michigan and that, of course, we would all be going, Michal expressed the greatest interest. He asked if there were Indians living in Michigan, and when I admitted I hadn't seen any, he looked disappointed. I quickly added that there were still many Indian tribes in such a large country, and perhaps we'd go see them. They would have school vacations there as well, which we would take advantage of to travel around America. My son wanted to know if that meant he would have to attend school, and when I said of course he would, he asked if they taught in Czech.

I explained that he would be going to a local American school.

The idea that he would have to attend a school where he wouldn't understand a word almost made him cry. Hana, on the other hand, was most excited about flying in a plane and seeing the ocean. My wife didn't say anything. At night when the children were asleep, she asked if I had thought this through. If we really did leave, weren't we betraying our friends? I objected that many of our friends had left with the apparent intention of not returning, and no one had considered it betrayal. We were just going there for two semesters. It was an extraordinary opportunity to get to know another way of life, for me an opportunity to do something completely different, and for the children an opportunity to learn English.

She asked what opportunity awaited her.

No obvious answer came to mind except the fact that she would have the chance to live in a free country and, at least for a little while, escape an environment that was becoming more and more oppressive.

"And what if everything changes here, and we won't be able to come back?"

"If it gets that bad, we'll be glad we were gone."

"You think I'd leave my mother and father here?"

"Then we'll come back," I said angrily (and presciently); "they'll always let us in, just not out."

———✸———

There was more and more work at the editorial offices, and because so many experienced editors had emigrated, it seemed silly, or even indecent, to leave. Also, I was frightened by the idea that over the course of the next six months I would have to prepare, as responsibly as possible, at least forty two-hour lectures in English on a subject I had indeed studied, but for twelve years—with the exception of several months spent writing my monograph on Karel Čapek—had had nothing to do with.

On January 16 I took an unpaid vacation and promised that if the editors considered it necessary, I would be glad to write an article.

It only gradually dawned on me what sort of task I had taken on in Ann Arbor.

I studied at a time when all science and scholarship, including literary history and criticism, had become tarnished by Marxist exegetes. Instead of literary values, they appreciated revolution and class origin. They didn't even mention our greatest Czech authors, or, if they did, it was only in order to censure them.

I also realized that many of the authors who were promoted held only local significance at best. During the period when Lope de Vega, Shakespeare, and Molière were writing, theater was practically nonexistent in the Czech lands. Only two centuries later did Václav Klicpera and Josef Tyl undertake their naive comedies, primarily for a rural audience who understood only Czech. It was the same in both poetry and prose. I decided to devote myself to a handful of figures in my lectures, for example, Jan Hus, Jan Amos Komenský, and, in the modern period, Karel Hynek Mácha, Božena Němcová, Karel Havlíček Borovský, Karel Jaromír Erben, and Jan Neruda.

From the interwar period, when Czech literature finally started to approach the level of other European literatures, I included Jaroslav

Hašek, Karel Čapek, and Vladislav Vančura, as well as Franz Kafka. Although Kafka wrote in German, he was famously associated with Prague (about which he said, "This little mother has claws" because one cannot tear oneself away). Also, Kafka was the most famous of all the authors who had written in the Czech lands. There were several generations of extraordinary poets (more good poets, in fact, than prose writers), but poetry from a different country is always difficult. The translator's abilities are much more crucial to reception.

I also planned to discuss the literature I thought would most interest my students—that is, the work of my contemporaries.

I prepared my lectures while corruption, which for the time being seemed far away, was slowly creeping into the country.

Allegedly, "healthy forces" (in Communist newspeak, those who welcomed the occupation) quickly came to power. The Communist Party chose Gustáv Husák as its head. Several years earlier he had belonged to a group of prisoners sentenced to life and had escaped the gallows only because he had refused to admit to fabricated crimes under torture (he was not prosecuted for his real crimes). Thus, some believed he would resist the pressure of the occupiers (as if allowing something like this were possible).

Our journal was once again proscribed, this time irrevocably, and I was once again kicked out of the party. Inasmuch as during the time after my ID card had been returned, I hadn't paid dues or gone to meetings, my expulsion was so incontestable that I wasn't even informed about it, nor did anyone demand I submit my party card.

—∞—

Two days after we left for the United States—the penultimate day of August 1969—our government, which by then had been completely altered, tightened the rules regarding exit permits. The borders securely—or, rather, dangerously—closed behind us.

Once again we were greeted at the Detroit airport, this time by representatives of the department and Professor Matějka. During the drive to Ann Arbor, the professor explained how to proceed with the teaching of Czech and pointed out the building that housed our department. He also suggested I stop by and see the secretary, Mrs. Parrott, who would help me out and offer advice. Apparently she was the angel of the entire Slavic department.

Then we stopped in front of a large apartment building on Geddes Avenue. They had assumed we would want something fairly inexpensive, and this apartment was only three hundred dollars a month (about four times as much as our apartment in Prague and roughly the same size), but we would also have to pay a three-hundred-dollar deposit, which would be returned to us when we moved out. The apartment had the advantage of being close to the department, and I could easily walk to work. So at first I could get along without a car but, as I would discover, I would need one as soon as possible.

The apartment was on the second floor and had two bedrooms, a living room, a dining room with a kitchen corner, and a large bathroom containing two sinks. The bedroom windows looked out on the low walls of a cemetery across the street. I was surprised that instead of paths, there were little roads running between the individual graves. The living room looked out on an asphalt courtyard that primarily served as a parking lot. In the kitchen there was an electric stove and a large refrigerator. The cabinets were loaded with pots and pans.

While my wife unpacked and the children explored the apartment, I set off for the department. Immediately I was struck and amazed by an enormous and familiar symbol of communism: a hammer and sickle. Someone had painted it on the carriageway of a bridge I had to cross on the way to school.

I was greeted in the department by Mrs. Parrott, a young, slender, elegant, and helpful woman. She acquainted me with my teaching schedule and gave me a list of my students, some of whom had beautiful Czech names such as Janáček, Lišková, Jelínková (of course, without the diacritical marks). Then the secretary gave me lots of other good advice: which health insurance to choose, which schools would be best for our children, where the nearest grocery store and shopping center were. She also pointed out that the university operated a bus, which students and faculty could ride free, and that I would receive all necessary office supplies from her. Then she led me to my office, which, unlike all my previous workspaces, did not overlook a courtyard. It had a beautiful view of the tall tower, the dominating feature of the city. Then I noticed a bottle standing on my desk. The secretary informed me the dean had sent it as a welcoming gift. The bottle, which I immediately placed in a cabinet, contained an entire half gallon of sherry.

———

I had eight students. Some of them, despite their Czech names, knew not a word of Czech. Yet there was a student from a Czech community in Texas that had survived for over a hundred years. She'd brought with her an endearing archaic form of our native tongue.

Even during my own student days, I hated it when a professor simply read to the class what he could have handed out at the beginning and allowed the students to read at their leisure. But was my English good enough to allow me to improvise? In the end, at least for the first few lectures, I compromised: Some passages I read, and in between I would digress into history or touch upon the present day.

Certainly in part because their ancestors (if not they themselves) came from other countries and continents, Americans behave graciously and good-naturedly toward foreigners. From the very beginning, my colleagues invited Helena and me to parties and introduced us to another dozen or so colleagues and their wives, and they all told us to call them by their first names.

The children started attending school. The mother of one of her classmates took Nanda under her wing and invited her over for help with English. Michal complained that he understood almost not a word, but unlike some students, he had no problems distinguishing individual letters.

Those first few weeks must have been difficult for them. A veil of linguistic incomprehensibility concealed their world. My daughter enjoyed the fact that instead of sitting in the classroom all the time, they often went outside; and in the park there was something she'd never seen in Prague—rocking animals on springs. Once, when the radio was on, Nanda started yelling excitedly for us to come listen. To our amazement, a local Detroit station was broadcasting in Czech. Much to their disappointment, the children soon learned it was only once a week for thirty minutes. It was paid for by a local funeral home trying to secure all potential clients of Czech extraction.

We saw funerals almost every day from our window. Grave diggers always arrived first, and if rain threatened or if there was too much sun, tarpaulins would go up around the grave site. Then the hearse would arrive along with other cars bearing the bereaved. The cars parked wherever they could near the grave site. If it was raining, the mourners wouldn't even make use of the tarpaulins but stayed in the car. Then the priest would appear and speak to both the people and the automobiles.

When there was no funeral, black squirrels dashed about the cemetery grounds, and students played soccer between the graves. I soon learned that in this country, it was not becoming to speak or even think about death, and it did not seem necessary to demonstrate any special respect toward the departed, since death, in fact, did not exist.

We soon discovered that it was difficult to cope without an automobile. Ann Arbor is a medium-sized university town with about a hundred thousand inhabitants, but because America has much more open space than Europe, the city is spread out. So I started looking for a used car in the classifieds. I was intrigued by an ad by a certain Mr. Zizala, who I correctly assumed was formerly Mr. Žížala. He lived at the other end of the city, and one of my students gladly drove me to see him. Mr. Zizala was a mechanic by trade, and this aroused in me the hope that the Chevrolet Impala he was offering—the color of a light coffee—would be in decent shape. This man, whom I met only once in my life and for less than thirty minutes, remains fixed in my mind. He had emigrated less than two years earlier but already owned a small house and workshop (certainly mortgaged). It was his unbelievable mixture of English and Czech that stood out. He assured me his car was *super-duper* and that since I was from Prague, he would give me a special *férst reyt prais*. He sold me a brand-new automobile for seven hundred dollars and wished me *fayn draivovat*.

The car altered our way of life entirely. Until then, we had walked to the local grocery store, made our purchases, and then, to the aston-ishment of everyone looking on, pushed the clattering shopping cart home past university buildings and the cemetery on Geddes Avenue while motorized argosies roared past us. Now, for the first time, we drove to the shopping center outside town.

As slightly awestruck visitors from a country that was in the midst of constructing the most advanced system of society where every per-son would soon be able to take according to his needs, we entered an immense (and ridiculous) empire of overabundance. To the sound of elevator music, we walked among piles of blouses, skirts, dresses, scarves, coats, and underwear; among millions of shoes, boots, perfumes, pow-ders, forest scents, and eliminators of all unpleasant smells. We could touch anything we wanted and try on anything that could be tried on, and, according to hypotheses of scientifically based marketing studies, we were supposed to fall into that state of ecstasy so often described as a loss of all judgment within these cathedrals of capitalism.

———

At first money was tight. Fortunately, I started receiving invitations to lecture at various universities, including Indiana University in Bloom-ington, a university in Kansas City, and Columbia University in New York.

I prepared a fairly political talk in which I tried as best I could to summarize the central ideals of the Prague Spring and describe the way the official policies of the Communist Party differed from the demands of its citizens, who longed for a renewal of democracy, free elections, and an independent judiciary. At the time, interest in occupied Czechoslovakia, and primarily the Prague Spring, was enormous.

The young generation had succumbed to left-wing ideals: The most radical wore T-shirts sporting pictures of Che Guevara, Castro, or Chairman Mao; they read Daniel Cohn-Bendit or Sartre. Among their idols were Noam Chomsky and Rudi Dutschke. Now these idols were joined by, at least for the more moderate, Alexander Dubček and his "Socialism with a Human Face." (Of course, almost everyone at the university, especially the students, was against the war in Vietnam.)

Then an unsigned (and sensibly so) document containing ten points arrived for me from Czechoslovakia. The preamble read:

> Many capable, enthusiastic, and duly elected people have been compelled to leave their jobs or their appointments. . . . Societal organizations are being undermined by violent intervention; the public has been excluded from participation in national politics; questions of deep consequence are being decided by groups of individuals instead of democratic organs of the country. Not a single Czech agency has arisen from the will of the people. . . . On top of everything else, censorship is making it impossible to discuss these issues publicly, which is quite convenient for people of limited thinking and a dictatorial disposition, for old opportunists and new careerists, because they can claim what they want, falsify facts, slander individuals, and organize campaigns in newspapers that are responsible to no one. At the same time, they tell the people straight to their faces that now the truth can finally be told!

The authors and signatories of the ten points demanded the departure of Soviet troops, whose presence they considered the cause of unrest in society. They protested against the purges, against the dissolution of most voluntary civic organizations, and against the renewal of strict censorship. The important point was number five, which began with this proclamation:

> We do not recognize the role of the Communist Party as an organization of power and its primacy over government organs that should be answerable to the people. Placing party membership above citizenship is repugnant.

The ninth point called for civil disobedience.

> When censorship silences critics, when crude intervention into government organs is supposed to frighten people, when dishonorable journalists with miserable standards are obviously preparing the atmosphere for worse things to come, we announce plainly and clearly that the right to disagree with the emperor and his rule is an ancient and natural right of man. Even the enlightened monarchies were able to make use of it as a constructive force. Therefore, we ask how this question will be resolved here. And we reserve the right to disagree, which we will express by resisting, through lawful means, everything that goes against our reason and against our conviction as citizens attempting to achieve a socialism that is both democratic and humane. . . . We express our solidarity with people who are persecuted for their political views.

The sender of the document, whose handwriting I recognized in several of the passages as that of my friend Ludvík Vaculík, added a postscript noting that some of the signatories had already been arrested.

———∞∞∞———

To make up for the little time I had been devoting to the children, I decided we should take a trip to Lake Erie, the closest of the Great Lakes. We parked in a spot that seemed suitably close to the water and, without suspecting anything ill, set off on a path that seemed to lead to the shore. We did not notice the sign informing us this was private property.

Suddenly, a man appeared out of nowhere pointing a rifle at as and shouting something I took to be: Not one more step or I shoot! As in a scene from a fatuous gangster film, we were told to raise our hands. In vain, I tried to explain to the apparent owner that I was not a criminal but merely a foreigner teaching at the university who wanted to show his children the lake. We made an about-face, were allowed to put our hands down, and, under the constant watch of the man with the rifle, we marched back to our car. Thus we became vividly acquainted with one of the pillars of American civil liberties: the inviolability of private property.

At the beginning of winter, an unfamiliar man called and informed me in Czech that he was a professor at a Catholic college in Saint Louis. He taught drama and invited me to the premiere of my play *The Master*, which he had been putting together.

Since childhood, I'd loved Mark Twain and, because of him, the Mississippi, the queen of rivers. Saint Louis lay on the bank of this river.

I succeeded in getting away for three days. I traveled to Hannibal, where I visited the house in which the famous boat pilot had spent his childhood and where, for myself and millions of other readers, lived Tom Sawyer and Huckleberry Finn.

I awaited the premiere of *The Master* with trepidation. It was supposed to be performed on a small stage belonging to the college. The director was a Czech postwar émigré who confided to me that at home he had been sentenced to death in absentia. The previous spring he was informed that he could be rehabilitated, but the Soviets had invaded before he'd had a chance to reply. I was surprised by how ardently he followed the events back home; he even allowed himself an idiosyncrasy: His wristwatch was set to Prague time, which differed from the Mississippi basin by seven hours. The director enthusiastically talked to me about my plays. He liked *The Master* because of the image of a fanatical faith in the redemptive role of desolation. Then, with some embarrassment, he admitted that he'd run into a little problem while putting together the play. The college was exclusively women, and there were two female roles in my play and three roles for men. It was this play, however, that he wanted to stage, so he took the liberty of turning one of the male roles into a female one.

He glanced at me and added that he understood my misgivings, but I would see that it worked quite well. To my relief, he revealed to me that he himself would be playing the role of the grave digger, and the woman who would be playing the old male professor was an old professor herself. She was extremely talented, and he was convinced I would be hearing of her in the future.

Armed with this information, I took a seat in the front row of the theater.

To my astonishment—perhaps this was due to my reduced sensitivity to the English language or my expectations of the worst—it really did work quite well.

I consoled myself by imagining that instead of the *Three Sisters*, I would one day see the *Three Brothers* (in a men's university production), and the uninitiated spectators would be none the wiser.

———

Christmas was fast approaching. A compatriot of mine named Timoteus Pokora was on a study trip through the department of Asian languages and literatures. We'd met here in Michigan and knew each other more by sight. He had come here with his wife and son, and his stipend was barely sufficient. He stopped by my office one day with the departmental newsletter, in which he'd circled a small announcement. The members of some sort of Reform church in Midland, Texas, were inviting foreign students to spend the week of Christmas with them free of charge. The application deadline was today. I agreed that it was a generous offer, but Texas was a bit out of the way and, besides, I wasn't a student. I refrained from mentioning to Mr. Pokora that his half-bald head and elderly appearance did not strike me as exactly boyish.

He objected that they wouldn't check up on us and, besides, he still considered himself a student, and this invitation was interesting if only because it was Texas. When else would we be able go there?

It slowly dawned on me that he'd be glad to accept the invitation but didn't have enough money for the trip. It would be cheaper if we went in my car; of course, he said he would contribute money for gasoline. Gas was so cheap, though, that I didn't need any contribution. It just seemed embarrassing to try to pass myself off as a student.

Mr. Pokora maintained that we were all essentially students until the day we died, and most of the students here had more money than the two of us put together. Could either of us afford a weeklong vacation in Texas? Did I realize what an opportunity this would be for our children?

I said that, in my case, an entire week was out of the question; I'd feel like a fraud.

With this decision, my compatriot left to telephone Midland and in less than an hour delightedly informed me that we were expected— and, of course, we could extend or shorten our stay as we wished. He was of the opinion that my worries were exaggerated. Timoteus learned that Midland was the business center of Texas petroleum production and one of the richest cities in the United States. The Midland church would assuredly not be impoverished.

So a few days later, the seven of us crammed into the Impala and embarked on a trip to Texas.

When you drive through this vast country from north to south, you realize that in addition to the America of extravagant residences, mansions, skyscrapers, slums, farmhouses, and wooden colonial structures, there is another America—an America of freeways, a landscape of gas stations, billboards, and neon, enormous signs providing directions and distances in hundreds of miles, signs with highway and freeway numbers. There are speed-limit signs, signs with telephone numbers in case of emergency, repair shops, fast-food restaurants, rest stops for truck drivers, an America of motels and hotels, where you can spend the night without anyone demanding to see your identity card, just the license plate number of your car, and that's in case it gets stolen. When I was reading Nabokov's *Lolita*, I had the feeling that the author was much more fascinated by this bizarre and colorful world of free-way anonymity—in which you can conceal infidelity and much worse atrocities—than he was by the love affair between a grown man and his underage stepdaughter.

We drove through several large cities which, unlike the freeway subculture, were gray, uninteresting, and usually featureless. The most depressing was Dallas, the embodiment of concrete vacuity, a city well suited to the recent presidential assassination.

We reached Midland on Christmas Eve. Skyscrapers jutted up above the flat countryside; everything here was new and evidently constructed only recently (the city was not founded until the last quarter of the nineteenth century). We had already grown used to seeing skyscrapers, and there was nothing else here that struck us as exceptional. (I don't wish to do the city an injustice; it had two theaters, a concert hall, and a museum.)

We easily located the enormous church, an establishment that performed many functions. Besides rooms for rent, there was a kitchen, dining room, fitness room, and, of course, several rooms for congregational activities. We were welcomed, housed, and notified when the next religious service was to take place.

At supper, we made the acquaintance of the other participants in this Christian Christmas; everyone did indeed appear younger than we did.

Each evening, both the genuine and the spurious students were invited to the home of a different family. One evening, a minister of the congregation invited my wife and me to his home. We were treated to an enormous beefsteak, wine, and a cake. Afterward, when we were munching the Christmas cookies, it was time for conversation. Although we had already become accustomed to avoiding anything serious or controversial, we searched in vain for a topic of discussion. Our hosts were not interested in art, politics, or Europe. They knew nothing of such a small country as Czechoslovakia; the tragedy that had occurred would not be of interest to them. For a while we chatted about the flight of Apollo 11, the weather, potential day trips from Midland. Then—I don't know what got into me—I started talking about marriage as an institution undergoing a crisis and that sometimes dissolving the marriage was more ethical than maintaining a strictly formal relationship in which two people persevere without love. Fortunately, my wife kicked me under the table, and only then did I register the horror, consternation, offense, and absolute disapprobation on the faces of our hosts.

After four days in Midland, I could no longer stand it. We decided to take a trip to the nearest national park, Big Bend (only a couple of hundred miles away), and spend the night there. The next morning we set off on an exquisite and all but empty freeway through scenery that is so typical for a significant part of the United States—a landscape dominated by semideserts and very little vegetation. Every now and then we caught a glimpse in the distance of a herd of grazing horses or cows, but only rarely did we come across a farmhouse.

In the park, we climbed along several hills covered with some sort of unfamiliar vegetation. For the first time in our lives, we saw cactus growing somewhere other than in a flowerpot and made it to a magnificent canyon formed from the erosion of the Rio Grande River. At our own risk, we boarded a ferryboat that transported us and a few other passengers illegally to Mexico so we could brag that we had stepped onto Mexican soil.

We also joined an excursion to some caves, which, although in German transcription, were called Karlovy Vary, or Carlsbad. Max Frisch, even though he doesn't call them by name, describes them beautifully in his novel *I'm Not Stiller*.

After less than a week, we embarked on our return trip and finally made Michal's wish to see real American Indians come true. We arrived just as the celebration was beginning. We fell in with a group of tourists who'd come for the same reason: to experience something of the life of the original inhabitants of the continent.

The Indians—a number of them were only a little older than Michal—stood in a group. Some were partially naked, some were covered in buffalo skins that were old and had seen better days, just like their headdresses. Then drums and tambourines started up, and the dance began. Despite the cold weather, I noticed there was no smoke rising from most of the old-fashioned dwellings, and I realized that most of the dancers no longer lived here. They came as a folklore group to sell something of their former glory and make use of their decaying animal skins, which they had inherited. It was more sad than anything else, like a memorial celebration of a lost culture and its rituals.

The next day we covered almost a thousand kilometers (Timoteus and I took turns driving). Outside Chicago, we were hit by a blizzard, and we could see only a few meters ahead of us. I happened to be driving just then, and I knew we should pull over, but I stubbornly wanted to get as far as we could, all the way to Ann Arbor, if possible. The highway was becoming more and more snowbound, and at one point, as I was passing an enormous truck, I was blinded by snow kicked up by its wheels. Fearing I would steer the car under the truck, I veered too much in the opposite direction, and we drove into a snowdrift in a ditch.

The driver of the truck stopped and jumped out. I got out as well. An icy wind lashed my eyes and face. The driver looked over our snowbound automobile and said he wouldn't be able to help, but he offered to drive one of us to the nearest gas station or repair shop.

Timoteus got in with him, and I returned to our car, completely frozen after those few minutes outside. Fortunately, I'd left the engine running, and the heater was on. I can't imagine what would have happened to us had the engine died. Timoteus's wife—usually quiet and nearly silent—now burst into a paroxysm of hysteria and started screaming that she shouldn't have gone anywhere; she shouldn't have come to America, let alone on this trip. We were going to die here with the children, and no one would come to our rescue.

On one account she was mistaken. As for the other, over the course of the next fifteen minutes, several cars halted to see if anyone was hurt or if we needed assistance. One driver even went to the edge of the freeway, in this dreadful storm, took a rope from his trunk, and, though I told him a friend had already gone for help, tried to pull us out. To no avail, of course.

While the children were enjoying our shipwreck and Timoteus's wife was sobbing, I kept revving the engine to keep it going. After about half an hour, a tow truck arrived with Timoteus in the passenger's seat, and a minute later, we were back on the road unscathed. We saw that we'd gotten stuck about a hundred meters from a small motel where we could spend the night.

The next day around noon, we safely stepped out of the car in front of our transient home overlooking the cemetery.

I realized that during our entire two-week trip, including a several-hour illegal stay in Mexico, we hadn't had to show anyone our identity cards.

⁂

The sense of freedom in this country was strong. I could say anything I wanted in public or in my lectures; I could go wherever I wanted, and if I was just a little frugal, I could acquire anything I wanted. At the same time, I couldn't rid myself of the feeling that the whole thing was inappropriate. I was enjoying freedom and prosperity I didn't deserve, whereas I was needed at home, where one had to somehow fight for everything.

I started subscribing to a newspaper with the paradoxical name *Lidová demokracie* (People's Democracy). The department also received the Communist Party paper, *Rudé právo*. This was not encouraging reading. It appeared that everything was returning to the way it had been before the Prague Spring, and because it is impossible to go back in history, I assumed that everything would naturally be much worse than when I'd left a few months ago.

I also saw that the Chamber Theater, which had staged my *Jury*, had removed the play from its repertory even though, I knew, the performances had been sold out.

In my correspondence with friends and family, I was trying to find out something more, but their answers were either evasive or ambiguous because they knew they had to be careful.

After the trip to Texas, I found a letter from our embassy informing me that as a result of new decrees concerning the residence of Czechoslovak citizens in capitalist countries, our exit permit would be revoked on December 31, and we would have to depart the United States as quickly as possible and return to Czechoslovakia. I immediately wrote back asking for an extension because I was teaching at the university until the end of the spring semester.

I also called my parents (they had stayed in Switzerland only a few months; my mother refused to live abroad). First, I mentioned our trip to Texas and then I started to complain about the authorities who were apparently forbidding me to conclude my teaching duties.

Father said with unexpected earnestness: It's good that you're getting to know everything you can there. You must realize that this will be your last opportunity for a long time to travel and teach.

When I considered that he was aware the telephones were bugged, it sounded as if he was telling me not to return, that prison awaited me or, I hoped, he meant just some sort of moderate form of persecution.

The thought of emigrating frightened me. I didn't sleep properly for several days, and I kept going over different scenarios.

When I confided everything to Professor Matějka, he consoled me by saying I could take a librarian's course and work in the library. I would make enough money to be able to live here decently. Professor Benešová called me from Bloomington, where I had recently lectured. She'd heard that I wouldn't be able to go back to Prague and informed me she would be retiring and had spoken with the dean. She assured me I could work as a regular professor there in Indiana.

All of this consoling news was alarming—for me, the only meaningful work was writing, telling stories that were somehow connected to my life, and this was interwoven with my homeland. The thought of writing in a foreign country about things that deeply touched me but with which I had cut off all ties seemed foolish. To teach modern Czech literature, which I'd just abandoned, would definitely be a painful blow. I would forever be aware that I had voluntarily decided to call it quits with the only work I cared about.

One day, my students came to see me and very politely, almost humbly, asked for a favor. They were planning a trip to Washington to protest the Vietnam War, and the demonstration was scheduled for a day we had class. Would I be so kind as to reschedule it for another day?

Of course, I was glad to. They had rented a bus, and it occurred to me that Helena could go with them and find out at the embassy if, despite the new decrees, we could extend our stay, at least until the end of the spring semester. For several years, my wife reproached me that I had sent her instead of going myself. But I thought that if I were to show up, the embassy would be afraid to deal with me at all.

Two days later, the students returned. The demonstration had been excellent and, unlike that of a year ago, peaceful. Helena told me that after long deliberations, the embassy had agreed to extend our stay until the end of March.

I told the department that I would evidently have to cut short the semester because our offices refused to extend our visa, but I said I would do everything possible not to cheat my students out of anything I thought they should know. I don't think anyone took my news very seriously. I wasn't about to return to an occupied country whose authorities assumed the right to decide how long their citizens could stay abroad, was I?

I received a letter from my parents saying that they were looking forward to all of us being together again. Father had intended no hidden meaning in his assertions concerning my last possibility to travel. He was merely pointing out that as soon as I returned, I wouldn't be allowed to leave. Even without Father's warning, I knew this much from the newspapers.

I was relieved nonetheless. I was going home. I didn't know what I would do, since our newspaper had been banned. Obviously they weren't going to let me publish, but perhaps they could let me continue working at the publishing house as a copyreader. Helena hadn't once considered emigration. She had her parents and sister at home, and she was certainly not going to abandon them. As far as the children were concerned, they considered it obvious that their real home was Prague, and they too looked forward to seeing their grandmother, grandfather, and friends.

Before long it was time to start thinking about saying goodbye. I invited all my students over. Everyone came bearing gifts and promises to come visit (almost every one of them came to Prague, two of them even for an entire year). We drank wine and bourbon, and then the students pulled out bags of marijuana and rolled joints, which they passed from person to person.

The chair of the department also organized a farewell party. He invited the members of the department as well as Mrs. Cisney, who had directed my *Castle* a year ago.

I remember that almost everyone expressed surprise that we had decided to go back to an unfree country; some even tried to talk me out of it. The director, who had the most experience with Soviet friendship, foretold that I would end up in a concentration camp in Siberia. She even knelt down before me (she had a theatrical sense of effect, but I'm convinced she was serious) and begged me to change my mind and not to go back to that concentration camp of a country.

They treated me very generously at the department and paid me for the next two months. Even our landlord returned our deposit, something he had a full right to keep because we'd broken the rental agreement. And we sold our Impala at the used-car lot. Besides the trip to the Mexican border, we'd driven to New York, Chicago, and several other places I don't recall. Despite the mileage, I was offered seven hundred dollars. My former compatriot Zizala really did give me a special *férst reyt prais.*

In the last issue of *Rudé právo* that I read on the American continent, there was invective directed at the former chair of the Writers' Union, Eduard Goldstücker:

> The first thing he did in this capacity was to try to reinstate the membership of those who had been justifiably expelled from the party: A. J. Liehm, L. Vaculík, and I. Klíma. . . . It is interesting that even as recently as 1967, E. Goldstücker was trying to distance himself from these people. Less that a year later, when their opinions and activities were openly directed against the party, he is once again taking them under his patronage and creating conditions for further detrimental exploits.

Finally I called my aunt Ilonka and Josef Škvorecký in Toronto to inform them I was returning to Prague. My aunt admitted it was my decision; I knew what was happening in Prague better than she did. Father had returned from Switzerland, even though she had tried to talk him out of it. Perhaps we knew best what we were doing. My colleague Škvorecký asked me to pass on his regards to all his friends. He still wanted to finish the semester, and then he would go back too. (He didn't return for a visit until twenty years later.)

As we were leaving for the airport, I felt a strange mixture of uncertainty, fear, and relief.

Essay: *Life in Subjugation,* p. 507

16

Surprisingly, we were allowed to walk through customs at the Prague airport without any inspection and thus were able to bring in the dollars we had saved, of which I carried some in my wallet and some, without a great amount of ingenuity, stuck between the pages of *The History of Czech Literature*.

Our apartment had been cleaned and aired out. My considerate mother-in-law had even prepared food for us and placed it in the refrigerator. On my desk lay a pile of letters and a recent newspaper.

I was home. I didn't know what I was going to do—today, tomorrow, or next week.

I telephoned various friends. Most welcomed me home, but a few were taken aback to hear that I was calling from Prague. Their news about the current situation was depressing. A great many people who had worked in film, radio, television, or publishing or taught college or even high school had lost their jobs. The shooting of several films had been interrupted indefinitely, and others that were ready for release could not be shown. Our books had been removed from all bookstores, and newspapers were forbidden to publish any articles by those who were on a secret list of "flawed" writers. Who was on the list? Almost everyone. I also discovered that a meeting of the central committee of the Writers' Union was to take place, and I was expected. Apparently, it would be the last meeting.

From the telephone booth on the corner of our street, I called Olga and told her I was back in Prague.

"Klímka," she said, "you can't be serious! Have you gone insane?" She then added: "No, you're still over there. For me, you left and remained there."

⸺◦⸺

> I was waiting for the tram in front of the Mánes Gallery. Two boys
> and two girls were sitting on the sidewalk; all were wearing jeans
> and tennis shoes, and the boys were as hairy as forest people. One
> of them got up and walked over to me.
> Him: My friend, what sort of problems are you having?
> Me: The tram isn't running.
> Him: You don't have any other problems?
> Me: Not right now.
> Him: Strange. You're not suffering?
> Me: No more than anyone else.
> Him: In that case, I can't help you. Keep waiting for the tram. It
> might never come.
>
> From my diary, January 1970

⸺◦⸺

I was received with astonishment at the writers' meeting. To them, I seemed like an extraterrestrial standing right before their eyes. Then Jaroslav Seifert, who was chairing the meeting, welcomed me home. I think he was touched that at least one of his colleagues had decided to return from the free part of the world to our present misery. After the meeting, I went to see my former colleagues at the publishing house and learned that the entire print run of my last book of short stories had been confiscated and pulped. I asked if I could work for them as a freelance copyreader. They promised to look into it and during my next visit informed me that it was out of the question. Then I was asked, almost in a whisper, not to come back. The new director ordered everyone to tell me my visits were not welcome. Since I could no longer publish, the director would have to explain my visits not as work related but as social calls from someone who has shown himself to be an enemy of socialism. I soon learned that people who, in the eyes of the occupying power, committed an offense through their recent activities had no chance of securing any sort of professional work.

I overheard that acts of revenge were taking place in the Communist Party. Screening committees composed of the most obdurate and unrepentant opponents of the recent reforms were now deciding the fates of the other party members. These members were required to reject all attempts at reform and, most important, to express their support of the occupation, which now, in Communist newspeak, was referred to as brotherly assistance in the defense of socialism. Whoever did not agree with the occupation was either cast out of the party or crossed out. Being crossed out was somewhat better than being cast out. Everyone who was cast out was relieved of his job, and his entire family was subjected to persecution. The only encouraging thing was that even under these circumstances, there were plenty of those who refused to accept these degrading requirements. As one may assume, hundreds of thousands were cast and crossed out.

Our Writers' Union was once again banned and, just as after the February coup, a new one was being organized. It did not matter if someone wrote a good book; what was important was the author's stance toward Soviet occupation. Nevertheless, it took a while for what Communist newspeak referred to as normalization to solidify. Helena could still return to her job at the Sociological Institute (the fact that she'd never been a member of the party and therefore could be neither cast out nor expunged became, at least for a short time, an advantage). The institute, however, had not counted on her return and so did not even list her name as among the team. It took her in on a temporary basis.

To let us know it hadn't forgotten about us, the Department of Passports and Visas summoned Helena and me to appear with our passports. A government official took the passports, looked them over to make sure they were ours, and kept them.

As my colleagues in Ann Arbor had warned, the gates of the camp called Czechoslovakia were closing behind us.

⸎

Pavel Kohout was trying to legally publish our writings abroad. He found a man in Switzerland willing to do everything he could to help banned Czech authors. Jürgen Braunschweiger worked in the Bucher publishing house and prepared contracts for seven of us: Jiří Gruša, Alexandr Kliment, Pavel Kohout, Eda Kriseová, Jiří Šotola, Ludvík Vaculík, and myself. The Dilia literary agency executed the contracts and acceded to the important point that Swiss law would govern any dispute.

Jürgen came to Prague (shortly thereafter he was not allowed to travel to the republic), signed the contracts, invited us to dinner, and asked us to provide him with more manuscripts soon. He promised to publish my collection of stories, *My First Loves*, immediately and even my plays; he also pointed out that plays and short stories did not sell well, and so I should write a novel.

Eric Spiess, of the German publishing house Bärenreiter, also came to Prague to represent Pavel Kohout and myself. Unlike Jürgen, who was bulky, cheerful, and bursting with optimism, Eric gave the impression of an ascetic. He was always broody and pensive—even skeptical. He said my plays were being staged quite successfully. Some had made it all the way to New Zealand in radio adaptations. As far as the stage productions were concerned, the one-act plays were usually performed on the smaller stages, but he was convinced that my royalties would allow me to support myself. Unless, of course, our government did not compel me to forbid the production of my plays abroad or even worse.

I asked if he'd heard that something was in the works.

No, but he added that he could imagine it happening. He was already over forty and remembered the history of his own country; anything could happen when the riffraff took power. Besides, he knew as well as I did what had happened to Boris Pasternak when his *Doctor*

Zhivago was banned in Russia and he undertook to have it published in Italy. And Andrei Sinyavsky and Yuli Daniel had been sentenced to prison for the same thing not so long ago.

I still retained some of that American optimism and energy. Certainly the money I had saved while in America contributed to this feeling; my material cares were, for the time being, taken care of. I recalled the parties in Ann Arbor, where everyone ate, drank, chatted, listened to the latest records of Iron Butterfly, Joan Baez, Bob Dylan, and Cream, and maybe even smoked some pot. This gave me the idea that my friends and I could organize something similar perhaps once a month. And to give these gatherings greater meaning, someone could read a piece he'd just written.

My friends took to the idea. Although it was a small gathering of a few friends, it was a chance to bring our writing out into the open. We agreed not to mention our get-togethers to anyone and would invite only those we trusted. Our parties took place for over a year without drawing the attention of the omniscient secret police.

Once Ludvík Vaculík brought a little-known author from Ostrava, Ota Filip, who had recently been released from prison. He'd been arrested for writing and distributing some leaflets. Soon a television show was broadcast in which Filip discussed our meetings. (My friends had to tell me about it because I refused to own an apparatus that was at liberty to transmit only programs approved by the censors.) The newly hired television reporters were trying to demonstrate their industriousness by airing photographs of guests arriving at my home. The images supplemented the claim that representatives of the defeated right-wing and counterrevolutionary forces were continuing their activities.

The likelihood that from then on our meetings would be observed carefully and everyone who visited assiduously noted down was discouraging, to say the least. We decided discontinue our readings.

I was banned from the Writers' Union. I didn't have a job, so the only way I could spend my time was reading and writing. (However, they hadn't forbidden me to play tennis, so about once a week I played with my brother—he had also come back from England—on one of the courts near the math and physics department where he, by contrast, was still allowed to teach.)

Until then I'd written mainly stage plays. Even though I'd never worked with any theater, I realized that writing without the possibility of seeing even at least one of my plays performed—that is, without being able to see how the actors played their roles or the audience's response—wouldn't be very satisfying. Furthermore, my publisher in Switzerland kept asking me to send him a novel.

I was forty years old and had written one novel, but it had been based on a screenplay that I'd reworked several times with a screenwriter. I didn't have a good subject to write about—I didn't want to return to the war, and I didn't want to write about what I was currently going through because it was too depressing and ridiculous, and, as critics usually point out when they notice an author hasn't dealt successfully with a contemporary subject, I lacked a certain distance from current events.

I wrote several short stories based on dreams. The longest story relied on a dream from about ten years earlier. I was trying to board a train which, to my horror, was transporting a group of lepers. Meanwhile the train had started moving, and in a panic I jumped from the steps and injured myself. When I asked around to learn the details of the strange train, no one knew what I was talking about—or, more precisely, no one wanted to know. The image of lepers being secretly transported struck me as an excellent metaphor for a world in which hundreds of thousands of the rejected disappear behind the wire fences of camps.

I reworked the story at least five times and so thoroughly that the shortest version was 10 pages and the longest 120.

I also started to write a love story: about an older, somewhat starchy and prudish scholar and a young actress studying puppetry.

I wasn't seeing Olga anymore, but what we experienced together stayed with me.

The story consumed me. When I took my family on vacation to a village in the Bohemian-Moravian Highlands (we couldn't afford to stay in a hotel or even rent a cottage somewhere in the countryside), all four of us lived in a cubbyhole with small windows and only one chair. When the children went out to play, I pulled out my papers, pencil, and suitcase, which I used as a desk, and continued writing.

The heroine had many of Olga's traits. I could almost hear her voice talking about the topics that obsessed her: Italy, the heat, the often bizarre stories she told about herself, her desire to have a villa somewhere in Italy, making love with passionate boys, living life to the full in the present moment. But I was afraid to make it too personal, so I invented most of the situations, characters, and dialogue. Besides, inventing is always more fun, and made-up conversations and events always sound more realistic than a transcription of what actually happened.

This novel, which I gave the somewhat mawkish title *A Summer Affair*, was the first of my novels translated into foreign languages and was even filmed in Sweden.

———— ∞ ————

The fact that our plays were being performed, and our books, and sometimes articles, were being published abroad, irritated our government. When they learned that everything was executed according to valid contracts, which could not be abrogated without our consent, they decided they would deprive us of our royalties (torture or crude physical coercion was no longer used).

At this time, banks exchanged foreign currency (possession of foreign currency was a crime) at a ridiculously low rate. Therefore, anyone who received foreign currency at the bank could request payment in so-called Tuzex vouchers. They were used in special Tuzex stores where the price of goods was about a fifth of that in normal shops that used crowns. Because Tuzex stores frequently offered otherwise unavailable imported goods (such as foreign automobiles, liquor, cigarettes, cosmetics, and clothing), it was possible to sell the vouchers on the black market for their actual value, one Tuzex crown for five Czechoslovak. The official exchange rate was around seven crowns to the dollar; thus one dollar had the value of thirty-five normal crowns.

At the beginning of 1972, the Ministry of Finance banned the only bank authorized to exchange hard currency for Tuzex crowns for foreign editions of works of an *antistate or antisocialist character and for works of authors whose distribution in the ČSSR is forbidden.*

The bank received (probably from the Ministry of Culture) a list of writers who were not allowed to receive their royalties in Tuzex crowns. We received only one-fifth of the amount we actually earned. But even this measure was not sufficient. Besides normal taxes, a special contribution for the Literary Fund was taken from all royalties. This was 2 percent. For banned works, the contribution was increased to 40 percent. When their attorneys pointed out that this directive was illegal and could be deemed overt persecution, the "normalizers" thought up something else. A ministry (it's not important which ministry because the secretariat of the Communist Party created similar stunts) issued an injunction according to which all payees (there were thousands of them because 2 percent was also taken off every newspaper or specialized article) had their contribution increased to 40 percent. At the same time, this special fee was reduced to 2 percent for everyone except those on the "blacklist."

The result was the same but less assailable because leniency, or relief, could be granted, but it didn't have to be. In total, we were deprived of 90 percent of our earnings. Instead of accepting this state of affairs, we asked our publishers and agencies to stop sending us royalties or, if they did send any, we refused to accept them and asked that they be returned to the sender.

From then on, our publishers and agencies would come to see us and present our money in person, and if the officials refused them a visa, they could always find messengers. Because the state needed hard currency so badly that it allowed it to be exchanged anonymously, we could then use our hard currency like any other citizen. In the end, these exemplary models of persecution had a single result: The government was deprived of any way of keeping track of our royalties.

⸺⧉⸺

A former colleague at *Květy* informed me that it was a guaranteed truth (like most guaranteed truths, it was false) that if we didn't get a job, we would be accused of parasitism and would lose our claim to retirement pay. Most of my colleagues who had been forbidden to publish landed jobs elsewhere. Saša Kliment was a doorman at a hotel; the former editor in chief of *Literární noviny*, Milan Jungmann, was washing windows; one of my university professors was helping build the metro; some of my friends got work in water resources. This last job was considered the most advantageous for philosophers and historians. They were usually housed in a trailer somewhere in the middle of a field, and they had only one duty: Every three or four hours, both day and night, they were to measure the copiousness of the stream. They were supposed to alternate in three shifts, but usually only two of them worked, sometimes one. So the others were free to focus on projects for which they were more qualified.

My wife and I still had enough money for subsistence. If accused of parasitism, I could, in the worst case, go sweep the streets, but in the dark recesses of my mind I recalled something from a lecture on Russian literature about Russian populists of the 1870s going out among the people. I dimly recollected that Maxim Gorky—whom I considered a good writer after I'd read some of his short stories—had recommended this to young authors. If I had to go to work, I would get to know a new environment and perhaps happen upon a good subject.

Just then Helena and I were invited to the home of our foremost pediatrician, Dr. Josef Švejcar. During the visit, I mentioned that I would have to find some sort of employment to avoid any trouble with the authorities, but I wanted a job that required absolutely no qualifications. Could he find something for me in the hospital?

The professor was naturally surprised, and when I explained that I wouldn't be accepted anyplace else, he told me there were jobs at the hospital for orderlies, cleaners, maybe some work in the kitchen, but those positions were so badly paid that no one stayed for long. If I really wanted something like that, he would let me know when there was an opening.

The next day someone called to inform me that an orderly position was available.

<hr />

At the personnel department, I had to fill out all sorts of questionnaires. As my last job and place of employment, I wrote: professor in the Slavic department of the University of Michigan, Ann Arbor, and gleefully imagined them writing to the university for my political profile.

The personnel woman saw that I was asking for only part-time work and sent me for a medical examination.

The following Tuesday I reported to the nurse on duty. She'd apparently been given preliminary information and didn't ask me anything, just told me my responsibilities. There were not many. In the morning I was to take the trash out to the furnace and burn everything, deliver containers of blood and urine samples to the laboratory, pick up the daily allotment of medicine from the pharmacy; in case of an emergency, I was to hurry immediately to the laboratory or the pharmacy. According to what was needed, I was to ferry patients in their wheelchairs to other exams or transfer them to another ward. Of course, I was to be available during the entire time of my shift.

I could have a twelve-hour shift, which, at part time, would be two days a week. Then the nurse showed me the orderlies' room where I could stay if I didn't have any work, even though, she was required to inform me, it was disallowed during work hours.

Thus I once again fell into the labor force, which is what such activity is called in a Socialist country. Each workday, as I soon learned, was divided into two parts of equal length. During the first, work took place; during the second, everyone pretended that work took place. Everyone simply killed time.

Socialist health care was free, and looked like it. In the morning, shortly before six o'clock, the merry-go-round of duties began for the nurses and orderlies. The ill were mercilessly awakened to have their temperature taken and their beds made up. Then the cleaning women burst in, and the nurses distributed medication and took blood and urine samples. Then came the doctors' visits. In the meantime, I would take the trash out to the incinerator. Besides ordinary refuse, the trash contained, as is usual for a hospital, medicine packaging and lots of bloody bandages, broken casts, and, every now and then, a finger or an amputated leg, but I never had to remove any human limbs. I also often helped change the elderly who couldn't control their bowels. Then I completed the rest of my duties and around ten o'clock went back to the orderlies' room, pulled out a book, and devoted myself to reading. In the afternoon, there was practically nothing in the ward that required my attention. In a short time I read three volumes of Chekhov's short stories (well suited for this place), a pocket edition of Kafka's *Amerika*, Kierkegaard in the same format, and the memoirs of Stalin's daughter, Svetlana Alliluyeva, in an English translation.

After their rounds, the nurses also gathered in a room that served as the medicine disposal site and as a room for the deceased. The nurses smoked, drank coffee, and chatted. If I ever joined them, they would ask me why I was there. If a patient kept buzzing, trying to get their attention, they would usually wait for him to stop; if he didn't, one of them would go see what was the matter and then come back to continue their amusements. The pay corresponded to our essentially part-time work. Even had I been working full time, I'd never be able to support my family, let alone drive to work, which I did once when it was pouring rain and another time when I'd overslept.

A hospital is, of course, a place where people die. If a patient died during my shift, one of my duties was to transport the body to the morgue after an hour had passed (all the patients who died had to remain in the ward for at least an hour, probably in case they woke up—something that never happened during the three months I was there). If he died during the afternoon or night shift, an orderly specially entrusted with carting away the dead from the various hospital wards would come for him. If someone died toward the end of a shift, the nurses would hold on to the body for a bit and save "their" orderly from the unpleasant journey to that gloomy place containing refrigerators filled with the deceased. During my three months as an orderly, I had to go to the morgue only once.

I didn't get very close to the other orderlies; only one of them had been doing this work for more than two years. He was a powerfully built man who worked in surgery, that is, during operations, where he brought the patients and then afterward transported them back to the intensive care unit. Because he actually did support himself with this job, he worked thirty-two-hour shifts, which were not difficult because most of the time he could sleep. My other colleague was a gangly asthenic with the movements and thoughts of a felon. If I overheard correctly, he had come here immediately after being released from prison. Both men were distinctive, and since I had decided to follow Gorky's advice to go among the people, I tried to take firsthand notes as much as I could.

Directly across from the orderlies' room was the intensive care unit where, of course, the work was much more accountable, and the best nurses worked there. One of them was Soňa, and sometimes when she stepped out to have a smoke, we chatted a bit. She didn't strike me as belonging to this environment; although it was certainly not professional, she always shared some of her patients' pain. Once during a downpour, I drove her home to Kobylisy. Then I sat for more than an hour in her little room. She put on a piano concert by Paderewski and then told me the story of her life. She'd been in love with a doctor and fled with him to Germany after the Soviet occupation. She had come back, but he had stayed and told her that she would join him in Germany when he obtained a job. Perhaps they would have allowed her to go, but even if they didn't, at least she would have known that some higher power had kept her from her great love. But she never heard from him again, and now she was alone, living with her father and a stepmother who hated her.

She started asking about my writing and wanted to know if I'd write about things that were not supposed to be written or talked about. I assured her that if I thought there was something that needed to be discussed, I would not remain silent. The difficulty was that I wasn't allowed to publish a line. She was surprised and almost in a whisper confided to me—I was sworn to secrecy (and I couldn't mention her name if I wrote about it)—that upstairs, when they received a patient they assumed wouldn't make it, they mixed a special cocktail of barbiturates. No one ever woke up afterward. "While down below," she concluded, "we fuss to keep them from the worst."

I wanted to know if this sort of thing happened often. She refused to say anything more on the subject but added that it took place without the knowledge of the doctors.

I realized that this was a Socialist version of euthanasia—it was done in the interests not of the suffering patient but of those who were assigned to him and who, at least according to the letter of the law, ruled the country.

During my three-month stint as an orderly, I never harmed anyone, and I never accepted a single crown from a patient. However, one day I was transferring an ailing old woman to another ward (I knew she was being sent there to die), and while we were waiting for an examination, she asked if I would hold her hand. I took it—holding her cold, wasted, shaking hand was disagreeable. When we moved on, she tried to force a ten-crown piece on me and begged me to come see her in the ward because she didn't have anyone left in the world. I didn't take the money, but even today I am ashamed that I didn't go and hold her hand. I only hope that some higher justice does not exact retribution when my turn comes.

No totalitarian regime can persist if it provides people with basic free-doms. There are always individuals or groups who attempt to acquire these freedoms, but the regime, no matter how charitable it pretends to be, can never debate with them; it cannot answer questions or criticisms. It must silence them and thereby instill fear in others who might be tempted to raise criticisms.

The occupying regime in our country could not behave otherwise. As I've noted, the first arrests and subsequent trials took place when I was teaching in Ann Arbor.

In our group of authors, whose works had been banned with particular thoroughness, it was Pavel Kohout who refused to accept the current state of affairs. Without overstepping any laws, he offered the occupying powers the opportunity to show their true character.

And so just before Christmas of 1972, Kohout put together a petition to send to the president of the republic, General Svoboda. The petition expressed a reasonable and in no way antigovernment request that the president provide amnesty to political prisoners (there were more and more of them every year) or at the very least issue a directive allowing them to spend the Christmas holidays at home. *Although the views of the undersigned differ widely on various fundamental questions,* read the petition, *we agree that magnanimity regarding political prisoners cannot in any way threaten the authority and capacity of the state's power; quite the opposite, it will testify to its humanism.*

We rewrote the text several times and then divided up into pairs to go collect the signatures of other writers (both legal and banned).

I was supposed to enter the hospital in a few days to undergo an operation on my gallbladder, but I didn't see this as a reason to avoid these activities. Ludvík and I agreed on the text of the petition and then visited several writers. Some of them signed; others refused with a bit of embar-rassment (because most of them are dead, I will not give their names).

The following day I was called for, and my first involuntary "visit" took place at Bartolomějská Street, secret police headquarters. As soon as I came home, I carefully wrote down what had happened at the interrogation:

They took me up to the third floor and down several hallways to a small office. They allowed me to take off my coat and then hung it (fortunately not me) up.

A large man around fifty years old, who vividly reminded me of Vítěslav Nezval, was sitting behind a table. Off to the side sat a lanky blond fellow. The man behind the table told me to sit down and prattled on that I was there according to paragraph such and such and then asked his first question.

"What do you know about the meeting of the PEN Club in Berlin?"

The question surprised me. I said truthfully I didn't know anything.

"Do you know what the PEN Club is?"

"Yes. An international organization of writers. I am a member."

"Do you know who the chair is?"

"Heinrich Böll."

Only later did I come to understand that the first questions are always supposed to appear innocent and that refusing to answer them would seem ridiculous and even indecent. But as soon as a person acknowledges something other than that these questions are, just like the entire interrogation itself, indecent, he acknowledges his position as the interrogated.

"So you're a member of the PEN Club! And as a member, you didn't even know there was a meeting?"

I tried to explain: "None of us were informed. I happened to overhear it from a German broadcast." (That was a senselessly accommodating answer to a question that hadn't been asked.)

"And what did you hear in this broadcast?"

"Nothing. That the meeting was taking place in Berlin."

"What was discussed at the meeting?"

"I have no idea."

"So you don't know that a special group of writers in exile was formed to assist persecuted writers?"

I answered again truthfully that I didn't.

Nezval looked surprised and with exaggerated irony declared, "So, despite being a member, you don't know. Do you at least know who was elected its head?"

I had no idea.

"Pavel Tigrid!" (He got up and started pacing behind the table to emphasize that his own loathsomeness excited him.) "Did you know that a resolution was passed with regard to Czech political prisoners and sent to Comrades Husák and Indra?"

"How would I know that?"

"What do you know about a letter sent to the president of the republic?"

"What letter?" I asked to stall for time.

"But you signed a letter to the president of the republic!"

I hesitated for a moment, and he picked up a piece of paper from the table and waved it in front of me.

"I did," I admitted.

"What kind of letter was it?"

"It was a letter requesting amnesty for political prisoners."

"Who else signed this letter?"

"I don't remember!"

"So, you don't remember?" He was starting to shout. "Who brought you this letter?"

I finally managed to bring myself to protest. "Look, I don't actually know why I'm here. Nothing is being taken down—and that letter was absolutely legal according to the law concerning petitions. So I will not give evidence about it."

The blond fellow noted ironically, "Law concerning petitions! What's that?"

"It's guaranteed in our constitution—everyone has the right to appeal to the representatives of the country with requests and complaints," I explained. "We learned that in school."

"Yes, such a law does exist," admitted Nezval. "But doesn't it seem to you, after I told you about the meeting of the PEN Club, that your petition seems to be something else?"

"No!"

"They drew up a resolution, and you hurried to sign it."

"But I told you I didn't know anything about that meeting."

"Perhaps not you, but we know the petition was prepared there."

As if we couldn't come up with things like this ourselves. "I don't believe it," I announced.

"You are either naive or at least pretending to be. We know who prepared the petition, we have proof. Who came to you with the resolution?"

I repeated that I had no intention of giving a statement concerning a letter to the president authorized by law.

"Then you won't talk about it, since you think there's nothing wrong with it?"

"That's precisely why."

"But we see it differently. We will prove that all this was not so naive. Why did you sign this letter?"

"I myself have been locked up. I could imagine what those people are going through, and I felt sorry for them." I was trying to play on their feelings, as if I thought they had any.

"When were you locked up?"

"During the war."

"During the war, innocent people were sentenced. Do you think innocent people are sentenced in our country?" asked Nezval threateningly.

"We were asking for amnesty. This has nothing to do with guilt."

"So you were asking for amnesty for people who you admit have committed a crime."

I said I had nothing to say to that.

"Do you have children?"

I acknowledged that I did.

"You have a daughter and a son?"

"Yes."

"Imagine your daughter is walking home from school, and a drunk driver runs her over. He's sent to prison. Would you also seek amnesty for him?"

"But he wouldn't be a political prisoner," I objected.

"Besides, what you're requesting in your petition, some sort of Christmas vacation, where did you ever hear about prisoners going home for Christmas?"

"In Sweden, prisoners are let out on Sunday, for example."

"Fine, I'm not saying our laws don't allow for such cases. If a fellow's in the lockup because he got drunk and got in a fight and then behaved well, let him go home for Christmas, but those who are there according to Chapter One are enemies. Do you understand? They won't be released even a day early. So, who came to see you with this letter? Vaculík or Havel?"

I said nothing.

"Let me tell you something. You should hear what people working in factories think; you should know what the public's opinion is. They write to us and demand that we finally deal once and for all with our enemies."

"But I think the people . . ."

The blond got up behind me and interrupted: "Do you mean to say you know a different public opinion?"

"I'm sort of interested in it because of what I write. Public opinion does not always have to be entirely one-sided."

"So you're writing something. For the desk drawer or for somebody else?"

"I write for myself."

"Have you written anything lately?"

"I've written a novel. A love story." (Once again, owing to inexperience, I jabbered too much about things they didn't ask and perhaps even didn't know.)

"And what's going to happen to it? Is this one for the desk drawer? Or is anyone publishing it?"

"It will be published in Switzerland."

"So you do have outside contacts, after all, since you sent them your novel."

"I sent it by mail."

"Do you have connections with a publisher or not?"

"I acted in accordance with a contract."

"What sort of contract?"

"Dilia has been shut down here. It's an official literary agency," I added.

The blond behind me spoke up, as if very well informed: "Yes, you have a contract with a Swiss publisher and according to Swiss law. It's interesting that you, a Czechoslovak citizen, have a contract based on Swiss law."

"Lawyers from Dilia secured the contract."

"How much are the Swiss paying you?"

"Whatever they pay authors all over the world."

"We're interested in how much you're getting."

I started to realize the absurdity of this line of questioning. They forbid me to publish, try to deprive me of all my money, and then reproach me for publishing a book somewhere. "I don't know. Ask someone from Dilia."

"You're getting enough to live on. At least for now. Does your wife work?" The blond was getting worked up.

"Yes."

"Where?"

"I don't know."

"Come on, you're trying to tell me you don't know where your own wife works?"

"Even if I did, I don't have to tell you anything. I don't think that's why you called me in here."

Nezval once again joined in: "Yes, it seems we've gotten a little off track." He was shouting again. "Now, for the last time, tell us who came to see you with this piece of paper. Was it Vaculík? Havel? Kliment?"

I remained silent.

"What were you talking with Kliment about yesterday? You think we don't know you were at his place?"

"I don't remember."

"What don't you remember?"

I said nothing.

"You were elaborating—what were you talking about?"

"I don't remember exactly."

"You really do have a bad memory."

The blond: "Isn't it instead, Mr. Klíma, that you don't want to remember? Who else signed this letter?"

"I don't know."

"Did you sign the first or the second page?"

"The second, I think."

"And whose signature was above yours?"

"I don't know. I didn't notice."

"Let me help you. Adolf Hoffmeister signed on the first page with a felt-tip pen. Do you remember?"

"No, not at all."

"Where were you last employed?" I didn't understand why they were suddenly changing the subject, but I answered nevertheless. "I taught at a university in America."

"Fine, fine, but here."

"For three months I worked as an orderly."

"So who came to see you: Kohout? Vaculík?"

They were angry; Nezval was shouting. But it was clear they had no idea that I was one of those who had had been collecting signatures. The informer knew only about Vaculík. I remained silent.

Then another agent entered the room, apparently a superior because Nezval reported to him: "Mr. Klíma has decided not to tell us anything." The new arrival merely said at the door, "You are naive, Mr. Klíma; your friends Vaculík, Kliment, and Havel have already told us everything anyway. They'll be laughing at you later. And what are you so worried about? It was all within the law, wasn't it? You assumed well enough that we wouldn't lock you up for it." He must have given a signal to release me because Nezval then said, "Since you're not going to tell us much, we'll bring this to an end in order to detain neither you nor ourselves."

He called in a typist. When she'd taken her seat behind the typewriter, Nezval leaned over to me and, with feigned friendship, suggested, "You know what? Dictate it yourself. How did this letter come to you, who came to see you?"

I must have looked astonished because he immediately added, "We won't even put your name down, if you don't want us to."

He finally dictated several meaningless sentences with the concluding formula: "I have read everything and agree."

Thirty-four writers had signed the letter before the secret police found out about it. Several more signed after Vaculík was arrested with the text in his possession.

Essay: *Occupation, Collaboration, and Intellectual Riffraff,* p. 511

17

At the beginning of the 1970s, the foremost international, especially American, writers started coming to Prague (the Czech government was still graciously granting them visas).

One of the first to arrive was Arthur Miller, at that time, along with Dürrenmatt and Beckett, one of the most famous living dramatists, and a recent president of the PEN Club. Miller traveled to Prague as a private citizen and, to the dismay of the official Writers' Union, was interested in meeting with only proscribed authors.

I first met him in the Alcron hotel, showed him around Prague, and the following afternoon invited him and several of my friends to our apartment in Hodkovičky.

Before our guests arrived, two black Tatra 603s parked around the corner of our street. I went over to one of the cars and asked the driver if he was looking for anyone.

He told me not to worry about it and rolled up the window. His physiognomy told me more about him than if he'd presented his service card.

That evening, we spoke uninhibitedly with our celebrated colleague about what had befallen Czech culture as well as all of the intelligentsia.

We were probably being monitored, but it was all the same to us.

I think Miller was trying to encourage us when he shared his experiences with McCarthyism; U.S. publishers had refused to publish his book, and films based on his screenplays had to be shot in Europe. But after a few years, all the nonsense about un-American activities had

come to naught. Then he told us a story from the time he was chair of
the PEN Club. He had been invited by a Soviet-American commission
to speak on the significance of freedom for scientific research. In his
speech, he criticized the lack of freedom of expression in the Soviet
Union and the fact that several outstanding Soviet researchers were not
allowed to publish. At this, a Soviet professor, a world-famous specialist
in cancer treatment, spoke up. He was offended by Miller's assertions
and denied them outright. There was nothing like that going on in the
Soviet Union. In fact, unlike those in America, Soviet scholars enjoyed
unprecedented support and absolute freedom in their work.

The following day, a secretary handed Miller an envelope with a
gift from the aforementioned Soviet professor. He couldn't believe the
professor had sent him a present after their argument. In the envelope,
he found a portrait of Pasternak with two words below it written in
pen: *Spasibo vam* (Thank you) along with the professor's signature.

―∞∞∞―

A few months later, William Styron and his wife visited Prague. Unlike Miller, he was more or less our own age and yet he was one of the
most famous American writers. I invited him over along with a few of
my friends.

Like most American intellectuals—I'd noticed this from my time
in the States—he had a lot of reservations about life in America. Society there would perish of overabundance. Americans, he claimed, will
drown in material goods; they will go deaf from the constant roar of
commercials and inane television shows. They were losing their taste,
their feeling for reality. Deaf citizens lose their discernment; objects
become goals in themselves, often the only goals in life. No matter
what we might think about Marxism, Marx was right about one thing:
Capitalism transforms material goods into a fetish. He thought that we
Czechs, along with the entire Eastern Bloc, were different, he explained
to our astonishment. For us, money was not the only goal; people were
looking for meaning in their lives other than the accumulation of goods.

He'd come to this realization from his stay in Russia. The only problem was something that was taken for granted in the United States: the opportunity of free expression.

It was bizarre that a writer, who everyone assumed possessed a heightened sense of perception, could be deceived by Communist propaganda and believe that platitudes concerning the construction of a Communist society could, after all the horrible experiences, offer some kind of higher meaning.

A few days before Styron's arrival, the trial of a twenty-two-year-old woman named Olga Hepnarová was taking place. She had intentionally driven a truck into a group of people waiting at a tram stop. She had killed eight people and seriously injured twelve. Hepnarová became the largest mass murderer in Czech history. She justified her act by saying she wanted to take revenge on the people who had hurt and wronged her. She was sentenced to death, and because she saw in her sentence only a confirmation of her opinion of human society, did not seek an appeal.

To my surprise, Styron knew about Olga Hepnarová's trial and brought it up himself. He claimed that the experience of the last war had demonstrated that it was necessary to ensure no one had the right to take another's life, even a murderer's. When he saw that some of us were surprised, he added that the woman had clearly deprived several innocent people of their lives, but this did not give us the right to take hers. She was obviously insane and required treatment. She should have been treated before she committed what she did, but even now she deserved medical care and not the gallows. (Indeed, as I later learned, she had tried to commit suicide at thirteen and had spent a long period of time in an asylum. Years later, Bohumil Hrabal said that he had spoken with her executioner. The woman was terribly afraid of her own death and had to be dragged to the scaffold. Apparently, until that moment, she had lived in some sort of dark pall of injury and injustice that detached her from reality.) Someone then objected that murderers were also sentenced to death in the United States. Yes, Styron admitted, but he was decidedly against it. He was horrified that some states were even trying to reinstate the death penalty. Europe should serve as an example; practically every country—he certainly meant the countries to the west of our borders—had abolished the death penalty.

This conversation later influenced me when I had the protagonist of my novel *Judge on Trial* contemplate the death penalty.

———

Philip Roth, the third American prose writer who visited us several times during the first few years after occupation, seemed to me unlike other Americans in one noticeable way: He was not fond of polite, social conversation; he wanted to discuss only what interested him. Primarily this was Jewish identity and the calamity that had befallen the Jews during the last war. It seemed that Roth had brought his interest in Franz Kafka to Prague. He lectured on him back in the States and had written a fairly long and entirely unrealistic story— in it, Franz immigrated to the United States. He had succumbed to Kafka's style and dreamlike vision of the world (fortunately only once) in his novella *The Breast*, in which the protagonist turns not into a bug, but into a breast.

Because Pavel Kohout and I were just then preparing a dramatic version of Kafka's *Amerika*, we spoke quite a bit about it. Roth thought it weaker than his other works. He considered it a story about a still immature young man who, in all innocence, comes into direct conflict with a ruthless world. Kafka's power, however, was in creating an ambiguous hero: simultaneously innocent and guilty. Josef K. also was not aware of his guilt, but he had committed an offense and was condemned.

Roth surprised me by asking if I thought Kafka had been impotent.

I had gathered from his correspondence with Milena that he hadn't been impotent at all but was simply so fastidious that whenever he was supposed to meet with a woman he was in love with (or tried to convince himself he was in love with), he perceived it as interfering in his daily routine. In order to somehow renew the order of this routine, he would try to think through what he would do and say, how everything would go. He was so disturbed by the planned meeting that he wouldn't sleep for several nights before. In the climactic scene of *The Castle*, a tall castle official named Bürgel somewhat absurdly receives the land surveyor in his bed and says all he has to do is express his wish, and it will be fulfilled. But K. is so tired that, at that very moment, he falls asleep. In my opinion, this scene was precisely an image of such a breakdown, which could influence all subsequent encounters.

When we had concluded this somewhat eccentric investigation of the love life of a writer who had been dead for half a century, I realized how unusual this conversation was for me: Our lives in an occupied country, the problems we thought and talked about, were entirely different from those that occupied my colleagues in the freer part of the world.

Of course, Roth was among those who tried to understand our situation. Given his interest in the fate of Jews, of course, he could not ignore one of the most fundamental Jewish experiences: persecution. However much he had managed to evade it in a free country, he harbored a feeling of solidarity with those being persecuted in a country that had been deprived of its freedom. I don't think any other author has written with such understanding and earnestness about the oppressive fate of Czech writers and Czech culture. He too, however, was denied further entry visas to Czechoslovakia.

⸺ ⸙ ⸺

We started to realize that, in addition to foreign readers, Czechs should know what we were writing about.

Of course no journal here would publish even a single love poem by any of us without the permission of the party overseers. All modern means of textual reproduction were strictly controlled, and using them surreptitiously was considered an actionable offense.

We met with some lawyer friends who told us that an author could not be punished for a copy made on an ordinary typewriter.

We agreed to have new works typed up, in several copies. We would sign the copies to emphasize that these were our own private manuscripts. Then we would get them to readers one way or another.

But even this primitive method of distributing our works required someone to organize it. The laboriousness of the task was difficult to imagine; it was essentially doing the labor of several publishers. Ludvík Vaculík volunteered. He would take the manuscripts to his girlfriend, Zdena, who would be able, just barely, to make eight copies on her typewriter. For this, however, she worked ten hours a day.

Michal observed our somewhat childish activity. He was a technically adept and enterprising young man. Sometimes at a second-hand shop, he would find a broken tape recorder, buy it, and fiddle around with it until he got it running. Then he would sell it at a profit. Once he noticed a used but perfectly functioning and cheap electric typewriter. He convinced us that we'd be able to make up to fourteen copies on it. Bearing in mind that it was more than five hundred years after the goldsmith and printer Johannes Gutenberg's revolutionary invention, this was not a breathtaking number. Nevertheless, we bought the typewriter and then searched around stationery stores for bundles of paper that was lightweight but of good quality. What we found was surprisingly inexpensive and well suited for duplication.

The first volumes of our manuscript series were quite appealing, and the best publishers in any free society would have expressed interest in them. Vaculík inaugurated the series with his novella, *The Guinea Pigs*, which had already come out in German translation. (Tomáš Řezáč, one of the most agile agents of the secret police, had managed to penetrate Bucher's publishing house in Switzerland and blatantly lied in one of his articles when he said that *not a single copy had been published abroad*.)

Among the first volumes of our typewritten series were verses by Jaroslav Seifert, Karel Šiktanc, and Jiří Gruša; Havel's original version of *The Beggar's Opera*; and novels by Pavel Kohout.

Ludvík started making the rounds of his friends, colleagues, and acquaintances (because of his long journalism career as well as his

Wallachian gregariousness, he had a lot of them) and provided them with freshly copied works. At first, they looked more like official files clamped in three-ring binders. To make them more resemble books, Zdena cut the pieces of paper in half. When the book had been typed, Ludvík would take it to Tomos, the only legitimate bookbinding firm, and the books received a binding. We decided to place a warning on the title page: *Further Copying of the Manuscript Expressly Forbidden.* Thereby it was made clear to the authorities that the author's intention was not to distribute the manuscript. Furthermore, the first letters of this phrase in Czech, which even the least astute secret police investigators could understand, spelled the word "Resistance."

Vaculík sold the copies for the price of the paper and wages for the copier, who received five crowns per page. The authors received not a crown. Not only would this have increased the sale price, but it would have also exposed the author to accusations of publicizing his work illegally. For New Year's Eve, Vaculík sent around a hand-painted postcard on which he'd sketched the initial works of the series. The names of the authors were listed on the spines of the books, and the entire bundle was enclosed in a large padlock. From this time on we called our series, which endured until the end of communism, Padlock.

At the beginning of the spring of 1974, Bohumil Hrabal—whom I considered the most remarkable Czech prose writer—was going to celebrate his sixtieth birthday. If the conditions in our country had been only a little more seemly, his birthday would unquestionably have been an occasion for newspaper articles and radio and television discussions, and thousands of his admirers and even government functionaries would have sent him their congratulations. If he'd belonged to the small group of collaborationist authors, he would probably have received the title of national artist. But he was classified among the prohibited writers and essentially did not exist for the current government and all publishing houses.

I was not among the circle of Hrabal's close friends who regularly met at the Golden Tiger pub. But I knew Hrabal from our brief encounters when we were still members of the Writers' Union. It struck me that we should render our colleague an appropriate honor, and my friends agreed. So we wrote up a sort of bull in archaic-sounding language in which Bohumil Hrabal was named *Prince of Czech Literature with the right to wear a diamond crown*. Saša Kliment secured a Latin translation of the text. We got an artist (I don't remember who it was, but a little later Nanda created a similar document) to embellish the bull. We convinced the orientalist Oldřich Král, one of Hrabal's friends, to sign the bull. (His first name had naturally preordained him for the task.) We didn't have a diamond crown, but I pulled together a collection of contributions from other writers, and Ludvík arranged for it all to be recopied and superbly bound.

Hrabal was waiting for us in the street in front of his building. He greeted us somewhat awkwardly and suggested we not go inside because the whole building was bugged.

We explained that we needed to go upstairs because he was going to be presented with a document requiring a seal that had to be made of wax. We couldn't do it on the street and, besides, the street was not sufficiently solemn. Hrabal acquiesced and led us up to his apartment.

There we presented him with the collection of articles along with the bull.

The Prince of Czech Literature was indeed moved. Several times he repeated, "This is wonderful, fellows, you didn't have to do this."

Then he opened the collection, which was titled: *What I Would Write If I Had Somewhere to Publish It, So I'll Write to You, Mr. Hrabal.*

Then the prince signed copies for all of us who brought one: *B. Hrabal received the original of this text on 28 March 1974.*

Then we took a seat at a round table and affixed the seal. It was indeed a solemn occasion. I held the burning candle while Saša heated the sealing wax and dripped it on the bull. Then Saša pressed an old Swedish coin into it. Hrabal brought out a bottle of Egyptian cognac, poured us all a glass, and then began telling us about his childhood, about his mother and how he was conceived out of wedlock. When she revealed her condition at home, her father was going to shoot her, but his wife took the gun away from him and said, "Knock it off and come eat!" He told it so convincingly, it was as if he'd seen it with his own eyes.

———

Sometime later that spring, I received a message from Jürgen that the Munich publisher Blanvalet, which published children's literature, was interested in a collection of fairy tales by prohibited Czech authors, but it needed the manuscripts by the summer. I asked Jürgen to thank Blanvalet for us and said I'd try to get the fairy tales as soon as I could.

There were still more than a hundred banned authors, but I wanted the connecting link between the writers of this collection to be not their illicitness but rather the quality of their work. In addition, I soon discovered that many authors were afraid to publish abroad and didn't want to end up in prison as enemies of the Socialist system. Many still (naively) believed that if they behaved inconspicuously, the rulers would show mercy and eventually allow them to publish again.

I received contributions from the excellent modern storytellers Jan Vladislav and Jan Werich as well as from the poet Jan Skácel. I succeeded in convincing Václav Havel to write something for the collection, and that is how *Pižďuchové* came into existence, the only one of his texts intended (at least to a certain degree) for children. In the fairly short time of five months, I managed to collect stories from thirteen authors.

I had all the manuscripts copied and assembled, placed them in an envelope, and, with a delay I thought excusable, sent them to Munich by certified mail. I knew mail going abroad was monitored, but I told myself they wouldn't find anything objectionable in a collection of fairy tales; maybe they'd find fault with a couple of my sentences from the introduction, but they wouldn't confiscate the entire package just for that.

Apparently they did, because after about three weeks I received a polite but slightly admonitory letter from the publishing house asking when I was sending the fairy tales. The publisher had to have them translated, and that would take time.

I replied that the package containing the texts had apparently gone astray, and so I put one of the copies into another envelope and sent it off. Then I went to the post office to reclaim my previous package.

After about another month, an editor I didn't know called me and could not understand why she hadn't received the manuscripts I had sent twice. Just in case, she repeated to me the address of the publishing house. The only problem was that it was located in Munich.

I didn't know what to do. As far as I was aware, none of Jürgen's messengers were planning a trip to Prague in the near future, and sending the package a third time by the Czech post seemed futile.

Fortunately, I ran into Jan Vladislav, one of the authors. When I told him about my difficulties with the manuscripts, he said it had been very naive of me to send the texts by mail. I was to get them to him as soon as possible, and he would see to their delivery. He had friends in the French embassy.

I brought him the manuscript the next day, and a few days later the fairy tales arrived at the Munich publishers.

I finally received an explanation from our post office. The second package had departed Czechoslovakia in good order, but it had apparently gotten lost in the Federal Republic of Germany. I therefore ought to turn to the German postal service. *Regards.* Signature illegible.

Jürgen advised me somewhat emphatically to write novels rather than short stories. The reason, as far as I understood, was strictly profit related. Novels sold better and, if the author was lucky, might be made into movies. Antonioni had made the famous *Blow-Up* out of Julio Cortazár's story, but this was anomalous.

So I told him I would write a thousand-page novel. Of course, this statement was made in jest, but the truth was that I had long wondered if I had it in me to write a novel in which I described my fundamental experiences and expressed something of what I thought about the time I was living in.

Of everything I'd experienced, it was the ruthless murders I had witnessed for over four decades of my life that had affected me the most.

I still woke up in the middle of the night and vividly imagined the horror of the victims driven into the gas chambers or the anxiety of those sentenced to death during the absurd show trials.

After the war, it was with a feeling of satisfaction that I read about the trials of the Nazis who were sentenced to death. When Adolf Eichmann was hanged in Israel after a long trial (it had been the only death sentence pronounced and carried out in that country), I accepted it as the appropriate punishment for a man who had been in charge of the internment and subsequent extermination of millions of people. But then I started to doubt the motivation for such punishment.

The death penalty is an important subject for judicial institutions in every society. Several centuries earlier, the death sentence was one of the most frequent punishments carried out, even for negligible infractions or even deeds that had often not actually been committed. Confessions were exacted from the accused through torture. Those who arbitrated justice and the law often transformed a place of adjudication into a place where criminals in gowns sent innocent victims to hangmen. That's how it was in the twentieth century, as well, where organized and legalized mass murder took place. How does even a slightly responsible judge reconcile himself to this in a country in which so many judicial murders have taken place and where the death penalty was used, or even required, for a number of offenses? I decided to make my somewhat autobiographical hero a judge.

At this time, my life was becoming more and more monotonous. I had been kicked out of all organizations and deprived of the possibility of working anywhere I might be able to employ my knowledge and skills. Furthermore, all decent films had been removed from the cinemas, there was no modern drama in the theaters, and the radio, if it was not broadcasting classical music, was impossible to listen to. My disposition required movement. Writing remained the only space in which I could move about freely. And so I started to write; I worked from morning till evening on my novel about a judge named Kindl.

A person can never be sure if what he has written is worth anything, but when constructing such a long piece of prose, he is even more unsure. I tried to banish my uncertainty with intensity. I kept writing even when I suspected that the following day, when I read over what I had committed to paper, I would almost certainly throw it out. Of course I consulted with my lawyer friends about many of the questions my hero grappled with, whether it was the law expert Pavel Rychetský; someone from his family, including his first wife; or Petr Pithart, who transferred his law erudition to the field of contemporary historical events.

I'm reading the criminal code from 1951, which Communist lawyers quickly cobbled together (based on the Soviet model). The legendary first chapter, according to which they executed dozens and dozens of innocent people, is chilling reading. Almost every paragraph, whether it deals with treason, sabotage, or espionage, allows for the death penalty, for instance, for putting the country at risk, and finally: "if there is any other especially aggravating circumstance." How did the agents of the secret police, and later the judges, construe these especially aggravating circumstances? Could it be, perhaps, class origin?

Leaving the republic without permission (when permission was for most citizens unattainable) incurred a punishment of up to five years, if, of course, the fugitive did not have on his person a piece of paper that could be construed as treasonous or espionage material. In any case, even without this paper, contingent conviction was precluded. Anyone who "belittled the reputation of the president of the republic or his deputy" faced three years' imprisonment. As we know from Švejk, the Austro-Hungarian law codes had already come up with this one.

From my diary, April 1975

Of course there were days when I put off writing. One spring day, Vaculík talked me into going to visit some of his friends in Bratislava who shared our fate of being prohibited writers. The sense of solidarity would boost their spirits, claimed Ludvík. (There were only a few banned writers in Slovakia, certainly because the leader of the country was their countryman.) Ludvík had no idea that on the same day several Czech politicians, who had also been expelled, had set out to Bratislava to visit Alexander Dubček, a man who, although he had pusillanimously signed the Moscow Protocol, was still considered, even by the secret police, a symbol of the Prague Spring reform movement.

It seemed that the government did not want me to succumb to indolence. The day after my return from Bratislava, our doorbell buzzed. When I opened the door, I saw an entire pack of fellows whose profession was obvious even before they presented their warrant to search the house.

The piece of paper headed RESOLUTION explained the reasons for the search:

Upon the resolution of investigators on 22 April 1975—document number 11/120-1975—according to article 160, paragraph 1 of the criminal code, the initiation of prosecution for the punishable offense of national subversion, which was to be committed in a manner specified below. After initiating prosecution, a suspicion arose that the apartment of the aforementioned individual contained written documents pertaining to the investigation of the punishable offense, which will be demonstrated.

It is necessary to determine how this occurred.

The document bore the stamp of the general prosecutor. The method by which I was supposed to have committed the punishable offense of subverting the republic was not provided. This was not surprising. I was, however, somewhat surprised that these henchmen were accompanied by a "disinterested" witness (the criminal code required that an independent witness be present). He had the fine Jewish name of Kauder (obviously they had thought up this name especially for me, since that was the name of my ancestors), and for all his disinterestedness, his features looked more coplike than any of theirs. I was still drowsy from sleep and did not protest and allowed them to come in. Helena was more intransigent and yelled at them that no one was allowed to trample around in his shoes. Amazingly, the entire commando squad took off their shoes and thereby were immediately deprived of some of their superiority. This reminded me that the true horrors of the Stalinist years were over.

This was the second house search I had experienced. I had simply gotten mixed up in the first one and was worried that the snoops would discover my notebook from my military preparation class. This time I was worried they would find and confiscate the novel I had begun.

They discovered it, but fortunately I was writing in ink instead of typing it—typed documents attracted their attention more than handwritten ones. The chief of the trespassers wanted to know if the manuscript was mine, and when I said yes, he asked what I was writing about. Of course, I should have said it was none of his business, but I chose a more conciliatory answer and replied that I was writing something of my experiences from the war. This seemed to diminish his suspicions.

Just as with the house search preceding my father's arrest, I had the feeling that they had no idea what they were looking for. (It obviously had something to do with our visit to Bratislava; perhaps they assumed we had prepared some documents for Dubček, some sort of new "Two Thousand Words," and they were trying to track down copies.)

Vaculík once told me that after a house search, it was as if a dark force had swept through the apartment, and he felt as though he should call a priest to have it consecrated. A house search, especially if a person knows he's not hiding any weapons, drugs, or other sort of contraband (even though the greatest contraband in a totalitarian society is any kind of uncensored declaration, whether written, spoken, sung, or painted), arouses more disgust than fear—as if a revolting insect had been crawling all over everything, leaving behind a sticky phlegm or spiderwebs.

Hour after hour they searched impotently through drawers, wardrobes, and especially my bookcase, which contained around five thousand volumes in Czech, Slovak, Polish, German, English, and Russian (they didn't notice the volume of Virgil's *Aeneid* in Latin). Most of it was fiction, but there were also essays as well as works of history and philosophy. What could they find that was subversive? It was beyond their powers to recognize it, and they would need dozens of boxes to confiscate all of it. They took a dislike to an English translation of Solzhenitsyn's *The First Circle*. I also had a copy of the novel in Russian, but they left that alone (obviously they didn't know Cyrillic). They commandeered everything if they thought it was samizdat, or if the title looked suspicious, and piled it all on the daybed.

They also noticed a framed original of one of Hadʼák's caricatures, which had been published in *Literární listy*. It was a replica of a Soviet poster of a Red Army soldier pointing at the viewer. Hadʼák had replaced the Russian text, *Have you signed up as a volunteer?* with the inscription, *Have you also signed the Two Thousand Words?* The large and threatening *You* was spelled in both Cyrillic and Latin.

Was I aware I could be tried for sedition?

I objected that I could hang on my walls at home anything I wanted, couldn't I? It was inciting neither my wife nor myself to sedition.

The chief informed me that my penchant for such impertinent remarks would soon pass and tossed the picture onto the pile of confiscated artifacts.

Whenever my wife or I went into another room, one of the rogues followed us, but the children could move about at will. Michal felt sorry for the caricature and, without any of the search team noticing, grabbed the picture and slid it under the daybed. Michal truly did evince extraordinary enterprise, for he himself was actually in possession of the greatest piece of "contraband." He had been preparing copies of a large portrait of Dubček for his friends. He managed to place the pictures in a large envelope of photographic paper. When one of the snoops grabbed it, Michal stopped him and warned that the envelope contained still unused and sensitive material that would be destroyed if opened. Surprisingly, the fellow put the envelope back in its place. Michal also managed to disconnect the telephone, so we looked on with not a little schadenfreude when the boss of the search unit—most likely in the expectation of further instructions—vexedly attempted to compel the silenced instrument to function.

Finally they went down to the basement, where the lowliest of them poked around with a shovel in the pile of coke to make sure it wasn't concealing a printing press or a machine gun.

When the head miscreant ended the search, he ordered a typewriter to be brought in, and one of his subordinates started typing up the individual items they were confiscating.

The chief suddenly noticed that the picture was missing. He started yelling at me and demanding to know what I'd done with it. As he perfectly well knew, I pointed out, he hadn't let me once out of his sight.

He apparently considered berating children inappropriate and was too lazy to look through the entire apartment again for the picture.

The list, which was also signed by the disinterested witness Kauder, contained fifty-six items. Among the documents that were supposed to prove subversion of the republic were manuscripts of the poetry collections of Karel Šiktanc and Oldřich Mikulášek, books by Pavel Kohout, the text of a fairy tale by Jan Trefulka, bound (but incomplete, owing to the events of 1968 and 1969) issues of *Literární listy* and *Listy*, as well as 28 sheets of typed letters from the writer Václav

Havel addressed to Gen. Sec. Dr. Husák; three sheets of Abraham begat Isaac, Isaac then begat Jacob, Jacob begat Judah and his brothers . . .

Of course there were 122 sheets of foreign correspondence in green folders that seemed to them auspiciously dubious and *1 letter of two pages, typewritten from 16 March in English, addressed Dear Isaac, in a plastic folder with the business card of Rabbi Isaac Newmann, Barnet Synagogue* (to the disappointment of the investigators, who probably had it translated, the letter contained nothing except news of how the children were doing in school and what we'd been reading lately).

Helena insisted on verifying once again that everything was written down, which, after a moment of hesitation, the chief allowed, but he required Helena to sign that she herself had requested the verification and that everything was in order.

Then the members of the search team donned their shoes and as they were carrying the confiscated items to the car called out threateningly, See you later.

⟨∞⟩

Although the search team had departed and there was nothing among the things they had confiscated that was illegal even according to our oppressive laws, in the evening when we went to bed, the arrogant faces of the police kept flitting before my eyes. What was their intrusion supposed to mean or prefigure? Were they trying to frighten me? Or had they finally found something for which I could be punished? The next day I was laid out once again with the spasms that had afflicted me before my recent gallbladder operation.

So I went, as I usually did when an attack of colic set in, to see Dr. Šetka at the hospital on Charles Square. He prescribed a strict diet.

Because the experience of the house search was still fresh in my mind, I complained about it to him. I added that they could lock me up; this was just a prelude.

Besides being an excellent specialist, the doctor was sympathetic to my plight. He said the colic attack was obviously due to nerves and offered me asylum in the hospital for a few days. If I were in the hospital, he assumed, they wouldn't come to arrest me. And then . . . then we would see.

And so I became a patient. The doctor prescribed a gallbladder diet and said he would conduct a couple of unpleasant examinations of my pancreas and stomach.

Over the next few days, my memory of the shadowy figures faded, my pains went away, and I felt absolutely fine. My asylum, however, continued. The doctor was perfectly willing not to rush the examinations.

The facilities of the general hospital were in a worse state of neglect than those of the hospital in Krč, where I'd been employed as an orderly. The building was from the eighteenth century, and it was swarming with beetles and cockroaches that crawled over the floors and walls and especially in the drawers of the night tables where patients stored their food. The rooms had high ceilings and were so spacious that plenty of beds were squeezed into them—a patient would never be wanting for company.

To my left lay a well-built old man who said he had been member of a Czech unit of the Red Army. I didn't know what was wrong with him; he probably was just old and doddery and had no one to care for him. The doctor prescribed him no medication or examinations, just a healthful diet. The Czech Red Army soldier told me about the battles—or, rather, skirmishes—he had participated in; he recalled hearing Trotsky speak (and all sorts of situations where Czechs were present). The president had even awarded him a medal for his services. It was in the drawer of his bedside table if I wanted to have a look.

When I opened the drawer, it was not the pointless piece of beribboned metal that intrigued me but the mass of hard-boiled eggs the drawer contained. The hands of this warrior, who had been present during Lenin's reign of terror and had been weakened by age and life, shook so badly that he was unable to peel the egg he received each day for breakfast. Apparently, he'd once asked a nurse to peel an egg for him, and she retorted that if she had to peel everyone's eggs or butter everyone's bread, she'd never be done with her work by evening. From that time on, I peeled his eggs and buttered his bread for him.

I spent three weeks in the hospital. The kind doctor informed me that all the tests had come back negative. My colic was definitely due to nerves—not surprisingly given my recent stressful conditions. Nevertheless, he suggested I eliminate fatty and fried foods from my diet and then added almost in a whisper that none of "them" had been asking about me, so they would probably leave me be. If there was any immediate danger, however, I should not hesitate to come back. More tests could always be arranged. He looked again into my file and noted, "You also suffer from hay fever? Maybe you could apply for partial disability. That's always a good thing," he added. "They seem to behave more decently toward the infirm."

I thought it improbable I could be considered an invalid, but if I did become one, my employment worries would be assuaged. I would have a legal income and could not be accused of parasitism. I started to hunt down doctors' confirmations attesting to my condition. The allergists were very charitable and slightly exaggerated my difficulties when they wrote that during the hay fever season—which in my case lasted from March to September—I was unable to work for longer than four hours a day.

Because I'd been in a concentration camp during the war, I came under a special doctors' commission, which had apparently been given orders to be kind to survivors.

I concluded that the searchers had only wanted to frighten me or perhaps they'd learned that I really had nothing to do with the people who went to visit Dubček.

I now spent most of the time working on my novel.

At the beginning of January 1975, a repulsive and intellectually sterile literary tabloid, which in the spirit of the Communist newspeak called itself *Tvorba*, printed a conversation with the Prince of Czech Literature.

To the horror of his readers, he expressed support for Communist policies. Hrabal announced:

> I do not want anyone to brandish my name about who does not wish our country or our people well, people I live among and am fond of. . . . I am not a political person; it takes me a while to become acquainted with everything, but there is one thing I have come to understand well: the XIV Congress of the Communist Party of Czechoslovakia was a challenge and a summons to all writers of this land to enrich the lives of our people. . . . As for me, I do not wish to stand aside but rather to contribute to creating, in my own way, relationships among people the way they should be among Socialist people. I think that it is important to today's Writers' Union that all honorable Czech writers understand that the most important thing is what our readers say about our work and not what some foreign broadcast reports.

He added that he could not conceive of the present, or even the future, without socialism. Then he spoke with incomprehensible enthusiasm about some kind of Slavic standard-bearer and then about soccer.

To endorse policies that suppressed every attempt at free creation was depressing as well as indecent. But I told myself that if by this embarrassing and blatant act of sycophancy, Hrabal was redeemed and allowed to publish—and this was the only conceivable reason for him to have done something like this—the newspaper article would be forgotten while his work would persist. Not everyone, however, was willing to accept such a justification for Hrabal's actions. A group of admirers of the underground, under the direction of Ivan Martin Jirous, known as Madman among his friends, burned several of Hrabal's books on Kampa Island. (This was an ostentatiously stupid act. The public burning of books, even fiction, is an expression of villainy worthy only of Nazis, Communists, Muslim fanatics, and other such bearers of barbarism.)

Hrabal explained to his friends that they'd come to him from *Tvorba* themselves with the text already prepared. He tried to keep them at bay, but they harangued him and said that readers were awaiting his works, and they only wanted him to espouse his support for socialism. This couldn't go against his own views, could it? He said he'd argued over every sentence, but they finally got the better of him and stuck in that bit about the Communist Party congress and their damn union.

I could imagine how it had all played out. The Prince of Czech Literature was happy to believe that the nation was awaiting his books—he was also a generation older than we were, and not so long ago he had experienced the plight of the outcast. He probably didn't think he had much time left to speak to his readers. Self-justification is not difficult. During a period when most citizens had given in, why should a writer have to play the hero?

In one thing, however, he was mistaken. It was less significant that they had elicited from him a statement than that he had let himself be dragged into a trap which, like most traps offering a tiny morsel, deprived him of his freedom. In return for once again becoming an "approved" writer, he was forced to heed the orders of various censors, along with their superiors and subordinates, who arrogated to themselves the right to tell him what and how to write. It soon became clear what they were requesting of Hrabal, or, more precisely, what he had to accede to for his writings to reach his readers in printed form. One can find many examples in his now "official" work, but I will present one that illustrates how far the author was compelled to withdraw from his original aim.

In one of his best prose works, *The Little Town Where Time Stood Still,* Hrabal has a brief scene in which his father, who was at the time a brewery owner, had to move out of his office during the Communist takeover. In the original typewritten manuscript, that is, the uncensored version, the scene reads:

When Father had carted off the last box of pens and tiny cal-
endars and notebooks, he opened the cupboard and took out
the two round lamps, the light of which he had used to write by
all those years ago, and which were ready and waiting, in case
the electricity went out, the lamps with green shades, and as he
was carrying them off, the workers' director remarked, "But those
lamps are listed in the brewery inventory . . . ," and he took them
out of Father's hands. "Then I'll buy them," said Father softly.
But the workers' director shook his head and said in an alien
voice, "You've raked up enough as it is, and you've built yourself a
villa." **And when Father left the office, this was what the workers' director had been waiting for. He took both lamps with
their green shades and threw them out the window onto a
pile of lumber and scrap, and the green shades and cylinders
smashed to pieces and Father clutched his head and there was
a crumpling sound inside, as if his brain had been smashed.
"The new era's beginning here too," said the workers' director
and walked into his office.**

I think that in our prose, no one else had captured in such an
image, so forcefully, simply, and precisely, the perverse, arrogant, and
arbitrary nature of the administrators of the February Communist
takeover and, in a single sentence, all the portentousness and inhuman-
ity of that "new era."

In the official version, *Harlequin's Millions*, Hrabal inflated this
scene with a lot of words and, at the censor's request, changed its meaning into its opposite:

And when he came back for the rest of his things, he took from
the wardrobe two old oil lamps with rounded wicks, the lamps
that hummed when they were lit and gave such warmth to the
writer's hands, so the workers' director said, "But those lamps aren't
yours, they're in the brewery inventory that we've just taken over."

Francin felt a prick in his heart, turned red, and said, "Then I'll buy them, these lamps are witness of my good old times when I was happy." But the director insisted. "These lamps aren't yours. You've raked up enough as it is, and you've built yourself a villa while we had to live by begging. Just remember the servants' room in the brewery where your own brother, Mr. Pepin, had a bunk next to the maltster Mára, just think about our children living in hovels where in winter the water froze in the pots on the stove, just remember how you took such care not to make anyone on the board angry. **But in the end, what do you think, comrades? We'll be generous and let you have the lamps as memorials to your good old times.**" Francin carried out his last things, but the director called after him when he was in the courtyard, "Because those good old times of yours will never return."

History provides countless examples of people recanting their beliefs before an inquisition and later privately adding, "And yet it moves!" In place of such a postscript, Hrabal would sometimes send his uncensored versions again to samizdat.

Essay: *Self-Criticism*, p. 517

18

As the pages of my novel accumulated, my original joke about a thousand-page book stopped being a joke; at the same time I began to fear that the marauding search team might invade again and this time confiscate my manuscript and thereby lay waste to the result of almost two years of work. I was tempted to type up the unfinished manuscript in several copies, which I would then hide with various friends. But as soon as I finished the manuscript (if I ever finished it), I would start making the final corrections, rendering the typed copy pointless. Finally, I took everything I had written to my father-in-law, who was happy to hide it among a pile of old magazines.

My manuscript worries were not the only thing troubling me. My writer's insurance had been canceled, and from that moment I was considered a parasite according to Socialist laws, especially since I could not demonstrate a legal income. It was just another way to make the lives of my wife, my children, and myself more unpleasant. Nanda had already finished elementary school, and my "parasitism" and "antisocialist" stance might jeopardize her further studies. She was an excellent artist, and we'd heard that the graphic arts school in Žižkov was very good. It was not out of the question that she would be accepted if she aced the entrance exam. Two of our acquaintances taught at the school, and one of them promised to give Nanda drawing lessons to prepare her for the test.

But our daughter started complaining that she had to keep drawing chairs, boxes, wrinkled rags, and her relatives' faces over and over. Her drawings, we were assured, were getting better and better and something truly unforeseen would have to happen for her not to be accepted.

Around that time, Zdeněk Miler stopped by. He was the kind, good-natured author of the popular animated cartoon *Little Mole*. We had been neighbors and friends for quite some time, and our families had gone camping together in the Tatra Mountains.

Zdeněk came with an offer of work. German television had ordered several five-minute films featuring Little Mole. I could write a couple of screenplays, he would conceal my name under his, and I'd earn a few crowns.

His offer appealed to me. It wasn't only the money; I needed to publish something legitimately without undergoing some sort of self-criticism. It would help Nanda get into the school, and I could try to renew my writer's insurance. I explained this to Zdeněk and admitted that it would be difficult to get my name past the overseers. I'd be very obliged, however, if he would try.

Zdeněk didn't hesitate for a moment and said he would give it his best shot.

I wrote seven brief screenplays, and Zdeněk took them to the studios. To my amazement, they were accepted, and I was to stop by to sign a contract.

Even today I'm not sure how this happened. The regime was thorough in this area. Anyone who appeared on a secret list of prohibited writers could not publish a single word. How was I suddenly and undeservedly an exception? One explanation is that I have an ordinary name, and those who had approved the screenplays (if they'd even ever heard of me) must have assumed it belonged to one of my namesakes. Another explanation, however, was more likely. After the Soviet occupation, a man with a very dark past—and apparently with the rank of secret police colonel—took over as the studio's director. It was difficult to tell, but perhaps he'd had an attack of conscience or perhaps he was trying to demonstrate his own independence and disdain for the official obstinacy with regard to artists. He provided many prohibited or persecuted artists either full-time employment or other work opportunities.

Then I was called before the doctors' commission so my recommendation for a partial invalid stipend could be evaluated. The members did indeed treat me considerately and inquired about my stay in Terezín. When they learned I had spent three and a half years there, they admitted that my state of health could be attributed to that.

My partial disability pension was approved. It came to 630 crowns, which wasn't something I could live on for more than a few days, but it was a legal income, which shielded me from charges of parasitism. I think the doctors knew what they were doing but pretended they had no idea who I was.

—⚬⚬⚬—

I soon finished the manuscript of my novel, or at least I thought so. I had never undertaken such an extensive work. I combined a great number of experiences I had lived through or heard secondhand or invented out of whole cloth.

However, I was still uncertain whether I was leading my characters to despair. What could they actually discover in a world that was still running wild and in which people were looking for a way to fill the void, a way to escape the hopelessness of their own destinies? On the final pages, I tried to show what my hero had discovered as an answer—an answer for both of us.

> He also knew by now that one would never find freedom in this world if he didn't find it in himself—however perfect were the laws and however great one's control over the world and people. And nobody could endow someone with moral grandeur if it was not born in one's soul, just as nobody could release someone from one's bonds if one did not cast off the shackles of one's own making.

I recognized that this was not particularly original; I was doubtless influenced by Karel Čapek (who had been influenced by Masaryk), who repeatedly tried to point out that if a person doesn't know what to do with himself, he will long to change the world. But this had been my experience in life as well: In the name of magnificent ideals, a person will lose himself, his conscience, and his freedom. If he pulls himself together and realizes this, he will never again dare to return to self-deception, no matter how merciful it pretends to be. If a person wants somehow to participate in the fate of the world, of society, of other people, he must first of all take responsibility for himself and his own actions.

I began to type up my handwritten novel, and when I was nearing page 950, I started to sense a childlike excitement. I drew out the last pages a little by adding a few nonessential sentences, and when I reached the final page, it was with a feeling of exhilaration that I wrote the number 1,000. I had fulfilled my promise and written a thousand pages. I had proved to myself that I was a "professional." At the journal, when I was supposed to write an article of sixty lines, I wrote exactly sixty. This time I had promised a thousand pages and had written precisely a thousand. But I wasn't able to think of a title. Finally, I chose a not very cheerful line from a song: *There Stands a Gallows*.

With both eagerness and impatience, I lent my copies to friends.

Apparently my manuscript preoccupied them a little too much, and they started discussing it, because once again, I received a summons for an interrogation at the dimly lit offices of the secret police on Bartolomějská Street.

The interrogation began with the usual query: Did I know why I was here? Because my examiner already knew the answer, he immediately asked what I had recently published in samizdat.

I said I had no idea what he was talking about.

He meant the series we referred to as Padlock.

I said I knew of no such series, and unfortunately I was prohibited from publishing. My last novel had been a love story, which I'd proposed to several different publishers who had all replied in the same way: It didn't fit into their publishing plans.

"On the other hand, it fit extraordinarily well into the plans of Mr. Braunschweiger abroad, isn't that right?"

When I gave no answer, he posed another question. "What else are you planning to publish?"

I was now a little more experienced so I said I was not going to answer, since I did not consider him a representative of an enterprise that published imaginative literature.

Then he went straight to the point. "We have learned that you've composed a long novel possessing the character of antisocialist agitation. What do you have to say to that?"

I said I had nothing. Or rather: I have never occupied myself with agitation because I find it repellent.

He asked if that was true. I said it was.

"Fine, if that's what you think. But you must admit that a reader might perceive your novel as an attack against our system!"

I said that I was not responsible for the perception of every reader, and novels were not written to attack anything. A novel is not propaganda, ideology, or agitation. A novel is an artistic work that can be good or bad. I had nothing more to say about it.

To my surprise, he recited the following monologue: "We are not here to judge the caliber of your work. It is apparently well written and of high quality. But its contents are antisocialist, and we are here to prevent the dissemination of such works. I am warning you that if you publicize this work of yours called *There Stands a Gallows*, either abroad or in so-called samizdat, you will be in contravention of our laws and must be prepared to accept the consequences that such an action would bring."

Then he had me sign a document containing nothing more than this exhortation.

I said I would sign only with the addendum that I did not agree with such an evaluation of my novel. "Fine," he said, "but I would like to point out that this addendum of yours will not help you in the least when it comes to considering your responsibility in this matter."

After this warning, I decided to send the manuscript abroad as soon as I could and make as many copies as possible. My decision to secure copies, however, was somewhat hampered by the manuscript's extensive size. I sent the manuscript to Jürgen through a Swedish diplomat who was generously assisting us smuggle out our manuscripts and in return bringing back freshly printed books. So that I not become too conceited, an urgent request arrived a few weeks later from Jürgen that should I shorten the novel by at least a third, or a half, at best. He wrote that readers wanted novels but not thick epics like mine. Furthermore, he thought the title was bad if only because no one abroad knew the song from which it had been taken. He suggested the title *Judge on Trial*.

A person enters adulthood with many resolutions, expectations, scruples, and prejudices. During the time I am recalling, almost everything in which one could place one's expectations either had been made difficult or was forbidden. All higher goals had been degraded and disgraced. Surprisingly, it seemed that immorality, or at least insincerity within personal relationships, was acceptable to the reigning immoral authorities. So it was easy to persuade oneself that, at least in this area of life, one was not restricted any more than anywhere else in the world, perhaps even less. At least in one area of our lives we were free: Men and women took lovers. The government tolerated it just as it tolerated the battering of its citizens. The gremlins in the cadre offices cared more about relationships within the collective than their relationships to their own partners or children. Infidelity, therefore, was often limited only by material circumstances: a dearth of apartments or money.

I loved my wife and children, but I fell in love again—this time with Helena's colleague. She came to visit me and said she wanted to talk about my novel. She'd even copied out several quotes on index cards. Of course I was flattered; I was still too young to realize the futility of vanity.

We met several times before we started something. She was nine years younger, slender, with auburn hair; she had two little girls and was interested in Indian philosophy. She believed our fates were determined by the alignment of the planets on the day of our birth. She quickly created my horoscope, from which she determined I was a man of love but also scruples. She was interested in everything esoteric: She interpreted cards, poured lead at Christmas, read coffee grounds, and collected herbs. Whenever I suffered from some bodily ailment, she had a remedy. She was a prophetess peering down at me from another time or at least from other parts of the world.

She also possessed a special gift of transforming everything she saw or experienced into a thrilling and impassioned story. The border between her laughter and tears, between happiness and sorrow, was barely perceptible.

She wrote short books in which her entire being was exposed, even if the stories were about other people and from an entirely different period.

Both of us adored nature. I had been deprived of entire summers during childhood, and since then I've harbored the natural world in my thoughts like an articulated image in which forests merge with fields and fields with meadows and meadows with ponds. It abounds with nameless fragrant flowers, and anonymous birds warble around.

For her everything was composed of concrete things that she could identify: She knew the name of every plant we encountered; she recognized any bird by its song and knew the name of every bush we later made love beneath.

I believed neither her auguries nor her spells. It all seemed to me a tentative and noncommittal game, whether she was foretelling success and fame or rejoicing over my lengthy lifeline which, at least in this moment, she hoped we would spend together.

In one letter, she wrote:

> My dear, my dearest, I am home alone and the snow is falling gently outside. My eyes are hurting me so much that I cannot read, I can't distract myself with anything. So I close my eyes and feel that I love you, that it is not within my strength to offer any resistance. You have cast a spell over me, stung me, bewitched me so that I am able to think of nothing else but you. And I ask myself: How could I have let this happen? How did you become so close and so inevitable that I am afraid? . . . You say that I bewitch you, but you have been casting even more spells over me. You know this well enough yourself. You employ not only your feelings but also your mind, and I cannot resist.

I wrote similar letters to her. At the same time, I was afraid of my feelings, of what I was hurtling myself toward, of what we were hurtling ourselves toward.

I had no desire to prevaricate, so I told my wife about my outburst of passion.

I think she was hurt. Then, for a long time, we scrutinized our lives, our mistakes, and our setbacks. She wanted to know how I planned to continue. What did I want? At no time did I consider staying with both of them. Finally, I promised to end it.

But I do not intend to compose a chronicle of my love life and my infidelities. My wish is not to draw my loved ones into my tale; it's enough that I drew them into real life.

The house in Hodkovičky in which we lived was a little more than forty years old, but it shared the unsettled and crazy history of our country.

In the early thirties, the house was built by the owner of a barbershop. Today, Hodkovičky is one of the most expensive sections of Prague, but back then it was still provincial and modest.

It was populated mostly by successful businessmen and craftsmen. There were a few other ostentatious homes on our street, which obviously belonged to people who were better off or at least could afford a decent architect to design their dwellings in a constructivist or cubist manner.

Our apartment was ordinary but also practically designed—the living room windows faced south and north. The building had a basement apartment, but with the passage of time it became so damp that no one used it anymore. There were three-room apartments on the ground floor and first floor (where we lived), and at the top was a small two-room mansard rental, which the authorities refused to recognize as an apartment because the ceilings were too low.

The only son of the owners—this was during the First Republic—rose to the top ranks of the police force relatively quickly. He even spent the years of the Nazi occupation with the police and he was not certain whether he would survive liberation. He fled across the ocean while life in his homeland trundled from abyss to abyss. In a quick series of events, (some) collaborationists were sentenced and deported along with the Germans they had served, willingly or otherwise. The government also announced nationalization, which at first did not concern the barbers' trade or private homes, let alone small houses.

Meanwhile, the son of our landlords had gotten his footing in the United States and was trying to contribute to his parents' impecunious household. He sent them dollars, which his mother, like many people, exchanged for Tuzex crowns, which she then sold on the black market—but so openly that she was soon arrested and convicted. In addition to receiving a prison sentence, she had part of her property confiscated. Her husband claimed he had no knowledge of his wife's activities, and the court surprisingly chose to believe him. Therefore, half the house was confiscated, and he kept the other half. But now that he was alone, he was obliged to move into the mansard apartment upstairs, and tenants were installed in the two lower floors—two families on the ground floor because the government was trying to resolve the housing crisis after the Soviet model by dividing the home in two, with the tenants sharing common facilities.

This is the state in which we found the building in 1965 when we acquired an apartment in exchange for our cooperative apartment that we had been remodeling. The landlady was well into her seventies, but she played the part of a grande dame and covered herself so liberally with cheap Soviet perfume that whenever she walked down the stairs, the cloying scent hung in the air at least half the day. She had a subletter—a quiet, thin, old-world, and well-mannered waiter who sometimes played the accordion or trumpet. The neighbors claimed he was the old woman's lover, and she provided his lodgings free of charge as well as cleaned his clothes and fed him. This seemed unlikely—a waiter could eat at his place of employment, even if it was just a pub, and taking on the task of sweetheart seemed even more unlikely. One day, however, the waiter disappeared along with his accordion and trumpet, and we never saw him again. A little while later, when I'd all but forgotten him, I received a postcard from him bearing a Danish stamp (it was surprising that the post office had even delivered it). On the card he had written: *I'm doing wonderfully, I'm free. Please say hello to all the tenants, even my niggardly and perfumed old lady. Regards . . .*

So the landlady was left on her own. She was like an old tin can tossed out in the forest and quickly starting to rust. Sometimes she stopped by our apartment, especially if Helena was baking a cake (which wasn't very often); the old woman knew she would get a piece to taste. Sometimes she even came to borrow a small amount of money, which she never returned. She began neglecting herself more and more and started to look like a witch—understandably in view of everything she'd lived through. But she was also mean. For years, we had a sparrows' nest just inside the building's front entrance, so we had to leave the door to the building open even at night (crime was not so bad then). One day she pulled down the nest with the chicks and threw it into the trash.

Sometimes paranoia would get the better of her, and she would fly around the building looking everywhere for her passbook. Finally, she would call the police and say she'd been robbed. The police would come every time (explaining that they had to show up when someone called) and try to persuade the old woman that she'd simply mislaid the passbook; they assured her that they'd found no sign of a break-in, and this appeased her for a moment.

One day Helena said she hadn't seen the old woman lately. We hadn't heard the usual sounds from the mansard apartment either, and I realized that it had been a while since I'd noticed the reek of her perfume. We asked the neighbors, but they also hadn't seen her. This time we called the police. They arrived, pounded in vain on her door, then borrowed the stepladder in the garden and placed it on our terrace, and one of them climbed up and broke a window in the mansard. I still remember the police officer's pale face as he climbed back down, took a seat on the stepladder, and stammered that the old woman was lying on the bed, and the room was filled with the stench of decaying corpse.

Soon thereafter, new tenants moved into the mansard apartment—a corpulent fifty-year-old man with significantly thinning hair, his young and rather fetching wife, and their five-year-old son, Jindříšek.

A few days later, the head of the new household rang our doorbell to introduce himself. He presented me with a small painted box, which was trying to look like an antique, along with his business card. A doctor's title preceded his pithy and memorable name. (I soon learned that this title was as fraudulent as everything he did. His wife told me that he worked at the sanatorium in Bohnice, of course not as a doctor but an orderly, and he held this position only for the stamp it provided his ID booklet. Otherwise, he supported himself by trading in antiques.)

As soon as he opened his mouth, I realized I was standing face-to-face with a hero from a short story by O. Henry, Chekhov, Hašek, or Hrabal, or a story yet to be written—which I undertook a few months later. I changed his name and, as far as I remember, condensed several of his discourses into one.

I was given to understand that he had been everywhere, knew everybody, and could procure or arrange just about anything. In the concentration camp, he had shared a bunk with Prince Schwarzenberg. He was on a first-name basis with the prime minister's brother. He was trying to obtain a set of silver platters for the Belgian delegate at the UN. He had rebuked the deputy interior minister by saying, "You needn't think you can pull the wool over my eyes, I can see right through you!" When he visited Honza Schwarzenberg in Vienna the other day, he was introduced to Otto Hapsburg, a truly charming gentleman. An agent, of course. All those fine gentlemen were agents. Agents were in charge the world over—policemen of the world unite. Nixon and other clowns like him—he wouldn't even bother to name ours— were just their lackeys. One of these days, when he had more time, he would tell me more about all this.

After ten minutes, I was supposed to feel like a country bumpkin who had no idea about the big wide world out there. After twenty, I might begin to hope that despite all his knowledge and wide experience he might consider me worthy of his interest.

This fellow certainly deserved to be immortalized along with his splendid monologues and remarkably shameless dealings. (He once offered me an oil painting, claiming it was an original Picasso.) I was eager to write about him, but I didn't have a story yet. Then one morning I was home alone; the children were at school, and my wife was at work. I was sitting in my bedroom writing. Suddenly the door flew open, and in walked little Jindřich. His sudden appearance in our apartment, which no one could enter except as a thief, put me in such a state of shock that all I could do was stammer stupidly, "Jindříšek, where did you come from?"

And the child explained: "I jumped." He led me onto the terrace and pointed to an open window in the mansard above us.

Jindřich's butt and elbows were a little scraped, and while I was treating his wounds, I realized I had the story.

———✺———

Sometime at the beginning of December 1976, Nanda's homeroom teacher invited us in for a talk. Pretending to be crestfallen, she informed us that there was no way she could recommend our daughter for college. "You, Mr. Klíma," she turned to me, "certainly understand why. We are all very sorry; your Hanička is such a sweet and industrious girl. Her drawings are excellent, and she even helps with the May Day decorations." She advised us to send Hana to work at a factory for a year or two, then the factory could do what they at the school were not allowed to (she immediately corrected herself: what they couldn't do), that is, recommend Hana for college.

Soon thereafter, Helena's colleague from the university, Jiří Dienstbier, came to see us (I knew him from my time in Michigan, when he and his wife had stopped for a visit on their way north). Jirka was an unusually witty and clever observer. But I think at the time he was somewhat less skeptical than I was.

His optimism was now quite apparent. He said that several of our friends were preparing the text of a petition that essentially repeated the fundamental principles of the Helsinki Accords. Among other things, it required the countries that had signed the treaty to uphold basic human rights, and, as I was well aware, our government had signed it. The petition demanded nothing more than that the government actually do what it promised when it signed this document. With almost gleeful joy, he added that he truly could not imagine what they might object to in such a petition. And he took out of his briefcase four typewritten pages for me to look over.

The text, bearing the title Charter 77, did indeed refer to the International Covenant on Civil and Political Rights and the International Covenant on Economic, Social, and Cultural Rights, which had come into effect a few months earlier. But in the third sentence it announced that the promulgation, *however, serves as a powerful reminder of the extent to which basic human rights in our country exist, regrettably, on paper alone.*

The introduction itself would not please our comrades in power. Then, blow after blow followed, all of them well aimed:

> In violation of Article 13 of the second-mentioned covenant, guaranteeing everyone the right to education, countless young people are prevented from studying because of their own views or even their parents.' . . . Freedom of public expression is inhibited. . . . No philosophical, political, or scientific view or artistic activity that departs ever so slightly from the narrow bounds of official ideology or aesthetics is allowed to be published; no open criticism can be made of abnormal social phenomena; no public defense is possible against false and insulting charges made in official propaganda. . . . Freedom of religious confession, emphatically guaranteed by Article 18 of the first covenant, is continually curtailed by arbitrary official action.

In the enumeration of the regime's violations, it was pointed out that there were no nonparty authorities; the Ministry of the Interior monitored the lives of its own citizens, tracked their every move, tapped telephones and apartments, intercepted their mail, and conducted house searches.

> In cases of prosecution on political grounds the investigative and judicial organs violate the rights of those charged and those defending them, as guaranteed by Article 14 of the first covenant and indeed by Czechoslovak law. The prison treatment of those sentenced in such cases is an affront to their human dignity and a menace to their health, aimed at breaking their morale.

Finally, the text pointed out that Charter 77 was not an organization; it did not have any statutes. It sought only to serve the general good. It did not pretend to be a political organization but wanted only to introduce a constructive dialogue with the ruling power. It was represented by three spokesmen: Professor Jan Patočka, Václav Havel, and Professor Jiří Hájek.

I said they couldn't possibly expect our government to conduct a dialogue on these sensitive issues.

What could they do? Jiří wanted to know my opinion.

They'll raise hell.

But then they'd just be proving us right! He said the petition had already been signed by a lot of people and almost all of our friends.

But no one will ever know about it, I objected. You say right here that they monitor every means of communication.

I saw he was waiting to see if I would sign, but I said I would have to think it over. Even though I had no doubt, I added, that the proclamation was correct about everything, this was precisely what would infuriate the government the most.

Certainly I was doing some shuffling because I kept hoping that Nanda might be accepted at art school and, unlike my friend and courier, I was certain that my signature would be carefully noted, and they would then consider an appropriate punishment.

The police confiscated the final petition even before the three couriers managed to deliver it to the National Assembly, the government, and the Czechoslovak Press Agency. The charter had 242 signatories: writers, philosophers, journalists, priests, and scholars (some asked that their names not be revealed). Later, the number of signatories increased by almost a thousand (Helena was among them).

The secret police reacted more furiously than my friends had anticipated. Over the following hours, they began searching the flats of everyone who had signed the charter. They confiscated crates of printed matter and manuscripts and brought in signatories for interrogation; some of the signers subsequently lost their jobs.

For a few days nothing happened. Finally, *Rudé právo* came out with an article titled "Castaways and Usurpers." Although I expected the official reaction to be harsh, this piece by the representatives of the journalist cesspool exceeded all expectations. The article was lengthier than the charter itself and cited not a word of the text. It noted among other things:

> The international forces of reaction will employ all means and seek out all allies. They corrupt anyone who can be corrupted, they bribe whomever they can bribe, they count on apostates and deserters from the enemy's camp. They enlist emigrants but also castaways living in socialist countries, those who, for whatever reason—their class origin, their reactionary interests, their vanity, megalomania, apostasy, or notorious spinelessness—are willing to lend their names even to the devil. In their obdurate battle against progress, the international forces of reaction . . . often seek the impossible—to revive even political corpses, both from the ranks of emigrants from Socialist countries and from the ranks of class enemies, renegades, and even criminal elements. One of the forms of this pathetic cooperation is the fabrication of all manner of pamphlets, letters, protests, and other trivial calumny, passed off as the voice of "oppositional" individuals or groups, which are then, with great fanfare, disseminated throughout the world.
>
> Among these is the newest pamphlet, the so-called Charter 77, given to certain Western agencies by a group composed of individuals from the ranks of the bankrupt, reactionary Czecho-slovak bourgeoisie as well as the bankrupt organizers of the 1968 counterrevolution upon the orders of anticommunist and Zionist head offices. It is an antistate, antisocialist, antipeople, and dema-gogic piece of libel that crudely and mendaciously slanders the Czechoslovak Socialist Republic. It is a colorful mix of human and political castaways. Among them are V. Havel, a man from a millionaire's family; the obdurate antisocialist P. Kohout, the loyal servant of imperialism and his well-established agent, J. Hájek; the bankrupt politician who, under the slogan of neutrality, wanted to

detach us from the society of socialist countries; and L. Vaculík, the author of the counterrevolutionary pamphlet "Two Thousand Words."

The only thing missing was a demand that the aforementioned be summarily imprisoned and put to death as quickly as possible.

At least a few of the names mentioned must have suggested to some readers that the charter was, in all likelihood, thoroughly different from the way it was being presented. Nevertheless, the party functionaries pulled out all the stops, and *Rudé právo* began printing indignant letters from working-class citizens who railed against the charter, ignorant of its contents.

A couple of days after this furious campaign began, a group of three coal men were delivering some coke to my apartment. I was standing at the entrance to the basement counting the buckets. One of them—he must have heard something about me—leaned over and asked if I happened to have a copy of "that charter."

I brought them the text. Even today, I can see the three men with tubs on their backs (they had climbed up to the landing). They were carefully holding the onionskin paper in their hands as if it were an ancient parchment and reading the text with rapt and unfeigned interest. They returned it to me and asked if I could get them a copy; they wouldn't reveal it to anyone, they assured me. I gave them one, and they apparently didn't snitch.

———

Nanda's teacher called us in again and delightedly informed us that they had changed their opinion and decided to recommend her for art school. I thanked her, even though it was obvious that the school had simply been given new instructions. I was astounded that the secret police had so quickly made it clear to me that they had taken into consideration the absence of my signature on Charter 77.

The charter was signed by Christians and atheists, opponents of communism, and those who had been expelled from the Communist Party but had remained adherents of socialism. The fact that I did not sign perhaps surprised some of my friends, but no one ever asked me why and no one ever considered me a traitor. Of course, everyone has the right to act according to his own convictions and resolve, and everyone knew I was reluctant to lend my signature to material I had not written myself or at least collaborated on.

Voice of America and Radio Free Europe were repeatedly broadcasting the text of Charter 77 and reporting on how it was being circulated and copied. Now it was up to the government to demonstrate that the petition was actually the work of only a few bankrupt usurpers and castaways. Whenever someone calls its legitimacy into doubt, every totalitarian and occupying power requires that the public conspicuously (it says: "by acclamation") support it, in order that the greatest number of people abase and immerse themselves in collaborationist mire.

After the assassination of the Nazi Reich protector and mass murderer Reinhard Heydrich, the protectorate government summoned a gathering of more than a thousand citizens on Wenceslaus Square to swear allegiance to Hitler. They brought singers from the National Theater and forced them to sing the national anthem while everyone raised his right arm in the Nazi salute. (In their defense, any manifestation of resistance by those participating in this absurd performance would have resulted in execution.)

Thirty-five years later, during the Soviet occupation, the government, installed by the occupiers, called the foremost artists, primarily actors, to the National Theater. In this building, which from its inception has symbolized national pride, those summoned were supposed to sign a protest against Charter 77.

One of the most fanatical Communist actresses, Jiřina Švorcová, read a long, impassioned speech which, with the usual phrases, proclaimed her unity with the working people. She claimed that extraordinary works and achievements had been accomplished, *which have enriched the spiritual life of our people and received much deserved recognition both at home and abroad. These achievements were realized in conjunction with the everyday work of our people whom our Communist Party led out of years of disruption. They emerged as a part of mutual efforts to achieve the rich, Socialist development of life in our country. They emerged in the favorable atmosphere of devotion, understanding, and optimal conditions that our society is creating for art and culture.*

After all the usual curtsies to the progressive forces of the world, the actress came to the heart of her message:

> That is why—in accord with the Final Act of the Helsinki Conference—we stretch our hand across the borders of countries and continents, fully aware that true art and true culture should help individual nations and all of humanity move forward; they should create understanding among people of diverse countries; they should win people over to the humanistic perspective concerning peace and mutual cooperation in the interests of joyful human life. That is why we hold in contempt those who, in the unbridled pride of their narcissistic arrogance, for selfish interests, or even for filthy lucre all over the world—even in our country, a small group of such backsliders and traitors can be found—divorce and isolate themselves from the nation, its life, and its genuine interests and, with inexorable logic, become instruments of the antihumanistic forces of imperialism and, in its service, the heralds of disruption and discord among nations.

This document of protest against Charter 77, which outlined the optimal conditions for artistic development in a country in which censorship watched over every publicly pronounced word, where hundreds of thousands of educated people were unable to work, and where hundreds of artists were banned from making their work public, was signed, to their shame (with a few exceptions), by those who were willing to accept the occupying regime and its violence against culture.

Over the course of several days, *Rudé právo* printed more and more signatures, first of the most famous and then of entirely unknown actors, actresses, artists, musicians, and regional authors who perhaps believed that their signature would open their paths to fame. (It is difficult to find an excuse for such a deed.)

Apparently my deviation from this common enterprise interested the secret police agents. As far as I could judge, they considered me one of the more active opponents. Why had I suddenly pulled back? Was it a sign that I'd had some disagreement with the others, that I had become the so-called weakest link in the chain? They decided to look into it.

At the beginning of February 1977, an article appeared in *Rudé právo* about a German journalist named Walter Kratzer who was leaving Czechoslovakia on January 15. According to the article, a letter was found during the customs check with instructions concerning whom to turn to in Prague:

> The best contact is the writer Ivan Klíma, Prague 4, Nad lesem 8, Tel. 46 12 64. Klíma signed the Charter 77, knows all the signatories, and is a close friend of authors of the "Prague Spring." He will open doors for you. Should you be unable to reach Klíma, contact Klíma's friend, the American actress Marlene Manchini, who lives in the Intercontinental Hotel.

The rest of the article mentioned that my German publisher was subsidized by the West German intelligence service, and we were therefore reputed fighters for human rights, but *in reality were a bunch of castaways and political adventurers.*

The intent of this nonsense, especially the mention of an American actress whom I'd never laid eyes on, was apparent. The article was offering me an opportunity to publicly protest this mendacious information. The reference to the actress was simply intended to make this easier. I could get angry and say not only did I not know Marlene Manchini but I had not signed any pamphlet by a handful of castaways and political adventurers and then demand that the newspaper issue a retraction.

I did not allow myself to be tricked and refused to react to the article.

Around this time, I was invited to the Swedish premiere of a film adaptation of my novel *A Summer Affair*. Although I knew it would be futile, I decided to request my passport. I filled out a complicated form, listed all my relatives abroad (Aunt Ilonka in Canada), and proceeded to the People's Committee for the first stamp. The unsuspecting official took the form and said she'd be right back. She did indeed come right back and with some embarrassment—in fact, she seemed downright frightened. They couldn't give me the stamp, and I certainly knew why. I said I actually didn't.

"You signed," she said in a whisper, "that pamphlet . . . that charter."

I went home and, weighing every word, composed a letter of protest to the minister of the interior.

> I do not understand why someone who signed Charter 77 cannot receive a passport and even less why someone who didn't sign the Charter is refused a stamp on a request for a passport with the justification that he signed the charter.

I also wrote that I had been invited to the premiere of my film, as is quite common, and I would be ashamed to tell the studio I couldn't attend because, despite all promises by the government about upholding basic human rights, our offices refuse to issue me a passport.

About two weeks later, I was called in for an interrogation. The official had in front of him my letter to the minister, with about half the lines underlined in red.

"You think," he asked, offended, "we don't know you didn't sign the charter?"

I said I had no way of knowing what they knew, especially when *Rudé právo*, apparently on the basis of materials received from the powers that be, wrote not only that had I signed the charter, but that I was also the best contact because I knew all the signatories.

"So you read the article?" He was comforted. "Why didn't you protest, since you knew it was false information?"

I said it would have been senseless.

He wanted to know why I thought this. I explained, "Because I know that what *Rudé právo* writes is the truth even if it is erroneous."

He twitched his lips and quickly changed the subject.

This time he was almost collegial. Perhaps he was supposed to be playing the good cop, or at least they hadn't ordered him to play the bad cop. He said it might be possible to consider a passport for me as long as I was willing to show a little goodwill.

I said that it was not appropriate for anyone to judge my goodwill if I was asking for something to which I had an obvious right. All at once, I was afraid they would issue my passport and let me out but not back in. Without further ado, I informed him that the premiere had already taken place, so my intention to travel to Sweden had lost its justification, and I had no plans to go elsewhere.

"So you actually don't want your passport?" he asked, feigning surprise.

"I think I'll wait," I decided to say, "until all my friends receive theirs."

"Fine," he said, "but just don't go complaining to some foreign radio how we're suppressing your rights."

So I didn't get my passport. In addition, they disconnected my telephone and confiscated my car inspection certificate.

Marlene Manchini, if she actually existed and was even in Prague, had certainly departed by now.

Essay: *(Secret Police)*, p. 522

19

Over the course of several weeks, Charter 77 issued a number of thoroughly elaborated documents (a number of outstanding lawyers were among the signatories). They drew attention to, among other things, the fact that many young people were limited in their right to an education and that the government persecuted religious devotees. Some of the documents dealt with illegal trials or labor law violations. (When my friends were preparing a text on the suppression of freedom of expression, especially literature, they asked me to help them.) Václav Havel, one of the three spokesmen, was arrested at the beginning of January. The authorities knew that in him the charter had a person of exceptional political abilities. On March 13, after a daylong interrogation, Professor Jan Patočka, the second spokesman of the charter, died.

The death of an outstanding philosopher, whom State Security had treated as a criminal, was not in the best interests of the leaders of our country, but they remained true to their resolve that anyone who tried to reveal their villainies would remain an outcast even after death.

Despite the malevolent campaign against the charter, thousands of people attended the funeral of its first martyr. A number of us recognized our investigators making their way through the crowd of mourners and noting those who dared to mourn publicly. The funeral was taking place in Břevnov, where there was a motorcycle track nearby, so the secret police sent motorcyclists to ride around the track as fast and loudly as they could. Helicopters meanwhile hovered overhead to drown out the words uttered at the graveside.

As the funeral rites were being performed, the cops turned their backs to the grave and photographed those who came to pay their respects. These obstinate manifestations of disrespect revealed the pathetic nature of the country's rulers more than any critical document ever could.

The fact that I hadn't signed the charter and still seemed to be abstaining from all protest activity struck the secret police as extremely suspicious now. After Hrabal's self-criticism, they hadn't been able to persuade anyone else to abandon his erroneous ways—not to mention that Hrabal was nonpolitical and his self-criticism didn't have the appropriate impact.

A few weeks after my last summons to Bartolomějská Street, the mail carrier delivered to me the familiar subpoena.

At the porter's lodge, I was met by the same official who had investigated my complaint to the Ministry of the Interior. He feigned affability and asked after my health and whether I'd received any more invitations from abroad.

When he pressed the button in the elevator, I noticed that we were going to a higher floor than usual. I asked where he was leading me this time, and he said we were going two floors up. In every sense of the word.

I was led down a corridor that did indeed look less dreary. He knocked on one of the doors, and I unexpectedly found myself in a human environment. There were even pictures on the walls and a fairly decent rug covering the floor. Somewhat bewildered, I said hello to the secretary, and she replied in kind. Then she rose from her chair, opened a padded door, and said the colonel was expecting me.

In this room were bookcases overflowing with various collected works and a little gray-suited gentleman with the slightly puffy face of a civil servant.

He seemed pleased to see me. "Ah, Mr. Klíma," he said. He rose from behind his desk, shook my hand, and introduced himself as Mr. Irovský. He pointed to a leather armchair and invited me to have a seat. Then, like a good host, he asked if he could offer me something to drink. I thanked him and said I wasn't thirsty.

He informed me he'd invited me here because he wanted to speak about my future plans, as they say. He apologized for the official form of his invitation, but we definitely should not consider this an interrogation. He would have asked me to a café, where it would have been much more pleasant, but from everything he'd heard, in all likelihood I would have refused such an invitation.

Then followed a conversation that some instruction manual or textbook of the secret police probably referred to as "cordial and friendly."

The colonel assured me that, for him, our meeting was a rare opportunity. When would he ever have the chance to sit and chat with a world-famous author? He emphasized "world-famous" in order to flatter me or to let me know he was aware of the publication of my books and performances of my plays abroad, which could be considered an act hostile to the state, to socialism, and essentially to all progressive forces of the world in their battle for peace. Then, no matter how astoundingly incongruous it seemed, he started talking about literature. He mentioned Hemingway, whose book about the Spanish Civil War seemed to him quite progressive; and Howard Fast, who, on the other hand, had gone over to the enemies of socialism. "And what about your books?" he wanted to know. "I asked about them at the bookstore just around the corner in the building where you used to work, but they didn't have anything."

Had he yelled at me, had he interrogated me, it would have been very easy to keep quiet, to ignore the questions or say I wasn't going to give evidence. But when a person is sitting across from you and says he's surprised he can't get a copy of one of your books, it seems stupid not to reply even though I knew this was some sort of ludicrous game.

I knew he hadn't asked anyone about my books because he was well aware they were forbidden to appear in bookstores. It was entirely possible that he was the one who had issued the order to confiscate my books immediately if they appeared anywhere.

I said I was not allowed to publish here.

"That's a shame," he replied. "I'll bet that's really quite vexing. Or perhaps it's all the same to you?"

I said there were plenty of other things more vexing.

He ignored my response. "But you must be working on something now. One of those little novels of yours? And plays as well. A colleague mentioned that something of yours was playing in Switzerland and Vienna. You apparently poked a little fun at our circumstances here. But that's part of your trade," he quickly added. "Did you go to the premiere?"

I said my passport and my wife's had been confiscated.

"So why didn't you submit a request for them?" he mused and immediately added, "But I'm not going to sit here and ask you questions. It might seem like an interrogation."

Why else would I be sitting in this viper's nest? It was more like an insane dream.

Then the colonel decided to change the subject of this amicable conversation and began discussing mushroom hunting. He'd heard it was my hobby (his agents had provided him with even this information), but the regular forests had already been picked clean. "Where could one find a decent mushroom?" he complained. At least a parasol or rosacea mushroom. He offered to take me out to the military zone where there were plenty, and I'd have a full basket in no time.

Then he returned to my writing and said he'd like to read something.

I repeated that my books were banned from publication.

"But you must have a copy of what you send to Mr. Jürgen in Switzerland."

I said I had no copies of my books because I didn't want any trouble.

"That's too bad." He seemed saddened. "But have a look around at home. You must have some manuscript lying around." He neglected to mention that he could send a band of his subordinates to help me look. Instead he said, "Of course, I'll return it when I'm finished."

Then it was as if this charming fellow had suddenly remembered that the last time he spoke with the minister, he mentioned that perhaps their offices could accommodate my passport request. "That wasn't right. In fact it was downright wrong. We must support our artists—even if they can be annoying at times. You know what I mean; don't take it personally. You see, our people downstairs like to demonstrate their vigilance, but they overdo it. Mr. Klíma, if you ever have the feeling you're being harassed, give me a call and I'll look into it. Here," he added almost ceremoniously, "is my card with my direct number. I don't give this to just anyone. You see how much I trust you." Then he got up and walked over to me; I was afraid he was going to hug and kiss me goodbye, but he said, "And could I have your number in case I want to get in touch?" (As if he wasn't fully aware that my telephone hadn't been working for two months.) I said that my telephone had apparently been disconnected.

"Really?" He looked surprised. "A breakdown?"

"That's what they tell me. They say it can't be fixed."

"Odd." He feigned astonishment. "You see how people work in this country. They don't want to go to work, so they say it can't be fixed. Something should be done about this. If you want, I've got acquaintances in communications; I can press them on it."

It was a farce—the person who probably had my telephone disconnected in the first place, and whose power and responsibilities were certainly more extensive than seeing that my telephone be reconnected, was now pretending to be someone who availed himself of acquaintances at the switchboard. I merely thanked him and said that I found it quite pleasant not to have the telephone bothering me when I was trying to work.

Then my official, who had apparently been waiting for me in the other room with the secretary, escorted me out of the building.

Outside, I fondled the card in my pocket. No, it wasn't a dream. I should have tossed it into the garbage—none of my friends carried around the business card of a secret police colonel.

About a week later, a uniformed officer rang our door with a summons to appear at the district department of the district police precinct. I was to bring my car.

I objected that my car had been inspected less than a month ago, and although they had taken my inspection certificate, I had had the supposed defect repaired, and it was returned to me.

He hesitated for a moment but then said that my car wasn't to be inspected. "In Tábor a man was run over by a blue Zhiguli, and the perpetrator fled the scene."

I told him I hadn't been in Tábor for several years. He replied that if I did not report within two hours, I would be brought in.

I was alarmed by the thought of trying to prove I hadn't been in Tábor at a certain time on a certain day: They could simply claim to have found dried blood on the hood and accuse me of killing a pedestrian.

I remembered the colonel's card and his vow to protect me from needless harassment by overeager police officers.

After thinking it over a moment, I dialed his number and was indeed connected with him at once. I told him about the summons concerning the auto incident between a blue Zhiguli and a pedestrian in Tábor, where I hadn't been for several years.

"You see?" he said. "There you go. Instead of trying to discover where you were, they're harassing you. Don't go anywhere, I'll take care of it."

I thanked him and hung up.

Then I realized he hadn't even asked where he was supposed to take care of it, and he immediately believed my assertion that I hadn't been in Tábor. Why? I was starting to have my suspicions.

After another week, a young man appeared at our door and refused my invitation to come in. He explained he was only a messenger. When he saw my surprise (at first I thought this was a messenger from Jürgen), he added that he had a message from the colonel; he would like to get together.

I asked him if this was a summons.

"No, of course not," he said. "There isn't to be any interrogation. The colonel just wants to talk to you and was hoping you might have found one of your manuscripts at home."

I asked him when I should show up.

"The colonel says it's completely up to you. He'll find the time."

I didn't know what to do.

"And where should I go?"

"The colonel asks that you come see him at his office. He doesn't think anywhere else would suit you."

It was Monday. To put off the meeting as long as possible, I suggested Friday.

"Certainly," answered the messenger. "At what time?"

This ostentatious accommodation strengthened my desire to confirm my suspicions. At the same time, I kept telling myself, Don't get involved in any games with them. They are stronger and, more important, they have no scruples. But why was the colonel trying to engage me?

I suggested eleven o'clock.

On Friday I pulled from the drawer my manuscript of *A Summer Affair*, which had come out in several editions abroad and would show the colonel there was nothing seditious in a book that had been banned from publication in Czechoslovakia. When a person decides to do something stupid, he can usually find a reason to justify it to himself.

At eleven o'clock, I presented myself at Bartolomějská Street.

The same official met me at the porter's lodge and led me to the same office, where I was greeted by the colonel. He offered me wine, coffee, tea, or mineral water. I refused everything, and the secretary brought me a bottle of mineral water.

The colonel invited me to have a seat and began by noting that the summer holidays were approaching. He himself hadn't been on vacation for several years and asked if I was planning to go anywhere. He promptly corrected himself and said he didn't want this to seem like an interrogation, then he suggested it was best to spend the summer near the water, for example at Lake Balaton. The Lipno Dam was also nice. He mentioned his company cottage not far from Jevany and reported with excitement that according to meteorologists, the air was supposed to be better there than in the Giant Mountains because the currents above their cottage bring air all the way from the Alps. He asked if everything was fine with me. When I replied that it was, he said he was glad to hear it. Then he asked if I had brought any of my books.

I pulled *Summer Affair* from my briefcase. He seemed surprised and thanked me profusely. He was very much looking forward to reading the manuscript and said that, of course, he would return it when he was done. "Perhaps you need it," he added, "to send to Mr. Jürgen."

He stood up, extended his hand, and said he hoped I would go on to write something nice.

A few days later, I received a subpoena to appear immediately at the district authority of police.

When I presented myself, I was asked to hand over my identification card. The official examined it for a moment and led me to the second floor to meet with a military member of executive power, apparently the local commander.

He was handed my quite well maintained ID, glanced at it, and started shouting: How dare I present such a grubby and tattered document. Did I realize that this document was the property of the state?

I protested that the ID was neither grubby nor tattered.

He roared at me to shut my trap. He paged through the ID booklet and carried on shouting: Where was I employed? Why didn't I have a stamp?

I said I was not employed but worked freelance.

"So you're freelance? To me, you're a parasite, and that is how I will deal with you. I am hereby confiscating your identity booklet."

When I didn't budge, he advised me to clear out before he lost his patience.

After I spent an hour waiting downstairs, my information was written out on a form, and I was told that this was a temporary ID valid for one month. I must submit a request for a new one.

My suspicions were confirmed. Now I was supposed to call my colonel, who would claim I was simply being harassed again; I could pick up my ID first thing tomorrow, or perhaps he would order it to be brought to me with an apology. Then he would invite me to come see him and allude to all the things he was doing for me and even confide in me that he had some acquaintances in publishing. He could arrange for one of my books to be published if I would only do some minor favor for him in return.

Perhaps this district director was not aware that I was collecting partial disability pay, and the charge of parasitism would not stick.

I applied for a new ID and didn't call the colonel. I simply waited.

About two weeks later, another messenger stopped by to call me in. He was just as polite and just as accommodating.

When I took a seat in the colonel's office and received the usual mineral water (I'd never taken so much as a sip), I said I preferred to receive a summons. The colonel, however, gave me to understand that this was out of the question. This wasn't an interrogation, or did I have the impression, he asked, somewhat offended, that it was? He was simply interested in my fate and wanted to help, so that I would not be disturbed in my writing. Then he spoke for quite some time about vacation possibilities and mushroom hunting in the military zone, where he once again invited me to join him. When I asked if I could bring along a friend, he wanted to know whom. When I said Vaculík, he seemed thrilled by the idea. To enjoy the company of two such marvelous writers—what more could he wish for? He would definitely stop by my place soon.

He didn't ask me anything more. Instead, he waited to see what I would start talking about, but I kept silent and thought what I would do if he actually stopped by. There was no way I would go mushroom hunting with an officer of the secret police, let alone to the military zone, where I might be shot. Accidentally, of course.

The colonel then mentioned my novel. He said he found it quite absorbing and hoped I would forgive him if he kept it for a few more days. Lately he'd had little time for reading. Finally, he asked if everything was okay with me.

When I said everything was fine, he asked more specifically: No harassment?

"No," I said, "If you have in mind my ID booklet, they have to issue me a new one; otherwise they will be violating the law."

My answer seemed to take him by surprise, but he was a professional. He wished me a pleasant vacation and reiterated that he would let Vaculík and me know if he was planning a trip somewhere to the woods in the military zone. We simply had to go mushroom hunting together.

He never got in touch again. He, or perhaps somebody above him, had decided I was not a good prospect, and he never returned my manuscript. If he's not dead, perhaps he's still reading it.

Writers on Their Congress

Immediately upon the conclusion of the constitutive congress of the Czechoslovak Writers' Union, reporters from the Czechoslovak Press Agency invited several delegates for a discussion. . . . MILOSLAV STINGL replied: . . . In the speech by the chair of the party and the ruling delegation, I was fascinated by the genuinely deep interest and solicitude of the highest representatives of our society for the development of Czechoslovak literature. And what am I personally taking away from the congress? I want to dwell not on what I've already accomplished, but rather on what I still have to do. I want to put everything inside me in the books I

have yet to write—perhaps even more. Is the precept "Outperform
even yourself" meant only for miners? Through my humble works,
I wish to serve the Czech reader and Czech literature.

From *Lidová demokracie*, December 10, 1977

It was during this time that I received my first small royalty payment
for my story for the cartoon *Little Mole*. Aware I could be accused of
parasitism (my partial disability pension could be taken away at any
time), I decided to try to renew my writer's insurance.

And it worked! The moment a crack appeared in the seemingly
impervious fortress of prohibition, the bureaucracy fell into confusion.
I went to the offices of the Literary Fund and presented my signed contract along with confirmation that Krátký Film had paid me a royalty.
The source of my income was legitimate, and the appropriate official (I
sensed he was sympathetic) renewed my insurance according to the law.
A year later my name appeared on TV in the credits for the scripts of
the short films I had written, which surprised everyone including my
friends (those who noticed). Many began to hope that the ridiculous
proscriptions would finally cease. But in this they were mistaken. I heard
a rumor that someone from the ideological department protested that
I had been allowed to work on officially produced films. Nevertheless,
because the films had originated at a time when only permitted authors
could publish, my name was not removed from the credits. At the same
time, however, nothing else was allowed to appear with my name on it
until the end of the eighties.

I think it was Pavel Kohout's idea—it was definitely his wife, Jelena
Mašinová, who bought dozens of tickets to a railwaymen's ball. I
thought it would be ridiculous for me to go, since I didn't know how
to dance. But Helena was excited; we would see our friends there,

and the railway workers would be surprised when they saw who was in attendance.

So I bought tickets. Helena wore her graduation dress, I wore my Sunday best, and Michal donned his suit from his dancing lessons. Then we got into the car and set off for the dance, the first one in my life.

On the way from the Vinohrady Theater, where we managed to find a parking spot, we kept running into friends who warned us not to try to get into the dance. Secret policemen were standing at the entrance turning everyone away who wasn't a railway worker.

For a while we lingered in the little park out front, then we saw a limping Pavel Kohout being supported by his wife. Pavel had refused to leave and kept showing his invitation, claiming that anyone who had bought a ticket had to be admitted. Instead, he had been tossed down the stairs.

I offered to drive him to a doctor.

The closest clinic was only about four hundred meters away. I noticed two vehicles following me; one of them belonged to the secret police. When I stopped, and Helena and Michal took Pavel inside, two members of the secret police stepped out of their vehicle, which they had parked just behind mine. They asked for my documents. They didn't know what to charge me with, so they had me breathe into a tube. Only an idiot or a gambler would have drunk alcohol before such an event. They told me everything was in order and handed back my documents while I waited for my injured friend to return.

Then we set off across Prague. Pavel, who had just recently moved out of his apartment in Hradčany, was temporarily living at Václav Havel's in Dejvice. (I did not have fond memories of this place—at one of Václav's birthday celebrations, I had indecorously taken a seat on a tabletop displaying the family crystal. The tabletop, however, was not secured, and I sent all the crystal crashing to the floor. Only shards remained. Václav, magnanimous as always, consoled me and said it was his fault; he should have had the tabletop attached a long time ago.)

Now we drove to Dejvice with a police escort worthy of a ministry chairman from some friendly African nation. We then said goodbye to Pavel and headed home. As we were nearing the Braník brewery, one of the cars tailing us suddenly passed and ordered us to stop. When the police officer once again pulled out the Breathalyzer, I protested that I had breathed into it a moment ago, and everything had been fine.

He was an older officer and looked like someone from the countryside (apparently, they'd activated police from all precincts of Prague). He resorted to an explanation I would never forget: "You could have been drinking behind the wheel."

I blew into the device once again. The officer ripped the Breathalyzer from my hands and said in a direful tone: "Positive."

I asked if I could see the device, and he said that was not permitted. He seemed both truculent and somewhat embarrassed. Obviously, he was an ordinary traffic cop, and such mendacity was not part of his job description.

They confiscated both my driver's license and my car keys. They didn't think about Helena's set of keys, and she drove me immediately to the sobering station (this time without a police escort) for a blood test. When we explained to the surprised doctor on duty why we wanted the test, he gladly took my blood and promised to send the results as soon as possible.

For the next two weeks I searched for my driver's license, which was apparently roving around various police stations. Finally, I made it all the way to the head of a regiment of the riot squad. He admitted me, even though it was after business hours. He was in his shirtsleeves with his police trousers held up by wide suspenders, and told me fairly genially that he'd had my driver's license but he'd sent it to the police station on Náměstrí míru.

The person in charge there actually pulled out my driver's license and several sheets of supporting documents. He looked them over for a moment and then informed me, "You were subjected to a breath alcohol test. No alcohol was detected in your blood. Unfortunately, your driver's license was in such a state that it had to be confiscated."

Although my driver's license was almost new, their retreat from the ridiculous charge that I was driving drunk seemed to me a small victory.

⸎

Even in the Soviet Union, the government was treating those who criticized the regime more leniently. Andrei Sakharov was neither executed nor run over by an automobile. He was merely exiled to Gorky. Alexander Solzhenitsyn, that "mercenary in the pay of imperialists," whom Stalin would have had destroyed along with his family and friends, was now forcibly dragged into an airplane and sent to West Germany.

The rulers in Moscow advised the collaborationist government in Prague to likewise banish unpleasant critics.

I can imagine the embarrassment this advice must have aroused. The ruling rabble wanted to punish, discredit, and humiliate their opponents and cast them into poverty. But exile them to lands of abundance and unlimited opportunities? Send them somewhere they would be welcomed as heroes? Where the rulers themselves would like to live if they hadn't gotten mixed up with the current regime?

But, as usual, they were obedient. During an interrogation, an offer would be proposed, which usually went like this: If you feel so oppressed here, you can move to that free world of yours. Submit a request and it will be approved. When Václav Havel was in prison in the summer of 1979, two seemingly pleasant envoys paid him a visit and suggested it would be possible for him to move to New York. All he had to do was submit a request. He refused and remained in prison for an additional three years.

The regime tried to force others to emigrate. One of its most outspoken opponents was Pavel Kohout. Once, to the surprise of us all, he was allowed to leave in order to direct one of his plays. He left knowing full well that they didn't have to let him back into the country. Therefore, he refused to give any politically colored interviews while abroad—this was at least one way to keep him quiet. When they let him out a second time with his wife, he was detained on his return trip at the Austrian border and informed him that his citizenship had been revoked. Thus they forced him into exile.

—∞—

Writers and artists in general have a proclivity to form personal and professional associations on the basis of generational affinities, personal friendships, or artistic tendencies. Often they consider everyone who does not share their opinions as mistaken, blind, or at least ignorant. There are few environments in which you will find more competitive emulation than an artistic one. In its vindictiveness, contemptuous disdain for values and national culture, and subservience to the occupying power, the collaborationist regime succeeded in doing something that no democratic society ever could: It unified everyone who had been harmed or silenced, everyone who had refused to acquiesce to its demands without regard to artistic or political convictions.

None of my friends belonged to the classic underground (even though Václav Havel knew those authors well), but when the current government was preparing to sentence the underground musical group the Plastic People of the Universe to prison, most of us signed the petition against the trial.

When my friends, under the leadership of "the guard of the Loreta treasure," Jiří Brabec, were preparing their *Dictionary of Czech Writers*, perhaps the most remarkable book in our typewritten Padlock series, they included, without differentiation, all authors whose works between 1948 and 1979 had been banned, at least for a time. In all there were several hundred, many more than those who had been allowed to publish the entire time; it was a unique collection of authors who at some time in their lives had managed to resist the felonious power.

At the end of the '70s, society was much more heterogeneous than it seemed at first sight. Not everyone preferred open resistance, but at the same time many young people were looking for a way to demonstrate their dislike of the prevailing conditions of society. The current leaders were always announcing that they cared about the youth. They even tried to make it clear they were willing to put up with some things—long hair, jazz, and even songs that demonstratively ignored official ideology.

Whereas the censors had destroyed the repertories of the large theaters, a few small stages were allowed to continue. Contemporary life—albeit only via a few allusions—managed to make its way into the Semafor Theater, which had been established at the end of the 1950s. The Jára Cimrman Theater also survived from the end of the 1960s. It was primarily this second theater that I took a liking to. It defiantly ignored present-day politics and the demands the regime made of art. It brought into existence its own special world set somewhere in the idyllic time of the early twentieth century and created wonderful unique parodies, sometimes just for the laughter itself, at other times in order to grasp the absurdity of contemporary life.

The young evangelical minister Svát'a Karásek wrote protest songs, usually based on the melodies of famous Negro spirituals.

> *Man cannot rule*
> *he gets drunk on his own power*
> *the truth is firmly in his hands*
> *instead of above himself.*
> *Ruler, what are you saying to the crowds*
> *what if you fell silent for once*
> *what if you knelt down for once*
> *with your head in your hands.*

Our family visited him at Houska Castle, where he worked as a caretaker (he was not allowed to preach), and he sang his entire repertoire for Michal into our primitive tape recorder. Michal made copies of the songs for his friends.

There was also an entire group of protest singers who joined together under the name of Šafrán. I used to invite the singers over to my house along with my friends.

Several times I drove Jaroslav Hutka, with whom I had become close, to various places in Bohemia where he was performing. It was an extraordinarily powerful experience when the entire auditorium, filled with young spectators, enthusiastically greeted their singer. In 1979, Václav Havel was arrested again. Hutka made use of the similarity of names and composed a song about Havlíček, whom the Bach regime had not imprisoned but rather exiled to Brixen. There was no doubt as to the real meaning of his lyrics.

> Now sitting behind walls, they've placed you in a cell
> The angels of Brixen, exhorting death's knell.
> A tale for young children, a puppet ballet,
> They pull on the strings without coming out into day.
> By the letter of the law of the gavel,
> Now think about justice, Havlíček, Havel.

The ovation that followed exceeded all measure. The fact that such songs could be sung led one to suspect that the occupying regime was losing some of its capricious vigilance.

Paradoxically for singers, as well as artists who refused to bow to the people in charge, these times brought a certain satisfaction. The public was waiting for any kind of rebellious gestures and vehemently accepted them.

At the beginning of the '80s, more and more groups were springing up that, unlike the charter, were not political. They strove only for independent thought and action.

I was invited by a group of young evangelicals from a congregation in Vinohrady to say something about samizdat literature. After my lecture, they showed me a thick typewritten volume. They were publishing it four times a year. Every three months, each member of the congregation had to write or translate an article from his field and bring several copies to their meeting. There the contributions were compiled and bound. I liked this idea so much that I told my friends about it, and we started putting together our own monthly typewritten journal. Because publishing any sort of periodical (even a typewritten one) was still against the law, we listed the individual contributions on the first page beneath the word "Contents." And thus our journal became known simply as *Contents*.

—⚭—

More and more often I was visited by strangers, sometimes even students (there was also a young teaching assistant of Czech literature who came around once a month all the way from Olomouc), to ask if they could borrow some of our samizdat texts. They usually returned the books after about a month and then asked to borrow others. I soon realized that each of them had his own circle of friends to whom he was lending the books. These were not groups of rebels but simply people who saw the current regime as baleful, hampering freedom, and therefore worthy of contempt.

Of course we had to keep everything secret—what we were doing, where we met, what we talked about. Originally, there were eight of us who put together *Contents*, but the number of regular contributors soon grew to around twenty. We usually gathered at one of our apartments, but we alternated and never said aloud where the following meeting would be. We would finish our work and then pass around a piece of paper with the date and place of the next one.

These meetings were important. A person expelled from normal everyday life, shut out everywhere, and forbidden to work among people with whom he shared common values, or at least professional interests, needed to feel some sort of acceptance among friends. Therefore we met in private. These meetings were in no way conspiratorial. I sometimes organized evenings and we would play different games. Ludvík Vaculík hosted gatherings that regularly occurred during a weekend nearest an equinox or solstice—these meetings usually attracted more of us. Among those who came from Prague, in addition to those most persecuted by the police, were the theater critic of the banned *Literární noviny*, Sergej Machonin, Milan Jungmann, the prose writer Lenka Procházková (banned most likely because she was the daughter of Jan Procházka, a writer who was currently despised by the regime), Eda Kriseová (banned simply because she refused to join in passive assent), and the poet Petr Kabeš for whom it was unimaginable to publish work alongside the official versifiers. Friends also came from Slovakia: Milan Šimečka and Miro Kusý, sometimes even Ivan Kadlečík. From Brno, the prose writer Honza Trefulka, the dramatist Milan Uhde, Mr. and Mrs. Kotrlý, and sometimes the Catholic poet Zdeněk Roztrekl (he had barely escaped execution in one of the first show trials).

These get-togethers required much caution. We rarely met at home; preferably, either we went to someone's country house (if possible, one belonging to a nonmember of our group), or we rented a few cottages at the Brno Dam. The meeting always began with an encouraging evaluation of the political situation by our colleague, a congenital optimist and the author of many exceptional political essays, Milan Šimečka. He sensed our need to hear something hopeful and managed to find in Czech and foreign politics clear signs of approaching radical changes. He usually concluded: The occupying regime is in its final days and will be gone before our next meeting.

Then Milan Uhde would read his skeptical supplementary report in which he would overturn most of what his predecessor had said; he would reel off all the depressing and retrograde signs of contemporary societal development as too many people accepted the policies of those in power. (Unfortunately, for many years, he was correct.) Then Ludvík Vaculík usually read a feuilleton he had prepared for the new issue of *Contents*. Of course we also used these meetings to drink beer, grill food, and revel in the feeling that we were free people living in a society of other free people.

It was heartening how this solidarity helped us overcome the absurd situation in which, as writers and literary critics, we could not publish or even appear in public. On the other hand, there emerged a ridiculous and harmful professional divide between banned and unbanned. We had definitely been locked up in some sort of ghetto, but we were also locking ourselves in. (During this entire time, I never met with a single officially published colleague, with the exception of Jaroslav Dietl, whom I regularly visited to play Mariáš, and I think some of my friends held even this friendship against me.)

To our surprise, the secret police never once interrupted our meetings. I think they were unaware of them. They hadn't been able to secure a single informer among us, and we told no one, not even our closest friends, about our gatherings.

⸻

I no longer remember who lent me the samizdat edition of *The Limits to Growth* by Donella Meadows. It summarized the findings of a team of scientists who had been studying the effects on the environment of our speedy industrial development and the finitude of natural resources. Few texts spoke to me so forcefully, and its message stuck in my mind. I realized that we were all so wrapped up in our own everyday affairs and struggles with the discreditable regime that we couldn't think about anything else. In the meantime, however, another specter was emerging that did not differentiate between the free and unfree parts of the world. It was engendered by the same selfishness, the same careless relationship to nature, something that we could not live without but that our greed was destroying. For *Contents*, I wrote a short essay on a rather unusual subject (unusual at least for us at the time) called "The End of Civilization."

> People now have a life-and-death connection with our civilization, and if it dies, they must die with it. They will die by the thousands and the millions, perhaps in famines or epidemics that can no longer be conquered, perhaps in a desperate and unwinnable war that will destroy everything.
>
> But even if they manage to avoid war, people will die just the same. They will die of despair or because they have lost

the ability to earn their daily bread or because they will have destroyed nature, which sustained them from time immemorial. Entire regions of the world will be depopulated and places that had recently radiated light will reek of the plague. *At the end, I stepped back from my impassioned tone and pessimism and concluded with a belief that our machine-age civilization would perish, but after a while* mankind will return to human space and time from a world of planetary dimensions. People will enjoy silence and hear birdsong. Of course their lives will be more difficult and precarious. The foolish dream of utopians who believed that man would be made happy by being freed from the need to work will be forgotten, as will refrigerators, air-conditioning, aircraft, nuclear reactors, printing presses, artificial lungs, automatic washing-machines, television sets, rockets, and bugging devices. This crazy century, when man, in a meaningless effort, raised himself so high that he managed to escape the planet, will increasingly blend with legends and fables from an earlier time. One day, future scholars or priests will declare it to have been a mirage, a fiction perpetrated by ancient poets, or one of the many illusions shared by vast numbers of people. Perhaps scholarly debates on the subject will take place, but it will not affect most people because it will not touch their lives, their potentials, their goals, or their happiness.

And what about their happiness? I see no reason why they should be any less happy than we who have lived in this singular and crazy century.

—◦◦◦—

The secret police had apparently agreed with the party bigwigs that it was necessary to expel from the country everyone who was disturbing the image of a contented society. During his interrogation the rock singer and artist Vlastimil Třesňák was burned with a cigarette and became so frightened that he asked for permission to emigrate. Michal and I visited him the day before his departure. He was taking all his things in a single suitcase he had found in a scrap yard—three meters of canvas, nine half-squeezed tubes of oil paints, a camera, a guitar, and a typewriter. No clothes, no valuables, just an extra shirt and three pairs of new socks.

One of my friends, the talented author Karol Sidon, did not consider political activity an important part of his life. Immediately after the occupation, Karol wasn't even forbidden to publish. At the time, he wrote mainly dramas; one about coal miners was broadcast by Czech Television. Then the small Rubín Theater took up his new play, *The Latrines*. At the time, every play had to have official approval. A whole group of party members came to the preview, led by the head of the ideological department himself. Karol later told us how he had been overcome with the sense that he had suddenly found himself in the times of Nazi occupation and that the gestapo had come to the theater. In a sudden panic, he couldn't wait for the end of the performance and, although it was pouring outside, fled from the theater without even picking up his coat from the cloakroom.

This play and his disdain of the authorities exiled him among the banned authors. He secured a job, however, at a tobacconist's at a lucrative spot on Jindřišská Street.

One Saturday, a defamatory article about Ludvík was published in the illustrated magazine *Ahoj* along with intimate photographs the secret police had confiscated. Karol carried out what I would call a unique and, at the same time, touching act of nonviolent protest: From each issue of the magazine in his shop, he cut out the article with the disgraceful photographs.

He was interrogated, but it was such an odd act of resistance that they couldn't find anything in the law to charge him with, so they just arranged for him to be fired from his job, and he couldn't find another one. They even made it impossible for him to work at water resources near Mníšek or as a grave digger. Finally they forced him to emigrate.

Czech writers to L. Brezhnev

The chairman of the Czechoslovak Writers' Union sent a congratulatory letter to the General Secretary of the Central Committee of the CPSU and the Chairman of the Highest Soviet of the USSR, L. Brezhnev, for receiving the Lenin Prize for Literature. The letter states: It was with great joy that we learned you had been awarded the Lenin Prize for your trilogy *The Small Land, Rebirth,* and *Virgin Lands.* We hold your books in high esteem. They are an outstanding contribution to the history of the present time as well as a shining example of a party approach to the calling of literature. In Czechoslovakia, your titles have met with extraordinary interest not only among writers, but throughout our society, as can be seen by the print run of book and magazine editions of your books—around two million copies. Your books have indeed become the subject of tens of thousands of conferences, seminars, and discussions, which are still continuing and in which millions of our citizens are participating.

Czechoslovak News Agency

In our day and age book-writing has become so poor, and people write about matters [to] which they have never given any real thought, let alone experienced. I therefore have decided to read only the writings of men who have been executed or have risked their lives in some way.

Søren Kierkegaard, Diary, 1844

I don't remember exactly when I started working as a mailman.

Because my plays and books were being published and performed abroad, I was often invited to meet various diplomats. When I got to know them a little, I sometimes asked them to carry out a manuscript, whether it belonged to me or one of my colleagues. Usually they were happy to oblige, even though they were breaking the rules and risking their careers. I will not name names, but we were assisted by Swedish, American, and Canadian diplomats. The English cultural attaché was prepared to bring in any sort of literature but opposed taking anything out. He was most likely afraid that I'd foist some espionage material on him. There is one man whose name I must mention, however. At the beginning of the 1980s, I met a councilor in the West German embassy named Wolfgang Scheur. He was a remarkable person with willingness to assist those who, in his opinion, needed help. Thanks to strangers, he himself had managed to escape Hitler to Palestine, where he spent more than a year in a refugee camp. Later he ended up fighting against Hitler as a volunteer.

He offered to take something out or bring something back in if we desired.

In this way, I soon found myself behind an invisible counter of an invisible post office, and Wolfgang became a special courier who at least twice a month carried out letters and primarily manuscripts whose number was increasing with all the new samizdat series. On the way back, he would transport bags of Czech books and magazines that had been published abroad.

Wolfgang had a rather good idea of what conspiracy involved. He was constantly on the lookout for cars tailing him, and when he was certain he wasn't being followed (as far as one can be certain in this time of surveillance), he would drive to our home, where the gate and doors were always unlocked, run upstairs with two or three full bags, take from me a bag with outgoing mail, and be gone in less than a minute. On occasion, when he was not so certain, he would call to pass on regards from his wife or something along those lines. This meant that the bags were waiting at his place on Hradešínská Street.

My amateur delivery service was fraught not only with dangers but also with difficulties. If I didn't find someone at home, I couldn't leave the package in the mailbox or with the neighbors. I also couldn't call ahead of time. In many cases, the addressee's telephone had been disconnected, and even if it worked, it would not be wise to announce my arrival beforehand.

Of course, I wasn't the only mail carrier. I saw only to writers' consignments. During my postal activities, I was never caught, and I cannot say if the sentinels of the regime knew about what Wolfgang and other diplomats were hauling into and out of the country. Or perhaps they just told themselves that if I were not doing it, someone else would.

It's also possible that they were gradually beginning to realize that they had no idea what was going on.

⎯⎯∝⎯⎯

Since Helena and I were in the position of persecuted dissidents against the reigning societal order, our children didn't feel the need to rebel against us. On the contrary, they shared our fate and sympathized with us. At the same time, of course, they led their own lives.

Nanda had barely turned eighteen when she got engaged. Unlike us, her fiancé was an Orthodox Jew. In 1981, for the first time in our family, a genuine Jewish wedding took place (including a ritual bath in the chilly Vltava). Michal constructed for them a hi-fi record player as a wedding gift. Our son-in-law had a small apartment in a housing development in the same quarter in which we lived (also near the forest). But as soon as Nanda moved out, our home suddenly felt empty. I missed her voice, her joy, her messy artsy room, her drawings and sketches strewn about. There was one fewer listener and narrator of everyday events, and one empty chair at the dining table. Suddenly I remembered all those times she used to sit beneath my desk and play while I was writing. Later—she might have been ten—we took a skiing trip to the Giant Mountains, something she had been excited about for a long time, and on the very first day Nanda came down with a sore throat. There was also our trip wandering around the Bohemian-Moravian Highlands and her almost nightly request that I tell her another installment of the unending story of the kitten and the puppy.

Once she decided to give me a birthday present of my choosing, and we went to the stationery store, where I selected a magnifying glass to better examine the old maps that I collected. She poured from her purse all her coins and spent almost everything she'd saved up. I was touched by the love that lay behind the gesture. And there were the times I sat patiently while she drew my portrait.

Michal was less communicative. He had no need to confide in us, or, if he did, he could never overcome his inhibitions. I was surprised to see him cry at Nanda's wedding, even though her departure meant he would have their room to himself—something he'd been looking forward to. Unlike me, Michal was manually dexterous and was interested in contrivances he could fix or improve. He read a lot and was curious about politics, perhaps excessively so, considering his age (but understandably in view of the circumstances in which he grew up). Ever since childhood he had been a member of the water sports club, an organization that became popular after the scouts were banned. They tried to preserve something of the values and traditions of scouting. The club was governed very strictly with a semimilitary or, rather, seminaval hierarchy. Each member began as a seaman and received tasks that were often extremely difficult, and if they were not fulfilled, he could expect punishments. But everyone who was persistent and diligent advanced until the most dogged made it to the rank of captain, who saw to all the activities and made sure the age-old traditions were upheld. Michal was dedicated to his club and did indeed achieve the rank of captain.

One of their traditions was that members would get together years after they had left the organization and help each other out in our society, which had been founded on oppression, self-criticism, and injustice.

When Michal graduated from high school, he applied to study at the Czech Technical University in a new field to train executives (Socialist, of course). At the entrance interview, they did not even take into consideration his family's doubtful history or the fact that he had not joined the Socialist Union of Youth.

We saw him less and less at home now too, and soon after Nanda moved out, he managed to acquire the mansard above us. Our apartment had become orphaned.

At the beginning of 1982, Nanda gave birth to a daughter, and they named her Anna. Naturally, she was beautiful.

And so we became grandparents, and after a while, our home, at least from time to time, was brought back to life by the sobbing or prattling of a child.

Early in the morning, Radio Free Europe mentioned that a rumor was circulating in Moscow about the death of someone important. Then the television program changed, and the announcers were all wearing black. About an hour later, in the middle of the news, the station repeated the same thing, but then around 9:05, the announcer said, "Dear listeners, Radio Moscow has just announced that the chairman of the Highest Soviet and the general secretary of the Central Committee of the Communist Party, Leonid Ilyich Brezhnev, has just passed away." Except for the "dear listeners," the news was read absolutely dispassionately (they must have thrust the report at him in the middle of his broadcast), and then he continued like a consummate professional, making me hesitate for a moment and wonder if my ears had deceived me.

I called Father, who was surprised: "Really? Are you sure?" Then he added, "God knows what villain is going to come next. They've got warehouses of them over there."

From my diary, November 11, 1982

Why did they announce Brezhnev's death a day late? They were waiting for Ilya Muromets whom they had sent to the West for magic water. But he didn't come back.

From my diary, November 13, 1982

Father went to see his sister for a few weeks in Canada, and when he came back, he was a little gaunt and had no appetite. We made him go see a doctor. He was told he had a tumor in his intestines and had to undergo an operation immediately. At this time, surgery, if undertaken in time, was the only chance of survival, albeit a small one. I accompanied Father when he went to receive the diagnosis. He told me about it as if he were informing me he had a cold. He was seventy-seven years old, but with his thick and only slightly graying hair, he looked at least ten years younger and was full of life. I couldn't imagine he would soon be vanquished by death.

They operated on him a few days later. The doctor said the tumor had been almost as big as a child's head, but he hoped he'd managed to extract it all.

When I spoke with Father, he was glad it was over with. The doctor had assured him everything had turned out fine. Then he added, "The main thing is that it wasn't cancer." I don't know if this statement concealed anxiety, a conscious self-deception, or the successful suppression of grim reality, but I expressed my agreement. When Father was released from the hospital, he seemed once again to be full of energy. But his condition continued to weigh on me. My personal hardships paled in significance before the anticipated approach of death.

I was at least somewhat distracted from my worries by a letter from Markéta Goetz-Stankiewicz, a professor of Germanic studies and translator from Czech. She was one of the fortunate ones who had managed to escape Hitler's claws at the last moment. Although she had emigrated as a child, she never lost her connection with her native land, and now, since a new occupation had befallen Czechoslovakia, she was prepared to be of service. She wrote that the University of British Columbia was preparing a conference for the hundredth anniversary of Franz Kafka's birth and wanted to know if I could contribute a talk.

After I had written my *Castle*, I was considered to have an affinity for Kafka. This was not true: In addition to other things, I didn't know much about him, and his works didn't especially speak to me. Except for the title, my *Castle* had nothing in common with Kafka's. I wrote back that I wouldn't be able to attend the conference, even though I would have liked to, but I would try to prepare a contribution. I added that, unfortunately, few of Kafka's works were available here and nothing at all about the writer himself. I gave the letter to Wolfgang, and soon thereafter he brought me a package from Markéta with the latest studies on Kafka in English and his recently published letters to Felice Bauer with an excellent and extensive introduction by Elias Canetti.

I dutifully read through several monographs and even found something in the university library. It was Franz's letters to Felice that interested me the most. From them I learned about his odd relationship to this woman he claimed to love. I found a similar relationship to Milena Jesenská in his letters to her. To my surprise, Kafka suddenly started to appear differently than he did to most scholars working on him (with perhaps the exception of Canetti). They searched his works for a symbolic expression of abstruse ideas about justice, human fate, society, man's alienation, and even the future fate of the Jews. I was almost certain things were precisely the opposite.

Literary theorists, critics, and historians are used to moving in a world of ideas, and they express generalizations and then force their abstract world onto the writer they're studying. When they criticized the works of Franz Kafka, whose often dreamlike visions seduce one to ambiguous interpretations, a drastic discrepancy arose between Kafka's ideas and theirs.

In my opinion, Kafka was not interested in the world of ideas; even the world around him held little appeal. Kafka was concerned almost exclusively with himself. He wrote most of all about his imperfections, his inability to grow up—that is, to extricate himself from his father's influence and become a mature man who builds a family. He was also shy and possessed the vision of an artist, and because his fantasy had greater significance than any kind of intellectual system, he expressed himself in apparently ambiguous and mysterious images.

His inability to grow up expressed itself even in his inability to complete a more extensive work. However, even from those unfinished fragments and several prose pieces that he nevertheless finished, one can deduce, in my opinion, the source of his inspiration.

As an example, I adduced the ostensibly indecipherable and bizarre story of one of the more extensive works he completed, "In the Penal Colony." Kafka writes about a traveler who arrives on an island and meets with some sort of conservative officer. Most of the story is devoted to the officer's explanation of the execution device, their traditional system of justice, and, finally, a demonstration of the device. Its mechanism is composed of a system of needles that slowly impale the body of the condemned man. The officer sets the device in motion. We learn about the prisoner, a man who *looked so like a submissive dog that one might have thought he could be left to run free on the surrounding hills and would only need to be whistled for when the execution was due to begin.* He has been convicted for an infraction that really wasn't an infraction but just an unwillingness to be beaten. This seemingly incomprehensible, even absurd story has received bizarre interpretations. I was intrigued by Kafka's diary entry about his first engagement to Felice, when *he seemed tied hand and foot like a criminal.* Furthermore, Kafka broke off the engagement after six weeks and journeyed with a friend to the seaside, where he composed the story.

Then I noticed in a letter to Milena a remarkable passage concerning Kafka's idea of marriage.

> You know, if I want to write something about [our engagement,] swords slowly begin to circle around me and approach my body, it's the most complete torture; when they begin to graze me it's already so terrible that at the first scream I betray you, myself, everything.

This was a condensed description of the execution device from "In the Penal Colony" from his *Selected Short Stories*, and, if I understood the motifs that inspired Kafka, he saw himself in the man condemned to lie on the bed beneath the approaching needles. I was almost certain that in two of Kafka's last unfinished novels I saw an image of his self-tormenting relationship to women. He tried to draw close to them, but owing to his inability to consummate any sort of relationship, he was condemned and punished like a criminal. For him, women became an impenetrable castle, and when they finally accepted him into their beds, he was overcome with weariness, anxiety, and his own indecisiveness and could not avail himself of the opportunity and could not accept their favors.

He could not effectuate any substantive relationship, just as he could not complete any extensive work. Finally, death was the only resolution for him, and he accepted his tuberculosis.

My talk was too long for someone to read at the conference; nevertheless, I took it to Wolfgang to send to Vancouver.

Markéta translated and read part of my paper at the conference. The text then came out in an English edition of my essays and later in many languages, even Chinese.

I once again applied for my passport. To my surprise, I received it. Although it didn't allow me to go to Vancouver, I could travel to the so-called people's democracies.

Helena's fearless colleague, Dr. Lukavský, offered her a part-time job in his marriage counseling office, but she had to travel all the way to Mělník. The trip across Prague and then farther by bus was tiring, so Helena slept there once or twice a week. In her free time, she attended secret psychoanalysis training (psychoanalysis was forbidden).

Alone at home, I was depressed. Time seemed to me unfilled and directionless. The most varied images started coming into my mind. What was love: blindness, passion?

The opposite of love seemed to me to be refuse: garbage—not only real garbage, but emotional and intellectual as well. Images of garbage and love alternated through my thoughts. But I knew nothing of garbage with the exception of when I burned it during my short tenure as a hospital orderly.

What kind of people came into contact with real garbage most often? Those who stood only on the lowest rungs of the social and economic ladder—street sweepers. I still wasn't sure if I could somehow lay out these thoughts and string them together into a story, but it couldn't hurt to get acquainted with the job of a street sweeper.

Street sweeping seemed to me to be a job requiring so few qualifications that whoever applied would not be asked if he'd ever held a broom before; if he'd previously been a priest, a university professor, or a writer; if he'd just been let out of prison; or if he was a student or retiree who needed a few more crowns.

One morning I presented my identity card to the work center in our district and was issued an orange vest and a broom. A permanent employee of the sanitation department formed us into a group and distributed more valuable equipment such as a wheelbarrow and shovels. Then we set off at a sluggish pace to the location we were supposed to clean.

All types of people imaginable worked as street sweepers. I soon learned that their efforts were applied not to cleaning streets but to waiting out—as effortlessly and unperturbed as possible—the necessary time between starting work and collecting the day's pay. After two hours of work, we sat for a long while in a pub and then dawdled away another couple of hours, since all we had left to do was finish cleaning a street that had previously been scrubbed with a street-sweeping machine.

I listened to some of the workers' stories and gossip, but everything I heard was drowned out by thoughts of Father's illness. His health had suddenly taken a turn for the worse and he was seized by bouts of fever. His temperature would suddenly rise to forty-two degrees Celsius over the course of two hours, as if he had malaria, and then a few hours later it would come back down to normal. This happened every day, and the doctor had no explanation. Father obediently submitted himself to ice packs and swallowed pills to lower his temperature, but it seemed that this peculiar illness was not responding to any external stimuli; it had its own rules. Father grew weak, and his usually clear mind became confused. When he awoke from a feverish state, he would lose all sense of time. In the evening, he thought it was morning, and when I tried to convince him otherwise (as if it was important to him), he would obediently admit that he believed me, since I, as a healthy person, maintained it.

After several weeks, when his condition improved and then worsened again, he was taken to the hospital and placed in a room with two other patients. The doctors were able to reduce his fever, but I was told his fever was coupled with the cancer, which had spread to his kidneys and other parts of his body. We had to assume he had only a few days left. Nevertheless, especially after a transfusion, Father felt better and, suddenly lucid, said he was looking forward to going home and seeing Mother and—something more enticing—his computer. He mentioned the poor fellow in the next bed who coughed throughout the night and was probably on his last legs. Then Father's state worsened and he started complaining that he couldn't sleep because of his neighbor's cough.

I offered the doctor some money and asked if Father could be moved to a private room. And so for his final days, Father received his own room with a bathroom.

I went to see him every day at the hospital. Although he was extremely weak, he still believed his health would improve, and just before the end, he told me he would fight his illness. He really didn't feel so old.

The day before he died, he complained he had fallen on the way to the bathroom and couldn't get up. When he called the nurse, she started shouting at him to pick himself up off the floor; she had enough work without having to get him back into bed. He asked me how people could be so insensitive to someone who had lost his strength.

In his final hours, I sat by the bed holding his hand. I don't know if he sensed I was there, but I hoped at least part of him registered that someone was trying to hold him from departing, that he was not alone. His breathing became more and more intermittent; a few seconds would pass between the individual breaths, and I knew the moment was approaching when they would cease altogether.

Certainly I had witnessed too many deaths in my childhood, but I had never been present when someone close to me was dying. I had never experienced firsthand the moment of the irrevocable leap from the last breath to eternal nonexistence.

That moment kept coming back to me, and I knew there was only one way to overcome its morbid insistency.

Perhaps it was the final impulse for me to start writing the litany I called *Love and Garbage.*

I had filled various notebooks with fragments of love declarations, letters, and unhappy meditations about our precipitous and self-destructive civilization. I had noted down a word or two about Father's death, but now I could think of little else. I loved my father, and nothing could tarnish or impugn this love—it would endure for as long as I lived, perhaps even longer, since things in this world cannot vanish entirely. Angels or some other ethereal beings carry scales in their hands upon which are weighed all the love and hatred in this world, and life inclines to that which predominates.

The news came that Václav Havel was seriously ill in the prison where he was being held for defending the unjustly persecuted from despotism. Finally, fearing that the world-famous author might die from pneumonia in a cell, the custodians of power commuted the few months remaining of his sentence and released him. He lay in the hospital near Petřín Hill, and as soon as he was doing a little better, we went to see him. I don't think this tiny hospital had ever had a patient so besieged with visitors.

Václav was pale and thin, but otherwise it seemed his long stay in prison had neither broken him nor dulled his interest in public affairs.

When they released him into home care a few days later, we invited him to a meeting where we were composing our journal *Contents*. We told him about the events that had unfolded since the last time he had met with us—who had allowed himself be exiled abroad, who had written something new, what we thought about the political situation after the change of the Moscow potentate. He listened attentively and then, with a certain matter-of-factness, gave us his assessment of the situation. In his opinion, changes were happening beneath the apparently unvarying surface of society. The Communists, who assumed they were destined to remain in power here and in every other country in which they had seized power, were demoralized and so intellectually barren that they were gradually losing the ability to alter anything. Without change, no future was possible, and so the heterogeneous society of those who refused to accept the current state of affairs would become more important. The Communists had already lost the majority of their ardent followers, and even though they lived with a certain self-deception, they knew well enough that all the Socialist euphoria was feigned, and they were supported by the people less and less. They remained in power only owing to the police force, but at the same time they did not dare resort to their previous violence. Havel also discussed the international situation, the attempt to suppress Solidarity in Poland and the alternation of old men in Russia. His "lecture" lasted about thirty minutes. When we expressed our collective surprise that a person who had just returned from three and a half years in prison possessed such an overview of events, he explained that it was quite simple. All you had to do was read *Rudé právo* thoroughly. You don't read it, he admonished us, and have no idea that everything is right there between the lines—what's happening, what rankles those at the top, and what kind of miracle they are still hoping for.

I wrote to Jürgen Braunschweiger that I had something resembling a novel in my head, and a large part of it on paper. Also, I had unexpectedly obtained my passport. Then I explained to him the limited number of countries I was allowed to travel to. I immediately received a proposal that all of his authors—the ones who had passports, at least—meet somewhere in Hungary. He had purchased an old castle in the town of Motovun in Slovenia, which he had converted to a summer residence where he spent almost every weekend. From there, it wasn't far to Hungary, and he'd almost certainly be allowed into Hungary. First off, he didn't publish any Hungarian authors, and, second, the Hungarian authorities behaved much more civilly than ours.

With Wolfgang's help, Jürgen and I agreed in writing on a place and time to meet. In the end, only three of Jürgen's authors attended the meeting—Kohout and Gruša were already living in Austria and Germany; Ludvík Vaculík was refused a passport; and my former boss at *Literární noviny*, Jiří Šotola, had gone so far as to be published officially. I was somewhat alarmed by the idea that, like Pavel Kohout, I could be deprived of my citizenship and thereby exiled from my country, but I didn't think it probable that the authorities would allow me to go to Hungary with such perfidious intentions.

We decided to gather at a small summer resort near Lake Balaton, and after a span of ten years I saw my publisher and my friend Gruša again. My friends consumed a great deal of truly superb wine (I was rather abstemious as far as wine was concerned) and discussed the possibilities of further publications. Some time ago, Jürgen had left the publishing house that had brought out our works and established his own company, which published illustrated books—studies, for example, about the history of flags or a pictorial devoted to different countries or nature reserves. Publishing any sort of prose literature did not fit into his plans, but he was prepared to continue working with us as a literary agent. He lacked experience, of course, in publishing books other than in the German language, but he promised to help us as much as he could. If we found a better agent, he would have no objections. He also said that the worst was behind us. We had successfully gained access to the book market—we were now known and he had no doubt we would become established. I saw that he would have been relieved to be released from the burden of his friendly duty to help us.

It was discouraging to think of losing a friend from a country where blacklists of authors did not exist. It wouldn't be easy to find a new publisher or agent abroad, even if one were to write a book that publishers wanted.

On top of everything else, our faithful courier Wolfgang was concluding his diplomatic career and preparing to leave our country. He invited us whose mail he had delivered to his abode in Vinohrady. We racked our brains over what to give him to express our gratitude. Finally, I had an idea: Just as we had awarded Hrabal the title of Prince of Czech Literature, we would bestow an order on Wolfgang. My friends took to the idea, and we wrote an accompanying text for the order, which stated "for assistance to Czech literature during times of darkness." Once again, Saša obtained a Latin translation, our Nanda copied out the text in old-fashioned lettering, and one of our friends and foremost sculptors created the order in the form of a bronze book brooch (it weighed at least a kilo and was certainly not suited for pinning on a lapel). Václav Havel, Ludvík Vaculík, and I signed the document, and thus we usurpers, as current propaganda would have designated us, elevated ourselves to spokesmen for Czech literature. During the first farewell toast we solemnly presented the unsuspecting Wolfgang with the order. I don't remember who symbolically pinned it on him. It was probably the oldest of us, Vaculík. Václav had no idea he would soon be pinning several dozen awards every year, and among the laureates would be Wolfgang himself.

It was our order and accompanying text that our extraordinary courier hung on the wall of his home in Melsungen and claimed it was the highest award he had ever received.

———

On her fourth try, Nanda was accepted at the Academy of Performing Arts in a field with a somewhat mysterious description: educating students in the craft of theater and broadcasting with an emphasis on puppetry; her major—design and technology. It was a subject we resorted to out of necessity, but it turned out to be serious and multi-faceted. Nanda learned not only how to draw and paint but also how to fashion puppets and work with different materials.

At the same time, more and more people were coming to see me to borrow books from our typewritten series. I think I could tell who visited upon the assignment of the secret police, who out of sympathy, and who out of an interest in what was new in a literature that was not subject to censorship. Several times I was invited—usually outside Prague—to someone's cottage or a private apartment to read something or talk about literature. I was usually led into a roomful of guests I didn't know, but I believed that no one came out of ill will. It was encouraging to meet with people who themselves were not among the persecuted but had enough courage and curiosity to meet with those who were.

After four years of commuting, Helena finally got a job in Prague at a couples' therapy office beneath the Nusle Bridge. One evening, she was invited to an acquaintance's place in Hanspaulka. Apparently, she and her husband had gotten their hands on a rare film about Dubček and the events of 1968. It would have been a shame to show the film just for themselves.

Helena accepted the invitation. Before we set out, I heard some news that no longer surprised anyone: Another Bolshevik leader had expired (the second in ten years), and the hearts and minds of all the vassals in the entire camp of peace were filled with the deepest sorrow.

When we arrived in Hanspaulka a little late, we saw that the hostess had fulfilled her intention to show the film to more than her immediate family. Around fifty guests crowded the apartment, among them many of our friends who were banned from publishing or re-search. I saw sandwiches on plates in the kitchen, but first the film started. Just at the moment when the ingenuous and smiling face of Dubček peeped out at us, something prompted me to turn around. To my astonishment, I saw a man in a police uniform standing in the doorway. Where had they come from? Were they among the invited guests?

After about twenty minutes they let us off on Bartolomějská Street. Even though it was nearing ten o'clock at night, the lights were on. The secret police had apparently been on high alert, and only then did I realize that the projection of the rare documentary occurred on the day of the unplanned death of the Soviet leader, Konstantin Chernenko. Such events were always accompanied by greater police vigilance.

We were led into some sort of large hall (I didn't know they had anything like this) and, from there, were taken individually to be interrogated. It went slowly, and we didn't see those who were led away again; they were either locked in cells or let out through another door. Time dragged on more than it did in a dentist's waiting room. The officers watching over us demanded we not speak to one another. Then one of the women started singing "Kyrie eleison." The hymn sounded powerful and, in view of the situation, absurd. To compound the absurdity, our host protested that we were starving—he'd prepared food at home, and now it was going to waste. To our amazement, the officers bundled him into a car and drove him back to Hanspaulka, where he grabbed the trays of sandwiches and returned.

After midnight, they came for me and I was led to an office where I saw "my" official behind a desk. He had been interrogating me for the past two or three years—he seemed like a typical police official of the times. He demanded that I report to him whenever summoned and that I not demonstrate disrespect for his office. He never once yelled at me. (If he'd been given the order to yell, I'm sure he would have done so.) Usually he asked questions about our samizdat journal, or my meetings with some journalist from Britain or another free country, and when I said I didn't remember or refused to answer, he didn't press me. He would note down everything briefly, hand me the minutes to sign, and, with an ironic comment, perhaps concerning my faulty memory, let me go. This time he greeted me once again ironically: "We should have known. Wherever something provocative is going on, we are sure to find Klíma." I said that I didn't do provocative things. Besides, I had no idea what was supposed to be going on. It occurred to me that I wouldn't be harming anyone by telling the truth, and I explained that my wife and I had been invited over by an acquaintance and, to our surprise, we were met with a large gathering.

He released me after ten minutes; Helena had been released a few minutes before. A number of my friends were led to a cell for the night and let go the next day.

Once again at liberty, we learned the name of the man who had been chosen for the Soviet throne. I had never heard his name before: Mikhail Sergeyevich Gorbachev.

Essay: *The Elite*, p. 530

20

The pension insurance I had managed to acquire, thanks to Zdeněk Miler when he filmed seven cartoons based on my stories, lasted for several years. Each year, I declared at least part of my foreign income in order to keep the insurance.

Because I had spent three and a half years in a concentration camp during the war, I had the right to retire a little earlier, and the time was approaching. Two years and three months before the target date, a new and ambitious collaborator, boasting the regal name of Kaiser, was assigned to head the Literary Fund. Kaiser decided to cancel my insurance with this intriguing justification: *Please find enclosed the supporting documents you submitted with your request for artists' social security. It is not possible to demonstrate unequivocally that your income was the result of artistic activity.* This determination was maliciously timed. The law stated that every insured person must work at least one day during the two years before retirement—that is, he must receive an income from a proper and approved work source. If I didn't, I would lose my entitlement to any sort of pension.

Of course, getting proper employment for a single day was impossible. Therefore, I had to look for someone who would employ me. I knew I would not be allowed to perform qualified work. I couldn't publish my books; I couldn't write reviews or work as a copyreader, so I tried to think up some kind of job that would be at least a little interesting and that I could actually perform.

Engineer František Kocina, who also regularly played Mariáš at Jaroslav Dietl's, worked at the Institute of Geodesy. I recalled Kafka's two characters who were the surveyor's assistants, and the protagonist in my first novel who was a land surveyor. I went to see František at the institute and confided to him that I needed to be employed for at least a short time.

He told me that they took on externs, usually students, and he could get me a job if I wanted, but I would have to work at least two months. Then he tried to talk me out of it. We would be surveying in the fields, and not only would my job consist of holding the surveyor's pole, but most likely I would have to do quite a bit of digging as well.

I told him I would get used to it and that I was counting on the job.

We agreed I would start at the beginning of September. Until then, he added, I could still change my mind.

I had found work but I was still uneasy. What if I got sick in September or didn't get the job in the end?

After he finished college, Michal found a position at a computer technology firm and heard they were looking for a messenger. I did have, after all, some postal experience, and he suggested this would be much less hazardous.

And so, almost fifteen years after my time as an orderly, I once again found myself in a normal job, a Socialist job, I should add. When I had finished reading the newspaper or part of a book I had brought with me, I was politely asked to deliver a package to one of the offices. Sometimes it was a fairly large package of computer disks—their enormous computers were located in Vršovice, while my office was in South Town. The central office was in Old Town, where I sometimes took the regular mail. Nobody checked up on how long I spent on my errands, and sometimes when I came back, my amicable boss would say, "If you're not having any fun here, you can go home. We won't need you for anything else today."

My "work" here was indeed quite pleasant—things were worse with my other, more risky postal work. Wolfgang's replacement was much more careful, and he asked me to request his services only when it was truly important. He didn't want to risk meeting unnecessarily and decided we would use a trash can in front of his house as a dead letter drop, something he'd unimaginatively come up with himself. I thought this much more risky than delivering the material in person. Fortunately, we met the American attaché, and it was to him that I would deliver the outgoing mail.

After two months, my official postal duties at Michal's company came to an end. To bid my fond friends farewell, I cooked up an enormous pot of Russian borscht in honor of the auspicious perestroika under way in Russia.

Thus, I had ensured I would not be deprived of my miserable pension. But suddenly I was sorry that I had missed out on the opportunity to work as a surveyor's lineman.

I went to see František and told him truthfully that I no longer needed the work, but I had made a promise, and I was here to announce that I was ready. František was astonished. He said this had made sense when I explained it was a matter of my pension, but now that I didn't need it, he couldn't understand why I was eager to take on such a difficult job, especially as someone unused to physical labor and for such poor pay. Of course, he was right. I was interested in the work precisely because I'd never done anything like it before. My friend again tried to talk me out of it but finally shrugged his shoulders, flipped through a batch of papers, and then said I should report on September 1 to Engineer Beránek in Městec Králové at 7 a.m. at the latest. The building was on the right corner of the square coming from Prague. That was where we would be staying, but as far as he was aware, we would have to obtain our own beds. He also said that Engineer Beránek was a decent fellow and would certainly understand my situation.

So on the appointed day, I became a surveyor's assistant. František was not lying when he said the work would be exhausting. During the first week, I woke up every morning feeling that I wouldn't be able to raise the pickax.

I also mailed off two letters to Kaiser, who had so brazenly dispar-
aged my writing at a time when every government-approved grapho-
maniac was being insured. The first letter read:

Dear Director,

Because you doubted the character of the previous activity,
which I and perhaps other people consider artistic, you certainly
deserve to be informed that, at least for a time, I worked as a
surveyor's assistant. I consider it necessary to inform you of my
activities, among other reasons, in order that your ignorance of
this fact not afford you the opportunity to once again doubt my
current activity.

Therefore, I am now informing you of my activities as a surveyor's assistant: During the month of September, I sanded and
later painted seventy-nine poles, excavated approximately eight
cubic meters of earth, implanted twenty-seven concrete footers
and five millstones. Into various walls, including mostly church
and cemetery walls, I hewed out openings for five apex stones and
assisted with measuring and associated work. Of course, I am aware
that only with the approval of the authorities do facts become facts
and activities activities, and I do not delude myself as to what I
actually accomplished in the surveying field.

The second letter was somewhat more substantial.

Dear Director K.,

While meeting with my colleagues, I learned that you impugned the character of not only my work but theirs as well; you
have determined their artistic endeavors to be undemonstrable.
I have also learned that most of them have decided to defend
themselves and are attempting to provide evidence of their artistic work. As proof, they are bringing in their books and news

of productions of their plays on various world stages. Are you surprised that I did not undertake similar steps? I could simply claim that I do not consider such efforts to be dignified, but I would be lying if I pretended that it was not my wish for people such as yourself to disappear from the armchairs from which you conduct your contemptible work. The question is, how to make you truly disappear? It is only your armchair that provides you with your seeming power, raised high above, not only above the ground, but above all life, above humaneness—not to mention justice. Whoever undertakes a fight with you—I mean an honorable fight—not only cannot win, but also thereby recognizes your tyranny as legitimate; it raises even higher your armchair and affirms you in your feeling of superiority.

Your body, your entire being can certainly be exchanged and replaced. What cannot be exchanged and replaced, however, is the world that you and those who appointed you have created for yourselves, the artificial world that you proclaim the only real one, because only those laws apply which you have laid down, and truth is only that which you proclaim to be true. You can be struck only when a force appears that will destroy your sacrosanctity and your world and thereby hurl you back down among the people.

That force, Director, is the story. A story from the real world. You can toss a hundred requests into the wastebasket, but you will not silence a hundred stories. These stories, whatever they may tell, whether of love, suffering, or tenderness, will always be pointing a finger at your contemptible work. Finally they will smite you, and you will tumble from your seemingly unassailable heights, from your impregnable world, back to the void from which you arose. I want you to understand, at least during your fall, that these stories will outlive you.

Sincerely,
Surveyor's Assistant Klíma

The end of our surveying job was symbolic in a way that I couldn't have imagined. In the enormous barn in which we'd been assigned to sleep, there was nothing when we got there except a sink and two coiled flags: the Czechoslovak flag and the one with the hammer and sickle.

We gradually acquired two bunks and two chairs (which served as night tables), and my engineer got a small table that served as his worktable in the evenings.

At the end of October, when we were preparing to leave our transient abode, we received an order from the city to hang out the flags because the anniversary of nationalization was approaching and, for all decent people, it was the birth of our not overly cheerful republic.

The next day we were awakened by a curious clatter above our heads. When we went out to investigate, we saw roofers gradually removing the roof. They explained that this shack was going to be torn down. This shack was our country.

We grow old, and even if we're still full of energy (at least that's what we tell ourselves) we start to remember the children. Our granddaughter, Andula, just like our own children, demanded that I tell her stories of the kitten and the puppy. Michal started fixing up his mansard apartment above us because he was getting ready to marry. His intended was delicate, shy, and almost unsuitably bashful. Unlike Michal, who had graduated in enterprise management, his Jana graduated in the field of aesthetics in the school of humanities, which meant that their interests could be antithetical or, on the other hand, that they could be complementary. Fortunately, Michal was not a one-sided technocrat. He read a lot; loved music, especially folk music (he was acquainted with perhaps every folksinger in the country); and was also becoming more and more interested in political events. Certainly this was influenced not only by our fate but also by that of our friends whom he considered his friends, despite the difference in age. When Vlasta Chramostová decided to turn her apartment into a theater, Michal worked as the soundman as they privately filmed a performance of Shakespeare's *Macbeth*.

To our surprise, Michal received an exit permit for a business trip to Sweden. There he met with the publisher Adam Bromberg. Michal explained to him that I had recently lost my agent and was therefore "available."

Mr. Bromberg immediately telephoned and asked if I had any interest in accepting his services. I was overwhelmed by his interest and said of course I was interested. He said he had been counting on that and had reserved a plane ticket to Prague for tomorrow so we could agree on a contract.

We negotiated for half a day. He assured me that he was connected with the best publishing houses in the entire cultured world; he represented two Nobel laureates, and I could be certain that in a few years, and owing to his services, I would become a world-famous author. I didn't understand at the time how great a role a literary agent played in the life (and celebrity) of an author, and I attributed even less significance to such avowals, which seemed implausible. But it was high time; my fiftieth birthday had passed some time ago.

At our meeting on the first summer day of 1987, we argued at length over what should be done now. Should we too invoke Gorbachev's democratizing socialism or aspire for a democracy in our own tradition, that is, should we strive for a society entirely free of the dogmas of Soviet socialism as created by the single ruling and irrevocable party? Finally we agreed that our country had a future only if it succeeded in linking up with our prewar democracy. This would most likely be achieved through small steps; for us, the most natural step would be to work for the freedom of art and speech in general.

Most of my friends and colleagues had signed Charter 77, which demanded the same thing, but the government still refused to deal with its representatives. Although I had no illusions that they would behave differently with me (my letters were always either ignored or passed on to the secret police, who called me in for interrogation), I offered to write a letter to the prime minister and then give it to the others for their signature. Among other things, I wrote:

Dear Mr. Prime Minister,

It was with satisfaction that we received the recent announcement by our institutional functionaries calling for changes that should be under way in our country. We expect that these changes will also affect policies in the area of culture. After all, the number of artists, thinkers, researchers, and journalists who have been silenced and are prohibited from carrying out their jobs totals several hundred. . . .

For seventeen years, the practice has continued whereby any writer who participated in (or was influenced by) the reform movement is not allowed to publish. More than half of Czech writers have been affected by this prohibition, which is in contravention of constitutional laws and with international conventions our republic has entered, not to mention the entirety of our cultural tradition. During this period, nearly a thousand books, poems, essays, memoirs, and theater plays have come into being, many of which have achieved world renown. In our country, however, they may not be made public. With every passing year, this state of affairs is becoming more and more unjustifiable. It currently persists only because it brings personal advantage to several official writers who have been relieved of all literary competition.

I went on to say that the perpetuation of the current state of affairs would have tragic consequences for the morality of society and would harm the reputation of our country abroad. I also noted that a great number of our colleagues had been expelled and that not only were Czech authors on this list but so were the best foreign authors.

We demand that this list be destroyed and that readers here be given back the opportunity of acquainting themselves with the values of world literature as well as Czech and Slovak.

I wrote the letter, insofar as I was able, if not in a respectful at least in a decorous tone. My friends corrected a few things and improved others. Finally, the letter was signed by twenty-nine writers and journalists.

I received not a single sentence in reply and wasn't even called into interrogation for it.

But slowly there began to appear signs of change. The secretary of the Central Committee's ideological department—a boozy, half-educated man beneath whose auspices the destruction of Czech culture had proceeded—was replaced, as was the secretary of the official Writers' Union. Both were replaced by younger functionaries who had the reputation of being more moderate.

Several of my silenced colleagues began something heretofore unthinkable. They decided to publish *Lidové noviny* (for now as a monthly), and not as a samizdat journal but as a legal periodical with a print run of a thousand copies. The two editors in chief endorsed the newspaper and approached the Federal Press and Information Office to request a publisher (this was a requirement in order to publish any periodical). Although they were refused, more and more authors began to contribute to *Lidové noviny*, and the circle of readers became much wider than it would have been for any typewritten journals. Meanwhile, the names of the editorial board were published, and most authors signed their articles. All along, they also managed to conceal the location where the journal was reproduced.

─────

Helena saw to it that the entire family (our children, her parents and sister, and my mother) got together now and then. We celebrated birthdays and of course Christmas. Even though our children were grown up, we still decorated the Christmas tree.

After a time, you forget the gifts you have received unless they are truly exceptional, but one present, although it was only promised, was among the most unforgettable. Michal and Jana informed us that their gift would be ready at the beginning of the summer.

Her name was Manka, and during this Christmas we foretold, or at least promised, she would be born in a better world, a free society —but this kept vanishing into the distance.

Soon after the holidays, I stopped by Michal and Jana's upstairs apartment and was surprised to see bundles of pages of *Lidové noviny*. They had been tasked with compiling individual issues, something they'd been doing for several months, but they hadn't told me because they didn't want me to worry.

I said it wasn't a matter of my worrying, but this building was probably not the most appropriate place for such activity.

"On the contrary," explained my son. "This is the perfect place because the secret police think just the way you do." Besides, they were trying to publish the journal legally. As f~ ~s the first point was concerned, Michal was right—the secret police had never entered his apartment.

January 16, 1989, was the twentieth anniversary of the death of Jan Palach. A humanities student at Charles University, Palach had set himself on fire in front of the National Museum in 1969. He'd done it to protest the Soviet invasion, or, more precisely, as he said later when they took him to the hospital mortally wounded, to protest everything that was happening here at that time.

I had wanted to buy some flowers, but none of the flower shops had even a sprig of anything left. Slowly and dutifully for almost an entire afternoon, Helena and I had moved forward in the column on Old Town Square in the direction of the Karolinum. The air in the hall where the coffin stood had been redolent with the aroma of flowers, and everything was silent, just the sound of soft footsteps and intermittent sobs.

For several years, the anniversary had been celebrated with a quiet gathering at the statue of Saint Wenceslaus. The police usually dispersed the people; this time, however, it was the twentieth anniversary, which especially unsettled the reigning power. The police were waiting with truncheons and water cannons for those who wanted to pay tribute to Palach.

During the demonstration, Václav Havel was arrested again, but something had changed. Many prominent people, who had previously put up with police despotism, decided to lodge a protest against the arrest.

⸺⚮⚭⸺

After the demonstration, when we had been driven from Wenceslaus Square with water cannons, I and a few others dropped into a pub on Vodičkova Street. The waiter briskly sat us down at a table and then said to me (because I was obviously the oldest): "This is the fourth day in a row we've had such an unexpected rush. I say: A wet Czech is a good Czech. There's nothing seditious about that." After a while, he came over again: "Yesterday a woman showed up at the demonstration and told the police she wasn't there to protest, she was just going to the cinema. Then she showed them her ticket. They seized it and said, 'Sure you were.'" I don't know if I inspired his trust or if he was simply trying to get something out of me, but he came over a moment later and said, "You know, I apprenticed across the street at the Hotel Šroubek." He pointed in the direction of the square. "Whoever studied the best was sent abroad for a year. I was in London and learned English for a year, not like those who stuff a couple of words into their heads. Foreigners walk in, order some beef, and they bring out a beer. And there were worse things. Those idiotic riot police sprayed water in here until all the chairs were soaked. Once we had a Dutch woman come in. She went to the toilet, flushed, and the entire toilet collapsed on her. A week earlier, we'd had the place painted, and the painters had scraped the walls. Now the Dutch woman was covered with plaster. So we wrapped her in a tablecloth and called a taxi. She showed up a half hour later wanting supper. Of course we had to give it to her gratis. And they want us to be self-supporting? How can anyone prosper under such conditions?"

From my diary, January 1989

⚬⚬⚬

My agent Bromberg was keeping busy. The last issue of *Svědectví* in 1988 arrived a little late, and there I saw that my *Love and Garbage* had been published in England and Holland. I also saw my first review:

> In his latest novel, Ivan Klíma has once again demonstrated that he is heir to masters of Czech prose such as Karel Čapek and Egon Hostovský. He is able to endow a simple sentence with the poetic charge of artistic conviction, amazing and enrapturing the reader. He induces that magnificent, blissful feeling that we experience whenever we come across a genuine artistic work. In reading Klíma's novel, the conviction grows in the reader, from page to page, that one has encountered a Czech author on a world-class level. And this conviction deservedly arouses pride.

I was still not permitted to publish a single line at home.

⚬⚬⚬

Michal brought me an instruction manual for operating WordPerfect and told me this was a new era of computers, and whoever didn't know how to use them was finished as an intellectual.

I looked at the instructions and saw an image of a keyboard with many incomprehensible designations such as F1 to F12 along with mysterious abbreviations such as Ins, Del, Home, Alt, and Ctrl. From time to time, Michal would quiz me on cutting and pasting or how to save a new text, and he was usually not satisfied with my answers. He nearly exploded when I called the Ctrl key the central key. (It didn't matter whether the key was called central, control, or casserole; what was important was its function, which seemed incomprehensible.) All the same, a few months later, he brought me a brand-new and, most important, portable computer as a gift and once again quizzed me on its operations.

Over the next few days, I became addicted to this new device. In the morning, I couldn't sleep and was at the miraculous keyboard at six o'clock. Not only could I write a new text, but I could even print the whole thing out on the attached printer, and the lines were perfectly aligned as if they had come from a real printing press. Until then I had to rewrite each page several times, cut the pages up, paste them together, type a clean copy, and then correct it again. Now my work flowed astonishingly quickly. During the next few weeks, I completed *My Golden Trades* and printed out twenty copies to share with my friends. But this amazing device could not alter my situation—I could print more copies, which looked nicer, but they were still only typewritten facsimiles.

⚬⚬⚬

From the very start of 1989, we met more often than in previous years. At the beginning of April, Yevgeny Yevtushenko, the Russian poet known for his rebellious verses, came to Prague. His translator, Václav Daněk, convinced him to skip lunch with the head of the official Writers' Union and visit us instead. Daněk assured him I would definitely invite more interesting guests. I did indeed invite most of my friends, among them our two celebrated travel writers, Jiří Hanzelka and Miroslav Zikmund. These two had traveled through the Soviet Union and composed their devastating findings and sent them to the Communist Party.

Yevtushenko arrived with his typical self-confidence and enthusiastically described the changes occurring in his country. He also recited his poem "Russian Tanks in Prague," which he had written, he said, two days after the Soviet invasion of Prague and sent it to the misguided rulers of his country. For its time, the poem was quite courageous. The first verses read:

Tanks are rolling across Prague
in the sunset blood of dawn.
Tanks are rolling across truth,
not a newspaper named Pravda

Tanks are rolling across the temptation
to live free from the power of clichés.
Tanks are rolling across the soldiers
who sit inside those tanks.

The conclusion was very personal and, as was fitting for Yevtushenko, even affected:

Before I bite the dust,
no matter what they call me,
I turn to my descendants
with only one request:

Above me without sobbing
let them write, in truth:
"A Russian writer crushed
by Russian tanks in Prague."

Then the Russian poet proclaimed that he had always believed in the ideals of the Prague Spring. Now he believed we would return to them.

To this, my colleague Hanzelka replied that it wouldn't be so easy, and then he availed himself of the following image: A criminal breaks into a house, ties up and gags the owner, places a guard on him, and leaves. After twenty years, the criminal's son remembers the victim; he even feels somewhat sorry for him and tells him, Father overdid it a little; now you can do what you want. But the victim is still gagged and bound. The guard hasn't even been called off. Even if he managed to free himself, could anyone expect that twenty years in fetters hasn't changed him?

Yevtushenko suggested that Hanzelka write a description of our situation, and he would make sure Gorbachev himself got it, or at least his trusted associate and adviser, Alexander Yakovlev.

But Hanzelka had already sent too many letters with no results.

A few days later, we convened another interesting meeting. Along with my usual friends, I invited members of the underground who, just like me, were prohibited and illegally published the typewritten journals *Vokno* and *Revolver Revue* as well as a typewritten series called *Popelnice*. I had assumed that although we had different literary convictions, we all wanted everyone to be able to publish freely. But our guests accused us of remaining official authors—more precisely, officially prohibited authors—and now we were attempting to reestablish our bygone prestige. Most of us unjustly considered ourselves creators of underground literature, but we were nevertheless publishing abroad and giving interviews to foreign journals. Unlike us, they had always remained secluded, off to the side because they were interested in authentic art, not some kind of consumer production that was forbidden only because of some official idiocy. We tried to explain that we too were trying to create authentic literature. But we couldn't come to an agreement. Who can judge what is authentic?

At another meeting, this time without our critics from the underground, we agreed that we should establish an independent writers' organization with a mission to stand up for freedom of creativity for every author, however he was characterized. But such an organization would have no hope of being recognized and permitted by the authorities. It would just bring further interrogations and, most likely, renewed assaults. It occurred to me that the PEN Club was still alive (and some of us were still members). The authorities hadn't banned the organization because it was an international group with its seat in

London, where their authority did not reach. They did, however, try to hobble its activities (which, among other things, included defending freedom of expression and creativity), and in the early seventies the Prague office was designated a sleeper office. What if we attempted to resuscitate it now?

My friends liked the idea and, as usual, I was punished for it by having to put it into action.

I decided to get thirty signatures from Czech writers, which would revive the Czech office of the PEN Club. My thinking was that these thirty signatures would represent all of Czech literature.

At the time, writers could be divided roughly into three groups based on their relationship with the authorities, not on their artistic convictions. First were the writers who were most acceptable to the government, members of the official Writers' Union. The second group, referred to as the "gray zone," comprised authors (usually younger) who, although they were permitted to publish, were not members of the Writers' Union and often had difficulties with the censors. Finally there were the prohibited authors. I asked those who kept away from political activities to sign the request to renew the PEN Club in the name of all banned writers. Then I turned to several of my colleagues in the "gray zone." Some were excited about our project.

Then I visited Mrs. Marta Kadlečíková, who for twenty years had remained the secretary of our sleeper office. She was still receiving documents from London, which were sent to all active or sleeper offices. I asked her in the name of thirty petitioners to inform London that we were renewing our activity.

Receiving recognition from London was easy; we expected more trouble from our authorities. Marta and I sent to the Ministry of Culture our notification that we were reestablishing the activities of the PEN Club, and, without waiting for an answer, we assembled the standing members of the committee from 1968 (I had been one of them) and immediately co-opted several more members, among them

Václav Havel. We immediately planned our first meeting for the end of the summer.

To my surprise, the response from the Ministry of Culture was not wholly negative. They were willing to meet with the members of the original committee and listen to our plans.

We were received by a deputy who told us that, in principle, they would have no objections to the club's activities as long as the PEN Club held to its statutes and did not pursue political activity. The statutes, which had been ratified sometime in the 1960s (and which the assiduous ministers had dug up), included a communal dinner associated with the meeting, to take place once a year and always during the first quarter. Our ministry bureaucrat informed us that we could not have our meeting as late as August as we had planned.

I protested that not a single anniversary meeting had taken place over the last twelve years, and it would be ridiculous to wait another six months, especially when, on the matter of freedom of expression, there was something to talk about.

But the state official insisted that we hold to our own statutes.

Even before we left, we had agreed to organize the meeting, whether the ministry approved it or not. Ultimately we were an international club, and we had informed the ministry only out of goodwill.

———

We succeeded in putting together a list of potential members, but our provisional committee had decided on too large a number for our regular meeting space—and we wanted to invite all of them. My colleague and translator, Jaroslav Kořán, suggested that we have it in the Chodov Citadel, where the curator was willing to accept the risks associated with an unlawful meeting of a lawful or, more precisely, not prohibited organization.

Around eleven o'clock on the day the meeting was to take place, the aforementioned curator called and told me to come see him right away. I asked if there was a problem with our using the hall for our meeting, and he said that was precisely why he was calling, but he didn't want to discuss it on the phone.

It was clear what had happened. Members of the secret police had strongly recommended that he not allow us to gather in the citadel.

There were only a few hours left before the meeting was supposed to convene, not enough time to inform everyone that it was canceled; besides, we wanted to have it. Marta Kadlečíková said she had the keys to the apartment of a writer who was now abroad, Jiří Mucha. One of the rooms was large enough to accommodate a few dozen people. She suggested we move the meeting there. We would have to call and inform everyone of the change of venue.

I wasn't going to say anything over the telephone that would inform the secret police where we were meeting. Two members of the committee had automobiles, and we could assume that several of the attendees also had cars and could drive those who arrived at the citadel by metro.

We did indeed manage to transfer everyone to Mucha's flat on Hradčanské Square. (It is difficult to imagine a more worthy place than this apartment filled with antiques and pictures by Jiří's father Alfons Mucha and other masters of art nouveau.)

Nevertheless, the secret police somehow found out about our new meeting place and detained several writers, including Vaculík and our Brno colleagues.

A few days before the meeting, I had received a long letter from Václav Havel. It began with an apology:

> Dear friends, a concurrence of circumstances has seen to it that I will most likely not be able to participate in your meeting, or that I will be able to participate in a limited capacity. At that time, I am to be meeting with representatives of the People's Militia where we will probably talk about whether they will fire upon people on the 21st of August. You will certainly realize that this meeting is, at the moment, of utmost importance.

There followed a series of instructions concerning what we should discuss and what to endorse.

Václav suggested accepting everyone into the organization who had been accepted by the PEN Club abroad. These were writers who had been the most persecuted.

The old committee, *which has in fact long been defunct, should resign and charge one member with conducting the remainder of the meeting.* Then we should elect a new committee to accept new members but not accept anyone who had publicly committed an offense against the charter of the PEN Club by participating in the suppression of the rights of his colleagues to publish. Then Václav asked that we ratify two documents immediately if we didn't want to make fools of ourselves at our very first meeting: one to demand that the political prisoner Ivan Jirous be pardoned and the other to take a stance on the case of Salman Rushdie (the fanatic Ayatollah Khomeini had issued a fatwa, that is, a death penalty on him for apparently offending the Prophet Muhammad in *The Satanic Verses*). It would also be good, continued Havel, if we requested the pardon of others imprisoned exclusively for distributing literature or other alternative culture.

Havel's suggestions seemed to me reasonable, but the meeting was being led by someone who was trying by all means to avoid any political discussion, let alone any protests or petitions. The most peculiar thing was his insistence that we conclude the meeting by seven o'clock (even though we'd begun nearly an hour late because of the location change).

The chair's attempt to avoid complications and conclude our first meeting in twenty years as quickly as possible met with such resistance, even among the official authors, that he finally gave up chairing the meeting. We understood his reasons when, just after seven o'clock, our friends started arriving after having spent the afternoon locked up for various reasons. Obviously, the secret police had been assured that the meeting would be concluded by then.

We quickly passed the necessary resolutions and elected Jiří Mucha president of the club. I was to be his deputy, but because Mucha was abroad, I was to head the PEN Club for the near future. (Soon thereafter, at Mucha's request, I was elected president in his place.)

Soon after our meeting, I was called in for an interrogation, where I was asked, at length and almost politely, about the PEN Club, its mission, and its charter. They said they had nothing against our electing Jiří Mucha president. It was now in fashion, added one of them ironically, that every organization have a president, but they knew I was the organizer. They understood our protest against Khomeini's fatwa on Rushdie; writers should not be sentenced to death for their literary works. They said nothing about our protest against our colleagues' imprisonment or our announcement that literature should enjoy freedom. Finally, I realized that the only point of the interrogation was to warn us not to elect Václav Havel, instead of Mucha, as president. This would threaten the existence of our club as an independent and nonpolitical organization.

I received this warning approximately three months before the Federal Assembly elected Havel president of the republic.

Helena said that a march to Albertov was going to take place on November 17 to mark International Students' Day and asked if I wanted to participate. I was much less a student now than twenty years earlier when I allowed myself to be convinced to go to Texas as a student, and I was not fond of marches or any kind of demonstrations. I preferred to stay home and write.

So Helena went by herself. At Albertov, she listened to a passionate speech by a student spokesman whom, to her surprise, she recognized as our nephew Martin. Then she traveled with the entourage all the way to the National Theater, where she just barely managed to avoid police truncheons.

I heard the reports (including the false information that Martin Šmíd was dead) on the radio—not the one broadcasting from Prague, of course.

The very next day I called a meeting of our PEN Club at the apartment of Karel Šiktanc. Karel, one of our best poets, never cared to involve himself in politics, so I thought his apartment would be safer than ours. Just in case, however, I arrived at his place an hour early.

In fact, a moment after I arrived, the police appeared in front of the building and were displaying the uncertainty characteristic of the time. They detained several members of the committee and led them off for interrogation. Other, less well-known members had their IDs checked but were allowed inside.

We were the only writers' organization able, or even willing, to publicly speak out against the events, and in view of our tradition and historical experiences, the position of writers could influence the behavior of the citizens. Therefore, we formulated our proclamation as emphatically as we could. Among other things, we wrote:

> The Czech Center of the PEN Club expresses bewilderment and anger at the brutal intervention by the forces of law and order, supported by members of special units, against a peaceful student demonstration. During the demonstration, not a single rock was thrown at the armed units; not a single window was broken; the students sat on the ground with lighted candles and, face-to-face with the armed forces, called out, "Our hands are empty" and "Dialogue, dialogue." . . . The authorities, not for the first time, responded to this call with violence, but this time it was more brutal than in the past.
>
> The Czech Center of the PEN Club appeals to the employees of all news media: Tell the nation the truth about the tragedy that has come to pass. Let the victims have the final word. The PEN Club appeals to all writers and translators to join this call.

We sent our proclamation to the Czechoslovak Press Agency, but just in case, we also immediately telephoned Radio Free Europe.

Two days later, I was invited to the New Stage of the National Theater. As in all other theaters, the actors here were on strike and, instead of continuing with their planned performances, they were calling various personalities onto the stage, usually those who hadn't been permitted to appear before any kind of audience for twenty years. Essentially, we all talked about the same thing: free elections, basic human rights, how freedom of speech and association had to be guaranteed, and that the constitutional article guaranteeing the leading role of the Communist Party had to be abolished.

I don't remember what I said. I do remember the feeling when, after almost two decades, I stepped onto a stage and the people in the hall began applauding even before I said anything. Somewhere in my subconscious was huddling the idea that at any minute, one of those gentlemen would appear whom I knew all too well and who for years had been on the lookout for anyone who, in their opinion, threatened the safety of the country, socialism, peace, and, thereby, all of humanity. Where were they? Where had they disappeared?

While I was thinking that the moment had arrived, the moment we had imagined over these years, the moment of change, I was overcome with an excitement similar to what I had felt when I stood by the collapsed fence at Terezín and waved at the passing soldiers who I knew were bringing with them the end of the war.

There are few experiences as strong as that of freedom, especially when it seemed for decades so unattainable. The most uplifting thing at this moment was the feeling that people in the audience were experiencing the same thing I was. Never had I longed to merge with the masses. In fact, such feelings frightened me. But once or twice in one's lifetime, for a few climactic moments of shared history, one can allow oneself precisely this exalting feeling.

—⚬⚬⚬—

During those days, writers who had been assiduously writing and publishing started calling me (apparently they had heard I was the head of the Czech PEN Club, which, unlike the current collaborationist Writers' Union, seemed to be the primary writers' organization for the near future). Only a week earlier, it was as if they hadn't known who I was, but now they were all but declaring their love and admiration for everything I'd ever written and done. Then they usually alluded to the fact that, although they had been publishing all along, they had actually been sacrificing themselves. They had longed to say something of import to their readers, but with censorship—certainly I could recall my own experiences—life was almost unbearably difficult. Then they tried inconspicuously to turn the conversation to the future: Would only certain people be allowed to publish, and others be banned? Would the roles now be reversed? Could they join the PEN Club?

These were difficult conversations, and I tried to cut them as short as possible. Freedom of the word and expression, I tried to assure these writers, was taken for granted. There was no force that could limit someone's freedoms. The telephone (at least at that time) did not permit one to see the face of one's interlocutor, but I imagined I could see the uncertainty in their faces: How could it possibly happen that suddenly everyone was permitted? This was against all their experiences, even common sense. Fortunately, I was difficult to reach at home.

Someone from among the group of students striking in the School of Humanities of Charles University invited me to a discussion and introduced me as a banned writer. I was asked to say something about how I had supported myself and how we smuggled our manuscripts abroad.

Finally, the students asked me to accompany them to northern Bohemia to meet with the workers. We agreed to go first thing the next day.

From the School of Humanities, it was only a brief walk to the School of Performing Arts, so I went to see Nanda. I bought her some food, since I'd heard from her husband that she hadn't been home for several days. It turned out to be unnecessary because, in their sudden revolutionary fervor, people had been bringing the students more food than they could consume.

I went straight to the classroom where students were cranking out slogans, proclamations, and posters as if on an assembly line. Nanda was excited, and when I asked her if she wanted to go home for at least one night, she said she wasn't about to lounge about when something so marvelous was going on.

I read the slogans on the posters and signs: CZECHS, COME WITH US! STUDENTS OF ALL DEPARTMENTS, UNITE! DOWN WITH THE CPČ! END THE RULE OF ONE PARTY! THIS COUNTRY IS OURS!

Scarcely had I arrived home when I received a call from the Central Students' Strike Committee, which had convened at the School of Performing Arts. They wanted my advice concerning an important matter. Could I come back? I had no idea what it could be, but they were wisely avoiding any sort of telephone conversation. I said I could be there in thirty minutes.

On this visit—unlike my visit an hour earlier to the same building —I was met by a guard who checked my ID. Then I was led across a courtyard and up and down stairs, and at another entrance I was transferred to another guard. It was all impressively conspiratorial. Finally, I was let into a room where a committee was in session; at its head was my nephew Martin. He welcomed me and said they needed to establish that the prime minister of the government, Alexander Adamec, was a member of the presidium of the Communist Party. I said yes. I waited for another question, but none was forthcoming.

On my way home again, I kept running into people coming from a protest demonstration. They were carrying bundles of banners as well as signs, many of which I had seen shortly before spread out on the floor and tables in Nanda's classroom.

I noticed that people were stopping or at least greeting one another. In the tram, I asked an older woman holding a small flag how it had been.

She said that Dubček and Havel had spoken and, had Masaryk been alive, he would have definitely been on the balcony as well.

This striking image stuck in my mind.

Of course, it was a time of striking images and unexpected changes (and metamorphoses), and, just as in a real drama, the tension and uncertainty were increasing.

The improvisation on the part of the victors, who were unprepared for victory, and the helplessness of the defeated, who could not imagine that over the course of a few days the structure that had been prophesied to endure for eternity would collapse, stood behind this remarkable, bloodless transformation.

The unexpected development of events also led to a strange compromise, which resulted in the Communist parliament unanimously electing Václav Havel president of the republic, and Havel appointing the Communist Marián Čalfa prime minister. As the brewmaster in Havel's play *Audience* says, "Them's the paradoxes of life, right?"

The most important thing, however, was that the heavens of freedom, imperceptible only a short time ago, had finally opened before us.

EPILOGUE

Most of my life up to now, I have lived without freedom. This lack of freedom assumed different forms and different intensities. Sometimes it was a matter of one's very existence, other times prison, and other times only the loss of a job and constant police persecution. To my discredit, for several years I had been a member of the party, the party that had this lack of freedom on its conscience, the party that had enthroned terror and was responsible for one of the most loathsome periods of our history. When I understood this (fortunately, fairly early), I did everything in my power to reestablish this freedom.

I gradually came to realize that there were two kinds of freedom, internal and external. One can behave unfreely even in free circumstances, and one can behave freely (with all the risks it entails) in unfree circumstances. I believe that for almost my entire adult life I tried to behave like a free person; I wrote about the world not the way I was ordered to but the way I perceived and experienced it.

Now I could choose many paths upon which to continue in life. I was offered various appointments, including membership in newly arising parties. I rejected them all. I had left behind me the brief period of my life when I believed that the duty of each person who did not want to waste his own life was to try to save the world. The world did not need saving; humanity did not need the prophets who, until recently, had led it to unimaginable heights. It needed decency, work, honor, and humility.

I wanted to keep doing what I knew how, at least a little. To write.

ESSAYS

Ideological Murderers

History can be seen as a series of bloody acts to which entire nations often fall victim. In some cities or areas humiliated during wartime, every living creature, including cattle, was exterminated. Sometimes, however, the slaughter following a victorious battle was carried out by the celebrating soldiers, and their behavior has been metaphorically described as "drunk with blood." It is a sort of afterglow of battle during which "drunken" men, before they sober up, carry out even more devastation. The occupying German forces would continue their destruction of conquered territory in Poland, Yugoslavia, and the Soviet Union, where soldiers often assassinated, burned alive, or hanged the inhabitants they considered defiant.

In the slaughter of the Jews, there was something even more appalling. This had no connection with soldiers who had survived the moral peril of battle and continued killing in rage and ecstasy. It was a carefully planned operation, the goal of which was to destroy an entire, precisely defined group of citizens in the shortest amount of time, without regard to sex, age, profession, creed, or religion. Thousands of men and women, officials, guards, cold-blooded killers, sadists, and obedient administrators participated in this slaughter, and they were clearly not in the condition of a soldier drunk with blood. They had days, weeks, and months to consider what they were doing. They painstakingly—and soberly—carried out orders, whatever they were, whether they impinged on their emotions or perhaps were in conflict with whatever remnant of morality and conscience they had.

A similar slaughter, just as senseless and cold-blooded, took place two decades later in the Soviet Union. Certain individuals or entire groups, often chosen at random—there was a quota of enemies that had to be annihilated—were loaded onto trucks and executed somewhere in secrecy. Those who were not murdered outright were carted off to one of thousands of Siberian camps, where most of them, under the leadership of similar hatchet men, sadists, or obedient administrators, perished.

Where did so many people, who were suddenly willing to commit such villainy, come from?

Several years after the war when I was sojourning in Poland, I dug up the memoirs of Rudolf Höss, the commandant of the Auschwitz concentration camp. I've never read a book so many times as this dry, matter-of-fact record of mass murder. I don't think I was the only one fascinated by this memoir. It inspired the French novelist Robert Merle when he was writing *Death Is My Trade*. Today Merle's novel, along with the Auschwitz commandant's memoirs, has been almost forgotten, overshadowed by the more recent massacres in the Soviet Union, China, and Cambodia or the murders committed by Muslim terrorists and other fanatics. I believe, however, that there are few texts that demonstrate the degree to which one can be driven by blind obedience to an aberrant doctrine, when the fanaticized mind enables a person to concede responsibility for his actions and suppresses his last tremor of conscience.

In the spring of 1942 the first transports of Jews arrived from Upper Silesia. All of them were to be exterminated. They were led from the ramp across the meadow, later named section B-II of Birkenau, to the farmhouse called Bunker I. Aumeir, Palitzsch, and a few other block leaders led them and spoke to them as one would in casual conversation, asking them about their occupations and their schooling in order to fool them. After arriving at the farmhouse they were told to undress. At first they went very quietly into the rooms where they were supposed to be disinfected. At that point some of them became suspicious and started talking about suffocation and extermination. Immediately a panic started. Those still standing outside were quickly driven into the chambers, and the doors were bolted shut. In the next transport those who were nervous or upset were identified and watched closely at all times. As soon as unrest was noticed these troublemakers were inconspicuously led behind the farmhouse and killed with a small-caliber pistol, which could not be heard by the others. . . .

Many women hid their babies under piles of clothing. . . . The little children cried mostly because of the unusual setting in which they were being undressed. But after their mothers or the Sonderkommando encouraged them, they calmed down and continued playing, teasing each other, clutching a toy as they went into the gas chamber.

I also watched how some women who suspected or knew what was happening, even with the fear of death all over their faces, still managed enough strength to play with their children and talk to them lovingly. Once a woman with four children, all holding each other by the hand to help the smallest ones over the rough ground, passed by me very slowly. She stepped very close to me and whispered, pointing to her four children, "How can you murder these beautiful, darling children? Don't you have any heart?" . . .

As the doors were being shut, I saw a woman trying to shove her children out of the chamber, crying out, "Why don't you at least let my precious children live?" . . .

According to Himmler's orders, Auschwitz became the largest human killing center in all of history. When he gave me the order personally in the summer of 1941 to prepare a place for mass killings and then carry it out, I could never have imagined the scale, or what the consequences would be. Of course, this order was something extraordinary, something monstrous. However, the reasoning behind the order of this mass annihilation seemed

correct to me. At the time I wasted no thoughts about it. I had received an order; I had to carry it out. I could not allow myself to form an opinion as to whether this mass extermination of the Jews was necessary or not. At that time it was beyond my frame of mind. Since the Führer himself had ordered "The Final Solution of the Jewish Question," there was no second guessing for an old National Socialist, much less an SS officer. "Führer, you order. We obey" was not just a phrase or a slogan. It was meant to be taken seriously. . . .

Since my arrest I have been told repeatedly that I could have refused to obey this order, and even that I could have shot Himmler dead. I do not believe that among the thousands of SS officers there was even one who would have had even a glimmer of such a thought. Something like that was absolutely impossible. . . . I am convinced that not even one would have dared raise a hand against him, not even in his most secret thoughts. As leader of the SS, Himmler's person was sacred. His fundamental orders in the name of the Führer were holy.

Rudolf Höss came from a narrow-minded Catholic family. His father had destined him for the clergy and inculcated in him a boundless respect for authority. His father, however, died when Höss was young, and at sixteen he enlisted in the army against his mother's protests. After the war he joined the semilegal units of the *Freikorps*, and when he heard Hitler's 1922 speech in Munich, he joined the Nazi party. He and his pals then participated in the murder of a teacher whom they believed to be an informer. Höss always considered this murder an act of justice, and it was correct to carry it out because *it was highly unlikely that any German court would have found him* [the teacher] *guilty*. Höss was sentenced to ten years in prison for the teacher's death but was released after five for good behavior. Before he joined the SS, he had made his living as a farmer. He writes that he enjoyed this work and harbored a love of horses. When the war ended, he evaded arrest and worked as a farmhand under the name of Franz Lang. During these eight months before he was captured, he didn't kill anyone and probably didn't feel the need to, since no one was giving him those orders, and the architect of the iniquitous ideology to which he subscribed was dead. In a letter to his wife just before his execution, he writes about himself: *How tragic it is that I, by nature kind, good-natured, and always obliging, became the greatest mass-murderer . . . , who cold-bloodedly and with all the attendant ramifications carried out every single order of extermination.*

Adolf Eichmann, the man who, with wholehearted diligence, ensured a steady supply of victims, lived after the war as a more or less respectable Argentinean citizen for fifteen years without committing any crime. Eichmann, who during his trial in Jerusalem declared that he was no anti-Semite, explained his criminal activity as mere obedience.

> Had they told me my father was a traitor and I had to kill him, I would have. At that time I followed orders without thinking about them. . . . Orders were given, and because they were orders, we obeyed them. If I was given an order, it wasn't meant to be interpreted. . . . Do you think such an insignificant person as myself was going to worry his head about it? I receive an order and look neither right nor left. It's my job. My job is to listen and obey.

When the elite representatives of the Nazi regime stood before the International Military Tribunal in Nuremburg, all of them, except a few, pretended to be astounded and shocked by the atrocities committed by the regime. During the screening of films from concentration camps or even when bearing witness to what went on, some even broke down in tears. Of course emotion can be simulated, but it is also possible that the moment Nazi ideology was defeated and it was clear that the consequences had inflicted misery not only on those at war with Germany but also on Germany itself, the accused, stripped of all glory and inviolability, suddenly saw the world and their deeds from another point of view.

One of the most barbarous and vindictive SS men in Terezín was Rudi Heindl, an electrician by trade. Witnesses at his trial in Litoměřice testified that he had placed an old man on a red-hot stove. One witness testified that he had kicked her mother so hard that she died from the wounds inflicted. Many others related tales of his barbarity. After the war he again worked as an electrician and mistreated no one. In court he claimed that he didn't want to cause anyone pain. Everything he did was upon orders from his superiors. Now he asked only that he be allowed to go to his family, his two daughters and his son who needed him. To them and to everyone around him he had always been amiable and good-natured.

They sentenced and hanged him.

One wonders. If Nazism had not existed, would these men have gone through life as honest, respectable farmers, workers, electricians, officials, or shopkeepers and committed no crimes? Without criminal ideologies which, often in a sophisticated way, deceive those who believe in them, would these slaughters have occurred, slaughters symptomatic of the entire first half of the twentieth century? One of course also wonders if these criminal regimes would have existed, whether hundreds of concentration camps—from Kolyma to the banks of the Rhine—would have come into being if such acquiescent people as Rudolf Höss, Adolf Eichmann, and those who had wept before the tribunal in Nuremberg had served them.

Höss was put on trial by the Supreme National Tribunal in Poland, which on April 2, 1947, *for all the evil he inflicted upon humanity . . . and at the behest of the world's conscience*, sentenced him to death.

In a farewell letter to his wife, the commandant of Auschwitz admits:

> Based on my present knowledge I can see today clearly, severely and bitterly for me, that the entire ideology about the world in which I believed so firmly and unswervingly was based on completely wrong premises and had to absolutely collapse one day.

For the several million who were slaughtered in Auschwitz, this insight came too late. And we can certainly assume that it never would have come if it had not been preceded by the absolute military defeat of the regime that the fanatic perpetrators of these crimes served.

Utopias

It sounds paradoxical, but all escalating violence, all barbaric and unparalleled murder or theft usually occurs in the name of the good, of morality, or of reason, or, during the modern period, in the name of the people, progress, and finally the common good. All great ideologies, such as the utopian projects of the ideal communities, sought those lofty goals, or at least professed them.

Plato emphasizes that a person tasked with protecting the good of the community must be brought up from earliest childhood with that goal in mind. Then Plato poses the logical question: Can a bad example serve the reinforcement of the good in education? The presentation of a lie as something beneficial? And from this basic premise he draws conclusions, which have always suited those who justify censorship: *Let none of the poets tell us* . . . *and let no one slander Proteus and Thetis, neither let any one, either in tragedy or in any other kind of poetry, introduce Hera disguised in the likeness of a priestess.* . . . And he adduces entire passages from Homer and Aeschylus that cannot be approved. Then he enumerates what is necessary to reject in poetry. Education is perverted by everything that elicits horror, everything that describes suffering, the moaning and lamentation of those in torment or dying, or the description of death at all. Furthermore, events that elicit laughter cannot be depicted because laughter transforms a person in inauspicious ways.

More that two thousand years later, Bernhard Bolzano was living in the Czech lands. All of his activities were aimed at strengthening democracy, eliminating social differences, and expanding education.

In his utopian *On the Best State* (from *Selected Writings on Ethics and Politics*), however, he draws conclusions similar to Plato's:

> As books may never become the property of individuals, they shall be published at the expense of the state. From this it obviously follows that not everything anyone wants to publish shall in fact be printed. . . . Those who urge us to accept an unrestricted freedom of the press no doubt also wish it to be accompanied by an unrestricted freedom to read. Thus once a bad or dangerous book is printed and distributed, one could hardly prevent it causing incalculable damage. . . . Concerning . . . the production of new works of art, one is not nearly so mild in one's judgments. . . . For this reason, one will not so easily permit someone to make poetry or musical composition, etc., his primary business when he does not show promise of accomplishing something truly extraordinary.

As far as censorship was concerned, as a man of the Enlightenment, Bolzano wanted an enlightened, educated, and strictly limited censorship. It should be aimed primarily at immoral works, *when a book contains scenes depicting lewdness or other vices in a provocative way, or even defends such vices.*

It is true that freedom of the press and freedom of expression provide an opening for many depravities, but censorship in itself is a depravity that harms society more than any erotic scenes. Moreover, the linking of censorship with the Enlightenment is a contradiction.

The Frenchman Étienne Cabet, the founder of the Icaria movement, was even more radical in his relationship to freedom of the press. In his utopian *Voyage to Icaria* he envisions that only his enlightened republic would have the right to print books. *The republic [would be] able to rewrite all the books that were imperfect . . . and to burn all the books judged to be dangerous or useless.* Cabet later moved to the United States and in the middle of the nineteenth century attempted to create a model republic based upon his ideas, which of course, at the beginning, would assume the form of a pure dictatorship and would compel the inhabitants to adhere strictly to all established norms of life in the colony. He forbade drinking and smoking and instructed the denizens to establish families and turn over to the community the responsibility of raising the children. Cabet's ideal republic (like all ideal communities), however, had no hope of succeeding and rapidly disintegrated.

Bolzano too planned out the life of his society in detail. He did away with property inheritance and outlawed youth organizations unless each meeting was overseen by an elder who had the proper worldview. He planned education and determined how many workers would be needed in various places. Everything was to be done, of course, *in such a way that they would be happy.*

All architects of the ideal state appealed to the happiness of the citizens. *It is I,* claimed Charles Fourier, *who will be thanked by current and future generations for initiating their happiness. . . . We are going to witness a spectacle which can only be seen once in each globe, the transition from incoherence to social combination. This is the most brilliant movement that can ever happen in the universe, and the anticipation of it shall be a consolation to the present generation for all its miseries. Every year of this period of metamorphosis will be worth centuries of ordinary existence.* But humanity did not thank him, and he did not become an actor in his theater.

The mistake of the utopians lay in their assumption that it is possible to build the ideal state with the agreement of the people. They believed in the ideal person who, as soon as he is afforded the opportunity to act honorably and fairly, would be transformed into a conscious citizen doing his utmost to serve, happily and willingly, the good of the community. And so was born the image of the joyful, enthusiastic citizen for whom the enlightened ruler would plan all of his feelings, activities, and mutual relationships (including amatory ones) and rigorously subordinate him to discipline—which was, however, gladly accepted. He who does not submit has chosen the fate of the pariah. It was a logical conclusion. As soon as the incontrovertible good was discovered, it would be possible and correct to require that everyone be in its service. Those who did not, were violating it, and because the community embodied the good, it would be necessary to deal with them as criminals.

It is here that the onetime advocates of the ideal community are in agreement with their modern successors. When we read not only the works of Marx but also Plato's *Republic*, More's *Utopia*, Tommaso Campanella's *City of the Sun*, or Bolzano's vision of the state, we are amazed that all these dreams of justice and the new arrangement of the community actually epitomized the despotisms or at least the precursors of dictatorships as they are commonly understood. Their authors rightly suspected that people would hardly wax enthusiastic over artificially created relationships. Therefore, they mercilessly put to death everyone who wrenched himself out of the established order. Thomas More suggested imprisonment for those who engaged in premarital sex, and because the parents were responsible for such corruption, they should be imprisoned as well. Marital infidelity would be punished even worse; the serial transgressor would pay for it with his neck. More also advocated the execution of anyone who dared discuss public affairs unofficially and would proclaim war on every state that possessed uncultivated land and did not allow the immigration of surplus citizens of the Utopia. We do not know if Adolf Hitler read *Utopia*, but at least on this point he decidedly acted according to its principles.

In Cabet's *Icaria*, there is not a police uniform to be seen. But this is not important. Uniformed policemen are unnecessary because ***in our community all citizens must keep watch over the upholding of the laws and pursue or report criminals.*** How accurate this two-hundred-year-old characteristic of the police state is.

In his turn, Campanella demands the execution of everyone who deviates from the strict order of his state. For example, he would punish with death a woman who *uses high-heeled boots so that she may appear tall, or garments with trains to cover her wooden shoes.* His image of prisons and hangmen in the future ideal state is prophetic of Bolshevism, which came several hundred years after Campanella's death. *They have no prisons, except one tower for shutting up rebellious enemies. The accused who is found guilty is reconciled to his accuser and to his witnesses, as it were, with the medicine of his complaint, that is, with embracing and kissing. No one is killed or stoned unless by the hands of the people. . . . Some transgressors are allowed to put themselves to death: they will place around themselves bags of gunpowder, light them, and burn to death, while exhorters are present for the purpose of advising them to die honorably. . . . Certain officers talk to and convince the accused man by means of arguments until he himself acquiesces in the sentence of death passed upon him. . . . But if a crime has been committed against the liberty of the republic, or against God, or against the supreme magistrates, there is immediate censure without pity. These only are punished with death. He who is about to die is compelled to state in the face of the people and with religious scrupulousness the reasons for which he does not deserve death, and also the sins of the others who ought to die instead of him, and further the mistakes of the magistrates. If, moreover, it should seem right to the person thus asserting, he must say why the accused ones are deserving of less punishment than he.*

It is as if the modern era were begun by Rousseau's *Social Contract* which, just like many other utopias, begins from the proposition that at one time people lived in a state of marvelous innocence. Their primary luxury was freedom and will. This paradisiacal condition was destroyed by the emergence of private property. Rousseau does not suggest doing away with private property, however. He describes in detail the specter of *the people* or *the citizen* as a kind of revolutionary power, a source of truth, a guarantor of knowledge, and therefore the highest judge. Something incontrovertible and just, which is called the general will, emerges from the unified will of all citizens who have a common interest. This is expressed by the law. The state itself watches over the fulfillment of the laws and the carrying out of justice. This general will always embodies truth. He who refuses to submit can be compelled *to be free.* He who continually contravenes, he who scorns the will of the people, deserves nothing less than death. Rousseau deliberates over who should ensure that this general will is fulfilled and at the same time not abused, and he comes up with the enlightened ruler, *who would be able, as it were, to change the nature of every individual.*

The people, then, over the course of further centuries, would become the shield concealing the crimes of those who in their name act as their benefactors and enlightened rulers.

Karl Marx identified this revolutionary force, which alone could achieve a just society, with the proletariat. When it took power, it would create a revolutionary society different from all previous societies. Marx translates his utopian vision of the future society that would be built by the proletariat into the *Communist Manifesto*: He predicts that as soon as all property is in the hands of the proletariat, the bourgeoisie will be destroyed, and class warfare and contradictory social interests will disappear. *In place of the old bourgeois society with its classes and class antagonisms, we shall have an association in which the free development of each is the condition for the free development of all.* Just like all creators of utopias, he possesses the fantastic conviction that he has at last found the key to happiness, justice, abundance, and a dignified life—truth. It is possible that the struggle to create this happy society would require time, but the future would reward the people for it. The utopians managed to capitalize on people's longing for impersonal guidance in order to persuade them of their vision no matter how unreal or even absurd. In backward and impoverished Russia, the resolute, fanatical adherent of Marx's communist vision, Lenin, actually tried to build a communist society. In 1920 he did not hesitate to proclaim that *the generation that is now fifteen will live to see a communist society.*

In a Communist society, as Lenin understood it, each person had the right to satisfy all his needs. In ten to twenty years, the country in which prosperity was to reign was stricken with a famine that took the lives of millions of citizens. Further millions perished because they refused to proclaim, or did not sufficiently proclaim, their enthusiasm for the unreal vision.

The greatest danger threatens humanity when adherents of utopia succeed in seizing power in its name and try to realize their dreams of a better society. Their unrealistic visions make them blind to reality. The horrible crimes of communism and Nazism arose above all from the utopianism of these ideologies. This forced life into a brutal stranglehold of illusion. When the illusion collapsed, the regime could not disown it without forfeiting its legitimacy. Therefore, it suppressed life—that is, precisely the people whom it invoked.

Despite all the disastrous experiences, new utopian projects will emerge. People long to live in a better, kinder, and more just world, and are therefore prepared again and again to succumb to the seductive promises of tyrants, political or religious dreamers who promise it to them, either in heaven or in heaven on earth—in both cases, however, for eternity.

The Victors and the Defeated

Several days after the coup, the Communist weekly *Tvorba* printed an impassioned editorial. *The 25th of February is one of the greatest days in our history. On this day our nation for the first time in the history of its thousand-year existence actually created a government truly of the people. A government dedicated to realizing all the just demands of the working masses, who will be hindered by nothing in their constructive labor.* As one can see from this brief excerpt, the author, Arnošt Kolman, did not excel in literary style. It is likely, however, that at the time he believed what he was writing. (At the end of his life, he admits in his memoirs: *Heavy thoughts force themselves upon me near the anniversary of Victorious February 1948, the day that unfortunately also predetermined August 21, 1968. For the rest, I admit that I too had a hand in that Pyrrhic victory.*)

Meanwhile, the newspapers published a manifesto titled "Forward, Not One Step Back." The propagandistic text full of phrases about the people and progress, undoubtedly created in the ideological department of the Communist Party, implored all of the creative intelligentsia to support the new regime:

> The magnificent days during which the fate of our nation and our republic is being decided beckon all upstanding patriots, all people of goodwill, to a state of readiness and responsibility. . . . At this historical moment, we turn to all the workers of the mind, to the entirety of the nation's creative intelligentsia to take their place at the side of the Czech and Slovak people, who so readily rose to the defense of the country. The Czechoslovak working people . . . in

a powerful national uprising thwarted sabotage, prevented confusion and disruption, and are now flocking to the new and vital National Front, the genuine representative of the Czech and Slovak nation. Join the action committees of the National Front. Help exterminate the forces of darkness and obscurantism. Join us in the formation of the progressive powers of the nation, which will ensure a happy and joyful future for our glorious country.

Forward, not one step back.

This text, composed in the new language in which the proponents of democracy are referred to as the forces of darkness and obscurantism while the representatives of dictatorship are called honorable patriots laboring to create social progress, signaled the end of Czechoslovak democracy. Nevertheless, it was signed by hundreds of educated people—writers, actors, singers, and painters. Among the signatories devoted to the Communist Party, there were certainly opportunists, those with a bad conscience, but there were more who believed that the future belonged to socialism. Enchanted and confused by the illusion that existed only in the minds of dreamers, demagogues, and false prophets, they were prepared to sacrifice their own freedom as well as that of society.

Years later, on the anniversary of the February coup, we would see films of the ecstatic crowd in the Old Town Square. It is possible, by various means, to compel people to go into raptures. Enthusiasm can be feigned or organized, but one can assume that the enthusiasm of the crowd on this late February day was neither forced nor feigned. To bring the supporters of revolution to the square was not difficult for the conspirators behind the scenes.

The history of our modern era is permeated with revolutions and coups, which always proceed to the zealous consent of the crowd in the streets. The people of France thrilled to the execution of their king and queen. They then rejoiced at the beheading of the revolutionary leaders, and a few years later the same anonymous people welcomed Napoleon's coronation as emperor. There were plenty of people who believed that the Bolshevik Revolution would inaugurate a new era of history; it would banish inequality and return the decision-making process to the people—that indefinable but repeatedly invoked societal entity. They sang the glory of the leaders: Lenin, Trotsky, Zinoviev, Bukharin. (The first died in time, the second was murdered by his comrades, the last two perished on the scaffold to the excited or enforced agreement of the mob.) And throughout Germany, the crowds hysterically cheered the victory of Hitler's Nazi party, which promised to return glory and prosperity to the humiliated country.

It is as if a dream of paradise slumbers in our thoughts. Christian thinkers recognized that people would gladly believe in a new kingdom in which they would know more love and God's forgiveness. This kingdom, however, was accessible only after death. Now came a new promise: an earthly paradise in which equitable relations would reign here and now. The poor would receive property; the silenced would receive their voice; the suppressed and the dissatisfied would receive satisfaction.

If the appropriate historical situation arrives, or if a sufficiently powerful group of conspirators manages to change conditions, someone will eventually appear promising to lead those who yearn for the unattainable to the goal of their longings. The crowds will go out into the street and shout in beatific anticipation that their lives, heretofore tormenting in their everydayness, finality, loneliness, and banality, will be transformed. The crowds will acclaim the glory of the leader, the idea, the future, which they believe they are just beginning to create. The crowds applaud; wave banners, slogans, portraits; offer freshly picked flowers to the leaders of the revolution; sing and dance. For a moment, hope wins out over life experience. There is something magnetic about the ecstatic crowd, not only for those who participate in it but also for those who observe it, often with fear. This attraction overwhelms them. It inhibits their will to resist the progression of events, even though they are convinced the events will be destructive.

When we look back at those epochal times and the rejoicing mobs, we usually forget, or at least do not notice, that we're seeing only a portion, sometimes an inconsiderable one, even though it is the louder portion of the participants. Because besides its victors, every revolution has its losers, and they are usually greater in number than the victors.

When the Czechoslovak republic was coming into being, there were three and a half million Germans in the country. They were frightened by the emergence of a "republic of Czechs and Slovaks" because it meant the loss of their influence and their station as leaders. Not even the hundreds of thousands of citizens connected with the old monarchy rejoiced. Its downfall threatened the end of their world, or at least their careers.

When the German occupation ended, in addition to millions of Germans who had until recently been Czechoslovak citizens, there were hundreds of thousands of people who were somehow connected with the occupying power living in the country. They had served the Reich, informed on their fellow citizens to the gestapo. They hated both the Jews and the democrats. When the Communists carried out their well-planned coup, besides the jubilant crowd in Old Town Square in February 1948, besides the misled proletariat and several hundred deluded, naive, cunning, or party-disciplined artists who had signed the manifesto of cultural enslavement, there were many in our country who believed in democracy and had fought for it in armies abroad. There were many who refused to accept that in the works of Marx, Engels, Lenin, and Stalin human knowledge had reached its zenith. There were many who believed in God in the heavens, not in the palace of the Kremlin. There were thousands who owned something and suspected that the new regime would take everything from them, things that had often been the work of entire generations. But they were caught unaware by the impetuosity of the changes, numbed by the roar of the victorious crowd, the ruthless determination of the new leaders. Some decided to bide their time, others fled, and still others, out of anxiousness or calculation, decided to join the victors.

Every euphoria caused by societal change quickly disappears, and suddenly it turns out that the number of defeated outnumbers that of the victors. If the revolution enthroned a dictatorship, the new power tries to destroy the defeated by force, drive them from their cities, silence and imprison them. The most defiant are executed. Thereby an all-pervading terror is created, but at the same time disappointment, which gradually becomes apathetic inactivity or hatred, often precisely among those who allowed themselves to be lured by false promises. All of these will gradually prepare the fall of the revolutionary power.

If the dictatorship falls or even if it retreats in the face of democratic change, the elated victors soon realize with horror that the recently defeated representatives of totalitarianism are once more struggling to seize the power of which they have been deprived. One cannot defend against this intermingling of the defeated with the victors, not only because democracy refuses to persecute anyone who does not conspicuously commit an offense but also because it is often difficult to determine who is the victor and who is the conquered. It is precisely this condition that contributes to the fact that the expected societal rehabilitation seems to dissolve and disappear, and once again those who would welcome a more visible division between the victors and the conquered appear, assuming that they themselves would be among the new victors.

Thus swings the slow pendulum of history.

The Party

There were many who recognized that the goals of the Communist Party were subversive and nefarious. The moment the party took control after the war, these people were prepared to resist the new power. At that time, there were also many who believed the party would lead society to the goals that generations had longed for, and after the appalling experiences of war, the party would do everything to ensure that the long-awaited peace would endure. But even the faithful who joined the party, convinced of its ability to carry the people to lofty goals, must have seen relatively early on that it was an organization not above baseness, lies, intrigues, or even villainy.

When I joined the party, its name signified that it belonged to Czechoslovakia. In reality, however, it had long been a mere copy of the Communist Party of the Soviet Union.

The Communist Party arose in Russia (just as the Czech Communist Party did later) through the fragmentation of the Social Democrats. At the Second Congress of the Russian Social Democratic Party (it took place abroad because the activity of the party was illegal in Russia), the faction led by Lenin garnered the majority, and from that time on its shrewd leader used the epithet "Bolshevik" (that is, the majority). Lenin's group, composed of several thousand devoted revolutionaries, seized power relatively easily with several armed campaigns at the end of the First World War. They then announced a dictatorship. And since dictatorships like to veil themselves with lofty or at least seemingly altruistic attributes, they called themselves the proletariat and announced that they were building a Socialist society, which during the next generation would become Communist, classless, and prosperous—the most just society in history.

The Bolsheviks were victorious in a country where political life, as far as it went, had been playing out in secret and where not only nonconforming politicians but also many intellectuals and artists were forced to spend parts of their lives underground or in exile. The party, whose fanatical leaders lived as conspiratorial outlaws, could not but differ fundamentally from political parties in democratic countries. Like every conspiratorial organization, it had to preserve strict discipline and introduce a military hierarchy. There could be no doubt concerning the leader's orders; they were to be fulfilled without hesitation. In theory, this principle was called democratic centralism. The members of the party had the right to defend their opinions until a resolution was accepted, and then they had to comply. T. G. Masaryk captured the basic outline of Bolshevism in his book *The Making of a State*, published a few years after Soviet power took hold in Russia:

> Bolshevik centralism is especially rigid; it is an abstract regime deduced from theory and forcibly implemented. Bolshevism is the absolute dictatorship of a single person and his assistants; Bolshevism is infallible and inquisitorial, and that is why it has nothing in common with science and scientific philosophy. Science, which is what democracy is, without freedom is impossible.

Lenin's concept of dictatorship was merciless and was characterized by barbaric cruelty. Immediately after assuming power, he established a political police force that had the task of uncovering all genuine and imaginary enemies of the new regime. Lenin repeatedly demanded that the new power be ruthless. In the name of the revolution, it had the right to shoot, hang, or take hostages. Then it would take entire families hostage. If the enemies did not submit, the adults were executed and the children taken off to camps where most of them perished.

During the reign of Lenin's successor, Stalin, the leader had already become infallible. His views were indisputable. Anyone who dared act against them was branded as a deviationist. Even those who only appeared to deviate from the official dogma were not only expelled from the party but were also accused of antistate activity. Thus, political life, the exchange of opinions, disappeared from the only existing political party. The party was transformed into a mere privileged echelon whose task was to ensure that the orders of the dictator were carried out.

The First World War aroused a revolutionary mood not only in the Russian empire but also in most European countries. When revolutionary fervor cooled, Communist parties remained in these countries, and the Russian Bolsheviks saw them as allies. To ensure that these allies were truly reliable and would defend the interests of "the first country ruled by workers and farmers" (as the Bolsheviks craftily and deceitfully characterized their dictatorship), it was necessary to impose the same principles the Bolsheviks had employed in governing their own party. They founded the Communist International, which then arrogated to itself the right to intervene in the politics of the individual Communist parties anywhere in the world. The Soviet government—that is, the Soviet dictator—was supposed to stand atop the entire movement.

The history of the Czech Social Democrats was different from that of their Russian counterparts. From its beginnings, theirs was a legal party and had no reason to accept Bolshevik methods. Czech Communists who split off from the Social Democrats in 1921 were not denied a part in the political life of the new republic, and their leader, Bohumír Šmeral, believed that he could push socialism through parliament. Jacques Rupnik in his *History of the Ruling Communist Party of Czechoslovakia* cites the aphoristic assertion by the Austrian Social Democrat Otto Bauer: "I know two good Social Democratic Parties: the best is of course the Austrian Party and immediately after it is the Communist Party of Czechoslovakia."

The Communist International could not accept the moderation of a subordinate party. Following their conspiratorial tradition, Soviet

Bolsheviks prepared a putsch of Czechoslovak Communists. It had one goal: to exchange the current leadership for one that would accept Bolshevik principles. In 1929 the coup was realized, and Klement Gottwald, a man with neither education nor scruples, became head of the party. He revered Stalin and shared his hatred of democracy. Most Czech Communists departed the party in protest, but this did not bother the new leaders. They possessed the mind-set of a sect: Only they knew what was correct, and their goal was either to convince the others of their truth or to destroy them. There were far fewer Russian Bolsheviks when the party took power. Power—absolute, uncontrollable power—is what the Czech Communists had to acquire if they wanted to realize their plans, plans of which most citizens had no understanding. Twenty years later, Gottwald and his henchmen did indeed acquire this power.

They saw the victory of the allies as the victory of their Communist truth. With Leninesque deviousness, they exploited the fact that the Red Army had occupied most of the republic. They presented themselves as defenders of the interests of Czechoslovak citizens; they fashioned themselves as the true spokespersons not only for the workers but also the farmers, intelligentsia, tradesmen, and small-business owners. They promised to defend their interests, call to account traitors and the greatest exploiters, and quickly introduce prosperity throughout the land. They pushed through (with the assistance of three naively acquiescent or mistakenly calculating democratic parties) the nationalization of large enterprises, mines, and banks, and prohibited most prewar political parties, which they saw as threats dangerous to healthier social relations. In reality, they sought absolute power and attempted to infiltrate every institution of the still democratic state. They occupied the most important ministries and prepared their armed militia. It would be needed when the moment came to strike the final blow to democracy.

After the war, the Communist Party became a heterogeneous group in which the old adherents of the Communist vision were joined by both those who yielded to Communist demagoguery and those who rightly suspected where the rule of society was headed and, along with it, the advantages that come with loyalty. After the February coup, thousands more joined the party: former Social Democrats who were forced to unite with the victorious Communists, and also opportunists or just frightened citizens who were presented with an application form and made to understand that if they did not sign, things would go badly for them. Finally, there were the young, who knew little about the rest of the world and democracy. As early as the 1950s, the party was merely pretending to be just another political party. Although it appeared that members of the higher political organs were elected, in reality they were merely approved, since the candidates came from precisely these organs. The general secretary ruled the party without restraint. He then chose a small body of members to make up the presidium. The only task of these so-called elected officials was to carry out the orders of the head of the party (and as happens in a dictatorship, of the state). In his turn, the head of the party was obliged to conform to the orders of the Soviet dictator in all fundamental decisions.

The power the Czech Communists acquired was only seemingly absolute. It was primarily derived from and subordinate to a foreign power. This was ensured by Soviet advisers, the secret police, and party organs that had been painstakingly screened. Only discipline, subordination, and expressions of enthusiasm or hatred, depending on what the party needed at the time, was required of the party members. It was unthinkable that a member raise objections to party policies. If you refused to sign a petition, or even dared express disagreement with forced collectivization or political processes, you would appear as an enemy and be dealt with accordingly. On the other hand, if you painstakingly advocated everything considered proper policy, you could expect the appropriate rewards. The party leadership decided everything: which era was worthy of following, which should fall to the wayside; which thoughts were necessary to disseminate and which to forbid. Who was a hero, who a coward, who was an inventor, who a scientist, who a cheat, and who an ally, and, most important, who was an enemy, a subversive, a saboteur, a revisionist, a cosmopolitan, a Zionist, a Trotskyist. Nothing announced by the party could be doubted unless the party doubted it. The party decorated its general secretary with the highest honors and a year later had him hanged. The party had a monstrous monument built to Stalin, and then the party had it destroyed. Whoever refused to curse that which a year before he had to approve became an enemy. It was a period of perverted values. The uneducated were promoted to ministers, party secretaries to attorneys; tailors and lathe operators became army commanders, while the experienced pilots who participated in the Battle of Britain, army generals, and members of the democratic resistance were sent to concentration camps or even the gallows.

In the name of the party, the leadership seized not only most of the wealth acquired over generations but also—and this was worse—all spiritual values. It claimed it had replaced mistaken religious views with scientifically recognized truth, and that a dog-eat-dog society would be replaced with a society in which comradely relations were the norm. In fact, the opposite happened. The party destroyed all traditional relationships. It introduced the cadre questionnaire and interviews in which those who wanted to continue in their work were supposed to disown their relatives. It misappropriated history; it erased great personages and replaced them with people whose only merit was membership in the party. It misappropriated peace, since it labeled its confederation of dictatorships a camp of peace, which only with the greatest efforts was keeping the imperialists from starting a new world war. It misappropriated the idea of democracy because it called its dictatorship the highest form of democracy.

Political life in the party and throughout the country was dead. Votes on anything were unanimous. The party ruled without restraint and introduced into the constitution a clause stating that it was the sole governing power of society. But it was the members of the party who became the primary danger for the genuine occupiers of power. Therefore, it was necessary to keep even the highest members in a state of constant fear. Klement Gottwald accepted this policy of Stalin's along with all the other principles of his rule and did not hesitate to hang all of his closest collaborators even though they had stood at his side from the very beginning and participated in the murderous (and suicidal) Bolshevization of the party. He considered self-evident his right and responsibility to hang opponents of the Communist regime.

The theory of hidden and deceitful conspirators in the highest positions of the party could shatter the faith of even the remaining idealists or those who hadn't completely renounced their own judgment. These, however, were ordered: "Believe the party, Comrades. The party is becoming murky by the uncovering of hidden enemies." At the same time, it was not important if any Communists lost faith. What was important was that they be afraid. If the reign of terror for some reason weakened, the party could reawaken the slumbering dangers. To be sure, the Communist leaders constantly warned of the threats from imperialists, international reactionaries, the remnants of the defeated bourgeoisie, and various deviationists and saboteurs, but in reality they were much more afraid of those in whose name they repeatedly claimed to rule: the workers, farmers, and even the members of their own party.

Revolution—Terror and Fear

Fear is common to all living creatures. It is a manifestation of the in-stinct for self-preservation. We are afraid of pain, loss, death. If we want to live, we must be afraid. If we want to survive with dignity, we must overcome fear.

In general, we hope that the things with which we are happy will continue while the things with which we are unhappy will improve. In youth we believe that death will not come for us, that we won't lose our job, that a friend will not disappoint us, that if we're decent and honorable, we will not be punished. We will start a family and have children who, in some form or another, will continue the work that we must someday abandon. We assume that if we do good work, we will be rewarded and our position will improve, that no one will accuse us of crimes we did not commit, and, quite the reverse, genuine criminals will receive their just punishment.

The basis of every revolution is that it categorically declares all previous values and goals wretched and demeaning. The revolutionar-ies pronounce the old order corrupt, unable to suppress criminality, to erase poverty, to ensure the functioning of society and thereby a dignified life for its citizens. They must do away with this order along with its values, its morality. *According to the Communist Manifesto,* the proletariat's mission *is to destroy all previous securities for, and assur-ances of, individual property. . . . The proletariat . . . cannot stir, cannot raise itself up, without the whole superincumbent strata of official society being sprung into the air.* Mussolini was terser: *Everything that exists must be destroyed!*

In place of a corrupt order, revolution offers the people a vision of better justice, more prosperity, a more dignified life. It promises to correct wrongs, whether to a person or the collective, and it promises the entire society (with the exception of those who are designated as traitors and determined enemies) unprecedented prosperity, even glory because it is precisely glory that will become the banner of world progress and national renewal. Revolutionary leaders announce a new moral category, which they call revolutionary consciousness. By this they mean that every citizen who joins the revolution will be freed from the tyranny of his own consciousness. The leader, who is troubled only by the infringement of the revolutionary ideals, selects this new consciousness for him. In the name of the ideals it is possible to change all values that have previously been valid. Many values that until recently have been considered base or criminal become of service to the revolution. Whoever informs assists the new society to purge itself of sinister elements; whoever plunders is merely correcting centuries of injustice. Whoever murders an enemy of the revolution (it is sufficient for one merely to designate someone an enemy) is a soldier in the revolution and deserves to be decorated. Many succumb to this confusion of values. So it happens that people who were recently honorable commit deeds that only yesterday they considered repulsive and unthinkable.

For one revolution, nobility becomes an ignominious sign; for another, one's origin or property and resulting wealth. For another it is perhaps religious indifference or another faith, and almost always it is education, decency, and the conviction that one is not prepared to give up personal responsibility. The first great revolution of the twentieth century classified people according to their class origin. Their leaders placed those of the working class at the highest level of values. They still allowed smallholders, but they did not hesitate to divest the other levels of society of their fundamental rights. They tried to abuse some ill-fated individuals; others they banished, interned, or murdered. They murdered even the tsar along with his whole family, including the young children, since the dynasty was a deadly class enemy.

Another revolution only a few years later classified people according to their racial heritage and placed Germans at the highest level. It did not hesitate to persecute members of other races, and it resolved to exterminate those designated as Jews or Gypsies. As Albert Camus writes: *The unavoidable fundamental and intrinsic attribute of most revolutions is murder.*

A society that accepts such aberrant criteria, especially in modern times, cannot operate without inflicting grave trauma on its people. But the revolution takes this into consideration. In the beginning, it has its fiery supporters who are willing to sacrifice everything for their ideals. They believe in their greatness or at least assume they will create personal prosperity. The number of devotees, however, is never enough, so the revolution acquires adherents precisely among those who joined out of calculation or fear, and it succeeds in gaining supporters among those it had unexpectedly elevated. After the victory of the revolution, new members pour into the party, either the Nazi or the Communist. Whatever the party, it will differentiate between "old" and "new" members.

A common characteristic of every revolution is the co-opting of the dregs of society, whether judged from a material or moral point of view. Revolution offers them social security and inclusion in the functioning of governance, but primarily participation in the spreading of terror and the resulting fear, which in turn provides those beaten-down or inferior with a feeling of satisfaction. No revolution can do without its guard, which it quickly arms and endows with special powers. At its head it places fanatical and fiery leaders: Trotsky, Dzerzhinsky, Yagoda, Yezhov, Röhm, Himmler, Heydrich. Only with them can the government begin its revolutionary terror.

The architects of the revolution soon realize that there are quite a few who do not long for their rule and rightly fear the impending changes. As time goes by, it turns out that the system the leaders of the revolution are trying to implement on the basis of their spurious visions cannot function. Therefore, they begin to battle for its existence.

The police no longer pursue only criminals but also pursue those whom it designates as enemies of the new order. Newly appointed judges sit in judgment not in order to strengthen justice but rather to call it into question, in order to make it clear that anyone can be designated an offender and found guilty. The citizen must understand that at any time he can lose his work, his freedom, even his life, and the same can befall his loved ones. The citizen must live in constant fear.

The first demented adherent of revolutionary terror in the twentieth century, Lenin, announced: *You certainly do not believe that we will be victorious if we don't use the harshest kind of revolutionary terror. . . . If we're not capable of shooting a White Guard saboteur, what sort of great revolution is it? Nothing but talk and a bowl of mush.* In his decree "On Red Terror," he then orders: *It is essential to protect the Soviet Republic from class enemies by isolating them in concentration camps. Anyone connected to the White Guard organizations, conspiracies, and rebellions will be shot; the names of all those executed will be published. . . . We shall not hesitate to shoot thousands of people.* In the name of the revolution, he and his followers had thousands, hundreds of thousands, and later millions of people murdered.

Immediately after Hitler became chancellor, the Nazis began to arrest genuine and possible opponents. The arrests increased after the Reichstag fire on February 27, 1933. Hitler lost no time in forcing President Hindenburg to issue an "emergency decree," whereby all basic human rights ceased to be valid, from freedom of the press, expression, and demonstration to even the assurance that no one would be unlawfully deprived of freedom. This opened the door to unlimited terror, which continued for the remaining twelve years of the Nazis' "thousand-year" Reich.

In Nuremburg, a Social Democratic representative testified about what had happened to him ten days after the Reichstag fire. *Members of the SS and SA came to my home in Cologne and destroyed the furniture and my personal records. I was taken to the Brown House in Cologne, where I was tortured, being beaten and kicked for several hours. Over the* course of a single month in Germany, twenty-five thousand people were taken off to concentration camps. Prussian police were allowed to use weapons against enemies of the state, and many people branded as enemies were executed on the spot. Hitler noted somewhat later and in passing: *It is a good thing if the fear precedes us that we are exterminating Judaism.* The Nazis aroused fear not only among Jews but also among Christians, Communists, Social Democrats, and the democratically minded intelligentsia.

Fear gives rise to informers and collaborationists. It drives people to the ballot box, where they cast their votes for candidates whom they hate or to whom they are indifferent. They attend demonstrations and applaud murderers who speak from the rostrum. When the mob smashes a window of an enemy of the new order, a Jew or a kulak, those whose windows were not targeted draw their curtains. When the secret police take away the innocent, those innocent who were not taken away pretend to see nothing that does not concern them. When they are summoned, they sign resolutions demanding the death penalty for everyone designated an enemy of the revolutionary state. The regime thereby brazenly pretends that except for a handful of enemies, everyone is its supporter. And the masses that live in fear accept this role and hope that if they display acquiescence, they will be spared.

Not even the representatives of the regime and the implementers of terror can escape fear.

The mob in police uniforms then knock on the doors of their houses and lead them off to the torture chambers. With fiendish schadenfreude, they force from them confessions to implicate other revolutionaries. Since the French Revolution, hangmen have received their victims from the ranks of the defeated victors as well. Hence the maxim: Revolution devours its own children. This metaphorical formulation, however, is sentimental and indeed false. Revolution devours its own children along with their parents. It begins to murder not only its victims but also their murderers.

During the period of the greatest wave of Stalin's terror, to which hundreds of thousands of "parents and children" fell victim, Stalin delivered a grand speech:

Some journalists abroad are babbling that the purge of spies, murderers, and evildoers such as Trotsky, Zinoviev, Kamenev, Jakir, Tukhachevsky, Rosenholz, Bukharin, and other scum has "shaken" the Soviet system, it has injected it with "degeneracy." This disgusting babble is laughable.... Who needs this pitiful band of slaves who sold out? ... In 1937, Tukhachevsky, Jakir, Uborevich, and other scum were sentenced to death by firing squad. Then elections for the Highest Soviet of the USSR were held; 98.6 percent of voters voted for the rule of the Soviets. At the beginning of 1938, Rosenholz, Rykov, Bukharin, and other scum were sentenced to death by firing squad. Then elections for the Highest Soviet of the federal republics were held; 99.4 percent of all voters voted for the rule of the Soviets. I ask you: Where are there signs of "degeneracy," and why did not this "degeneracy" appear in the election results?

Indeed, fear did not fragment the society, for even fragmentation is movement. It killed it. The moment fear, without distinction, seized both the victors and the defeated, the rulers and the ruled, it immobilized the entire complex apparatus because no one dared decide anything. Everyone tried to avoid responsibility for this intractable situation. Terror brought society to the edge of annihilation.

There are only two points of departure in such a state of affairs. The first is war, that is, the transference of terrorist methods onto the international field. The second is the cessation of terror. The first subjugates the citizen even more in the name of war mobilization, but it leads nowhere. In case of a military defeat (such as that suffered by Hitler's Germany), the revolution along with its ideals and its representatives is swept out, and the country is destroyed. In case of victory (such as that achieved by Stalin's Soviet Union with the help of democratic powers), society returns to its prewar situation: Terror continues and with it the all-immobilizing fear.

The other point of departure, which calls for the renewal of at least partial freedom and thereby extricates itself from the rule of fear, likewise does not safeguard the revolution. Revolution and the dictatorship it establishes cannot survive for long without the coregency of fear simply because the ideals forced upon the people have been so compromised that almost no one accepts them.

Revolutionary power must necessarily die away, sometimes early, sometimes not for several generations. In both cases it leaves behind innumerable dead, a devastated country, an incomprehensible number of personal tragedies, frustrated possibilities, destroyed talents, subverted morals, and the memory of omnipresent fear, which will inhibit for a long time the activity of those who experienced it.

Abused Youth

On March 1, 2006, the Czech News Agency reported that around five thousand children from eight to twelve years of age gathered for a demonstration in Karachi, Pakistan, and called for the execution of the authors who caricatured the prophet Muhammad. (The children had certainly never seen the caricatures and had probably never seen a caricature in their lives.) The hijackers of the planes that hit New York and Washington, which took the lives of thousands of civilians in suicide attacks, were young people. Most Muslim suicide bombers are young. It also was young people, even twelve-year-old children armed with machine guns, who fought in most of the African civil and tribal wars. They fought enthusiastically and ruthlessly.

All totalitarian regimes, all fanatical ideologies see in the young the most appropriate executors of their goals. Here are the words of one of many Socialist songs from the '50s.

> *Forward, boys and girls,*
> *a new world we are building among perils.*
> *This one has but little strength,*
> *thus all must work together at length*
> *Forward, boys and girls,*
> *a new world we are building among perils.*
> *Lenin, Stalin, Gottwald as well,*
> *them we shall follow and enemies expel.*

The coup was supposed to be a new beginning of history. But there were, and still are, more convenient reasons to celebrate youth.

Radicalism belongs more to the young than to the old, just as does the image that the world could be better organized than it ever has been. The young have a tendency to question the values of their parents' generation and are more open to slogans and simplifying explanations of society's ills and the promise of a finer world. They cannot oppose a false ideology with their own insufficient life experiences, and they usually lack a deeper understanding of history and the inherent laws of society. On the one hand, the totalitarian regime flatters the young, and on the other it forces upon them its own image of the ideal person and the ideal society.

In 1920, Lenin outlined his ideal of a young communist:

The Union of Communist Youth will deserve its name and will show that it is a union of the young Communist generation only by linking up every step in its studies, training, and education with the continuous struggle of the proletarians and the working people against the old society of exploiters. . . . This generation should know that the entire purpose of their lives is to build a Communist society. . . . [Its] morality is what serves to destroy the old exploiting society and to unite all the working people around the proletariat, which is building a new, Communist society.

Fifteen or sixteen years later, it was precisely this generation that was killed off in Stalin's purges, and a new generation of fifteen-year-olds was bombarded with flattery. Pavlik Morozov, who informed on his own parents and fulfilled Cabet's vision that every citizen will be an informer, became the new official hero and role model recommended to Soviet youth according to Lenin's theory of the new morality.

At the same time (1935), Adolf Hitler was embodying his image of the young generation in images that corresponded to his poetic invention: *In our eyes, the German youth of the future must be slender and supple, swift as greyhounds, tough as leather, and hard as Krupp steel. We must cultivate a new man in order to prevent the ruin of our nation by the degeneration manifested in our age.* A year later the Reich government passed a law specifying that, among other things, all *German youth besides being reared within the family and school, shall be educated physically, intellectually, and morally in the spirit of National Socialism to serve the people and community, through the Hitler Youth.*

The first of the Ten Commandments for students, delivered in Nazi Germany in 1934, was: *It is not necessary to live, but it is necessary that you fulfill your duty to the German people. Whatever you are, you must be German.*

The Nazis emphasized the mission of the people, the Communists the mission of the working class; today's theoreticians of Muslim fundamentalism emphasize the cleansing mission of their religious faith as revealed in the Koran, from which they select those passages that justify the hatred and violence they commit.

The youth of postwar Czechoslovakia was an especially propitious section of society upon which Communist propaganda could concentrate. The life experiences of those born during the 1920s and '30s were one-sided and mostly negative. The way their parents' generation had organized society seemed unconvincing and had obviously caused, or at least allowed, not only a cruel economic crisis but even the war and an unbelievable number of casualties.

Politicians and thinkers of the older generation, even those democratically minded ones, admitted their mistakes. The president of the republic, Edvard Beneš, in a speech at the law school where he was receiving an honorary degree shortly after the war, criticized late-nineteenth-century liberalism.

> **Politically** this is a society with an expanded number of contending and anarchizing political parties, which are subverting the nation as a whole with their battle; **economically**—it is a society with a highly cultivated culture of capitalism and industrialism, which produces a relentless class struggle between the exploit-

ers and the exploited; **socially**—it is a society waging an exalted battle between the person of the past with his feudal aristocratic conceptions and the person with egalitarian ideas attempting to assert the equality of people; **culturally and artistically**—it is a superficial and aestheticizing society, a welter of opinions and chaotic conceptions without any literary or even artistic style; in short, it is a **sick society, uncertain, searching for something new and incapable of finding it.**

Even though Beneš reached the conclusion that the new society must be democratic, he defended friendship with the Soviet Union as well as a new social politics: *One of the most important issues is to open the gates to social change in the sense of socialism.*

It was not difficult for Communist ideologues to interpret this to the members of the younger generation, who barely remembered the First Republic, as a clear condemnation of liberalism and of an unjust social system, and emphasize the necessity of doing away with the bygone system and replacing it with a Socialist one.

To the naive or politically inexperienced, it could seem that democrats and Communists were in agreement on the need for societal and economic changes.

When the Communists achieved power after the February 1948 coup, they sought as quickly as possible to destroy or remove their political opponents from all important positions. It was, however, necessary to replace them posthaste. Suddenly there was an opportunity not only for the "reliable" ones—genuine believers in Communist ideology, or pragmatic careerists who understood that the new authority would reign for many years—but also, and primarily, for the young, who still had no political past and were now being offered a marvelous future as long as they assumed the proper form. And so, in only a few weeks, the young enthusiasts could become (as long as they underwent the necessary courses) attorneys, judges, teachers, officers, factory directors, even doctors, although they often lacked a degree.

At the end of the 1940s and the beginning of the '50s, young people voluntarily and often enthusiastically left home to construct huge smelters in Ostravsko and a Railway of Friendship into eastern Slovakia. News articles and films were produced upon the order of the party, celebrating their heroic feats of labor. Journalists praised these marvelous achievements with the pathos characteristic of the time. These disingenuous campaigns served several purposes. They provided an inexpensive labor force, and participation in a work brigade contributed to the further reeducation of people and transformed them into confirmed disciples of the new regime. At the larger construction sites, the organizers invited young people from democratic countries as well. Thus young adherents of communism from different countries came together to spread revolutionary ideology.

That some members of the young generation expressed their approval of the new regime and accepted its activities without suspicion was certainly due to the fact that they had grown up under Nazi occupation and had been denied education. These efforts produced a paradoxical result. Nazi propaganda was seen as deceitful and antagonistic, which was how all attacks against Bolshevism came to be perceived. (When the Nazis announced their discovery of the mass graves of Polish officers who had been murdered in the Katyn Forest by Stalin's secret police, few doubted that this was a Nazi lie.)

Who of the youth knew the details of the Soviet dictator's path to power? Who at ten or fifteen years of age was interested in trials in which the Soviet dictator liquidated his opponents group by group? Who knew that millions of innocent victims of the Communist regime were leading miserable existences or dying in Siberian concentration camps?

But because the trials of enemies of the people, reactionaries, conspirators, spies, and traitors became one of the fundamental and essential pillars of Communist dictatorship, it was necessary to acquaint those who suspected nothing, who were uninterested, with these methods.

And so, soon after the coup, carefully manipulated information concerning these events began to appear. Alongside the quickly translated and published transcripts of the staged trials (which were sometimes difficult to accept if only for their absurdity) or the boring and, for the uninitiated, incomprehensible *History of the Communist Party of the Soviet Union*, further works of Stalinist propaganda were published that were masterful in their mendacity. Among them was *The Great Conspiracy*, which pretended to be nonfiction: To provide it with the appearance of greater objectivity it was written (or at least signed) by two American Communists, Michael Sayers and Albert E. Kahn. This pamphlet about a worldwide imperialist conspiracy against the land of the Soviets skillfully and suggestively employed transcripts from political trials. It cited fabricated conversations and secret meetings between disciples of Trotsky and others later condemned as "traitors, spies, and terrorists" as if they had actually occurred and had been written down on the spot. From this the authors inferred the existence of an enormous conspiracy, whose goal was to destroy the first Socialist state of workers and farmers. Hundreds of thousands of copies were distributed and, like all similar works of propaganda, served as the foundation for wholesale slaughter.

For a reader unfamiliar with these events, it was easy to believe that sabotage units, conspiracies, and even cunning imperialistic spies in fact existed, that everything presented as historical fact was indeed true. There was of course no mention of the phony political trials that took place in the Soviet Union practically from its inception; that they were carried out upon the order of the steeled man of steel, Stalin; and that all confessions were acquired by means of unspeakable torture, signed beforehand by hangman interrogators, and then under threat of further torture repeated by the broken prisoners at their trials.

The Necessity of Faith

Since time immemorial, man has sought to explain the connection between himself and everything that is remote or estranged; he wants to uncover his own origin and the origin of the world. During different periods, people in different parts of the world hit upon a satisfactory explanation, which was handed down from generation to generation because they believed it was incontrovertible.

Faith helped them live in a world full of mystery, of inexplicable phenomena, when at times there was enough food whereas at others they were hungry, where one day a person was alive and the next he was some kind of lifeless, cold matter.

In various places on our planet, people accepted events as the work of someone or something much more powerful. One could perhaps implore the higher being to revoke his decisions, but even so, times would come when one could no longer implore. One must die. But while he was alive he could try to please the powerful one to avoid suffering while on earth and then be allowed live on in some other realm—perhaps beneath the earth, perhaps above it—or perhaps he would be reincarnated in another being or an inanimate object. And then this object would be revered.

Since long ago, the world was, in the imaginations of our fore-fathers, inhabited by gods and goddesses, powerful beings both good and evil. Some of these dwelled nearby, in trees, animals, or water; others inhabited the heights and revealed themselves only in the form of lightning, thunder, sunlight, or illness, which drew near from the unknown. In his relationship with the powerful forces, man was full of humility; nevertheless, he believed he would one day enjoy some sort of beatific condition that went by various names—heaven, nirvana—but was always a condition in which a person was happy, where all pain, all cares, all fears of the end ceased. In the Judeo-Christian tradition, it was even supposed that at one time we had lived in such a state, and only our own reckless longing for knowledge had deprived us of it. The longing for knowledge, however, although stigmatized, persisted.

Gradually the individual gods lost their concrete forms or retreated in the face of one most powerful God until they disappeared entirely or turned into his servants or lingered on as water nymphs, sprites, naiads, genies, or angels.

While the gods changed their form, the human need for faith changed only little. Man wanted to believe there was someone above him who would judge all his deeds, who would reward good and punish evil, who would right the wrongs, who would even arrange it so that after death he would encounter those he had loved.

Although human societies arose at different times and places, and they developed various and oftentimes very dissimilar religions, many things connected them: All religions had their own rituals. They celebrated the festival of the solstice, the arrival of rain, the metamorphosis of a boy into a man, the joining of man and woman, and the dead on their final journey. All of this persisted for generations, and it never occurred to anyone to doubt the usefulness and necessity of observing the rituals.

Every religion, every deity, had its own chosen people or caste, its own shamans, monks, lamas, or priests who ensured that all the prescribed commandments were obeyed.

Religion required unswerving faith in everything it claimed, in everything it demanded, even in what it promised. Only the insane, the outcast, or the blaspheming heretic could not believe.

As thousands of years went by, man continued in his aspirations, which caused his banishment from paradise. He wanted to know and discover new and better explanations for phenomena in his world. Reason appeared against the enduring faith in the constancy of ancient explanations. Reason announced that everything could be subject to doubt; it was necessary to examine and explore everything. Even the ancient Greek philosophers reached the conclusion that man was after all part of nature and like everything else was subject to old age and then death. Not even the Greek materialist philosophers doubted the existence of immortal gods, but they assumed that immortal beings cared little about the fate of mortals. They themselves had to seek how to avoid anguish from nonbeing, from the meaninglessness of their existence, and at the same time how to escape this meaninglessness.

In the seventeenth century, however, thinkers began to emphasize the significance of reason over the long-standing conclusions issuing from faith.

During the Enlightenment, reason became the instrument that should guide a meaningful life. In subsequent centuries, reason achieved unexpected successes. There is no sense enumerating them, but reason, along with its child science and its grandchild technology, altered essentially the conditions and utility of life. As knowledge and understanding developed, certain religious dogmas began to be doubted. Science arrived with a new conception of time; it began to explain the origin of man and the origin of the earth and the universe in an entirely different way. It began to investigate and finally even break down matter. Gradually, at least in people's everyday lives, the inexplicable diminished, and reason began to insinuate itself and take the place of God.

But the need of man to believe, to turn to some power greater than himself, a force that was certainly not rationally explicable but that one could approach through exaltation and with the aid of dance, music, or song, was not dead in the least. People missed the cults and rituals as well as the saints; they lacked an absolute superhuman authority.

Enlightenment reason cast God's power into doubt and, along with it, the earthly and religious rulers who were supposed to reflect that power. Emperor Josef II abolished monasteries and expelled monks as freeloaders; just a little while later the French king and his family were executed (rather, murdered), and not long after that, Russian Bolsheviks murdered the tsar and his entire family. Rulers and their ministers, people who only recently were looked up to with reverence, were dead or overthrown. But could their places remain empty? People wanted to look to something higher, an authority that determined what was good and what was evil, who deserved punishment and who deserved acclaim. New leaders exploited this need, but they derived their claims not from God's will (even though Hitler enjoyed announcing he had been chosen by providence) but rather from the will of the people who flattered themselves as the very embodiment of a wise and reasonable power.

It is significant that both of the powerful ideologies of the twentieth century were atheistic and professed scientific or, rather, pseudoscientific theories; at the same time they adopted signs of religious faith. At first this fascinated millions of both the educated and the unlettered.

The ideology of German National Socialism combined elements of socialism with an obscure racialist theory. It declared that the German race, which according to the Nazis represented the highest level of human development, was destined to rule the world. This theory was not based on contemporary, scientifically provable facts and therefore could be accepted only on the basis of faith. This faith, however, was indeed quite gratifying. It elevated its adherents above all others; it offered them a vision of a marvelous future, the building of something suprapersonal—a thousand-year empire.

Communist ideology emphasized its rationality even more; it claimed to have arisen on the basis of the most modern, ingenious, and fundamentally insuperable scientific method of Marx and Engels. The conclusions reached by these two thinkers while studying societal forces and their development were supposed to have eternal validity, like the laws of Archimedes or Newton, for instance. It was precisely the scientific basis of their teachings that was supposed to guarantee they would lead to a perfect society, to heaven on earth. In reality, this utopian vision was unscientific; it could be believed only on the basis of blind faith.

Textbooks of Marxism or historical materialism resembled a catechism in which every question had a prepared answer that applied irrefutably.

Historical materialism is a pragmatic and harmonious scientific theory that explains the evolution of society, the transition from one societal system to another. At the same time it is the only correct scientific method of investigating all societal phenomena and the histories of individual states and nations.

Everything that did not conform to the dogma of the new Word was condemned as heresy and had to be suppressed and punished.

Holy writ, of course, enjoyed natural authority. The wisdom of entire generations was collected in the Old Testament. There was no need to continually belaud its authors (disregarding the fact that according to the Orthodox interpretation the writers of the texts were merely interpreters of God's will). Marxist, fascistic, and Nazi ideology, however, brought a new faith, and their interpreters considered it necessary to convince the readers that the new prophets were the only genuinely elect and proselytized the only truth.

Fifty years after the death of Lenin, when it was obvious to everyone who had not lost his reason that the regime he created with unusual cruelty had plunged the citizenry of an enormous empire into poverty and subjugation and deprived several million people of their lives, Lenin's official biography was published in the Soviet Union with this evaluation:

Lenin's activity and his deep and noble thinking influenced and will continue to influence the course of world history and the fate of all humanity. . . . V. I. [sic] Lenin showed the nations of the world the path to genuine freedom and happiness.

Communist ideologues perhaps attributed the most oracular characteristics to Stalin. *Through his ingenious perspicacity he glimpsed the contours of future prosperity . . . and masterfully elaborated and sketched out a grandiose program of Socialist construction. . . . In his unrepeatable, ingenious analyses, he pointed out the abysmal difference between the world of capitalist decay and disintegration and the efflorescent and deeply humane world of socialism.*

Furthermore, like a true prophet, Stalin was *extremely simple, modest, far-sighted, uncompromising, ingeniously perspicacious; his logic was overwhelming, his thoughts crystal clear. Therefore, he became for us our teacher and father, the greatest luminary of the world, a coryphaeus of science, the great leader of the working class, an ingenious strategist who has written the indelible Word in the book of history.*

The miserable poet and Hitler Youth leader Baldur Benedikt von Schirach composed Hitler's panegyric:

> *That is the greatest thing about him,*
> *That he is not only our leader and a great hero,*
> *But himself, upright, firm and simple,*
> *in him rest the roots of our world.*
> *And his soul touches the stars.*
> *Yet he remains a man like you and me.*

The attempt by totalitarian ideologies to satisfy the traditional need to believe was remarkably consistent. Leaders renewed the significance of ritualistic gatherings, pilgrimages, and marches to the sound of monotonous music. They returned banners and images of their own saints to the hands of the people. They used religious-sounding words. They loved to talk about eternity and immortality. An often banal and vacuous statement was passed off as a prophetic revelation. *Because of his unlimited, mystical fascination,* remarked Goebbels on Hitler's address at a party gathering, *it was an almost religious rite.*

Every year the Nazis organized eight days of ritual celebrations that were supposed to function like religious pilgrimages. The American diplomat and author Frederic Spotts, in *Hitler and the Power of Aesthetics*, notes:

> The fifth day was the "Day of Political Leaders" and from 1936 this event culminated in the dramatic high point of the rallies. After sundown 110,000 men marched on to the review field while 100,000 spectators took their places on the stands. At a signal, once darkness fell, the space was suddenly encircled by a ring of light, with 30,000 flags and standards glistening in the illumination. Spotlights would focus on the main gate, as distant cheers announced the Führer's approach. At the instant he entered, 150 powerful searchlights would shoot into the sky to produce a gigantic, shimmering "cathedral of light," as it was called. . . . "Cathedral" was the apt term since the essence of the ceremony was one of sacramental dedication to Führer and party. Encased in a circle of light and dark, the participants were transported into a vast phantasmagoria.

Film clips of the enthusiastic crowds greeting the new gods embodied in the figures of Hitler, Lenin, Stalin, or their successors even today bear witness to the fact that many people upon meeting their leaders truly experienced the ecstasy of religious rapture and were prepared to do anything the new gods commanded—work oneself to death, go to one's own death, or put someone else to death.

Often fear lurked behind this ecstasy, but of course it was never very far from some sort of religious faith.

Totalitarian ideologies demanded devotion from their followers, absolute obedience in carrying out their (often absurd) commandments. They demanded that people believe the image of reality precisely in the form submitted to them. Millions of Germans believed so fervently in the villainy of Jews that they permitted their slaughter. Plenty enthusiastically made this perverted idea a reality. In the same way, many Germans believed they were destined for world domination and were willing to sacrifice their lives to the new divinity in the name of this horrible but suprapersonal goal.

The Communists accepted that entire groups of inhabitants had to be suppressed or killed if a new and better society was to be created. Absolute and uncritical faith was necessary to believe that the recently celebrated members of the party leadership were subsequently revealed to be traitors and must therefore be forcibly removed from the world of the living.

The faith of some was so strong that they were not willing to renounce it. They could not turn away from their villainous god even when standing upon the scaffold. When Hitler with the help of Himmler's SS suppressed a nonexistent conspiracy by the SA, the SS men led the alleged conspirators before the firing squad. Before dying they managed to shout out their elementary slogan, "Heil Hitler" (while the execution squad received the order, "Heil Hitler, fire!"). Many Communists sentenced to death during the trials, which took place upon Stalin's orders, died while crying out, "Long live Stalin!" They could not imagine that their god, in order to elevate himself, had demanded their death, and they did not have the fortitude to admit that the entirety of their faith had been an error, for which they had sacrificed their lives. It is probable that at least some of those who stood across from those carrying out the execution also invoked Stalin's name. It is even possible that several of those who were to die the very next moment believed that they were serving a magnificent goal to which society was allegedly drawing near. Paradoxically, fanatically believing hangmen and victims stood face-to-face, each convinced that everything he had lived through and everything he was undergoing served a great and laudable objective.

Many German citizens, almost to the final moment, believed in the megalomaniac who had driven them to death and to the very end glorified his name in the same way they glorified the name of God. Even after the defeat of Nazism, even after the disclosure of the crimes of the Stalinist regime, many refused to admit that their faith had been misplaced and even villainous. They remained true to their faith because without it their lives would have fallen into even greater meaninglessness.

Totalitarian ideologies built on faith collapsed, but the need for faith remained. Even where traditional churches retreat into the background, people look for some kind of replacement for traditional faith. They believe in astrology, in people from outer space, in the miraculous power of a faith healer, in alternative medicine, in karma, in clairvoyance.

Perhaps surprisingly, however, the strongest faith is evoked by that which faith has always denied: reason, science, and technology. At least in our part of the world, people began to believe in their own redemptive abilities, their own wisdom. Science should be able to reveal and explain the past and predict the future, ensure prosperity for everyone who tries hard enough, overcome illness and finally even death. Lately scientists have begun to experiment with decoding the human genome. More and more we hear in the popular press ebullient cries that man stands on the threshold of immortality.

People have once again begun to believe in the paradise that science will bring them from heaven.

Whenever people begin to believe in the attainability of paradise, they usually enter upon a path leading to hell.

Dictators and Dictatorship

The governments of two especially cruel dictatorships affected my life directly, but during the same time a Fascist dictatorship ruled in Italy; at the end of the 1930s democracy was suppressed in Spain; a totalitarian, or at least undemocratic, regime came to power in Poland, Hungary, and Romania. And outside Europe? Dictatorships persist today: in Communist China, North Korea, Cuba, and a number of Muslim countries in both Asia and Africa.

With the benefit of hindsight, people continue to wonder how, in a country with such a tradition of learning and culture as Germany, citizens could voluntarily entrust their fates to the hands of Adolf Hitler and the riffraff that surrounded him. One could say the same thing, of course, about the country in which Dostoevsky, Chekhov, and Tolstoy wrote.

Usually certain obvious arguments are adduced for a blossoming of such reckless dictatorships: the humiliation of defeat, the collapse of the economy and resulting world economic crisis (which in Germany deprived almost half its working-age citizens of work), the inability to resolve social questions, military traditions, even a fascination with self-sacrifice and death in Germany and conversely the ruminations and popular debates concerning a better society in Russia. But it is obvious that there was something more general and overarching.

Considerations of national character, culture, or people's behavior usually substitute the image of society for the image of the elite. Cultured Germans knew Goethe and Schiller (probably not all had read them), perhaps also Hegel and Kant (probably not all had studied them). Certainly some of the educated were acquainted with the German myth of the Nibelungs and might have considered that the meaning of German fate lay thus in self-sacrifice. It's safe to assume, however, that most citizens in these categories did not consider that most Germans were not knowledgeable about the great German minds, just as in semi-educated Russia most muzhiks had not heard of Tolstoy, Dostoevsky, Chekhov, Chernyshevsky, Berdyayev, or Plekhanov, let alone cogitated over their works and allowed themselves be inspired to action.

Who were the people of the twentieth century? How did our lives differ from the lives of our forefathers?

The twentieth century brought unprecedented technological progress, new revolutionary developments in communication, the automobile, the radio, and the smashing of the atom, as well as new forms of entertainment, which was dominated by the recording of pictures and sound. New heroes were proclaimed. Celebrities of the entertainment industry—film stars, athletes, and singers—replaced the spiritual elite. The twentieth century brought ruin to many traditional values: Religious faith flagged; the village community faded in significance, as did the feudal nobility; and the family started to fall apart. A spiritual emptiness suddenly opened up before humanity. The atmosphere of precipitous development compelled people to ask how they could fill this void. Movement, change, upheaval, the cult of the new—these were most clearly expressed in art. The modern began to disdain tradition, while everything new seemed to be a revolutionary contribution and was showered with praise. What had until recently been considered a virtue, for instance, communicability, clarity, or even an idea, was snowed under by the ridicule of those who saw themselves as adjudicators of art. An abyss opened up between those who considered themselves the creators and everyone else. The tragedy was that "everyone else" made up the great majority. This majority, now deprived of certainties that until recently had provided them with faith—the traditional arrangement of society and generally recognized values (even if most of those values were mistaken)—found themselves untethered. The overturning of traditional values was exacerbated by serious societal crises, the most serious of which was the world war at the beginning of the century, the largest and bloodiest thus far in history, both in extent and in its use of new, lethal weapons. The war, however, ended with the defeat of the militaristic and undemocratic regimes. In their stead, in the place of defeated monarchies, new democratic republics began to establish themselves. For a brief moment, the promised rule of the people aroused brash and grandiose hopes of a way to escape the void. Yet these hopes went unfilled, and the people were overwhelmed with disappointment. The poverty they had longed to escape persisted and, moreover, they found nothing suprapersonal, nothing absolute to cling to, nothing before which they could bow down in religious devotion.

What a splendid opportunity for fanatical prophets of hope, for demagogy promising to fill this void and endow life with a new meaning.

The first place where restlessness broke out was in Russia during the war, where they had deposed the rule of the tsar and tried to replace it with a democratic government. They decided not to end the war, however, and it didn't appear that the new democracy could fulfill any of the hopes the people had placed in it. Nevertheless, the fall of the authoritatian regime made it possible for freedom, which had long been suppressed, to enter into life. An expanse opened up for both reformers and revolutionaries. The first to avail himself of this newly formed freedom was Vladimir Ilyich Ulyanov, aka Lenin, a fanatic with a utopian vision He placed the value of the ideas he propagated above the value of human life and was prepared to spill any amount of blood on their behalf. As soon as he took power he announced he was immediately embarking on the creation of a new, just societal order and that he would end the war because the workers were perishing in the interests of their exploiters. He would carry out land reforms, fulfill projects that previous utopias could only dream about but that two Communist theoreticians in the modern period, Marx and Engels, had scientifically worked out and deemed realizable. The new arrangement of society—which was not to be limited by national borders, since it was in the interests of all of the exploited classes, that is, most inhabitants of the planet—was supposed to develop in two phases. The first was socialism, which would do away with property inequality, seize the means of production, and thereby develop production to ensure general prosperity. Over the course of, at most, two generations, a new, free, and classless society would arise in which all could satisfy their needs. This second phase, which was suspicious to thinking people as a delirious and unrealizable utopia, was to be called communism. To lead people to this freest of societies, a dictatorship was required.

Lenin's idea of revolution inspired enthusiasm even in other countries. The first reports of unbridled Bolshevik terror, however, also inspired revulsion and even fear among the propertied members of society as well as among enlightened intellectuals. Moreover, Lenin never denied that he despised democracy, which was supposed to exist (but in a distorted form) only inside his party. Despite troubling accounts issuing from the land of the Soviets, enough politicians in democratic countries agreed that the societal order that had heretofore existed was unsatisfactory. In a society laid low and impoverished by war, with an economy that had not yet managed to recover from its war wounds, future leaders eager to promise anything and commit any crime in order to acquire power began to prance about as prophets of new ideas and new hopes.

Two countries seemed to have been affected by war the most: defeated Germany and victorious Italy. Germany was humiliated, Italy frustrated in its hopes and cheated, it was assumed, out of the war booty it deserved. Immediately after the war, Germany was hit with inflation, impoverishing the majority of its citizens. Italy, weakened by worker unrest and quickly escalating violence perpetrated by members of the growing Fascist movement in their fight with Socialists, searched in vain for a government that could lead it out of recession.

It was primarily the workers in both countries, but also part of the intelligentsia, who saw a solution in Socialist rule. In both countries and at the same time, spokesmen and other opponents of democracy found receptive, eager adherents. In Italy it was a teacher and journalist, a demagogue intending to take power: Benito Mussolini. In Germany it was an unrecognized painter refused by art schools, a devotee of opera and ostentatious architecture, a half-educated deadbeat, pathological anti-Semite, and megalomaniac who was convinced of his calling: Adolf Hitler. They thundered against ineffectual democracy, warned of the dangers of Bolshevism (Hitler added Judaism), and promised to renew national glory and power and thereby provide their citizens with pride. They even offered a new savior who would solve everything and whose powerful will would rescue the country from all hardship. Everyone who believed in and followed him was promised a portion of the eternal glory in the new empire he would create.

Both men stood out as passionate opponents of Lenin's revolution and, when we compare their deeds with the benefit of hindsight, we find that the dictatorships differed from each other only slightly. At the same time that each was maligning the other, each also was looking to the other for inspiration as they introduced despotism.

Dictatorship as asserted and defined by Lenin means nothing less than *absolute power unlimited by any laws, absolutely unhampered by rules, and based on the direct exercise of force.*

Almost simultaneously, Benito Mussolini announced: *Now in light of new political and parliamentary experiences, the possibility of a dictatorship must be seriously considered.* And elsewhere: *Violence is not immoral; sometimes it can be moral.*

Only a little later did the Spanish leader General Francisco Franco formulate his credo: *Our regime is based on bayonets and blood, not on hypocritical elections.*

During his brief stay in prison (convicted for an unsuccessful putsch), Adolf Hitler formulated his hatred of democracy:

> For the view of life is intolerant and cannot be content with the role of a party among others, but it demands dictatorially that it be acknowledged exclusively and completely and that the entire public

life be completely readjusted according to its own views. Therefore
it cannot tolerate the simultaneous existence of a representation
of the former condition. . . . With this, however, the movement is
antiparliamentarian, and even its share in such an institution can
only have the meaning of an activity for the smashing of the latter,
for the abolition of an institution in which we see one of the most
serious symptoms of mankind's decay. *And in a political testament
only a few hours before his suicide, once more and for the last time, he
shouted out his tyrannical credo:* I am the last chance for [a united]
Europe. A new Europe will not be built on parliamentary vote, not
on discussions and resolutions, but only compelled by violence.

The fanatical revolutionary and prophet of class hatred, Lenin,
died too early to view with satisfaction how his theory would travel
around the world. He found, however, in his own country executors
of his legacy. The seminary dropout, reckless revolutionary, and crafty
intriguer Stalin transformed his theory into dogma no one could dispute. He who disagreed would not be convinced under Stalin's rule;
he would be executed.

On his path to absolute power, Stalin made violence the primary
tool of his politics. During the period of greatest terror he circulated
requirements as to how many people in a given district should be dis-
posed of and approved sometimes hundreds of death sentences a day.
During the trials, which were preceded by the torture of the accused,
he sentenced to death members of all strata of society, his closest collaborators, eminent artists, practically the entire leadership of the army
and clergy. Even his relatives were not spared. The wives of the executed
were either murdered as well or sent to concentration camps along with
everyone who questioned his unshakable leadership. Led by the logic
of dictatorship (and of all mafiosi), he executed those who could testify
to his crimes, since they had committed them on his orders.

Every dictator proclaims himself a spokesman for the people, that
is, for everyone over whom he holds power, and he expends much effort

to appear as a benevolent father. Dictatorship, proclaimed Lenin, cannot be administered by the entire working class (in part because they were not conscious enough and were *corrupted by imperialism*). It could be realized only *by the vanguard, which had absorbed the revolutionary energy of the class.* This is how terror is justified. In theory it is employed by one party with respect to all society. In reality it is employed by a handful of leading party functionaries and finally in the name of the one and only leader.

The great mass of a people, contemplated Adolf Hitler in *Mein Kampf, is not composed of diplomats or even teachers of political law, nor even of purely reasonable individuals who are able to pass judgment, but of human beings who are as undecided as they are inclined toward doubts and uncertainty.* Contempt for people and democracy is characteristic of all dictators. It allows them to conclude that it is possible to enslave the minds of the masses and that it is necessary—and correct—to devote all care and diligence to this effort if they are to rule. Dictatorships have gone as far as they can go in their methods of controlling human thought. To justify their deeds, which they claimed would protect society from ruin (whether from outside or within), it was necessary to create an image of the enemy who, no matter how weak and destined by history to disappear into eternal nothingness, is a constant threat and must be uncovered, isolated, and finally liquidated. Lenin had a wide range of enemies: the bourgeoisie, the White Guard, the imperialists, the members of all other parties, the nobility, and all of his opponents, whether they belonged to these categories or whether they were prominent artists or scientists who abhorred his terror. Hitler embodied evil, danger, and destruction in the figure of the Jew who was an enemy of culture, peace, and all humanity. (For contemporary Muslim fundamentalists, the United States and all democratic countries are the embodiment of evil. Among them, the most execrated is Israel.)

A dualistic view of the world, a strict delimitation between good and evil, is innate to human perception. Demons of darkness and light, devils and angels, the goddess of abundance and the god of the underworld—this division is found in all mythologies. Dictatorships bring this mythology to life: First they offer to rid the world of evil forever by simply exterminating evil's representatives. Some are murdered straightaway without trial. Others are carted off to concentration camps, where they are slowly destroyed by hunger, arduous toil, and finally gas, like troublesome insects.

The dictatorship announces a merciless battle or fatwa against enemies of the state, of the people, or of the only true faith. Genuine cohorts of criminals are formed in the battle against an imaginary evil (at one time they were called the Cheka, at another the SS or SA, and at another the secret police), and are determined in the name of an idea, a faith, or the unerring leader to commit violence, to torture and murder. Because the leaders well know the real character of their deeds, their rampages take place in secret. Often people living in the vicinity of an extermination camp had no idea what was going on behind the barbed wire. For months no news about the gas chambers leaked out, even though several thousand people were murdered there daily.

At its most glorious moments, a dictatorship appears to be indestructible and thus eternal. Even Hitler, for a short time, when he controlled an empire that encompassed almost all of Europe and reached from the Atlantic and North African coast to the Caucasus and the Volga, seemed undefeatable. Before his death, not only did Stalin rule the largest country in the world, whose territory spread to the Baltic republics and the eastern part of Czechoslovakia, Poland, and Romania, but he also controlled puppet governments in a series of European and Asian countries. In these others, often numerous and influential Communist parties were subordinated to his will.

The dictator lawfully fastens the fate of his regime to his own. Although his merits are set up as indubitable, his glory as immortal, and the idea he serves as eternal truth, one day the dictator will fall in the battle he himself has unleashed, or he will die a natural or violent death. And suddenly, perhaps in the small Dominican Republic, the larger Spain, or the enormous Russia, the ingenious creation of the dictatorship established will collapse or at least begin to deteriorate.

The Betrayal of the Intellectuals

At the head of the two powerful European empires, which in many ways defined the insane events of the twentieth century, stood two semieducated men, two apparently down-and-out individuals. Hitler graduated from high school, Stalin not even that—he fled from a seminary before he could receive any education. Both attempted to adopt the persona of intellectuals; after all, they lived in a century of science. Hitler was even a decent painter and considered himself an art expert. He was a compelling orator who could fascinate a crowd. Stalin was a bureaucrat who excelled at nothing but intrigue, villainy, and boundless cruelty. When we examine what both of these homicidal maniacs preached, we are amazed at the emptiness, the backwardness of their words. They were preceded, or accompanied, however, by others who were more educated and who gave shape to their lunatic visions.

The creators of the modern Communist utopia were intellectuals: Marx, Engels, and Lenin. Lenin, who consciously abolished any sort of law and replaced it with revolutionary justice (or as he called it: revolutionary terror), was paradoxically an erudite lawyer. Even Fidel Castro graduated with a law degree, and Pol Pot, the Cambodian organizer of cruel revolutionary slaughter, studied at the Sorbonne. Educated revolutionaries proclaim principles, even values, that often go against everything mankind has achieved.

It was also college graduates who helped formulate the basic principles of National Socialism. Hitler's right-hand man Joseph Goebbels received a doctorate in literature and philosophy. Heinrich Himmler, Hitler's second, was also educated. He too tried to justify the murderous goals of the SS with a mystical theory of the exceptional individual and the historical calling of the chosen race. Albert Speer was apparently a capable architect, and he later designed megalomaniacal buildings according to Hitler's ideas. Hans Frank was a lawyer by profession who, at least in the beginning, tried to get the regime to respect some basic legal norms such as the presumption of innocence until a defendant is proved guilty and the right of the accused to an independent defense. In the end, the opposite took place, and, as the absolute ruler of occupied Poland, he had on his conscience numerous illegalities, depredations, and murder.

The Wannsee Conference at the beginning of 1942 where the planned slaughter of Jews in all occupied lands was decided, as the historian Mark Roseman points out, was attended by primarily people with academic titles; *two-thirds had university degrees, and over half bore the title of doctor, mainly of law.*

One of the creators of the Soviet political or politicized trials, in which innocent people were condemned on the basis of forced confessions and name-calling that substituted for proof (*stinking carcass, fetid pile of human garbage*), was the knowledgeable prerevolutionary lawyer Andrey Vyshinsky. His Czech disciple, Josef Urválek, was a lawyer as well.

Far too many intellectuals were in the service of a fanatical idea that contradicted and betrayed everything humanity had thus far achieved.

In 1934, just after the Nazis took power in Germany, Karel Čapek published several remarkable reflections on the role of intellectuals in the political tragedy that was unfolding.

> An entire nation, an entire empire spiritually conceded to a faith in animality, in race, and in other such nonsense. An entire nation including university professors, preachers, men of letters, doctors, and lawyers. . . . What has happened is nothing less than the immense betrayal of intellectuals, and it has resulted in a horrifying image of what intelligence is capable of. Everywhere that coercion occurs on cultured humanity we find intel-

lectuals who are engaged en masse, even brandishing ideological arguments. This is no longer a crisis or the powerlessness of the intelligentsia, but rather its quiet and energetic complicity in the moral and political mayhem of today's Europe. . . . No cultural value can be exceeded if it is abandoned. . . . Destroy the hierarchy of the spirit, and you prepare for the return of the savage. The decline of the intelligentsia is the path to the barbarization of everything.

Nevertheless, it did indeed happen, and for decades scholars have repeatedly tried to explain this mass failure of the intelligentsia.

Thus far I have mentioned only the intellectuals who participated directly in the creation or the operation of totalitarian regimes. It is significant to note that, with only a few exceptions, these were not especially gifted thinkers. (This is particularly true of the Nazis just mentioned.) Goebbels was merely a capable demagogue; in reality, as his diaries show, he was inwardly insecure. For years he despaired over his fate, which seemed to him so hopeless that he considered suicide. Himmler was just as uncertain. His entire youth was utterly without success, and from his lack of confidence was born a raving fanaticism. When he finally decided to assume the mantle of the intellectual, he proclaimed only fatuous prejudices based on romantic German my-thology. Their ferocious anti-Semitism bears eloquent testimony to the base intellectual level of both men.

Not even among the Communist intellectuals do we find great minds. Although numerous paeans have been written about Lenin's in-tellectual achievements, no one has yet sought inspiration in his flights into the area of philosophy or the social sciences. When examined ob-jectively, his theses are a conglomeration of cranky polemics, simplifying interpretations, and, above all, errors and lies presented as scientific truth.

Otherwise, intellectuals did not participate directly in the achieve-ment of totalitarian power, but they either actively endorsed it or toler-ated it without objection. Of these there were millions.

During the birth of Communist ideology, enthusiastic supporters were found all over the world (even more than in the Soviet Union), and many were outstanding intellectuals. Artists were captivated by the utopian vision, the marvelous goals, and the skillful demagoguery with which Communist dictators managed to defend everything that took place in their empires (terror, famine, murder, and imprisonment). Some of these artists, at the beginning of the Bolshevik reign, were still allowed to work. During the first postrevolutionary years, Boris Pasternak, Vladimir Mayakovsky, Anna Akhmatova, and Isaac Babel even approved of and were willing to publicly defend the Communist vision of a joyous society, as if it had already been created. Although other recognized and influential minds of the time condemned Bolshevism immediately after the revolution, they also found positive things to say about Russia. H. G. Wells visited Russia in 1920 and was shocked by what he saw. However, he ended up writing several complimentary things about Russia and Lenin. He concluded his book about his visit, *Russia in the Shadows*, with the assurance that only the Bolsheviks were capable of preventing the collapse of Russia. It was as if he'd forgotten that it was precisely the Bolsheviks who had brought Russia to the brink of collapse in the first place.

In *The Practice and Theory of Bolshevism*, Bertrand Russell, who visited Russia at the same time as Wells, spoke more ambivalently about Bolshevism.

> One who believes as I do, that free intellect is the chief engine of human progress, cannot but be fundamentally opposed to Bolshevism as much as to the Church of Rome. [But] the hopes which inspire Communism are, in the main, as admirable as those instilled by the Sermon on the Mount [!], but they are held as fanatically and are as likely to do as much harm.

It is true that the First World War shook people's faith in current political systems, and this caused even educated people to look with

expectation upon this great social experiment the Bolsheviks were trying to bring about in Russia.

There were many intellectuals who supported Stalin even during
the period of his greatest cruelty. Usually they found a rational justification for their weakness concerning the merciless totalitarian regime.
Hewlett Johnson, nicknamed the Red Dean of Canterbury, one of the
most passionate advocates of the Soviet regime, considered it more
humane than capitalism. In his trilogy of journalistic books about the
Soviet Union, he writes only about that which lent itself to Soviet
propaganda. He enthusiastically praises free medical care, education,
and the tax system, and justifies his praise (like Stalin) by pointing
out the great support the regime receives in its elections. *If such a large
percentage of the population participates in elections—on May 10th, 1946,
it was 99.7 percent—and if 99.18 percent voted for the selected candidates,
there must be truth behind the elections in a country where there are equal
voting rights, where voting is secret, and where elections are direct.* Whether
this prominent intellectual public figure from a country of traditional
democracy actually believed this claim is difficult to judge. Lenin, however, called such intellectuals useful idiots. Useful idiots were used and
abused, often cited as authorities, and showered with admiration and
accolades. (Johnson was awarded the Stalin Peace Prize.)

Of course, it is true that Soviet politicians cunningly continued
the Russian tradition of showing willing visitors their country. After
the war they deftly exploited the atomic fears of a series of intellectuals, and although they themselves were feverishly producing atomic
weapons (intended to defend their camp of peace), they unleashed
an enormous political campaign against the spread of weapons of
mass destruction—and for this campaign they enlisted the foremost
scientific experts, the Nobel laureates Frédéric Joliot-Curie and Linus
Pauling.

A few decades later, just after the publication of *The Black Book
of Communism*, an editor for *L'Humanité* announced on television that
even eighty million dead did not tarnish the Communist worldview.

After Auschwitz, he opined, *one cannot be a Nazi, but after the Soviet gulags, one can be a Communist.*

Certainly it is possible to remain a Communist standing over the mass graves of the murdered (they were, after all, enemies of the greatest and most humane society), it is possible to remain a Communist on the scaffold (whether as the condemned or the hangman), but it is impossible to remain an intellectual or a cultured person. Because the betrayal of intelligence leads to the barbarization of everyone.

On Propaganda

Propaganda, although it has not always gone by this name, has existed since antiquity. Oftentimes a capable and demagogic individual would win over so many adherents through disclosures and promises and an ability to provide the people with bread and circuses that he would succeed in achieving absolute power. With a certain schadenfreude one can say that every leader, every regime prefers the darkening of the minds of its subjects (called citizens in modern times). More precisely, the subjects should possess only enough knowledge to confirm the rule of those who hold power.

Whereas democracies seek ways to limit the tendencies of governments to transform their citizens into a mere assenting mob, totalitarian regimes try to achieve the opposite.

These regimes have a certain number of loyal citizens, often even fanatically devoted adherents (and approximately the same number of determined opponents). They attempt to acquire the rest of the citizenry for their goals or at least compel them to obedient silence. First they must protect each of their subjects from the influence of all enemy elements and ideas, and all thoughts that do not support the vision upon which the dictatorship is built are considered enemy ideas. Then they must besiege their opponents with correct thoughts. In his first speech as newly appointed chancellor, Adolf Hitler announced his cultural (or, better, anticultural) program. *Concurrently with the political purification of our public life, the Reich government will undertake a thorough moral purification of the country. All cultural bodies, theaters, cinemas, literature, the press, and radio—all of this will be used as a tool to fulfill this goal. . . . Blood and race will once again become the source of artistic inspiration.*

A few weeks after this, purges were under way in all cultural organizations, in all media outlets, even in churches. Bonfires of "harmful" books blazed on city squares and in front of universities. Books vanished from libraries and bookstores.

Over the course of a few months, the ground was laid for the dictator and his helpers to gain control over the people's minds via propaganda in all media.

In modern times, propaganda has become an essential element of totalitarian power. In the first stages there is always the corruption of the people through the generous distribution of property, which was at one time stolen from the nobility, another time from the Jews, and still another from the capitalists. Then follows the attempt to control the minds of the citizens.

The clearest (and most cynical) function and mission of propaganda, as it is understood today, was defined by one of its creators, Joseph Goebbels, the author of the infamous dictum that a lie repeated often enough becomes the truth:

> The goal of the National Socialist revolution was to seize power because the idea of revolution remains empty theory if not combined with power. Revolutionary political propaganda brought the ideas of National Socialism to the masses, and therefrom arose Adolf Hitler's iron soldiers who, through faith in the gospel of his teachings, brought revolution all the way to the threshold of power.
>
> Propaganda is a matter of practice, not of theory. . . . In other words, propaganda is good if it leads to the desired results, and propaganda is bad if does not lead to the desired results. . . . Its purpose is not to be decent, or gentle, or weak, or modest; it is to be successful.

The Communists were somewhat less direct in their speeches, but propaganda occupied the same essential position. According to Stalin:

> There is probably no need to mention the great significance of party propaganda and the Marxist-Leninist education of our workers. I have in mind not only the workers in the party. I also have in mind the workers of youth organizations, trade unions, business unions, cooperatives, financial and cultural institutions, and others. . . . The attention of our party must be concentrated on propaganda in the press and in the organization of a lecture system of propaganda.

In reality, Marxist-Leninist "education" concentrated not only on party members but on all of society. Over the course of a few generations, it became the basis of education in the Communist empire, from preschool to doctoral students, and one could not receive a degree without successfully passing an exam on Marxism.

Modern means of communication transformed propaganda into a powerful medium; therefore, every totalitarian regime sought to bring them under its power as quickly as possible. The day after the Austrian anschluss, Goebbels, now the powerful Nazi minister of propaganda, noted: *I am giving Dr. Dietrich precise instructions for the reform of the Austrian press. We must initiate an enormous reshaping of personnel. . . . We are establishing a Reich radio in Vienna. At the same time, we are creating a Reich Ministry of Propaganda.*

In the days immediately following the February coup in Czechoslovakia, the Communists occupied the editorial offices of all newspapers and radio stations. They instituted action committees to expel tenacious editors and replace them with vetted personnel willing to cooperate. News organizations were purged, and those belonging to the party took power. Frightened non–party members often hastily joined their ranks.

In all totalitarian systems, the news media are directed by some sort of office (called varying names); however, it is always in the hands of the ruling party, or, more precisely, the group that rules in the party's name. The office dispenses orders concerning what may be written about and what may not.

In the first half of the twentieth century, when radio was the most important news medium, the Nazis condemned to death anyone listening to "enemy" broadcasts. A few years later, Communists made it impossible to listen to foreign radio broadcasts by installing a net of jammers—this was not for humanitarian reasons; it was simply more effective.

A sort of canon of propaganda quickly arises. The fundamental means, policies, and goals can be condensed into a few points.

First, propaganda must name and define the basic idea it is implicitly to serve. It does not matter whether the idea is called National Socialism, Marxism-Leninism, Maoism, or Muslim fundamentalism. What is crucial is that it be transformed into Goebbels's aforementioned gospel. The idea is holy, that is, unimpugnable, all-explaining, and eternal. Regimes based upon it will last for all time imaginable.

It is necessary to convince the citizens to willingly accept the fact that what has happened is irrevocable. The Soviet Union will endure forever because it embodies the most progressive and advanced societal order. Therefore, our friendship with it will endure forever. The Nazi empire will assume the rule of Europe. Nothing will change during those thousand years (a thousand years and eternity mean the same thing in the life of an individual), and from this it follows that only an idiot or someone on the enemy side would oppose it.

Article number two of the canon proves the existence of a cunning, deceitful, malevolent enemy intent on committing atrocities. (Without it, as I have indicated, no dictatorship can exist.) All effective propaganda is dualistic: It must battle for something the people long for, something to which they can fasten themselves, and at the same time it must battle against something or someone that is interfering with their desires and ideas. The enemy can be Jews, international imperialism, the United States, Israel, kulaks, the bourgeoisie, Trotskyites, plutocrats, Bolshevism, Zionism, cosmopolitanism, degenerate capitalism, seditious transmitters of Radio Free Europe, the CIA, German revanchists, Masons, or religious sects. The enemy can change shape over time too. It cannot, however, disappear from the world because the sanctity of propaganda is always strengthened by doing battle with satanic forces. The enemy is a pariah: deceitful, disgusting, dirty, corrupt, cunning, crafty, inordinately ambitious, treacherous, insidious, intriguing, destined to vanish from history. No comparisons are powerful enough. The enemy is a *blood-letting dog* (Stalin for Goebbels, Tito for Stalin). For Hitler the Romanian peasant is a *miserable piece of cattle*, Churchill an *unprincipled pig*. When Lenin writes his furious polemic with the foremost Social Democrat, the theoretician Karl Kautsky, he showers him with ever-new curses—Kautsky is a *renegade, a parliamentary cretin, a bourgeois lackey, a sweet idiot*. For Stalin, those he needs to divest himself of, the pariahs, are *a handful of spies, murderers, and cankerworms slinking in the dust before foreign countries, infected by a slavish feeling of groveling humility before every foreign stooge.*

Against the background of these repulsive monsters looms the refulgent yet almost kitschy image of the leader. He is kind, polite, wise; he has an understanding of the needs of simple people; he is uncompromisingly fair, works tirelessly, defends honor and decency, loves children, the elderly, and war invalids. Magazines and newsreels are chock-full of photographs of the leader and scenes from his life. Lenin with Gorky, with his wife, with his nephews. Lenin skates, collects mushrooms, and has a dog named Aida that he plays with. Hitler has his blonde. The führer also loves the children of his friend Goebbels. He skis and goes on walks, and we see him smiling and down-to-earth *mit der kleine Helga*. Stalin holds in his arms a pioneer schoolgirl, who has just brought him a bouquet of flowers. During the war, on the other hand, he inclines over a map of the front to demonstrate to everyone that it is he who is calling the shots in the final victory of his armies.

As soon as it seizes power, every totalitarian regime proclaims plenty of magnificent and lofty goals along with pleasing slogans. Soon, however, it becomes obvious that few of them can be fulfilled.

Another task of propaganda is to create a fictive world and persuade the people that only this fictive world is real, while the real world is a fiction that has been thrust upon them by the enemy, who has still not been uncovered. Propaganda seeks to convince its citizens that almost everything that was promised has been fulfilled. You just have to be able to see it, or, more precisely: You have to know how to look. Propaganda thus emphasizes a point of view: Whoever does not see it is looking at events from the enemy's point of view.

A new fictive reality full of zealous partisans swells to the deafening roar of the celebration of glorious and magnificent victories. The press abounds with enthusiastic speeches by shock workers, loyal party followers, vigilant citizens who uncover traitors and pen resolutions in which they announce their devotion to the government, demonstrators, sloganeers, voters who vote 99.18 percent for the candidates proposed by the government. (In Kim Il-sung's North Korea, it is reported that all were chosen without a single exception.)

Entire apparatuses are delegated to the organization of enormous mass demonstrations and parades. *Triumphant ride through the city. Hundreds of thousands rejoice. Fireworks rise into the heavens, celebratory salvos and the people rejoice. This is Berlin*, Goebbels notes in his diary. Radio announcers describe the rejoicing May Day parades in Moscow, in Prague, in Warsaw, and in other Communist dictatorships. They read out the soul-destroying slogans borne on red banners. The mass media follow these orgies of assent in word and picture.

In order to substitute this fictive reality for real life, isolation is necessary. Propaganda must proclaim the entirety of the rest of the world as a degenerate, rotten place, in which a relentless battle, exploitation, poverty, nationalistic prejudice, irresponsibility, and sexual perversion reign, where representatives of a lower race or international imperialism made their way to power, endeavoring to subjugate the rest of humanity.

On one day (January 5, 1953), *Rudé právo* published articles with the following headlines:

Barbaric Bombardment of Korean Cities and Villages

Strikes on the Rise in Canada This Year

Denmark's Grave Financial Crisis

Latin American Hatred for American Imperialism Is Growing

Escalation of American-British Tensions

New Provocation by West Berlin Police

Boycott of Tito Banners by Yugoslav Workers

The Brave Opposition of French Sailors to American Gestapo
Regulations

Italian Government Again Violates Peace Agreement

News reports are masterfully composed to confirm the fiction. The mayor of Detroit speaks out on the horrible poverty threatening the lives of the unemployed and their children in his city. This is accompanied by a photograph of Soviet Pioneers departing for vacation. These are children whose blissful lives are threatened by nothing because they live in a Socialist country.

Propaganda must assiduously lie about the democratic part of the world, but power must facilitate it: It must restrict the input of information, the exchange of individuals and ideas; it must strictly control everyone who leaves or enters its realm and declare foreign printed matter contraband. Finally it must build a wall and stretch barbed wire along its borders, obviously in order to keep diversionists out of the country. To overcome the recklessness of all its assignments, propaganda must fulfill yet another task, the confusion of language. George Orwell describes this ingeniously in his novel *1984*.

Propaganda labels wrongful situations—in which the police investigate, condemn, and execute whomever they want—the highest justice. Concentration camps are referred to as reeducation institutions.

Slavelike work under inhuman conditions is called the path to liberation. A system in which people cannot without permission leave their
region is called the government of the people, bondage is called freedom,
and poverty is prosperity. Their backwardness is an example for the
rest of the world; their empire surrounded by barbed wire is the only
place a person can live in happiness and contentment. Murder will be
called an act of justice.

In 1934 Hitler had his former collaborators and friends murdered
en masse so that he would not have to share power. When the citizens
wondered at the bloodiness and gore of the purge, one of the official
media (the *Westdeutscher Beobachter*) reported the following:

> Never before has a leader suppressed his own personal feelings so
> completely; never before has any statesman taken such extreme
> care for the welfare of his nation as the Führer. Not even Alex-
> ander the Great, no other king or emperor of ancient history,
> not Bonaparte, not Frederick the Great, has done anything like
> this. . . . One must follow the Führer for years, as we have, to be
> able to appreciate the enormousness of his sacrifice and to un-
> derstand what it meant for him to give the command to execute
> so many of his former friends.

When the Nazis installed a reign of terror against any kind of
opposition after the occupation of Austria, Goebbels noted in his diary:
The hour of freedom has arrived for this country as well.

At the end of 1918, when unforgivable massacres were taking place
in the name of the proletarian revolution, Lenin wrote: *Proletarian democracy is a million times more democratic than any bourgeois democracy.* A
few decades later, his student, the foremost Hungarian Marxist György
Lukács, elaborated upon this lie: *Our people's democracy, after the victorious
battle against bourgeois democracy, is fulfilling the function of the dictatorship of the proletariat.* This of course is not logical nonsense, not even
an outright confusion of concepts, Czech Marxists will explain thirty

years later. *One cannot identify the dictatorship of the proletariat with violence. It is a new method of democracy.* Every totalitarian power requires strict discipline and the obedience of all, and thus propaganda militarizes everyday vocabulary. It announces a **battle** to fulfill the plan, a **battle** for peace or Socialist morality. To help the workers, it sends **brigades**; it talks about **offenses** to exceed the quota, of the necessity to ensure an effective **defense** against enemy propaganda. It talks about successes on the **cultural front**, about **capitalist encirclement**, about the almighty **army of workers**. It emphasizes vigilance and watchfulness. The dictator himself (Stalin) proclaims: *The closest practical goal of the kolkhozes [collective farms] consists in the battle for sowing, in the battle for the spreading of the tracts of sowing, in the battle for the correct organization of sowing.*

But words are not sufficient. One can avoid them, refuse to read the newspaper full of catchwords, ignore the radio, and not go to the cinema. Therefore it is necessary to impose upon the citizen at least those catchwords and symbols of the current power. Everywhere he goes, he stumbles upon an abundance of swastikas: on the sleeves of pedestrians, on flags hung everywhere the eye can see. As soon as he enters the door, he must cower before hammers and sickles. They will be hung above factory entrances, pasted on windows, sewn or printed on red banners. State banners with their symbols wave on all holidays; they are hung on every column. No structure will be spared the symbols of perverted power. They are engraved on the graves of functionaries and soldiers who fall in battle.

Whenever a person enters a room, he hears not "Good afternoon" but "Heil Hitler!" He hears the same thing when he leaves, if people do not say to him, "Honor to work, Comrade!" Stalin's face, with its pockmarks smoothed over, stares down at his every step, and he will be forced to acclaim Stalin's glory at every meeting of the gardening club or trade union. And he will applaud and stand in tribute to the great führer or the immortal generalissimo.

The fictive reality, day after day, month after month, with the help of all media, insinuates itself into the minds of the people and, in technical terminology, brainwashes them. At least in some cases it achieves its goal, and people succumb to the repeated lies and begin to wonder which of the realities is the real one. Most people accept bifurcation: In all intrinsically societal situations they accept the fictive world of propaganda as reality, while in private they move in the real world—they grow lettuce in their gardens and during the Christmas holidays stand in real lines for tangerines or bananas.

Propaganda protects the fictive world to the very end. When the broken Adolf Hitler, whose hand shook so much that he could sign his name only with difficulty, organized in his shadowy bunker his own theatrical wedding, he cursed the German people for their inability to be victorious. He then shot himself and his newlywed bride. The abating propaganda informed the people, who were thinking of nothing but escaping their own destruction, that their führer fell in heroic battle while defending the capital.

Totalitarian power cannot survive without its thoroughly mendacious propaganda, and propaganda cannot exist without a regime hell-bent on every iniquity. When the regime falls, its propaganda dies with it. For most people, the long-awaited moment of truth arrives, but there are plenty of those who are frightened of this moment, which will throw them from the fictive world back to into real life.

Dogmatists and Fanatics

The *Encyclopedia of Politics* defines the concept of dogmatism as: *Dogmatism (from Greek dogma = opinion)—a persistence of views without regard to new findings. Dogmatism was used in the political sphere primarily in the 1960s in connection with the attempt to reform Marxist-Leninist theory and the political practices of the Communist Party.*

The *Academic Dictionary of Literary Czech* provides a more precise definition: *Dogma is an unproved assertion accepted on the basis of faith and considered incontrovertible, infallible, and eternal.*

For example, the basic Christian dogmas as established in the Apostolic Confessions of Faith prescribe that Christians believe that Jesus is the Son of God, born of the Virgin Mary; he was crucified, died, descended to hell, and on the third day he rose from the dead and ascended to heaven. The Confessions also include faith in corporeal resurrection after death and eternal life. The dogma does not concern itself with how a person can die and come back to life, or how we will all, on some unspecified day, perhaps millions of years after death, be resurrected in our bodily form, or what eternity means. Dogmas can only be believed.

It is natural to want to live in truth. People desire that what they affirm and stand behind—what guides their life—be correct and that other people believe it to be correct as well. But who is entitled to judge what is correct? Certain norms are generally accepted, and laws must be based upon them or society will descend into chaos. But what about those areas that do not fit into these norms? How should society be organized so that a person is assured he is spending the time he has in the best way possible? How can he tell beauty from ugliness? Art from mere diversion? Does something suprapersonal exist? If so, where do we look for it? Which of the various offers put forth by different prophets do we choose?

Most people incline to some sort of canonized guidance or explanation, to commandments, to ideals against which they measure their own deeds and behavior. The stricter and more apodictic these ideals appear, the more people are attracted to them. Whoever accepts them as his own is protected by their uncontestable authority, and he can feel safe. He abdicates all responsibility and, if necessary, renounces his own conscience.

We have no conscience, announced Hans Frank at the beginning of Nazism. *My conscience is Adolf Hitler.*

Dogmatists are usually uncreative people, but because they cleave wholeheartedly to some incontrovertible, infallible, and eternal truth, they acquire the certainty—the conviction—that they have the right to judge and to condemn all who do not recognize their truth.

Dogmatism, therefore, becomes dangerous and destructive when it joins together with power or when it seeks to attain power.

At the end of the Middle Ages and the beginning of the modern era, dogmatism was triumphant in the Christian church. In order to spread the Christian faith, crusades were undertaken whose participants sometimes slaughtered adherents of Christian sects and at other times adherents of Islam. The rabble would organize pogroms against Jews. To defend its dogmas, the Roman Catholic church established the Inquisition, an institution that suppressed manifestations of independent thought and killed heretics and women accused and "convicted" of witchcraft.

The infamous *Malleus Maleficarum* is the fruit of such a perverted spirit which, by appealing to the church fathers and the Bible, proved the existence of witches and their nefarious deeds.

But there is no bodily infirmity, not even leprosy or epilepsy, which cannot be caused by witches, with God's permission. And this is proved [!] by the fact that no sort of infirmity is excepted by the Doctors. For a careful consideration of what has already been written concerning the power of devils and the wickedness of witches will show that this statement offers no difficulty.

This preposterousness can by explained by the preposterousness of the era. Even in the Bible itself we find mention of witches and evil spirits. In Exodus we find: *Thou shalt not suffer a witch to live.* It was the merging of dogma with the enormous power of the Catholic church that led hundreds of thousands of women to be slaughtered.

The twentieth century is distinguished by the revolutionary development of science, and new dogmas adapted themselves to this reality.

The official explication of Marxism connected with the power of the Marxist state was fraudulent. Marx's dialectical materialism (later developed into Marxism-Leninism) was proclaimed as the highest level of scientific knowledge, as the only permissible method of research. Several fundamental dogmas—the decisive significance of relations of production, the economic basis (which defines the political and ideological superstructure) of sustained class warfare, the historical mission of the working class as the bearers of progress, and the felonious character of the exploiting class—were continually confirmed as ingenious by propagandists who feigned the scientific method. Most important, they transferred this dogma to all branches of human activity and production. Scientific work was judged not according to whether it was objective and revelatory, but precisely the opposite, according to how it managed to support derived and unoriginal claims, with citations from classical Marxism. The teaching of philosophy at universities was replaced by dialectical and historical materialism. No academic degree could be achieved unless the candidate passed a test in Marxism. Since all spiritual aspirations resisted this conception, it was necessary to establish strict control over them. One redoubtable interpreter of the Marxist doctrine, the Chinese Communist dictator Mao Zedong, provides the following definition of culture:

In the world today all culture, all literature and art belong to definite classes and are geared to definite political lines. There is in fact no such thing as art for art's sake, art that stands above classes, art that is detached from or independent of politics.

It is precisely a mind bound by dogma that is predisposed to believe it has discovered the truth, the one and only indisputable truth, which is therefore universally valid. And the duty of the one who has discovered this truth is to disseminate it and then, by all possible means, destroy its (that is, his) opponents. Fanaticism is characteristic of cells of enthusiastic militants prepared to unleash terror, revolt, or revolution and beguile those who merely look on.

Thus faithful Christians abetted (through their denunciations), or at least watched, the burning of heretics, just as during the French Revolution crowds of Parisians rejoiced at the execution of the opponents of the revolution and, a little later, the execution of its leaders.

Lenin was all the more convinced that he had uncovered the only valid truth concerning societal activity and history, and thus had uncovered the only correct evolution of society. The Bolshevik leader Grigory Zinoviev, a comrade of the beloved leader, characterized Lenin as a man who as early as age twenty-five *felt responsible for all of humanity.* Obsessed with his idea of constructing a communist society (against the will of everyone), Lenin declared the legitimacy, indeed the necessity, of dictatorship. *The dictatorship of the proletariat is a stubborn struggle—bloody and bloodless, violent and peaceful, military and economic, educational and administrative—against the forces and traditions of the old society. The force of habit of millions and tens of millions is a most terrible force.* For a zealot of the new faith, a new world, and a new society, the most dangerous things of all are the traditions of the tens of millions who refuse the salvation he wishes to impose upon them.

Lenin and his followers had the tsar and his family murdered along with hundreds of the monarchy's representatives. Those who surrendered to Lenin's vision, thinking, and conscience believed that each new murder confirmed the one and only truth, which they had accepted (or had been compelled to accept) as their own.

Lenin was firmly and fanatically convinced that in asserting his truth, he was authorized to do anything. No less thorough was his successor, Joseph Stalin, who rightfully proclaimed himself Lenin's pupil. This is how the Yugoslav politician Milovan Djilas characterized Stalin after numerous meetings with him:

> He knew he was one of the cruelest and most despotic figures in all of human history. But this did not bother him in the least because he was convinced he could, by himself, realize the intentions of history. Nothing bothered his conscience despite the millions slaughtered in his name and upon his orders, not even the thousands of his closest colleagues whom he murdered as traitors because they doubted he was leading their country to happiness, equality, and freedom.

Adolf Hitler believed he was acting in the interests of history and following the will of providence, and he therefore demanded unlimited obedience and servitude from all. In his programmatic book *Mein Kampf*, he claimed that

> the future of a movement is determined by the devotion, and even intolerance, with which its members fight for their cause. . . . The greatness of every powerful organization which embodies a creative idea lies in the spirit of religious devotion and intolerance with which it stands out against all others, because it has an ardent faith in its own right.

Through an unshakable faith in their own truth, their sense of chosen destiny, and their ability to bring salvation to the people, prophets of new truths and creators of new empires manage to acquire, at least for a time, masses of devoted and fanaticized followers.

Weary Dictators and Rebels

The beginning of every dictatorship appears to its contemporaries as solid and unyielding. The organs of a dictatorship function precisely according to calculations that suit the power being established. In their relationship with artists and the intelligentsia in general, their positions seem unequivocal. Those who glorify and subordinate themselves to the regime are praised. Those who refuse to subordinate themselves in thought and work are silenced by imprisonment, exile, or the scaffold. The new masters, the coffin carriers, appear as the guarantee that the dictatorship will persist undisturbed. In reality, it is precisely the opposite. The uncreative nature of the new masters, their dull-witted loyalty, is the beginning of a stagnation that will gradually mortify and kill off society, which begins to lag behind in all branches of human activity. Usually when the founding dictator steps down, is overthrown, or dies (one of these must inevitably happen), it is at once revealed that all that is left are masses of unfulfilled promises, slogans no one believes, absurd prohibitions, and directives that hinder life. Wearied by its own arrogance, weakened by its own dull-wittedness, rid of all personalities, hated by most of its subordinates, the dictatorship seeks some way to survive.

The new inheritors realize that as long as they continue the previous despotism, they cannot be sure their subordinates will not turn against them. They know they cannot trust each other. Some of them can turn to the subordinates, exploit their dissatisfaction, and deal harshly with the other inheritors who previously committed crimes under the protective hand of despotism. In the end, the inheritors of totalitarian power will decide not to risk it and instead flatter their underlings (including the army, police, and government authorities) by promising a renewal of law and order, a return to the original ideals, and a prosperity unseen anywhere else in the world. They will seek to retain absolute power without absolute repression.

The Communist dictatorship in Czechoslovakia was derived from the Soviet dictatorship in both form and content. During the very first months of its rule, it decided to suppress unconditionally every sign of resistance in all areas of life. It formed action committees made up of fanatical Communists tasked with screening the behavior of individuals and organizations. It immediately closed down newspapers and magazines not under the government's immediate control; it broke up and prohibited independent institutions. It nationalized all enterprises and later small workshops and businesses, and installed its loyal acolytes at the head of every institution. It took over film production, shut down theaters, closed private publishing houses, and began its attack against farmers. The richest were transferred to the border regions. Representatives of democratic political parties, if they had not fled in time, were sent to prison and concentration camps for long periods (some were executed when workers organized a mass campaign demanding the death sentence for the accused). Members of the Western resistance and army officers, university professors, journalists, and the educated in general who did not accept the Marxist doctrine were turned out from their jobs. The Catholic clergy, including nuns and monks, were locked up or at least silenced. Several Catholic poets were condemned to lengthy prison terms.

After the death of Stalin, however, and shortly thereafter that of his obedient vassal, Gottwald, a new, "wearier" form of dictatorship began to emerge.

The weary dictatorship no longer murders, it doesn't even pronounce lifetime prison sentences, but it tries to corrupt all the more. Corruption does not manifest itself only in its most brazen form, allowing the most loyal followers to steal unrestrainedly or at least to enjoy sinecures. The regime now behaves more benevolently toward most of its subordinates. Until recently it compelled them to ostentatiously declare their love to the regime, to devote time and money to it, and t o go to meetings, brigades, and rallies; and even when they were doing so, they could never be certain the police would not accuse them of some serious crime, then interrogate them, torture them, and finally hand them over to a court that would deliver a predetermined conviction. Now the powers make it clear that whoever works, refrains from any acts of opposition, and confirms his loyalty once every four years in elections will be allowed to purchase a weekend cottage and cultivate bourgeois amusements, such as attending jazz concerts or collecting stamps; he will be allowed to read lyric poetry and from time to time vacation at the seaside of some friendly nation. He can even steal—a little. In return the regime will provide him with peace. From now on only criminal elements and genuinely determined opponents will be persecuted. Even the innocent, whom it had previously accused and ordered servile courts to sentence, now, after long years of imprisonment (if they survived), are hesitantly and discreetly released—as long as they understand that they may not communicate to anyone the details of their imprisonment. For a short time, peace, or, more precisely, torpor, will reign in society, which compared with the recent terror will becalm or even arouse hope.

The regime will alter its relationship to intellectuals. In its benevolence, which should be appropriately appreciated, the totalitarian regime will provide intellectuals and artists with a little more freedom, with the proviso that any doubts and solutions cannot be aimed at it. At most they may request that the regime rid itself of several (now admitted) vices, and the artists will always submit their conclusions for approval. As long as intellectuals behave in this way, they will be tolerated. As a sign of its goodwill, the regime will allow some, who until now had to remain silent, to speak, even if usually only on some inconsequential topic.

The retreat from direct terror creates difficulties for the totalitarian power. Whereas terror drove the surviving, freely thinking intellectuals deep into the underground or compelled them to be silent, now many refuse to be bought, refuse to pretend that the ground disintegrating beneath the vigilant governance of a weary but still totalitarian power is an empire of unprecedented freedom.

In the first half of the twentieth century, plenty of intellectuals and especially artists believed the erroneous visions and promises of the Communist Party. Between those who supported, or even believed in, the regime and those who understood its true essence was a border that was difficult to traverse. Some (often in good faith but always blindly) supported the dictatorship and helped stifle freedom, and thus bore, to a greater or lesser degree, coresponsibility for the crimes committed. Others understood that without preserving basic freedoms, society was doomed to destruction. Some stood up to power; others remained silent, but they knew that all terror was self-destructive and thus condemned to extinction.

After the death of the Soviet dictator, however, another analogous border was created within the Communist Party. Some considered a partial admission of crimes as an unprecedented, even admirable, act of self-criticism, which all citizens should appreciate and which entitled the party to further lead society to the goals it defined itself. To admit that the goal was mistaken or at least unrealizable seemed unacceptable. But many Communists began to realize that they had become members of a felonious party that had committed unspeakable crimes. It is impossible to ascertain the number of such people, but they were often active in fields of the humanities: journalists, film directors, scriptwriters, authors, historians, sociologists, university teachers—that is, those who could influence the thought of others, even if only to a limited degree under the conditions of a totalitarian state. Most of them could not accept that those who had answered for crimes committed in the name of the Communist regime had gone unpunished, that they still participated in governing the country. At least in the domain of the spirit, they wanted society to be open to the world.

Those who stood at the summit of party power and henceforth considered all similar opinions as revisionist, opportunistic, bourgeois, or Trotskyist at the same time perceived that a good number of intellectuals in the party were "infected" with these opinions. It even seemed that most of the grumbling, most of the dissatisfaction, most of the criticism of the current power was coming not from democratic opponents but from a reckless and unruly section of the party.

The party (and the police) organs were most likely correct in their suspicions. After all, the only remnants of societal criticism (at least those that might be made public) and political life survived precisely in the party itself.

The metamorphosis of disappointed disciples of the Communist vision into its opponents occurred in all countries. Utter disappointment is one of the most powerful experiences, and it is not important whether it is disappointment in faith in man or in an ideal. The most persuasive texts revealing the crimes of communism were written by its former disciples, for example, Arthur Koestler and George Orwell, and, more recently Milovan Djilas. Throughout most of his adult life, Koestler fought against dictatorships, something with which this century is so rich, and compellingly described the monstrous political trials. In 1931 he was still, as a member of the German Communist Party, convinced that *communism is the global solution to all problems*. In *Animal Farm* and his celebrated utopian novel *1984*, Orwell depicted the horrifying possibilities of totalitarian states and their control over their citizens in both thought and action. During the Spanish Civil War, however, Orwell fought in the militia of the Workers' Party of Marxist Unification, and until the end of his life he considered himself a Socialist and adherent of that which he called democratic socialism. Milovan Djilas was one of the highest functionaries in the Communist Party of Yugoslavia and one of Tito's closest associates. Even Alexander Solzhenitsyn, who convincingly revealed the criminal foundation of the Communist regime, began as a loyal citizen of the Soviet state. He graduated from the university, joined the Komsomol, and during the war was a decorated captain in the Soviet army. In his polemics with a Czech agent of the Soviet secret police, Tomáš Řezáč, he noted: *I know how inexperienced and superficial our understanding of things is; after all, I myself began to sympathize with the unbelievably villainous Leninism. . . . I was entirely and fervently for the defense of Leninism.*

As soon as the most brutal terror had passed, the number of Communists who were fed up with the politics of their party began to increase. They considered the leading functionaries and their blindness the greatest danger for the future of the country. The impossibility of founding a new party or establishing a faction within the party itself led to the emergence of groups of party members who were against the dull-witted dogmatism and absolute absence of democratic principles in both the party and society.

After the official party doctrine had rejected its primary ideological pillar—Stalin's doctrine of the escalating class battle and his method of rule (that is, handing over every critic to the courts and then to the firing squad)—there was only one pillar left, one prophet: Lenin. The founder of the Bolshevik Party and the first architect of revolutionary terror was, after all, more educated than the Georgian seminary dropout. He had lived many years in Europe, even in democratic Switzerland and England. Even though he scorned democracy, his work contained defenses of, or even demands for, open criticism or at least a free exchange of opinions within the party he led. Now members of the party exploited this fact to defend their right to advocate opinions other than those of the leading functionaries.

By invoking Lenin, Communist rebels were demarcating another border they were not willing to cross. Even the most critical pronouncements tried to convince the ruling power that their advocates were actually acting in the interest of socialism, its development and enhancement. Their goal was not to overturn it but merely to return it to its roots. (The poison of these roots had already been forgotten, debilitated by myth.)

One of the leading lights of the nonparty opposition, Václav Havel, expressed his distaste for the "rebelliousness" of the Communists:

Please realize that your relativizing antidogmatism, which admires
itself for its tolerance, is tolerant of only one thing: itself, that is,
its own attitudinal amorphousness.

Rebellious communists, as long as they stayed in the ruling party,
could enjoy many advantages, even rights, that were denied the rest of
society. But in order to achieve some sort of change, it was necessary
to reestablish an independent, or at least less dependent, judiciary. It
was necessary to limit the influence of the semieducated and uncreative party apparatus and abolish censorship, which hindered the free
exchange of opinions and the development of the spiritual sphere of
life. It was necessary to extricate the economy from its dependence
on unattainable long-term plans. All of this the party rebels tried to
achieve, sometimes covertly, sometimes more openly. And even though
they often invoked Lenin or some party resolution, their demands
subverted the foundation of the ideology of exculpatory Communist
domination. A totalitarian power cannot coexist with an independent
judiciary, with free expression, or with an impugned ideology, which
tries to justify its irreplaceable societal mission. Thus it cannot exist
without absolute rule.

Dreams and Reality

There are moments in history when it appears that everything that recently seemed like destiny—for example, the unalterable run of everyday events—can be changed. It often seems as if a large part of a generation has been struck by a bedazzling flash of a belief in the possibility of change. People go into ecstasy; the vision of a better society (the bygone image of a paradise that preceded all the toilsome history full of cruelty and suffering) impels them to deeds they couldn't have imagined only a short time before. Because paradise can exist only in dreams, only in myths, a cruel awaking usually follows, and enthusiasm turns into a hangover. Even in our modern history, such moments of hope flare up.

Our forefathers were at first blinded by a vision of national independence and citizenship within the Slavic tribe, which would gain self-confidence by inclining toward the powerful "Russian Oak."

In June 1848, the Slavic Congress met in Prague. Pavel Jozef Šafařík read a fanatical speech ending with the challenge: *For me it is not the time for long speeches, for artificial speechifying; that is something for another place and time. Only deeds concern us, action. The path from serfdom to freedom is not without struggle—either victory and a free nation or honorable death, and after death glory.* The hall erupted in exultation.

Even the pragmatic František Palacký gave way to his feelings:

Something our fathers never dreamed of, something that in our youth kept entering our hearts like a beautiful dream, something we only recently did not dare to long for, today is coming to pass.

Soon after this congress, revolutionary events occurred that were connected with fantasies of establishing a democratic regime. As is well known, the revolution was suppressed (without blood, as is usual in Bohemia). Enthusiasm vanished, the participants in this Slavic and then democratic dream ended up in prison or retired into seclusion. Some—like Sabina—were bought off by the police; others—like Palacký—devoted themselves to scholarship.

Several generations passed without such fantastic visions. Only in 1918, at the end of the First World War, did a moment arrive that seemed to fulfill the dreams of contemporaries and forefathers alike. *The Prague people behaved in exemplary fashion*, recalls Jan Herben in his biography of Masaryk. *They rejoiced, hung banners, sang hymns.* (They also destroyed monuments. It's difficult to understand what was exemplary about the whole thing.)

A few days later the otherwise severely critical historian Josef Pekař gave an impassioned speech on the grounds of the Czech Academy:

> The day will come when they will tell us: You are free! This day of great tidings in which our joy tries to compensate for centuries of oppression and to measure our strength with the pain of entire generations who waited in vain for the morning star of freedom. They tried in vain, for years will pass before we will be able to consider and absorb the entire significance of this historical turnaround, the entire contents of our happiness. For the freedom that greeted us is not the freedom our fathers and grandfathers looked forward to: not freedom within Austria, but freedom from Austria, not the freedom of the feudal classes, but the freedom of all!

It also seemed that 1968 would bring a change that promised to touch the lives of most citizens. Not everyone saw it in the same way, however. For some, this was an attempt to cleanse the image of socialism in which they had once believed. For others, it was hope for the renewal of at least a limited democracy.

Substantial gatherings swelled with supportive petitions; enthusiastic ovations by courageous orators promised the end of dictatorship. A year earlier, people had participated in the May Day celebrations only with distaste. This time they went out spontaneously to emphasize and demonstrate their faith in the new leadership of the country. In an April public opinion poll, three-quarters of respondents expressed support for the process of renewal and the leading politicians Alexander Dubček, Josef Smrkovský, and the newly elected president, General Ludvík Svoboda.

Just as during the time the National Theater was being built and people donated their life savings and jewelry, the Fund of the Republic arose at the impetus of a few enthusiasts and collected almost eighty pounds of gold in two weeks.

When the Czech delegates left for Čierna nad Tisou at the end of July to meet with Soviet potentates, *Literární listy* accompanied them with a text by Pavel Kohout titled "A Dispatch to the Central Committee of the Communist Party of Czechoslovakia." This appeal reminded me of our recent and not overly encouraging history:

> All the more eagerly did our nations welcome socialism, which liberation brought us in 1945. It was an incomplete socialism because it gave its citizens neither civil nor creative freedom. We began obstinately to seek it out, however, and started to uncover it after January of this year.
>
> The moment has arrived when our country once again has become a cradle of hope not only for our nation. The moment has arrived when we can present the world proof that socialism is the only genuine alternative for all of civilization.

The dispatch went on to condemn the unacceptable pressure of *socialist community spirit* and appealed to the representatives of the party in the interest of our shared country and progressive forces on all continents to protect socialism, alliance, and sovereignty, and presciently pointed out that any use of force *will strike our judges as well like a boomerang, it will destroy our efforts, and, primarily, it will leave a tragic blot on the idea of socialism anywhere in the world for years to come.*

In order to understand this impassioned declaration of Socialist faith, we must enter into the tense atmosphere of the time. The Soviet leadership intended to halt, perhaps with force, the renewal of at least a few civil freedoms. The citizens sensed this. Thousands of Communists and others signed declarations. Suddenly the dream was revived that we were creating history, that our deeds were obtaining some sort of higher meaning.

For the first few days after the unbelievably massive invasion of the Soviet army, thousands of unarmed citizens tried to restrain the Soviet tanks and explain to the unknowing and manipulated soldiers that they were being abused, that what had been happening for the last eight months in Czechoslovakia was supposed to benefit socialism, not do away with it.

During these brief eight months, hopes for change for the better flared up. They even took (at least for many) the form of a dream of the fusion of democracy and socialism, despite the fact that history had shown that such a fusion was almost impossible.

Life in Subjugation

Our small country has been repeatedly afflicted with waves of emigration. The first big wave, following the 1620 defeat at the Battle of White Mountain, is half forgotten. But even then, it was the elites who fled the country.

Only in the last century have there been several waves of emigration. The first preceded the Second World War when, first from the republic and later from the protectorate, the leading democratic politicians, but especially the Jews, fled. (Most who did not manage to escape were murdered.) The second wave of emigration—more precisely, forced expulsion—affected almost three million Germans who (like their forefathers) had been born and lived in the territory of the republic. The next wave followed the Communist takeover when, within a brief period before the borders were closed, around fifty thousand people left the country. And after the Soviet occupation, more than a hundred thousand people emigrated. As is common in such cases, it was the more able and educated who left, those who believed that they would find greater opportunities in a freer world.

If we imagine society as a powerful body with a complicated circulatory system, then these waves represent huge bleeding wounds that are difficult to stanch.

But what does emigration mean for each individual?

Perhaps it is better to call emigration for political reasons escape from probable persecution, imprisonment, or even execution based upon a concealed verdict delivered by a manipulated court. It differs from normal relocation—that is, economic emigration. At the decisive moment, when a person crosses the border, whether legally or surreptitiously, his action appears as final and its results appear as irrevocable. A person on the lam must admit that unless the political situation changes in his country, he will never be able to return. He will never again see the places where he spent his youth, and he will probably never see his relatives and friends. With the exception of the displaced Germans, he knows he is leaving forever the home where he can best make himself understood in the language he has spoken since childhood. Emigration from a country that limits rights and freedoms offers the émigré more rights and better opportunities, but it also requires sacrifice, which to some might seem incidental, but to others might mean lifelong trauma.

Those who leave are, even if they refuse to admit it, surrendering a part of their soul. In more sober terms, they are interfering with the emotional ties that form the integrity of their personality. There will be some who seek out their compatriots and a certain nostalgia. At times they will recall their former homeland with satisfaction. Others, on the contrary, will avoid everything that might remind them of their former homeland and try to merge with the new society as quickly as possible; to achieve success, perhaps even property; to forget about both their previous home and their native tongue; to convince themselves that all their emotional ties were dispensable.

After the Soviets violently entered Czechoslovakia, for almost a year it was relatively easy to leave the country. Even during the first days after the occupation, the borders were open, and entire families were permitted to depart. Many abandoned property, employment, and even their country with the firm justification that they were leaving primarily for their children. At least they would grow up under free conditions. Of course, many of those who remained, or even returned to an occupied country, had children as well. Was their decision, therefore, bad or selfish?

We know that children quickly adapt to a new environment and a new language. They will accept the new country as their homeland. Nevertheless, even they are forced to break all previous ties. They are deprived of grandparents and other relatives, and if they are old enough to perceive their homeland, they lose that also. And what if the parents love their native land, their town, their language, their country and want to raise their children so that they have essentially the same values? Wouldn't emigration leave a spiritual or physical burden on the children as well?

Parents make decisions for their children until they are old enough to choose their fate themselves. It is possible that when they grow up, they will reproach their parents or, on the other hand, praise them. But the decision whether to or not stay is the parents'.

For many of those who left, the free conditions helped them apply their gifts and abilities. Others were overwhelmed by their new reality, the new conditions in which they felt themselves uprooted. After the Bolshevik Revolution, most Russian emigrants incorporated themselves into their new environment only with difficulty and, for the most part, never learned the language of the country that had offered them asylum.

For many, freedom that they do not earn becomes something foreign and false. If a person is threatened with almost certain death, as the Jews were during Nazism, the decision to leave or remain is a false dilemma. It is different for a person whose life will most likely not be imperiled.

In a country that suppresses freedom, each citizen has the right to freely decide which of his values are more important. One can say: I do not want to live under these degrading circumstances and will do everything to escape them. One can also say: They are depriving me of most of my rights, but I will not allow myself to be deprived of my home and everything that goes with it. Therefore, I will stay.

The wave of emigration after the Soviet occupation was tragic for life in Czechoslovakia. If we consider the intellectuals, we see that most remained, even though living in oppressed conditions meant for them, at the very least, losing their jobs and sometimes even facing imprisonment.

But in this recent history, we notice another outcome. Many who left felt so tied to their homeland and its fate that they did everything in their power to counteract this decision. Various cultural organizations emerged abroad, even political parties and publishers—the books published abroad were then smuggled into their homeland. Even though they were far from their home, these exiles remained connected to the life of their country, perhaps even more than those who remained.

There is no generally valid resolution to the dilemma of whether to go or to stay. Each point of view has its justifications. It is up to each individual to decide which values are the most important to him.

In conclusion, I would just like to mention one curiosity that is characteristic of our history: Except for Václav Klaus, each of our presidents has spent part of his life in exile—or in prison.

Occupation, Collaboration, and Intellectual Riffraff

A brief dictionary definition of "occupation" reads: *the seizure and conquest of a foreign territory.*

If we conceive of the situation in which the Czech kingdom found itself after the defeat at White Mountain as the seizure of territory for the benefit of a foreign power—with a definite part of the inhabitants of the kingdom accepting this state of affairs—we can declare that, beginning in the seventeenth century, most generations spent their lives in occupied territory. Although the ruling Austrian powers became more liberal during the last few decades before the First World War, at the beginning of their reign, just like almost every other occupying power in history, they ushered in murder. Furthermore, they executed twenty-seven representatives of the Czech elite in a manner that was cruel even for those times. The elite, especially the spiritual elite, are the first target of all occupiers, even revolutionaries.

After twenty years of freedom during the First Czechoslovak Republic beginning in 1918, there followed a further seventy years of direct and indirect, but much crueler, occupation. It is no exaggeration to say that we have had a long experience with occupation. (In this respect, we do not differ greatly from many other small European nations.)

In all cases, including the last two—the Nazi and subsequent Soviet occupations—the government of the entire territory was moved to centers of foreign powers. It is not important that in the second case, the first twenty years of the occupation took place without the presence of occupying troops but only with the assistance of hundreds of

Soviet advisers and hundreds of thousands of executors following the foreign power orders.

The phenomenon of collaboration is necessarily and legitimately connected with every occupation. Without it, the occupier could achieve its ends only with difficulty.

Collaboration, once again according to the dictionary, is determined by occupation. It is *dishonorable (usually voluntary) cooperation (both overt and covert) with a ruling enemy or occupiers.* If we focus our attention on the word "dishonorable," we can expand this definition. Collaboration is cooperation with any illegitimate totalitarian regime that systematically violates the fundamental human rights and freedoms of its citizens.

Determining the extent of collaboration after the enemy is defeated or the totalitarian regime eliminated is not easy. Except for a handful of those who openly or secretly battled against the enemy, most inhabitants, at least passively, accepted the occupation or illegitimate regime.

After all, it was necessary to sow the fields, go to work, and earn one's pay. The trains ran and the stores were open, even if at the same time thousands of people disappeared behind the fences of concentration camps, ended up before firing squads, or, in the case of Nazi occupations, perished in gas chambers. Occupying or illegitimate powers leave in peace most people who accept occupation as an unavoidable reality, even if it goes against their way of thinking. When necessary, the government is willing to corrupt this group of citizens—as the Nazis successfully did during the war—by offering them more money or greater rations of food.

Both occupiers and totalitarian regimes, of course, not only require this passive collaboration (they are well aware that it is legitimate and, in its own way, unavoidable for the subdued masses), but also seek support among those without whom it would be difficult to govern the country. They appeal to at least some of the populace and try to influence their thinking and to raise the youth in the "new" spirit. So they try to win over those who are most visible, whose positions or careers enjoy general respect or from whom society expects moral accountability, that is, politicians, distinguished journalists, well-known artists, and pedagogues. Essentially, all of the most well-known representatives of the intelligentsia are welcomed. In the entirety of modern history of war, occupation, and revolution, the victorious power always manages to acquire active collaborationists at all levels of society.

The minister of education during the protectorate and the founder of the activist youth organization Curatorship for Czech Youth, Emanuel Moravec—a symbol of collaboration with Nazi power—presents an admiring comment concerning Hitler, which he apparently heard from a German friend:

> I would like you to keep one thing in mind. The Führer meant what he said, and if he said that this or that must look like this or that, you may be certain that he will do everything he said he would. And here we are at the question of intelligence, which culminates in genius. Genius is not leadership but rather prescience, the premonition of progress. The world is being rebuilt; we are going through a great, historical spring cleaning which, as you can clearly see, requires a little time. The democratic order that is now exiting was built by the Jews. If we look back in history, we see that all kingdoms and orders built by the Jews and Semites perished precisely when they rose, so to speak, to the stars. . . . Of one thing we are convinced. Our Greater German Reich and its courageous army will destroy the enemy. We shall be victorious!

Instead of arriving at the culmination of genius, we ended up at the very bottom of Czech collaborationist thinking. A half-educated maniac and mass murderer was proclaimed a genius who was supposed to lead the Czech nation as well.

Only a few years later, Communist collaborators with the Soviets touted new mass murderers as ingenious leaders worthy of being followed. Klement Gottwald asserted:

Only loyalty to the Soviet Union and the teachings of Marx, Engels, Lenin, and Stalin can ensure the future triumph and prosperity of our nation and the well-being of our people and safeguard our country from the snares of imperialism.

Twenty years later, after the Soviet army invaded and occupied our country, other collaborationists publicly praised the occupiers. The Secretariat of the Central Committee of the Communist Party, Josef Kempný, claims:

More and more people are coming to the realization that in August of 1968, together with the armies of other members of the Warsaw Pact, the Soviet army arrived just in time. The Soviet Union did not hesitate to offer assistance to our working class and workers even at the cost of incomprehension and temporary damage to its international prestige. The Soviet Union succeeded in providing international assistance, and history will appreciate the intervention as an example of class assistance in the battle against international reactionary forces.

All totalitarian and occupying regimes, of course, have their ideological adherents. Hitler's Nazis, in the last free elections in Germany (like the Communists fifteen years later in the Czech lands), had the massive support of the citizens. Later, apparently only a small number of citizens, which included a minority of the intelligentsia, youth leaders, and artists (as well as those who emigrated), considered unacceptable the unprecedented persecution of ideological enemies and Jews.

German occupation, which for a significant part of Czech society was a shock, was welcomed by many who had an affinity for Nazism, militant anti-Semites, and various groups of Czech Fascists or staunch opponents of democracy. In the same way, Communist organizations established collaborationist groups. In complete disregard of the labor unions, they established the Union of Youth, the Pioneers for children,

the Union of Czechoslovak-Soviet Friendship, the Union for Cooperation with the Army, the Union of Anti-Fascist Fighters, artistic
unions that were supposed to ensure the loyalty of their members to
the new regime, the Czechoslovak Union of Physical Education, and a
reformed Pacem in Terris for acquiescent Catholic clerics. In addition,
they indirectly ruled all special-interest groups including the two legal
and entirely subordinated political parties.

These ideological kindred spirits become ever more dependent,
both materially and morally, on this felonious power. Soon, many of
them become its loyal servants and remain so even when their closest
comrades and friends end up in prison, on the gallows, or in mass graves,
murdered by other comrades and friends. They serve even though the
idea has lost its credibility, and the images of a victorious empire, an
earthly paradise, or at least a prosperous society have dissolved. Later,
being linked to the occupation or illegitimate power will become a
matter of life and death. Only in this way can we explain the desperate
affirmations of the incontrovertible victory of the Nazi Reich at the
very moment of its defeat.

Whereas German rule over the Czech lands lasted six years, Communist suzerainty over Czech society lasted four decades—and this
was during peacetime, when the pronouncements of the spiritual riffraff
did not have the appearance of treason. Perhaps precisely because they
occurred during peacetime, they can be considered even more abject
and disgusting.

The illegitimate power places in prominent positions only those
who are prepared to offer unconditional service, to collaborate. In every
society, one can find hundreds of thousands of those we call riffraff, the
dregs of society, without any moral scruples. Writers of anonymous
abuse letters, racists, followers of a ruthless government, or adherents of
hateful ideologies are always on hand. In return for their blind support,
the illegitimate power offers them a share in its prestige and its power,
and the chance to settle accounts with those they hate, those they envy,
those to whom they are inferior. They will write denunciations against

Jews who dare go out without their yellow stars, against neighbors who listen to foreign radio broadcasts. Often with gleeful satisfaction, they ally themselves with secret police, whether it goes by the name of the gestapo, the secret police, or Cheka. They will acclaim everyone whom the power designates worthy of respect and will demand the death of others (or even the same ones), if the powers proclaim them worthy of death. They will execrate businessmen, the university educated, and former factory owners just as they did Jews. They will hang banners with a swastika and, with the same alacrity, banners bearing hammers and sickles. The moment for the spiritual dregs of society arrives with the fall of democracy, with the suppression of the country's basic freedoms. In our country, these moments were connected with occupations and the violent establishment of totalitarian power.

The riffraff is not the same as the people, writes André Maurois in his *History of France*, whereby he clearly seeks to emphasize the difference between an individual's social origin and his behavior. Collaborationist and totalitarian regimes, however, usually call the riffraff the people and rule only on their behalf.

Self-Criticism

With the development of science and the method of its speculation, the notion spread that the knowledge of each one of us is limited by both our abilities and the overall level of understanding. It is therefore accepted that most of our conclusions will most likely not be eternally valid; we might be mistaken. We are willing to admit, even publicly, our mistakes.

Such a way of thinking was, of course, until recently unique and condemned. Our forefathers not only possessed a firmly established set of values but also professed firm and eternally valid truths. Even Socrates was accused and condemned for not recognizing the gods that were recognized by the community, and for thereby corrupting the youth. According to the Evangelists, Jesus was accused of blasphemy because he did not deny that he was the Son of God before the high priest and predicted he would be "seated at the right hand of the Power and coming with the clouds of heaven."

The majority of the most widespread religions oblige believers to accept the truth proclaimed in the recognized and immutable canon. There is one God, the creator of the earth and the heavens and all of creation. His Son, with whom he and the Holy Ghost form a unified entity, is the savior of all who believe in him.

There is one God, and (only) Muhammad is his prophet. Immutable and obligatory rituals were established. The Christian faith even conducted wars to determine whether believers could consume wine and bread as a symbol of the blood and body of the Lord or whether only the priests enjoyed that right. Other religions established how their temples or mosques could be situated and how one behaves in a house of worship.

For entire centuries in our lands, the Bible determined not only fundamental moral norms but also fundamental truths about history and the origin of the world and of life. (To be more precise: Those who arrogated to themselves the right to interpret the Bible determined which of the ideas of ancient pre-Christian philosophers and scholars could be reconciled with biblical tidings and what was necessary to reject and perhaps destroy.) Those who doubted their conclusions were pronounced heretics. For centuries, it was an indubitable truth that the earth was the center of the universe and the sun revolved around it. Not too long ago, it was thought that some women could be proved to be witches, that they flew around at night and participated in sinful sabbaths, that the devil traveled around the world trying to seduce people to sin, that it was possible to buy one's way out of eternal damnation. Then, one of the most serious sins was to doubt the truths of established power. For centuries, the church ruled over people's thinking. It introduced confession; it offered spiritual relief because it assumed the right to forgive the sins of all who humbly admitted to breaking the commandments. At the same time it ensured that the priests knew the thinking and disposition of their parishioners, their lesser and greater offenses, as well as any skepticism regarding the established truths.

At the end of the fourteenth century, the Roman Catholic church organized the Inquisition, whose mission was to make sure that Christians did not deviate from the truths or the practices the church had pronounced as immutable and infallible. Punishment for skeptics was sometimes exile, sometimes imprisonment, sometimes immolation at the stake. Tens of thousands of men and women were murdered for heresy, which sometimes consisted of casting into doubt the actions of the ruling church but often consisted of no offense related to the immutable truths. It was based only on confessions compelled by torture. Every institution, even the Inquisition, needs to prove the legitimacy and necessity of its existence. The inquisitor needed to fight heresy, and if he did not find it, it had to be invented.

At the same time, each person accused of heresy was offered the opportunity to recant what was called his error, to do penance, to loudly espouse the canonized truths. In a lengthy trial in which Jan Hus defended his teachings, even after he was condemned, he was offered the chance to recant. The proposed recantation read: *I have never held nor preached these articles of faith, and if I had, I would have been acting against the truth for I pronounce them as erroneous and swear that I would neither hold nor preach them.*

For the authorities, a heretic who recants is always more valuable than one who perishes in protest. The subjugated heretic is living proof of the invincibility of the one and only truth.

Two centuries later, Galileo Galilei recanted his teaching concerning the movement of the heavens and thereby saved his life. The Catholic church, despite wide acceptance of the fact that the earth rotates on its axis and orbits around the sun, rehabilitated Galileo only in 1992.

Totalitarian states, which derive their legitimacy from some modern ideology, likewise require faith in the immutability of proclaimed truths. Perhaps it was precisely this that increased their attractiveness; in the complicated modern world, with its crumbling traditional values, many people were enticed by a world in which values were once again established.

The sole truth became whatever the dictator proclaimed, whether it was Hitler, Stalin, or Mao. Furthermore, Communist ideology offered its holy writ in the classic works of Marx, Engels, and Lenin. (The collected works of these holy books stood in the libraries of all secretariats as well as the offices of university professors; no one read them, just as few Nazis read the entirety of Adolf Hitler's tome.) It was not necessary to read the books (those interested could get their hands on the most important extracts, so-called Red Books, and selected quotes). The dictator was also the highest priest who interpreted the word; he alone could give the eternal truths their obligatory form according to the demands of the moment. Because these truths mostly concerned everyday reality, which they unilaterally described or distorted, in addition to enthusiastic and infatuated followers of this new faith, skeptics could be found. It was necessary to uncover these modern heretics, incriminate them, and condemn them, sometimes to exile, at other times to prison or to death. (Over the course of the several decades of totalitarian rule, their number exceeded many times over the number of heretics condemned throughout the centuries of the Inquisition.)

Just like heretics, the contemporary skeptics were afforded the opportunity to repent, to recognize and recant their errors. Such repentance was called self-criticism.

In 1928, the Soviet dictator Stalin published a long article on self-criticism.

> The slogan of self-criticism must not be regarded as something temporary and transient. Self-criticism is a specific method, a Bolshevik method, of training the forces of the Party and of the working class generally in the spirit of revolutionary development. Marx himself spoke of self-criticism as a method of strengthening the proletarian revolution.

In a society where freedom of expression did not exist, where any attempt to place into doubt the canonized truths—or even the ruling party and its leadership—was considered a crime, self-criticism was accepted as an intellectual or even societal exercise. The action of self-criticism was supported in every permitted organization. Upon the orders of their superiors, it was undergone by functionaries even at the lowest levels, factory foremen, and members of individual organizations or trade unions.

Artists (always suspected of kowtowing to some decadent trend) were also prompted to perform this ritual act, as were scientists, who were predisposed to being misled by the decadent science of the West. Even the leading party functionaries subjected themselves to self-criticism, usually when the dictator considered it necessary to strengthen his power. Even Stalin himself saved his career at its beginnings through self-criticism.

Self-criticism became a ritual that had nothing in common with critical self-reflection or even with examining the legitimacy or illegitimacy of the ideas one espoused or actions one performed.

The not-very-long history of the Communist movement abounds with the self-abuse of prominent people. The leaders of the movement recant yesterday's assertions and repent of their previous deeds; writers apologize for their books; philosophers reject, in the name of the ingenious classics of Marxism, those other philosophers whom they recently praised as giants. Because the dictator sometimes changes his opinions, people often recant words spoken and deeds done when they were following orders. Their repentance is supposed to affirm the dictator's infallibility, and therefore it is accepted. Whoever submits to it heads off his condemnation, but the suspicion clings to him, nevertheless, that in the depths of his soul he has remained a heretic; at the very least he was at one time susceptible to dangerous opinions or skepticism.

Condemned Communist politicians in the Soviet Union, along with those residing in lands conquered by it, even before they were placed before a court, performed self-criticism in which they recanted and pledged loyalty to the dictator and everything he advocated and carried out. Such self-debasement was merely a desperate attempt to save one's life.

At the height of Stalin's terror, the logic of penitence, as it was understood, resulted in the most perverse form of self-criticism. During the political trials in which the accused, subject to long torture, submissively admitted to deeds they had not performed and to crimes they had not committed, they themselves even asked for the harshest punishment. Because they had in the past conducted self-criticism and promised atonement, their new repentance was no longer mitigating, and they were hanged as a warning to all.

Without the ritualized act of self-criticism, however, it is difficult for the dictatorship to resist the onslaught of doubt and distrust until the moment finally arrives when the fallacious principles on which it was built are cast into doubt even by those who are paid to endorse and defend it.

(Secret Police)

In his *History of France*, André Maurois writes, *Robespierre was all-powerful, and he was undone. For he lost all sense of proportion.*

The three great European revolutions were bloody, and their leaders indeed lost all sense of proportion. Each of them captivated at least a part of his citizens with magnificent plans and promises for a new and better arrangement of society. Among them were followers and admirers in the intelligentsia, workers, and people from the countryside, as well as people from the streets, the rabble, informers, and unreserved administrators of the dictator's will.

The dictators murdered their real and presumed opponents; they sent to death even their closest collaborators—Robespierre sent Danton and Hébert; Hitler sent Röhm; Stalin sent practically everyone who had helped him achieve power and perpetrate crimes. The number of victims during Nazism and the Bolshevik Revolution was much greater and the bloodshed worse than during the French Revolution.

Robespierre's dictatorship lasted less than two years, and he died on the guillotine. Hitler's lasted twelve years, until the moment when the führer, defeated in a war he had unleashed, committed suicide. Lenin's and Stalin's dictatorship endured for more than thirty-five years until each dictator, at the summit of well-organized ovations and all-encompassing adulation, had died, whether felled by a stroke or by a well-concealed murder.

What were the differences between Robespierre and these other dictators? Robespierre failed to organize the boisterous rabble, to bring the street completely into his service and under his control. He did not create a secret police force that would surround him with an impenetrable shield and would carry out his plans without bothering about the number of dead left behind.

The absolute power of the three modern dictators consisted precisely in the ruthless, illegitimate authority of a substantial police force and special guards whose activities were controlled to the very end by the dictators themselves.

In Russia, just as in Germany, such a police force existed even before the violent change of affairs. Because prerevolutionary Russia was swarming with agents attempting to overthrow the tsarist regime, the political police—called the Okhrana—was large, even by Russian standards, as well as efficient. It monitored revolutionaries not only at home but also if they ventured abroad to more democratic countries. Most scholars agree that the tsar's Okhrana was the largest and most efficient secret police force of its time (it employed around fifteen thousand agents). As a result of its activities, hundreds of opponents of the tsarist regime spent part of their lives in prison or Siberian exile. On average, seventeen opponents of the tsar perished on the scaffold every year. Among them was Alexandr Ilyich Ulyanov—who planned an assassination of the tsar—the older brother of Vladimir Ilyich Ulyanov, who later assumed the name Lenin. The leader of the Bolshevik Revolution, therefore, had a personal reason to detest the Okhrana, but he also recognized its usefulness for safeguarding the state. The architects had to guard vigilantly the postrevolutionary regime and at the same time condemn the police methods it employed. According to the classics of Marxism, all repressive roles of the state would cease to exist after the Socialist revolution. In his extensive study, *The State and Revolution*, Lenin attempts to lay out, with many citations from Marx and Engels, his opinion of the repressive role of the state after the revolution.

According to him, the consummation of the proletarian revolution would be *the proletarian dictatorship, the political rule of the proletariat.* Marxists, claims Lenin, *will recognize that it will be necessary for the proletariat to smash the old bureaucratic apparatus, they will shatter it to its very foundations, they will destroy it to the very roots, and they will replace it with a new one.*

∞

The necessity of state terror was theoretically justified. And who better to effect long-term terror than a well-organized police force?

Later, after Lenin had seized power, he founded a political police force (first it was called Cheka—All-Russian Extraordinary Commission for the Suppression of Counterrevolution and Sabotage). Over the course of three years, under the command of the Polish Bolshevik Felix Dzerzhinsky, this revolutionary police organization, whose task was to liquidate political opponents and essentially everyone who somehow represented the previous regime, employed around a quarter of a million fanatics resolved to carry out the dictator's will. The number of murdered exceeded ten thousand victims a month. At the same time, immediately after the revolution, the Cheka began organizing the first concentration camps. The Cheka was renamed and reorganized several times, but it continued to serve as a ruthless instrument of the dictatorship. During Stalin's reign, the number of murdered grew along with the number of concentration camps. After World War II, according to the Soviet model and under the direct leadership of Soviet advisers, affiliated organizations were founded in all countries where Communists had taken power.

The Nazi dictatorship could avail itself of traditions established by the Bolsheviks and the Italian Fascists, and even the German tradition itself, which had its own semimilitary organizations and associations.

A few years before the Nazi takeover, Hitler had at his disposal a million-strong organization called the SA, led by the retired artillery captain Ernst Röhm. His fanatical disciple, Heinrich Himmler, commanded a much smaller, but more elite, body: the SS, which he planned to employ as the political police. From the beginning, the members of the SS carried out their orders with ruthless, blind obedience. They committed appalling crimes, from the torture of prisoners to inhuman medical experiments to mass murder in gas chambers.

One of the leading Nazis, Hermann Göring, had commanded an eighty-thousand-member corps of the Prussian police. He then established the gestapo, based on that model, one of the most efficient secret police forces in the world. In outright cruelty, it was not far behind the state police in the Soviet Union.

Because the Nazis were the only political party that commanded such large armed units with members willing to do anything, their coup took place incredibly smoothly and much more quickly than the Bolshevik coup (certainly the fact that it took place in the middle of peaceful Europe played a role). On the very first day of the takeover, the police arrested more than fifteen hundred Communist functionaries, who were on a previously drafted list; later they started arresting the functionaries of other political parties. Because there were so many of these and they couldn't all be crammed into the existing prisons, on March 21, 1933—less than a month after the coup—Himmler established the first concentration camp not far from Dachau in an abandoned munitions factory. Originally it was intended only for five thousand people arrested for interrogation, but after a few years its population swelled to twelve thousand at a time.

The Nazis had been thoroughly prepared for the coup, so they easily seized absolute power in just a few weeks. Himmler's SS units quickly penetrated the highest ranks of the secret police, which also assumed control over a growing number of concentration camps.

In terms of the number of victims, one cannot compare the terror of the first years of Nazi rule to the Bolshevik reign of terror. Nevertheless, the Nazi terror afflicted tens of thousands of German citizens and in the end culminated in the extermination of six million Jews.

During the brief period in Czechoslovakia between the end of the protectorate and the Communist coup in 1948, the Communist Party did not have its own (at least, not its own legal) armed contingent;

however, a Communist named Václav Nosek headed the Ministry of the Interior.

Three days before the coup, members of the party quickly formed armed people's militias. (This obviously illegal and unconstitutional action calls into question the claim by the Communist leaders that they achieved power legitimately.) Armed members of the Communist Party marching through Prague certainly influenced the quick transformation of a democratic society into a Soviet-style dictatorship.

The Communist journalist Rudolf Černý compiled President Antonín Novotný's memoirs from a series of conversations. Here, the president and the highest representative of the Communist Party supposedly demonstrated unambiguously the necessity of police terror during the second half of the 1950s and most of the '60s.

The new Communist government immediately removed from both the police and the army its real and probable opponents and replaced them with reliable members of the party. The changes primarily concerned the secret police; the Soviet Union sent advisers who demanded the introduction of inquisitorial methods, which until then had been unthinkable, since the populace remembered all too well this practice by the gestapo. Some who survived questioning, and even some of the investigators, described how these interrogations were carried out. The accused were beaten, given electric shocks, deprived of water, and placed in unheated underground cells, and had their most sensitive parts burned. One of the most effective methods to break someone accused of an often nonexistent or absurd crime was to deprive him of rest.

Most of the important political prisoners were interrogated at the Ruzyně prison. The head of the interrogators there was Bohumil Doubek, who wrote about the methods employed: *Therefore, it was determined that if there was supposed to be a certain result in the investigation, it [the interrogation] must be conducted at least fourteen to sixteen hours a day. The prisoner was allowed to rest from ten in the evening till six in the morning. If he arrives at his cell at midnight, he won't fall asleep because he's still agitated from the interrogation, and in the morning he must get up at six. Moreover, he can be woken at night by the guards. Because he has to stand during the interrogation, he is then physically and mentally exhausted, and it is not difficult for the interrogators to acquire the incriminating evidence because the accused is more acquiescent.* The reality was even more drastic because the interrogated often had to walk the entire night in their cells; their feet would swell, and they often lost control over their own words owing to exhaustion.

The interrogations, conducted under the guidance of Soviet advisers, had only one goal: to compel the prisoner to confess to the accusation that had been prepared ahead of time: treason, espionage, sabotage, or another capital offense.

People broken by long and relentless torture were told repeatedly that they had no hope but to confess—then considered a mitigating circumstance—and admit to the most absurd crimes. The quickly "trained" judges and prosecutors, together with those who were willing to fulfill unquestioningly the orders of the new government, then sentenced the tortured prisoner to a long prison sentence or to death.

The investigators knew that the confessions had been coerced, that they lacked any real basis or were derived only from other confessions that had also been made under duress. Nevertheless, entire units of interrogators, without apparent hesitation, employed these methods, perfected during the Middle Ages. Just as in the Soviet Union, just as in Nazi Germany, the political police acted outrageously, not only with the awareness of the ruling power but also upon its orders, and the cynicism with which these deeds were carried out was stunning.

Primarily, the organization [CPC] exhorted all of its members to display perseverance during interrogation and, just like the leadership of the investigation and the leadership of the ministry, support the view that anyone who was arrested was an enemy of the state and must be convicted no matter what. Therefore, they were to assist the diligence and persistence of the investigative organs. For example, the organization also supported and oversaw

a competition for the best interrogation time, which was rewarded
with book prizes for those who achieved the best average interrogation times.

All this was made possible because the authorities abolished all
basic civil rights; they raised repressive organs above the law, above
judicial power. They adjudicated the status of those who had to take
even the most absurd accusations seriously.

Over several years, almost 200,000 citizens died in concentration
camps; 178 political prisoners were executed by Communists. The
secret police provided the material for the trials, which, like the Soviet
trials, had nothing in common with actual judicial processes. The secret
police also determined the judgments and the punishment, although,
especially in the case of the death penalty for prominent defendants, the
recommendation had to be approved by the highest organ of the party.

At the same time, the secret police in all dictatorships is an essential component of power. After the Communist coup, the small
unit of the National Security Corps became the most important security unit, which in the 1950s had five thousand permanent workers
and employed the services of countless agents, petty informers, and
denouncers. Even though secret police forces were also in charge of
espionage, from the beginning their primary function, as determined
by Lenin, was battling the internal enemy. Just after the coup, it was
mostly democratic politicians, Western resistance fighters, and those
with an inappropriate class origin (there were all sorts of those in our
society) who were persecuted. But soon prominent Communists also
were being victimized.

Although, after the death of Stalin, the most brutal repressions
ceased, the secret police became more important for the perpetuation
of totalitarian power. Fiendish terror was replaced by agents who monitored, overheard, and admonished. It was necessary to ensure participation in elections, rallies, and brigades; to know what people said in
private, what kind of jokes they told; to ensure that legal organizations

did not become cells of resistance (as happened in artistic circles in the 1960s); to know if any illegal organizations were being established, if anyone was listening to "seditious" foreign broadcasts, if people were meeting with foreigners or even foreign diplomats, if they were exchanging "harmful" literature. Even after the Soviet invasion in 1968, the secret police did not commit murder; instead it compiled long lists of unreliable citizens who were not allowed to go abroad, whose children were not allowed to study. No one from their families could be accepted into any qualified position, especially not one of leadership. It was necessary, at least on occasion, to monitor them, acquire informers from their neighborhood, photograph them, repeatedly summon them for interrogation, search their apartments (sometimes in their presence, sometimes in their absence), install listening devices. Secret police employees wrote anonymous, threatening letters and collected incriminating material that could be used in a political trial. Active opponents had their driver's licenses revoked and their phones disconnected. At times, the secret police bundled someone into an automobile, drove him out to a distant forest, threatened him, and dumped him as far as possible from any road or inhabited place. (The musicologist Ivan Medek, for example, was beaten unconscious in a forest and thrown into a ditch.)

The courts sometimes pretended to be real courts, and in some isolated cases they were not governed by the investigators. The fear of unfathomable repression combined with torture and the possible loss of life was lessening. The task of the secret police was now to keep the citizens aware that if they refrained from any manifestations of resistance or protest, they could live in peace. He who protested, on the other hand, had only himself to blame for the loss of this peace.

In its own way, this work was more demanding than outright terror. It came as no surprise, therefore, that when the secret police was dissolved after the fall of Communism, it had more than thirteen thousand employees, almost twice as many as during the years of Gottwald's terror.

The Elite

The dictionary definition of "elite" refers to the French word *élite*, which means select, the best. The elite of society are *individuals exceptional in education and morals; in the military, the bravest.* It is worth noting that the definition, stemming back to the middle of the nineteenth century, mentions education, morals, and bravery, not ancestry or property, both of which at that time were seen as entitling one to be considered a member of society's elite.

Of course, the concept of the elite was significantly influenced here by our National Revival. The property owners and the nobility belonged primarily to the German-speaking layers of society because revivalist thinkers, or simply Czech intellectuals, emphasized precisely these characteristics. However, in the Czech lands, just as in France at the time, those whom we called the cultural or spiritual elite enjoyed greater respect. Their members had neither power nor property but rather admiration and influence upon the behavior and thought of the people. (Let us recall the influence of Émile Zola on liberating the unjustly accused Alfred Dreyfus or Masaryk's participation in the battle against the apologists for ritual murder in the case of Hilsner.)

The respect enjoyed by Czech writers in the second half of the nineteenth century is well known. The funeral of Karel Havlíček Borovský became a sort of national demonstration; the funeral of the second-rate poet Svatopluk Čech, whose versified works came out in dozens of editions, looked like that of a leading statesman or a national hero. The collected works of Jan Neruda and Jaroslav Vrchlický, just like the *History of the Czech Nation in Bohemia and Moravia* by

František Palacký, stood in the bookcases of both intellectuals and commoners. Manifestos published and signed by Czech writers at various key moments in history often changed, or at least influenced, the course of events. At the very last moment, Vilém Mrštík's polemical essay "Bestia triumfans" roused the public and helped save historic parts of Prague from "modernization" (read: demolition). In May 1917, more than two hundred writers signed the "Manifesto of Czech Writers." They demanded that Czech representatives in the Viennese Imperial Council fight for the self-determination of the Czech nation, the renewal of constitutional rights, and amnesty for political prisoners. The language of the document seems today inconceivably presumptuous.

> We turn to you, to the delegation of the Czech nation, who well
> know that we Czech writers, figures who are in our public lives
> active and well known, have not only the right, but also the duty
> to speak for the majority of the Czech cultural and spiritual world,
> even for the nation, which cannot speak for itself.

In Prague's parks and squares and on the walls of buildings we can see statues and busts—not of politicians, nobles, or generals, but primarily of artists, scholars, and writers.

During the First Republic (1918–1938), this respect for writers continued. Several writers received more acclaim than members of other elites, for example, in the realms of finance and power. Even the president of the republic, Masaryk, who enjoyed extraordinary respect, was a representative of the spiritual elite and was characterized by the aforementioned characteristics: education, morality, and bravery. Masaryk also never severed his relationships with representatives of the cultural elite, the "Friday Men" in the home of Karel Čapek, where he met with the foremost Czech writers and journalists.

At the end of the First Republic, Czech writers composed and published the passionate and insistent manifesto, "We Remain Faithful," in which they asked society to defend democracy, freedom, and the integrity of the nation despite professional and class differences.

Besides the cultural elites, power, political, and military elites were beginning to arise in our free country (although before the Nazi occupation, many of their members emigrated). Even though it is often pointed out that in the modern period, Czechs have never defended their country with military force, it cannot be claimed that they did not fight. Czech officers, primarily airmen, formed units with the help of the allies and were integrated into the armed forces fighting against Nazi Germany.

Such activity is worthy of esteem if only because these forces were made up exclusively of volunteers who had chosen to take part in battle for the freedom of their nation.

Members of our army abroad also participated in the mission to remove one of the most powerful and influential men in the Nazi Reich, Reinhard Heydrich.

Even at home during the first months of occupation, there arose illegal resistance organizations composed of democratic politicians, citizens dedicated to democracy, members of Sokol (the youth sport and gymnastic organization), and officers of the former Czechoslovak army (they were joined by the Communist resistance after the Nazis attacked the Soviet Union). The gestapo (with the help of many Czech informers) uncovered most of these organizations, and their members were sent to concentration camps or executed.

With the rise of cinematography during the First Republic, celebrities—that is, those who enjoyed the respect and admiration of society without the need of education, morality, or bravery—started to appear next to the cultural elite.

The Nazi regime, which certainly did believe that persons it elevated would be well liked, did not object to the cult of Czech celebrities as long as they were loyal to the Nazis and if, when outbreaks of discontent threatened, they brought people consoling diversion.

The Communist regime, which soon took the place of the Nazis, like every totalitarian regime, considered morality, independent intelligence, or unapproved bravery unwelcome. Like all riffraff, the Communists hated the elite with a vengeance. Consciously and unconsciously, they tried not only to degrade their cultural influence but also to humiliate them. They were willing to pardon only those who submitted unconditionally to the party. Over the course of a few months, they also removed from schools (primarily the universities) all professional organizations, especially those that enjoyed any kind of natural authority.

Part of the elite, especially the political elite, managed to flee the country, as did at least some of those who were respected for their property or for their business success. Most intellectuals, however, stayed behind. The remaining political elite was replaced by the new Communist pseudoelite. Lack of education was given precedence over education, immorality over morality, and acquiescence over bravery. The primary virtues were supposed to be proletarian origin and class consciousness.

The misfortune among the Czechs and Slovaks was that, after the rule of the Nazis, who had murdered part of the Czech elite and deprived the rest of a voice, a new elite did not have time to establish itself. Those returning after the war, which included soldiers and airmen who had fought with armies abroad against Nazism, were imprisoned by the Communists or executed. Those who remained free were at least partially blocked from public work, and most were able to acquire only menial jobs.

The Communists tried to replace people who had achieved natural authority through their activities (the Communists had removed them precisely for this reason) with people they endowed with artificial authority. Loyal party members, who lacked even a college degree, received university titles; others were named lawyers or chief justices; second-rate artists or those who disowned their previous work and were willing to be propagandists received the title of Worthy or National Artist.

Even though the Communists quickly enthroned terror, affecting part of the cultural elite, it cannot be denied that a considerable number of the elite failed. Those who sold out and consoled themselves with the thought that they were spokesmen for the nation (and also National Artists) were mistaken. They were spokesmen for and servants of only a felonious power. On the other hand, the Communists, having acquired at least a few members of the cultural elite during those first years, never fully trusted them.

Many of those who failed gradually came to understand the wretched role they had been assigned and laboriously tried to win back some of their natural authority. This meant that they had to come into conflict with the current government.

Throughout the rule of communism—perhaps with the exception of the brief Prague Spring—this conflict never ended.

During the period of Soviet occupation, the cultural elite, in their battle with the illegitimate occupying power, acquired the credence and natural authority they had lost. (This applies not only to the activity of artists and intellectuals who had been officially repudiated but also to protest singers and artists from the so-called small theaters.) This went on despite the fact that the government did all it could to defile, discredit, and undermine this natural authority; it tried to elevate the false elite and especially the so-called celebrities, whose popularity and apparent significance were strengthened by their appearance on television. As long as they did not try to resist the government, the celebrities had unrestricted freedom.

For four decades, natural authority was banished to the underground or to the very edge of cultural activity, banished from the entire country or at least surrounded by official and therefore formidable silence, and the false elite were forced upon society. All of this could not be prevented from influencing the majority of society—the decline of morality and even the distrust of intellectuals, which persisted not only during communism, but long after the Communists had ceased to rule.